Munther Isaac's *From Land to Lasents a new and significant work the notion of "land" in Scripture against the backdrop of the biblical account of the Garden of Eden and then traces its use and significance in both the Old and New Testaments. Accordingly Isaac brings to light how "land" as gift, promise, condition, and covenant delineate the universal, territorial, and ethical dimensions of redemption and the reign of God. This work is not only a significant contribution to biblical scholarship, its contemporary relevance makes it a must buy for students of the Bible and theology alike.

Dr Thomas Harvey
Academic Dean, Oxford Centre for Mission Studies

This is an extraordinary book. It does not fall into the trap of playing Christian universality against Israel's particularity in view of the "Holy Land." It sees the unity of the Bible as a whole in regaining the universal scope of God's particular covenant with Israel to establish justice on earth. This calls both Jews and Christians to overcome imperial conquering of land and oppression of its inhabitants in order to walk humbly with God, the giver and owner of land, to be a blessing for all peoples.

Dr Ulrich Duchrow
Professor of Systematic Theology at the University of Heidelberg

From Land to Lands, from Eden to the Renewed Earth

A Christ-Centered Biblical Theology of the Promised Land

Munther Isaac

MONOGRAPHS

© 2015 by Munther Issac

Published 2015 by Langham Monographs
an imprint of Langham Creative Projects

Langham Partnership
PO Box 296, Carlisle, Cumbria CA3 9WZ, UK
www.langham.org

ISBNs:
978-1-78368-077-1 Print
978-1-78368-092-4 Mobi
978-1-78368-093-1 ePub
978-1-78368-094-8 PDF

Munther Issac has asserted his right under the Copyright, Designs and Patents Act, 1988 to be identified as the Author of this work.

All rights reserved. No part of this publication may be reproduced, stored in a retrieval system or transmitted, in any form or by any means, electronic, mechanical, photocopying, recording or otherwise, without the prior written permission of the publisher or the Copyright Licensing Agency.

Scripture quotations are from The Holy Bible, English Standard Version® (ESV®), copyright © 2001 by Crossway, a publishing ministry of Good News Publishers. Used by permission. All rights reserved.

British Library Cataloguing in Publication Data
A catalogue record for this book is available from the British Library

ISBN: 978-1-78368-077-1

Cover & Book Design: projectluz.com

Langham Partnership actively supports theological dialogue and a scholar's right to publish but does not necessarily endorse the views and opinions set forth, and works referenced within this publication or guarantee its technical and grammatical correctness. Langham Partnership does not accept any responsibility or liability to persons or property as a consequence of the reading, use or interpretation of its published content.

To the memory of my father, who brought our family back to the land;

To my mother, who raised me up in the land;

To Rana, Mona, and Ghassan, who share with me the love of the land;

To my colleagues and students at Bethlehem Bible College, who serve with me in the land;

To the family of the Oxford Centre for Mission Studies, who were a family to me when I was away from the land;

To the Palestinian Church, the church of the land;

And mostly, to Rudaina, the love of my life, whose love and support carried and accompanied me throughout the writing of this book, and to Karam and Zaid, our precious gifts from the God of the land.

To God be the Glory – لله المجد

Contents

Abstract xv

Introduction 1
A Biblical Theology of the Land
   Biblical Theology 1
   Terminology 3
   The Land in Recent Biblical Studies: A Brief Survey 5
   Thesis 8

Chapter 1 11
The Theology of the Land in the Garden of Eden
   Introduction 11
   1. Eden as a Sanctuary 13
      1.1. The Garden as an Enclosed Distinct Area in Eden 13
      1.2. Eden Mediated the Presence of YHWH Elohim 15
      1.3. The Work of Adam Is in the Garden 18
      1.4. The Landscape of Eden 18
      1.5. The Compound Name of YHWH Elohim 20
      1.6. Evidence from Genesis 4:12–16 20
      1.7. Conclusion 21
   2. Torah and Covenant in Eden 22
      2.1. The Commandment in Eden 22
      2.2. The Covenant of Eden 24
      2.3. Eden and Deuteronomistic Theology 27
      2.4. Conclusion 29
   3. Eden as a Kingdom 29
      3.1. Eden as a Royal Garden 30
      3.2. Adam as a Vicegerent 31
      3.3. The Image of God: Genesis 1:26–28 35
      3.4. Conclusion 38
   4. Eden and Biblical Theology 40
      4.1. Genesis 2–3 and Salvation History 40
      4.2. Adam Is Israel 43
      4.3. Eden Is the Land 46
   5. Conclusion: The Theology of Land in Eden 51

Chapter 2 55
The Land and Holiness
   Introduction 55
   1. Holy God, Holy People, Holy Land 55
      1.1. Holy God – Derivative Holiness 56
      1.2. Holy People – Mandated Holiness 60
      1.3. Holy Land: The Land Personified Demands Holiness 63
      1.4. Conclusion 66
   2. Sanctuaries 66
      2.1. From Land to Zion 66
      2.2. The Legitimacy of Zion 69
   3. Conclusion 73

Chapter 3 75
The Covenanted Land
   Introduction 75
   1. Covenants in the Old Testament: Two Main Types 76
      1.1. Covenants of Grant 76
      1.2. Treaty Covenants 77
   2. Land and Covenant 78
      2.1. The Land as a Gift within the Covenant 78
      2.2. Conditional or Unconditional Gift? 79
   3. Land as a Mandate 86
   4. Stipulations of Keeping the Covenant – Ethics in the Land 90
      4.1. Idolatry 91
      4.2. Sabbath, Land Sabbath, and Jubilee 92
      4.3. Social Justice 93
   5. Conclusion 96

Chapter 4 97
Kingship, Vicegerency and Universal Dominion
   Introduction 97
   1. Abraham as a Royal Figure 97
   2. The Royal Status of Israel 99
   3. The Theology of Kingship in Israel 103
      3.1. The Deuteronomic Account 103
      3.2. A King, or No King? 104
      3.3. The Vicegerency of the King of Israel 105
   4. The Failure of the Monarchy 109
   5. Universal Dominion 111
   6. Conclusion 121

Chapter 5 123
The Land in the New History
    Introduction 123
    1. From Crisis to New History 123
    2. Eschatological Holiness in the Land's New History 127
        2.1. The Sanctifying Presence of God 127
        2.2. An Inclusive Zion 129
        2.3. The Healing of the Land 132
        2.4. Conclusion: An Ideal Zion 133
    3. New Covenant in the Land's New History 134
        3.1. The Gift of a New Heart and Guaranteed Obedience 134
        3.2. The Land in the New Covenant: An Inclusive Inheritance ... 136
        3.3. Ideal Covenantal Society 138
        3.4. Conclusion: An Ideal Covenant 140
    4. The Royal Vicegerent in the Land's New History 141
        4.1. A Future Davidic Kingship 141
        4.2. The Servant of YHWH and the Kingship of YHWH 142
        4.3. Restoration, Justice and Peace in the Land 146
        4.4. A Kingdom of No Limits 148
        4.5. Conclusion: An Ideal Kingdom 150
    5. Conclusion 151

Chapter 6 153
The Theology of the Land in the Old Testament
    Introduction 153
    1. The Land as Eden Regained 153
        1.1. Canaan and Eden Parallelism 154
        1.2. Edenic Descriptions of Canaan 155
        1.3. The Restoration as Eden Regained 161
        1.4. The Eschatological Restoration as a New Creation 163
    2. The Land and Old Testament Biblical Theology 166
        2.1. The Land in the Biblical Narrative 166
        2.2. The Land as a Prototype for Eschatological
        Cosmic Restoration 169
        2.3. The Land as a Paradigm for Other Societies 169
        2.4. Conclusion: From Land to Earth 170
    3. The Land and Old Testament Theology – Concluding Remarks 171
        3.1. *Why* a Land? 171
        3.2. From the Particular to the Universal 172
        3.3. Theologies of the Land 174
        3.4. The Limited Importance of the Land:
        Ethics Trumps Location 176

First-Century Jewish Theology of the Land
- Land Theology in First-Century Judaism 179
- Expectations of Restoration..181
- A Different Perspective from the Diaspora 183
- Conclusion 186

Chapter 7 189
The Jesus-Event and the Land
- Introduction 189
- 1. The Study of the Land in the NT..189
- 2. The Jesus-Event as a Hermeneutical Key 191
- 3. The Jesus-Event Aftershocks..194
  - 3.1. The Arrival of the Age to Come 194
  - 3.2. Israel Rejects the Messiah...195
  - 3.3. The Inclusion of Gentiles...196
- 4. Conclusion 197

Chapter 8 201
Jesus and Holy Space
- Introduction 201
- 1. Background: The Temple in the Time of Jesus....................202
- 2. The Embodiment of God's Presence, and the Nullification of Holy Place 203
  - 2.1. In the Synoptic Gospels..203
  - 2.2. In the Fourth Gospel 208
  - 2.3. In Stephen's Speech (Acts 7)...211
  - 2.4. In the Writings of Paul...213
  - 2.5. In the Epistle to the Hebrews..214
  - 2.6. The Jesus-Event and the Parting with Judaism 216
  - 2.7. Conclusion 218
- 3. The Church as Holy Space 219
- 4. Universal Holiness 222
- 5. The Demand for Ethical Holiness 226
- 6. Conclusion – The Arrival of the Eschatological Temple....229

Chapter 9 231
Jesus and the Covenanted Land
- Introduction 231
- 1. Background: Covenantal Nomism 231
- 2. Israel and the Land Redefined...233
  - 2.1. Jesus the Faithful Israelite in the Gospels 233
  - 2.2. Jesus the Seed of Abraham in Paul 236

  2.3. Jesus Inherits the Land 237
  2.4. Conclusion 240
 3. The Covenanted People Redefined 241
  3.1. Covenantal Membership through Christ.....................241
  3.2. The Universalization of the People of God 242
  3.3. The Inheritance of the Land by the People of God.............247
  3.4. Conclusion 250
 4. The Inheritance as a Mandate 250
  4.1. Jesus Redefines the Covenant...250
  4.2. Paul and the Law 252
  4.3. The Jesus-Community and the Demand of "Fruits"..........253
  4.4. Conclusion 257
 5. The Nullification of the Old Covenant......................................258
  5.1. Who is Abraham's Seed?...259
  5.2. Israel Broke the Covenant...260
  5.3. Gentiles and Jews United..261
  5.4. The Jewish People Are Part of the New Covenant:
    Romans 10–11 262
  5.5. The New Nullifies the Old..266
  5.6. Conclusion 268
 6. Conclusion – The Church as the Eschatological Covenant
 Community..268

Chapter 10 271
Jesus and the Kingdom of God on Earth
 Introduction 271
 1. Background: Expectations of Restoration in Jesus' Time 271
 2. The Jesus-Event and the Reign of God on Earth 274
  2.1. The Kingdom Now, and the Vicegerency of Jesus 275
  2.2. The Kingdom Not Yet 292
  2.3. The Land of the Kingdom 294
 3. The Kingdom and the Vicegerency of Jesus in the Epistles 299
  3.1. The Kingdom of God in Romans......................................300
  3.2. Paul and The Vicegerency of Jesus:
    1 Corinthians 15:20–28 303
  3.3. Hebrews 1:8–9, 13; 2:6–9 305
  3.4. Conclusion 308
 4. The Mission of the Church and Universal Dominion..................308
  4.1. Jesus Bestows Vicegerency on His Disciples 308
  4.2. Conquering the Land: The Book of Acts..........................310
  4.3. Subduing the Nations and the Inclusivity of the Kingdom:
    Acts 15:6–21 313

    4.4. Conclusion: The Kingdom of God and the Mission
        of the Church...314
   5. A Future Israelite Kingdom? 315
   6. Conclusion: The Land and the Kingdom 319

Chapter 11 323
The Land as Eden Restored
   Introduction 323
   1. Echoes of Eden in the Jesus-Event.................................324
   2. Eden in the NT 325
       2.1. Luke 23:42–43 325
       2.2. 2 Corinthians 12:2–4 327
       2.3. Jesus as the Last Adam: Romans 5:17–19;
           1 Corinthians 15:22, 45......................................328
       2.4. Revelation 2:7...329
       2.5. Revelation 22:1–5..330
       2.6. Conclusion 333
   3. The NT and the Restoration of Creation 334
       3.1. Romans 8:18–23 335
       3.2. 2 Peter 3:10–13 337
       3.3. Hebrews 11 338
       3.4. Revelation 21: A Completed Picture......................340
   4. Conclusion: A Better *Place*..343

Chapter 12 347
Conclusions: Towards a Missional Theology of the Land
   Introduction 347
   1. The Land and Biblical Theology: A Paradigm...............347
       1.1. The Universal Dimension of Redemption 350
       1.2. Jesus and Adam, Eden and the Land....................351
       1.3. Subduing the Earth..351
       1.4. Redemption as Restoration of Commissioning 351
   2. A Christ-Centered Theology of the Land 353
       2.1. The Land Christified..353
       2.2. Land Matters 354
       2.3. The Universalization of the Land.........................360
       2.4. Two Testaments. One Story 362
   3. From Land to Lands: A Missional Theology of the Land...........364
       3.1. Israel as a Paradigm..364
       3.2. The Individual and the Community 366
       3.3. Territorial Ecclesiology...367

  3.4. Embodying the Presence and Reign of God on Earth 368
  3.5. The Cross as the Paradigm 369
  3.6. Practical Implications..369

Epilogue.. 373
  1. The Promised Land Today..373
  2. Religion, Christian Theology, and the Palestinian Israeli Conflict...375
  3. A Palestinian Christian Response: Towards a Shared
  Land Theology 378

Bibliography... 383

Abstract

The theology of the land must start in the garden of Eden. Eden is a sanctuary, a covenanted land, and a royal garden. Eden is proto-land, and Adam is proto-Israel. Starting in Eden underlines the universal dimension of the land promise and its conditionality. It also elevates ethical behavior above the gift.

The theology of the land in the Old Testament (OT) reflects these Edenic themes: holiness, covenant, and kingdom. First, the *holiness* of the land depends on the presence of God in the land, and on the holiness of its dwellers; there is no permanent holy place in the OT. Second, the land is a gift under treaty; the goal of the gift is establishing an ideal *covenantal* community that witnesses to other nations in other lands. Third, the land is the sphere of God's *reign* on earth through his vicegerent. The vicegerent brings justice and peace to the land. God remains the ultimate king in the land. The original promise to Israel is a promise of universal dominion.

After the exile, the prophets spoke of a time in which the land would become an ideal place. This ideal land is, effectively, Eden restored. The restoration of the land ultimately points forward to the restoration of the earth. The land in the OT underlines the social dimension to redemption. Yet, importantly, Israel's faith can survive without the land.

The Jesus-event is the starting place for the theology of the land in the New Testament (NT). Jesus restored Israel and fulfilled the promises of the OT, including the land. He embodied the holy presence of God on earth, kept the covenant on behalf of Israel, and brought the reign of God on earth. He inherited the land, and in him Jews and Gentiles are its true heirs. This radical new fulfillment, brought about by the Jesus-event, dramatically changed the meaning of the land and nullified the old promises in their old articulation. The NT points forward to a time of consummation when the whole earth will become an ideal place or a redeemed land.

The land has thus been universalized in Christ. Universalization does not mean the "spiritualization" or "heavenization." Instead, the theology of the land of Israel – modified in the Jesus-event – is a paradigm for Christian communities living in other lands. The theology of the land thus underlines the social and territorial dimensions of redemption. It also highlights the goodness of creation, and has many practical implications for the ongoing mission and practice of the church throughout the world.

INTRODUCTION
A Biblical Theology of the Land

Land is a central, if not *the central, theme* of biblical faith.[1]

The fate of the land is the focal point of biblical historiography.[2]

Biblical Theology

The land is an important theme in the Bible. It is a theme through which the whole biblical history – contained in both the Old and New Testaments – can be studied and analyzed. When it comes to the Old Testament (OT), it is no exaggeration to say that the land is the central theme in the narrative of Israel. This study is a "biblical theological" study of the land. Biblical theology can be defined as:

> A branch of theological inquiry devoted to identifying distinctive themes in various sections of the Bible . . . tracing them from one section to another, and discovering any overall unifying theme that draws the whole Bible together.[3]

---
1. W. Brueggemann, *The Land: Place as Gift, Promise, and Challenge in Biblical Faith* (Minneapolis: Fortress Press, 2002), 3 (emphasis in original).
2. M. Weinfeld, *The Promise of the Land: The Inheritance of the Land of Canaan by the Israelites* (Berkeley: University of California Press, 2003), xvi.
3. G. R. Osborne, "Biblical Theology," in *Baker Encyclopedia of the Bible,* eds. W. A. Elwell and B. J. Beitzel (Grand Rapids: Baker Book House, 1988), 339. The foundation of biblical theology was laid by J. F. Gabler, who argued in 1787 that biblical theology was a discipline independent from systematics, centering on the description of each biblical

This study, simply put, will trace the theme of the land from one section of the Bible to another, and will attempt to discover any overall unifying themes in the theology of the land that draw the Bible together. The assumption that there are unifying themes in the Bible is essential to biblical theology. "Biblical theology is concerned to describe the inner unity of the Bible on its own terms."[4] Yet this does not mean that the Bible by design has only one major unifying theme, or that there is a theological uniformity that runs through every section of the Bible. The diversity of the "theologies" that are contained in the Bible is well acknowledged:

> Yahwistic history and Deuteronomic history, the Sacerdotal tradition, the Wisdom tradition, the synoptic Gospels, the Pauline doctrine and that of the epistle to the Hebrews, the apocalyptic fresco of John and the fourth Gospel – all are so many "theologies" which can be explained in themselves. But likewise, from a much broader point of view we can consider the Bible as a whole. We can try to grasp the organic continuity and coherence which manifest the profound unity of these diverse theologies: this is biblical theology.[5]

In other words, biblical theology acknowledges the theological diversity in the different layers of the Bible. This diversity can be the result of historical developments in the biblical narrative, in addition to the unique theological perspective that each author brings. The biblical authors spoke from different historical and theological perspectives. Biblical theology is historical in nature. It traces the historical and theological developments in the biblical narrative as portrayed by the biblical authors. These developments or progression do not however mean that we cannot find some unifying

---

author's theology in its historical context. See also B. S. Childs, *Biblical Theology of the Old and New Testaments: Theological Reflection on the Christian Bible* (Minneapolis: Fortress Press, 1993).

4. C. G. Bartholomew, "Biblical Theology," in *Dictionary for Theological Interpretation of the Bible,* eds. K. J. Vanhoozer, C. G. Bartholomew and D. J. Treier (Grand Rapids: Baker Academic, 2005), 86.

5. X. Léon-Dufour, *Dictionary of Biblical Theology* (London: Geoffrey Chapman, 1973), xvii.

themes in the biblical narrative. As Brueggemann argues regarding the OT (and we can apply his argument to biblical theology in general): "The Old Testament is not a metanarrative but offers the materials out of which a metanarrative may be construed."[6]

Millar observes that a major problem facing any biblical theological discussion of land is that the theme seems, at first glance, to be limited almost entirely to the OT.[7] Yet, as will be argued extensively, the land proves to be an important theme in the NT. Furthermore, Christian theology "must not limit its reflection to either the Old or the New Testament but must account for its understanding of the Bible as a whole."[8] We must of course acknowledge that the Bible "consists of two parts whose points of *commonality* as well as *difference* must be equally appreciated."[9] As such, we must take seriously – in addition to the different theologies contained in the different layers of the biblical narrative in each of the Testaments – the different theological and historical perspectives between the Old and New Testaments themselves. The NT biblical theology of the land, as will be argued, adopts, redefines, and challenges the themes that are related to the land in the OT.

Terminology

We could refer to the land in the biblical narrative as the "Holy Land," "Canaan," "Israel," "Haaretz," "the Land," or "Israel's Land." This study simply uses the term "the land." By this term we mean the land promised to Abraham, settled on by the patriarchs, conquered by Joshua, and which was the arena of the monarchy. Moreover, the focus in this study looks at the land as a theological concept that is loaded with meaning:

---

6. W. Brueggemann, *Theology of the Old Testament: Testimony, Dispute, Advocacy* (Minneapolis: Fortress Press, 1997), 559.

7. J. G. Millar, "Land," in *New Dictionary of Biblical Theology*, eds. T. D. Alexander and B. S. Rosner (Downers Grove: InterVarsity Press, 2000), 623.

8. B. Janowski, "The One God of the Two Testaments: Basic Questions of a Biblical Theology," *Theology Today* 57, no. 3 (2000): 300.

9. Ibid., 297 (emphasis added).

> Land continually moves back and forth between literal and symbolic intentions . . . A symbolic sense of the term affirms that land is never simply physical dirt but is always physical dirt freighted with social meanings derived from historical experience.[10]

> In the Bible *erets* represents neither a geographical object nor a philosophical abstraction, but [is personified as] a person. *Erets* plays its role in the biblical drama alongside God, Israel, and the nations.[11]

It will also become apparent that "land" in the Bible is meant to reflect more than just one particular land (Canaan), but different "lands" in different places – indeed the whole earth. As such, the theology of the land is more than just the theology of the "Promised Land," as will be argued in the conclusion of this study.

The Hebrew Scripture uses two terms for the land: ארץ and אדמה. ארץ is the more frequently mentioned term and also the more comprehensive. It designates the entire earth (Gen 11:1), the earth in contrast to heaven (Ecc 5:1), and the known cosmos as over against the heavens (Isa 1:2; Gen 1:1). The term also refers to the land in general (Exod 8:12; Deut 11:25) and especially to the land as a territory (2 Sam 24:8), and as an area with political boundaries (Deut 1:5).[12] אדמה is connected to the root אדם, and reflects the soil from which humanity was taken and to which humanity returns.[13] It can be translated "ground."

---

10. Brueggemann, *The Land*, 2.
11. A. Neher, "The Land as Locus of the Sacred,," in *Voices from Jerusalem. Jews and Christians Reflect on the Holy Land*, eds. D. Burrell and Y. Landau (New York: Paulist Press, 1992), 19.
12. H. D. Preuss, *Old Testament Theology. Volume I* (Louisville: Westminster John Knox Press, 1995), 118. For more on the meaning of ארץ, see W. Janzen, "Land," in *The Anchor Bible Dictionary*, ed. D. N. Freedman (New York: Doubleday, 1992), 143–154.
13. Gen 2:7; 3:19; Ps 90:3; 104:29; Qoh.12:7.

The LXX translated both Hebrew terms ארץ and אדמה with the Greek word γῆ.¹⁴ This is also the most common word for the land in the NT. Γῆ could designate land in the geographical or territorial sense (Matt 9:26, 31), the land of promise (Acts 7:3), the inhabited earth (Rev 3:10), and the earth as a theater of history (Matt 23:35).¹⁵ In addition, two other words are used: ἀγρός refers to land with reference to agricultural or topographical features (Matt 13:31), and χώρα refers to a political region (Matt 2:12).¹⁶ The fact that ארץ and γῆ could mean both *land* and *earth* is significant. One needs the context to distinguish which meaning is applied, and in some cases this is not an easy task.

The Land in Recent Biblical Studies: A Brief Survey

Following the emigration of Jews to Palestine and the establishment of the modern state of Israel, there was inevitably an increased interest in the land, which led to it being a topic for academic studies. There was also a sensitivity towards understanding this in the context of Christian-Jewish relationships. The first major study on the land was the book by W. D. Davies in 1972.¹⁷ Davies devotes the bulk of this book, *The Gospel and the Land*, to how the NT treated the theme of the land. Only the first chapter dealt with the land in the OT; then after some reflection on the land in Second Temple Judaism, Davies devoted most of the book to the land in the NT, arguing that the NT's attitude towards the land is that of "rejection and spiritualization."¹⁸ For him, the Christian faith "cut loose from the land," and the Gospels demanded a breaking out of its "territorial chrysalis."¹⁹ Davies's book represents a landmark in Christian theology

---

14. G. M. Burge, "Land," in *The New Interpreter's Dictionary of the Bible. I-Ma (Vol. 3)*, ed. K. D. Sakenfeld (Nashville: Abingdon Press, 2006), 573.
15. H. Sasse, "γῆ," in *Theological Dictionary of the New Testament*, ed. G. Kittel (Grand Rapids: Eerdmans, 1969), 677–678.
16. Burge, "Land," 573.
17. A second edition was published in 1994. See W. D. Davies, *The Gospel and the Land: Early Christianity and Jewish Territorial Doctrine* (Sheffield: JSOT Press, 1994).
18. Ibid., 367.
19. Ibid., 336.

of the land, and his contribution was fresh and well articulated. However, his conclusions de-emphasized the importance of the land in Christian thought and mission.

The second major landmark book on the land was done by an OT scholar, Walter Brueggemann; naturally the main focus was on the land in the OT.[20] Brueggemann took a socio-historical approach to the text, looking at the role land played in the narrative of Israel through the different historical periods. He talked about the "dialectic" in Israel's fortunes between *landlessness* (wilderness, exile) and *landedness* (possession of a land, anticipation of the land, or grief over its loss).[21] Brueggemann devoted one chapter in his book to the theme of the land in NT, arguing that the kingdom of God in Jesus is a new way of being 'landed' in the Bible. Brueggemann's masterful work highlighted the importance of land across the whole of the OT, arguing that the land is "central, if not the central theme in biblical faith."[22] It offered wide range of new insights on the role of land in OT. It remains one of the key resources, if not *the* key resource, for any student of the theme of the land in the Bible.

Brueggemann's book was followed by another important book on the land in the OT by Norman Habel.[23] This book identified six biblical land ideologies in the OT: royal, agrarian, theocratic, prophetic, ancestral household, and immigrant. Habel's thematic/ideological approach differed noticeably from Bruegemann's historical approach, yet complemented it in an important way: it highlighted the diversity in the OT when it comes to the theme of the land. Habel, however, did not elaborate much on how these different ideologies relate to one another within the framework of the OT.

Another important contribution to the theology of the land is the work of Jewish scholar Moshe Weinfeld.[24] Weinfeld focuses on ANE (Ancient Near East) settings that influenced the Hebrew writers on the theme of the

---

20. The first edition of Brueggemann's book on the land came in 1977. A second and revised edition was published in 2002. See Brueggemann, *The Land*.
21. Ibid., xi.
22. Ibid., 3.
23. N. C. Habel, *The Land is Mine: Six Biblical Land Ideologies* (Minneapolis: Fortress Press, 1995).
24. Weinfeld, *Promise of the Land*.

land. His book adopts historical-critical methods and assumptions when analyzing the texts. Perhaps the most important chapters in his book are the ones on the borders (chapter 3) and the covenant (chapters 8 and 9).

In addition, we should also mention the book by Paul Tarazi[25] and that by Alain Marchadour and David Neuhaus.[26] Both of these books look at the theme of the land canonically in both the Old and New Testaments, arguing that the land in the NT has been universalized. This conclusion – that the land has been universalized – is also found in many Christian scholars who discuss biblical theology in general.[27] However, the nature and implications of this universalization are often left unpacked and unexplained. It seems that this universalization becomes a means of dismissing the theme of the land in the NT.[28]

A more recent book was written by Gary Burge on the land in the NT.[29] This book is a very important contribution to the discussion on the land in the NT, as it went beyond Davies's earlier work and managed to show that the NT does indeed have much to say about the land. The book is structured canonically, looking at the theme of the land in each section of the NT: the synoptic Gospels, the fourth Gospel, Paul, Hebrews and Revelation. The main thrust of the book is that the NT claims that Jesus

---

25. P. N. Tarazi, *Land and Covenant* (St. Paul: Ocabs Press, 2009).

26. A. Marchadour and D. Neuhaus, *The Land, the Bible, and History: Toward the Land That I Will Show You* (New York: Fordham University, 2007).

27. See for example B. Waltke, 2007, *An Old Testament Theology: An Exegetical, Canonical, and Thematic Approach* (Grand Rapids: Zondervan, 2007); G. K. Beale, *A New Testament Biblical Theology: The Unfolding of the Old Testament in the New* (Grand Rapids: Baker Academic, 2011).

28. A notable and very important exception is Chris Wright brief treatment of the theme of the land in the NT is his two major works *Old Testament Ethics for the People of God* and *The Mission of God*. Wright retains a missional implication for the theme of the land in Christian thought, and his thoughts on this will be advanced in this study. C. J. H. Wright, *Old Testament Ethics for the People of God* (Downers Grove: InterVarsity Press, 2004); C. J. H. Wright, *The Mission of God: Unlocking The Bible's Grand Narrative* (Downers Grove: IVP Academic, 2006).

29. G. M. Burge, *Jesus and The Land: The New Testament Challenge to 'Holy Land' Theology,* (Grand Rapids: Baker Academic, 2010). Prior to Burge, Peter Walker has written an important work on Jerusalem in the New Testament. Though the book deals mainly with Jerusalem, there is a lot of relevance and overlap with theology of the land. Walker looked at Jerusalem in each section in the NT, and argued that the NT de-emphasized and critiqued the theological importance of Jerusalem. P. W. L. Walker, *Jesus and the Holy City: New Testament Perspectives on Jerusalem* (Grand Rapids: Eerdmans, 1996).

fulfilled the promises of the OT, including that of the land. The tone in Burge's book is primarily a negative one, stressing the way in which the NT seemingly relativized or even nullified the significance of the land. It focused mainly on how the NT theology of the land differed from that in the OT and contemporary Jewish theologies of the land.

Finally, the Palestinian Israeli conflict in the land today and the use of religious languages in this conflict has drawn a lot of discussion, especially after Palestinian theologians began to write. There are many books that address the theme of the land in the Bible with a direct concern to the modern conflict; asking questions that arise from the context of the conflict rather than studying the theme of the land systematically. Notable books include Chapman,[30] Sizer,[31] Johnson and Walker,[32] Munayer and Loden,[33] and Katanacho.[34] These works and others are very relevant to our study and offer an important contribution. This study, though written by a Palestinian Christian, takes a systematic and comprehensive approach to the theme of the land of the Bible, constructing a Christian biblical theology of the land, while leaving the contemporary relevance to the very end.

Thesis

This study traces the theme of the land throughout the biblical canon. It starts in the garden of Eden, and ends in the book of Revelation. Eden, it will be argued in the first chapter, is presented in the OT as proto-Promised Land. By starting in Eden and by arguing for a theology of the land in Eden, we will be adding a unique contribution to the already existing discussion on the theology of the land. Three major theological themes are

---

30. C. Chapman, *Whose Promised Land? The Continuing Crisis Over Israel and Palestine* (Grand Rapids: Baker Books, 2002).
31. S. Sizer, *Zion's Christian Soldiers? The Bible, Israel and The Church* (Nottingham: InterVarsity, 2007).
32. P. S. Johnston and P. Walker, eds., 2000, *The Land of Promise: Biblical, Theological and Contemporary Perspectives* (Downers Grove: InterVarsity Press, 2000).
33. S. Munayer and L. Loden, *The Land Cries Out: Theology of the Land in the Israeli-Palestinian Context* (Eugene: CASCADE Books, 2012).
34. Y. Katanacho, *The Land of Christ* (Bethlehem: Bethlehem Bible College, 2012).

found in Eden: (1) Eden as a sanctuary; (2) Eden as covenanted territory; and (3) Eden as a royal garden. These three themes – which can be summarized under the three terms Holiness, Covenant, and Kingship – will then become three lenses through which we will look at the land in the rest of the biblical narrative. We will take a diachronic-thematic approach: looking at each of these three themes as they develop in the biblical narrative. This will provide a new structure for studying the theme of the land in the Bible. Chapters 2–4 look at the theology of the land in the OT up to the exile: chapter 2 looks at the land as "holy"; chapter 3 looks at the land as "covenanted"; and chapter 4 looks at the land and "kingship." Chapter 5 then looks at these three themes in the visions for the future (or the eschatology) found in the OT prophets. Chapter 6 argues that the land of promise in the OT is portrayed as Eden restored, and draws some conclusions regarding the theology of the land in the OT.

Chapter 7 introduces the theology of the land in the NT, arguing that the coming of Jesus is the essential foundation for any study of the land in the NT. We will then go back to our three themes and look at them with reference to Jesus: chapter 8 looks at Jesus and holy territory; chapter 9 looks at Jesus and the covenanted land; and chapter 10 looks at Jesus and the reign of God on earth. These chapters will argue that Jesus in his life, teachings, and ministry embodied *all* the realities that pertained to the land in the OT; also that as a result, in the new era in history, the meaning and significance of the land – as articulated by the NT authors – has been radically transformed by the coming of Jesus.

Chapter 11 then looks at the land in the eschatological vision of the NT authors (the consummation). The chapter focuses on the book of Revelation, and argues that the land points to the redemption and renewal of the earth. The final chapter draws conclusions from all the chapters, and proposes a paradigm both for biblical theology in general as well as for the biblical theology of the land. The study concludes by proposing a missional approach, based on an Edenic theology of the land, which gives an agenda for faithful Christian practice throughout the world today.

This study argues that the land has indeed been 'universalized' in Christ. However, this universalization of the land is not a denial, or even a dismissal, of the significance of the land in the NT. Quite the contrary. Rather, it is an affirmation of the importance of the land for Christian theology and the mission of the church. Thus, this work also argues against any 'spiritualization' of the land. There is indeed a movement from the *particular* (Israel) to the *universal* (the world), achieved through Christ and this is a non-negotiable element in biblical theology. The movement in the biblical theology of the land is thus a centrifugal one: out from the Promised Land, to every land, to the earth. However, this movement does not evaporate the theme of the land of its enduring significance and its potential applications. The theology of the *land* becomes the theology of *every land* – and is ultimately the theology of the whole earth. Its implications have gone global.

The main contributions of this study can be summarized as follows:

First, it offers a theology of the land that is rooted and established in the garden of Eden, and makes it the basis for the biblical theology of the land.

Second, it offers a new structure through which the theme of the land is studied and analyzed in the Bible. The three themes of holiness, covenant, and kingdom are considered in a diachronic-thematic manner, seeing in what ways each of them develops through the course of the biblical narrative. These themes create the framework of this study.

Third, it gives the Old and New Testaments equal space and importance, examining NT through the lens of what was discovered in the OT section. This creates a sense of continuity. The study neither stops with the OT, nor simply begins with the NT. The NT section thus uses the same three themes from Eden and the OT: holiness, covenant, and kingdom. This has not been done before, and brings a strength and freshness to the NT material.

Fourth, the main argument of this study is that the land has been universalized. In contrast to many land theologies that either spiritualized the land or rendered the promises of land for the future *only*, this study unpacks this notion of universalization and builds from it towards a missional theology of the land that is practical and applicable here and now – not just in the land itself, but throughout the world.

CHAPTER 1

The Theology of the Land in the Garden of Eden

Introduction

This chapter argues that the theology of the land should have its starting point in Eden, and not in the promises to Abraham. Failure to acknowledge this point minimizes the universal role of the land in biblical theology and the universal focus of the calling of Abraham and Israel.

Many theologians in studying the theme of land in the Bible have neglected this critical point.[1] The absence of an Eden theology in the major

---

1. Davies, who is considered the pioneer in the theology of the land, started his study on the land in the promises to the Patriarchs, and so did von Rad, Brueggemann, Weinfeld, and Burge. Davies, *The Gospel and the Land*; G. Von Rad, "The Promised Land and Yahweh's Land in the Hexateuch," in *The Problem of the Hexateuch and Other Essays,* ed. G. Von Rad (Edinburgh and London: Oliver & Boyd, 1966), 79–93; Brueggemann, *The Land*; Weinfeld, *Promise of the Land*; Burge, *Jesus and The Land*. Habel's study was a thematic one and he did not touch on the garden of Eden; and the collected essays on the land edited by Van Ruiten and De Vos do not mention Eden. The collected essays on the land edited by Walker and Johnston also do not touch on the issue, with the notable exception of Robertson. Habel, *The Land is Mine*; J. Van Ruiten and J. C. De Vos, eds., *The Land of Israel in Bible, History, and Theology: Studies in Honour of Ed Noort* (Leiden: Brill, 2009); Johnston and Walker, *The Land of Promise*; O. P. Robertson, "A New Covenant Perspective on the Land," in *The Land of Promise*, ed. P. Johnston and P. Walker (Downers Grove: InterVarsity Press, 2000), 121–141. On the other hand, Marchadour and Neuhaus, Tarazi, and Munayer started their studies on the land in Eden, but did not devote much attention to the narrative or to its importance to the rest of the study. Yet by starting in Eden, these theologians stress that the theology of the land has universal dimensions, and is not limited to a particular people and a particular piece of land. Marchadour and Neuhaus, *The Land, the Bible, and History*; Tarazi, *Land and Covenant*; S.

studies of the land is striking, especially when we take into consideration the importance of creation theology in the OT. Brueggemann in fact mentions the creation theme but only in the introduction to the second edition of his book. He observes that the creation theme should take on crucial importance since the term הארץ in the OT refers both to earth and land. He then says:

> Thus, it is entirely possible that Israel's land stands in for and epitomizes all lands. Consequently, in the Pentateuchal traditions, the final form of the text begins in an account of "earth" . . . but culminates with references to the "land of promise."[2]

On the basis of this observation, it is only proper that any theology of the land should start in the creation narrative, and in particular in the garden of Eden (Gen 2–3) – the particular territory in the creation narrative.

The first part of this chapter argues for Eden as a sanctuary, or the first 'holy' land. The second part discusses the importance of the covenant and Torah traditions in the formulation of the Eden narrative, and argues that Israel's salvation history is the background of this story. The third part discusses the royal theology in Eden and argues for Eden as the location of the first "monarchy." Lastly, in the final part, the place and role of the Eden narrative in salvation history is examined.[3] The main argument of this chapter is to view Eden as proto-Land, and Adam as proto-Israel. Based on this argument, a theology of the land in Eden will be proposed.

Munayer, "From Land of Strife to Land of Reconciliation," in *The Land Cries Out*, ed. S. Munayer and L. Loden (Eugene: Wipf &Stock, 2010), 234–265.

2. Brueggemann, *The Land*, xiii.

3. The focus of this study of the Eden narrative in Genesis 2–3 is on Eden as a place. I acknowledge the many different angles or lenses through which we can look at the story (Fall, sexuality, human condition, ecology, etc.), and I also acknowledge the validity of these readings. But for the sake of proposing a biblical theology of the land, which is the aim of the whole study, we will only focus on Eden as geography/place/land. Therefore there will be some selectivity, by focusing on certain texts and themes in the Eden narrative. We will not for example discuss the fall in Genesis 3. Instead, the focus will be on Genesis 2:8–17, where Eden is described.

1. Eden as a Sanctuary

There are strong indications in Genesis 2–3 that the garden of Eden is portrayed as an archetypal sanctuary.[4] By sanctuary we mean a place set apart by God where he encounters humanity and reveals himself to them in a special way. In the Pentateuch, a sanctuary refers to "the place where God appeared and/or dwelt as indicated by the presence of the ark."[5]

There is textual evidence and symbolic features that point towards the conclusion that Eden is portrayed as a sanctuary, in addition to similarities with ANE literature that describes cultic gardens. If Eden was a sanctuary, it follows that Adam was a priestly figure. The evidence for Eden as a sanctuary will be examined below. Though each point will be considered separately, these points overlap.

1.1. The Garden as an Enclosed Distinct Area in Eden

In Genesis 2:8 YHWH Elohim planted a garden *in* Eden (גן בעדן).[6] Eden is then the locus or site of the garden. Adam was formed outside of the garden, and then was brought *into* it. In Genesis 2:10 a river came out of Eden and watered the garden. All this tells us that the garden is a distinct place

---

4. G. J. Wenham, "Sanctuary Symbolism in the Garden of Eden Story," in *I Studied Inscriptions from Before the Flood: Ancient Near Eastern, Literary, and Linguistic Approaches to Genesis 1-11,* eds. R. S. Hess and D. T. Tsumura (Winona Lake: Eisenbrauns, 1994), 399–404. See also T. D. Alexander, *From Eden to The New Jerusalem: Exploring God's Plan for Life on Earth* (Nottingham: Inter-Varsity Press, 2008), 20–31; G. K. Beale, "Eden, The Temple, and The Church's Mission in the New Creation," *JETS* 48, no. 1 (2005): 5–31.

5. A. E. Cundall, "Sanctuary," in *Baker Encyclopaedia of the Bible,* eds. W. A. Elwell and B. J. Beitzel (Grand Rapids: Baker Book House, 1988), 1902.

6. For a etymology of עדן see A. H. Lewis, "The Localization of the Garden of Eden," *Bulletin of the Evangelical Theological Society* 11, no. 4 (1968): 169–175; A. R. Millard, "The Etymology of Eden," *Vetus Testamentum* 34, no. 1 (1984): 103–106; C. Westermann, *Genesis 1-11: A Continental Commentary* (Minneapolis: Fortress Press, 1994), 208–210; T. C. Mitchel, "Eden, Garden of," in *New Bible Dictionary,* eds. H. Marchal, A. R. Millard, J. I. Packer and D. J. Wiseman, (Nottingham; IVP Academic, 1996), 289–290; E. Noort, "Gan-Eden in the Context of the Mythology of the Hebrew Bible," in *Paradise Interpreted: Representations of Biblical Paradise in Judaism and Christianity,* ed. G. P. Luttikhuizen (Leiden: Brill, 1999), 21–22; B. Kedar-Kopfstein, "עדן," in *Theological Dictionary of the Old Testament. 10, naqam - 'azab,* eds. G. J. Botterweck, H. Ringgren and H. Fabry (Grand Rapids: Eerdmans, 2001), 481–491; G. Anderson, "Eden, Garden of," in *The New Interpreter's Dictionary of the Bible,* ed. Sakenfeld (Nashville: Abingdon Press, 2006), 186–187.

within Eden. Genesis 2:15, 3:23, and 24 call it the garden of Eden (גן עדן) after it was established that it was actually a garden in Eden.

How can we understand this garden? Dumbrell concludes from the definition of the Hebrew word גן as a "fenced off enclosure, particularly of a garden protected by a wall or a hedge," that the garden is "a special place which is spatially separated from its outside world."[7] The term used in Greek in the LXX is παράδεισος,[8] and "this term had established itself as a loan-word in the corpus of the sacred writings with the significance of 'park,' or 'orchard,' or 'royal garden.'"[9] Clearly, then, the garden is a distinct protected place, which had some type of borders or boundaries.

When Adam and Eve were expelled from the garden, they lived east of the garden of Eden (מקדם לגן עדן) (Gen 3:24). Beale has taken this to indicate that the entrance of the garden was from the east, a feature similar to the temple in Jerusalem.[10] In addition, the verb גרש used to describe the driving out of Adam and Eve is the same verb used to describe the cleansing of the Promised Land by Joshua (Josh 24:12, 18). Stordalen suggests that this lexeme "may imply a vague similarity between the Eden Garden and the land."[11] The land was cleansed because it specially had to be holy and clean of anything that defiled it – and so was Eden.

After Adam and Eve were cast out of the garden, it was guarded by cherubim (כרבים). In the OT cherubim guard the ark of the covenant (Exod 25:18–22) and are always associated with the tabernacle or the temple. The fact that cherubim are said to guard the garden suggests that the garden is a sacred and enclosed place, now out of reach to Adam. Accordingly, "the

---

7. W. J. Dumbrell, "Genesis 2:1–3: Biblical Theology of Creation Covenant," *Evangelical Review of Theology* 25, no. 3 (2001): 221–222. Similarly, Lewis sees in גן a term that argues for the localization of paradise, since it comes from "a verbal stem meaning 'to protect,' 'to defend,' it always describes an enclosed or fenced area." Lewis, "Localization of the Garden of Eden," 171.
8. For a treatment of this term in Greek, see J. N. Bremmer, "Paradise: From Persia, via Greece, into the Septuagint," in *Paradise Interpreted: Representations of Biblical Paradise in Judaism and Christianity*, ed. G. Luttikhuizen (Leiden: Brill, 1999), 1–20.
9. Lewis, "Localization of the Garden of Eden," 171.
10. Beale, "Eden," 8. See Ezek 43:1; 44:1; 46:1.
11. T. Stordalen, *Echoes of Eden: Genesis 2-3 and Symbolism of the Eden Garden in Biblical Hebrew Literature* (Leuven: Peeters, 2000), 457.

narrative clearly regards this tree garden as a *holy* region, enclosing God's presence and therefore guarded by cherubim."[12]

These pieces of evidence collectively indicate that the garden of Eden is portrayed in the narrative as an enclosed distinct area in Eden that is arguably marked by holiness – similar to that of the land and the temple.

1.2. Eden Mediated the Presence of YHWH Elohim

There are also strong indications in the text that the garden was the place where God visited and appeared to Adam. God regularly spoke to Adam (2:16, 19; 3:9), and since he created Eve from Adam, this means that he was actually in Eden (2:22). Eden was "a locus for divine activity."[13]

The strongest evidence however for the presence of God in the garden is in Genesis 3:8: "And they heard the sound of the LORD God walking (מתהלך) in the garden in the cool of the day."[14] There is a suggestion of a theophany in this verse that recalls divine appearances in the tabernacle and the temple, especially when compared with Leviticus 26:12, Deuteronomy 23:15, and 2 Samuel 7:6–7.[15] Stordalen also observes that the hithpael of הלך (Gen 3:8) is used elsewhere to describe the presence of God in the tent sanctuary and then reminds us that "a prime location for theophanies would be the Temple."[16]

---

12. G. Von Rad, *Genesis: A Commentary* (London: SCM Press, 1972), 77 (emphasis in the original). See also M. G. Kline, *Kingdom Prologue: Genesis Foundations for a Covenantal Worldview* (Overland Park: Two Age Press, 2000), 48.

13. D. E. Callender, *Adam in Myth and History: Ancient Israelite Perspectives on the Primal Human* (Winona Lake: Eisenbrauns, 2000), 41.

14. All Scripture citations are from the English Standard Version (ESV), unless other stated. *The Holy Bible: English Standard Version* (Wheaton: Standard Bible Society, 2001).

15. Beale, "Eden," 7; Wenham, "Sanctuary Symbolism," 400.

16. Stordalen, *Echoes of Eden*, 458. Niehaus goes as far as arguing that we should also read קול and רוח היום "theophanically" and suggests the following translation for Gen 3:8: "Then the man and his wife heard the thunder (*qwl*) of Yahweh God as he was going back and forth (*mthlk*) in the garden in the wind of the storm (*lrwh hywm*)." J. Niehaus, "In the Wind of the Storm: Another Look At Genesis III 8," *Vetus Testamentum* 44, no. 2 (1994): 266. For a similar interpretation of this verse, see: Kline, *Kingdom Prologue*, 129. Grundke in particular took issue with this interpretation and responded to Niehaus. He argued that: "there is no compelling logical connection between the textual features of Gen. iii 8 and its status as a storm theophany. Although Niehaus' proposal is not groundless, the cumulative power of his arguments seems insufficient to establish the case convincingly. Despite the admitted shortcomings arising from the lack of other biblical examples of the expression *lrwh hywm*, the traditional translation – 'at the windy time

Moreover, evidence from ANE myths suggests that Eden could be viewed as the throne or palace of the god. Callender, in his thorough study on Adam in Eden, says that in the ANE, a mountainous, oasis-like garden setting is one of the traditionally understood dwellings of the gods. Therefore, he argues that the garden of Eden was similarly understood to be a divine dwelling, a place where the divine could be encountered unmediated.[17] Callender relied on ANE material in addition to some OT texts to reach his conclusions on Eden.[18] Neiman, who sees strong mythical ANE elements in the story, has similar conclusions and even goes beyond to argue that Eden was the "throne of the creator King":

> His throne stands in the midst of the garden . . . The garden is on a mountain, the mountain of God, which may have temporal likeness, a miniature-scale model on earth in the form of a hill on whose top there stands a Temple where men can come to worship God in his House which is but his earthly dwelling, his various place of being.[19]

If we go along with this interpretation, we can conclude that this throne belongs to the "creator King."[20] YHWH Elohim is the creator of heavens and earth in Genesis 1. The garden is the locus of his throne.[21] The cherubim in Genesis 3:24 therefore can be compared to the seraphim (שרפים) surrounding the throne of אדני in Isaiah 6, and so there is justification in Neiman's conclusion that Eden was the locus of the throne of God.

---

of the day' – remains the preferable option." C. L. K. Grundke, "A Tempest in a Teapot? Genesis III 8 Again," *Vetus Testamentum* 51, no. 4 (2001): 552.

17. Callender, *Adam in Myth and History*, 49.

18. Ezek 28, Ps 36:8–10, Jer 17:12–13.

19. D. Neiman, "Eden, the Garden of God," *Acta Antiqua Academiae Scientiarum Hungaricae* 17 (1969): 121. Neiman's study focused on Ezek 28 more than Gen 2–3. He believed that Ezek 28 is more mythical in nature than Gen 2–3 and that the mythological elements were removed from Gen 2–3, but gives no reason or proof for this view.

20. Kline, *Kingdom Prologue*, 47.

21. See part three of this chapter: Eden and the Kingdom.

These evidences have led some to argue for Eden as a "dwelling place" of God – the garden of God.[22] Levenson says that paradise, like the temple, is a place in which God is "forever present in an intensely palpable sense, a place therefore of beatific existence, of perfection."[23] We have already noticed that von Rad considered God's presence to be "enclosed" in the garden.[24]

Stordalen and Gordon on the other hand do not go this far. For Stordalen, Eden mediates the presence of God, but God does not live there.[25] He also observed that deities in the ANE "would live in houses, gardens being hardly more than peripheral setting for the heavenly palace."[26] Gordon similarly argues:

> Although Eden may be regarded as having sanctuary features, it does not follow that it is depicted as the permanent home of God, any more than the tabernacle and temple traditions necessarily represent a limiting of the abode of God to an earthly shrine.[27]

Regardless of whether we can say with certainty that Eden is portrayed in Genesis 2–3 as a dwelling place of YHWH Elohim, we can safely conclude that it was the place or medium of God's presence with humans. In other words, if God was to appear to man, it would happen in Eden.

---

22. Kline, *Kingdom Prologue*, 60. See also H. N. Wallace, *The Eden Narrative* (Atlanta: Scholars Press, 1985).
23. J. D. Levenson, *Sinai & Zion: An Entry Into the Jewish Bible* (New York: HarperSanFrancisco, 1987), 131.
24. Von Rad, *Genesis*, 77.
25. Stordalen also observes that this is similar to Assyrian royal gardens. Stordalen, *Echoes of Eden*, 298.
26. *Ibid.*, 161.
27. R. P. Gordon, *Holy Land, Holy City: Sacred Geography and the Interpretation of the Bible* (Carlisle: Paternoster Press, 2004), 20.

1.3. The Work of Adam Is in the Garden

One of the strongest arguments for Eden as a sanctuary comes from the description of the task given to Adam in the garden in Genesis 2:15.[28] There we read that God placed Adam in the garden to "work and keep" it. The two Hebrew verbs used, עבד and שמר, are an unusual combination. The only other times they are combined in the OT they describe the work of the priest in the tabernacle or temple.[29] Stordalen hence argues that the guarding and serving imposed upon Adam in Genesis 2 "mirrors religiously and morally appropriate conduct – especially that of Yahwistic priests in service."[30] Walton sums up the argument in four points: (1) since there are several contexts in which שמר is used for levitical service along with עבד, and (2) since the contextual use of שמר here favors sacred service, and (3) since עבד is likely to refer to sacred service as to agricultural tasks, and (4) since there are other indications that the garden is being portrayed as a sacred place, "it is likely that tasks given to Adam are of priestly nature: caring for sacred space."[31]

1.4. The Landscape of Eden

Eden contained trees and rivers. When we look carefully at the symbols in the narrative,[32] a new light is shed on the meaning of the tree of life, the tree of knowledge of good and evil, and the river and other landscape features. The tree of life of course symbolizes life,[33] and so do the four rivers with their water (Ps 1:3, Ezek 47:8–12, Zech 14:8).[34] Life is to be found

---

28. See for example Dumbrell, "Genesis 2:1-3," 224; Beale, "Eden," 7; Wenham, "Sanctuary Symbolism," 401.
29. See Num 3:7–8; 8:26; 18:5–6; 1 Chr 23:32; Ezek 44:14.
30. Stordalen, *Echoes of Eden*, 461.
31. J. H. Walton, "Eden, Garden of," in *Dictionary of the Old Testament: Pentateuch*, ed. D. W. Baker and D. W. Alexander (Downers Grove: InterVarsity Press, 2003), 206.
32. As Wenham argues, the Eden narrative should be read "not a naive myth but as a highly symbolic narrative." Wenham, "Sanctuary Symbolism," 399.
33. See Stordalen, *Echoes of Eden*, 456–461.
34. Traditional scholarship considered the verses in Gen 2:10–14 that speak about the four rivers as a later addition. Von Rad for example says: "This passage has no significance for the unfolding action, not are its elements mentioned elsewhere . . . It must therefore be considered as originally an independent element which was attracted to the story of Paradise but without being able to undergo complete inner assimilation." Von Rad, *Genesis*, 79. Mettinger more recently echoed this sentiment: "What we have in the Eden

in Eden, and it comes out of Eden to other lands. This could be another lead for viewing Eden as a sanctuary, since the idea that life is to be found in the sanctuary is "a basic principle of the sacrificial law and a recurrent theme of the Psalms."[35]

As for the tree of the knowledge of good and evil, some scholars believe that it stands as a "symbol of the Law."[36] Thus Clines argues from Psalm 19:8–10 that the similarity of the Law to the tree of knowledge is "unmistakable."[37] However, a case could be made that the actual Law in the narrative was the *commandment* (מצוה) not to eat from the tree.[38] If the tree symbolized the Law, the Law itself was that Adam should not eat from that tree. In all cases, if the association between the tree of knowledge or the commandment itself and the Torah is true (and of course the Torah is to be located in the temple), then the association between Eden and the temple is further confirmed.

It is no surprise that Israelite sanctuaries were portrayed using garden images. A river appears in Jerusalem in Psalm 46:5 and Zechariah 14:7–8, and in the temple of Ezekiel's vision (47:1–12). Gordon sees that the tree of life "has its counterpart in the stylized tree of the menorah that stood in the outer compartment of the tabernacle."[39] Beale observes that that the wood-

---

Narrative is a unified plot, not an episodic one: all parts of the narrative have a necessary function . . . a possible exception would be the passage about the rivers of paradise." T. N. D. Mettinger, *The Eden Narrative: A Literary and Religio-Historical Study of Genesis 2–3* (Winona Lake: Eisenbrauns, 2007), 27. This critical view undermines the coherence of the Eden Narrative. In addition, despite the common consensus that Gen 2–3 is a composite unit, Stordalen observes that "modern scholarship has not succeeded in producing a 'composite' reading which is generally convincing." Stordalen, *Echoes of Eden*, 187.

35. Wenham, "Sanctuary Symbolism," 401.

36. Ibid., 400; M. Ottosson, "Eden and the Land of Promise," in *Congress Volume, Jerusalem 1986*, ed. J. A. Emerton (Leiden: Brill, 1986): 177–188. Morris on the other hand shows that in later Jewish thought the tree of life is in fact what becomes a representation of the Torah. P. Morris, "Exiled from Eden: Jewish Interpretations of Genesis," in *A Walk in the Garden. Biblical, Iconographical and Literary Images of Eden*, ed. P. Morris and D. Sawyer (Sheffield: JSOT Press, 1992), 118–119.

37. Clines believes that Psalm 19 is teaching "the superiority of the law to the tree of knowledge as a means of obtaining wisdom." D. J. A. Clines, "The Tree of Knowledge and the Law of Yahweh (Psalm XIX)," *Vetus Testamentum* XXIV, no. 1 (1974): 11.

38. Some scholars see the wisdom tradition behind the inclusion of the tree of the knowledge of good and evil in the story. For more on this, and for the place of the Torah in the garden, see below section 2 of this chapter.

39. Gordon, *Holy Land, Holy City*, 19.

carvings of flowers and cedar trees (1 Kgs 6:18, 29, 32, 35) also gave the temple "a garden-like atmosphere and likely were intentional reflections of Eden."[40] These garden features, according to Callender, are something logical that has long been established in the religious consciousness of Israel: "The association of the temple with the garden is a logical extension of the conception of the garden as a place of divine habitation."[41]

1.5. The Compound Name of YHWH Elohim

Stordalen gives further evidence that Eden was an archetypal temple from the compound name of God, YHWH Elohim (יהוה אלהים).[42] This combination is almost exclusive to the Eden narrative, with some notable exceptions. Stordalen notes that the compound name appears more frequently in the later Israelite period, especially in the book of Chronicles, and almost always in passages related to the cult.[43] He argues that "to a reader who shared the theological environment of the Chronicler, the compound name in the Eden story could imply a similarity between the garden and the Temple." His conclusion is that "for someone accustomed to encountering יהוה אלהים guarded by כרבים in liturgical life, the Eden story invites a view of the cult as acting out primeval events."

1.6. Evidence from Genesis 4:12–16

Gordon gives a fresh perspective on the "driving out" of Cain in Genesis 4 that strengthens the view of Eden as a "sacred" place.[44] "If Genesis 2–3 sees the primal couple ejected from an Eden sanctuary, chapter 4 seems to take this idea a stage further with the expulsion of Cain from 'holy land.'" After Cain killed his brother, the verdict was that he would be a fugitive and a wanderer on the land. Cain interpreted this as being driven out (גרש) from the face of the ground and from the face or presence (פנים) of God. We have already noticed how גרש is used elsewhere in the OT to explain

---

40. Beale, "Eden," 8.
41. Callender, *Adam in Myth and History*, 54.
42. Stordalen, *Echoes of Eden*, 457–458. For a comprehensive study on the name of God, see J. L'Hour, "Yahweh Elohim," *RB* 81 (1974): 524–556.
43. See 1 Chr 17:16–17; 6:41–42; 28:20, 29:1; 2 Chr 26:18; 30:19.
44. Gordon, *Holy Land, Holy City*, 17–23.

the cleansing of the land by Joshua. So in Genesis 3–4, the distancing of the first humans from God occurs in two stages, reflecting the stages of holiness in the tabernacle: there is first Eden as a sanctuary, then a holy land outside of Eden, and then the land of wandering in which Cain would find himself.[45]

1.7. Conclusion

The cultic elements in Eden have been well established among many biblical scholars.[46] Thus we can safely say that Eden was an "archetypal sanctuary"[47] or the "first temple"[48] that prefigured – canonically at least – Jerusalem and the Zion temple tradition. Eden "echoes the national temple in a sublime way,"[49] and "corresponds to and provides an archetype for the temple as the place where human and divine meet."[50] That is why the OT refers to Eden as גן אלהים (the garden of God, Ezek 28:13; 31:8) and גן יהוה (the garden of YHWH, Isa 51:3). As such it is a holy place – a holy land. In this sense we can argue that it prefigures the Promised Land in the history of Israel.

The penalty of eating from the tree of knowledge of good and evil was death (Gen 2:17). But the actual penalty was expulsion from Eden. Thus the expulsion of Adam and Eve from the garden was in the narrator's view the real fulfillment of the divine sentence. He regarded the alienation from the divine presence as "death."[51] This is mirrored in the history of Israel when Israel receives the ultimate judgment from God: the exile. The exile is like death. It is being away from the land and Jerusalem, the locus of the presence of God (Ps 137). The expulsion from Eden is in a sense a proto-Exile.

---

45. Gordon cites 1 Sam 26:19–20 to further support this interpretation.
46. Furthermore, as van Ruiten has observed, the rewriting of Gen 2–3 in the book of Jubilees is characterized (among other things) by "the fact that the garden of Eden is conceived as a sanctuary." J. Van Ruiten, "Eden and the Temple: The Rewriting of the Genesis 2:4–3:24 in The Book of Jubilees," in *Paradise Interpreted: Representations of Biblical Paradise in Judaism and Christianity*, edited by G. P. Luttikhuizen (Leiden: Brill, 1999), 80.
47. Wenham, "Sanctuary Symbolism," 339.
48. Beale, "Eden," 7.
49. Stordalen, *Echoes of Eden*, 457.
50. Callender, *Adam in Myth and History*, 42.
51. Wenham, "Sanctuary Symbolism," 404.

2. Torah and Covenant in Eden

The first eleven chapters of Genesis and, in particular, the story of Adam and Eve give an OT account of the first humans. Their reference is humanity in general. This section will take a look at Eden with reference to the story of Israel and, in particular, the themes of covenant, the Torah and Deuteronomistic history. We will examine the commandment and conditions appointed for Adam in the garden, and the nature of the relationship between Adam and God.

2.1. The Commandment in Eden

When YHWH Elohim brought and placed Adam in Eden, he *commanded* him:

> You may surely eat of every tree of the garden, but of the tree of the knowledge of good and evil you shall not eat, for in the day that you eat of it you shall surely die. (Gen 2:17)

A lot has been said about the tree of knowledge of good and evil. Many see the Wisdom tradition of Israel behind the inclusion of the tree in the story. Callender for example argues that "the centrality of wisdom in the Genesis account is expressed in the notion of the tree of knowledge of good and evil."[52] His conclusions are primarily based on 2 Samuel 14:17, 20 where the wisdom of king David is equated to the wisdom of the angel of God who discerns good and evil.[53] But whereas in Genesis 2 the knowledge of

---

52. Callender, *Adam in Myth and History*, 66.
53. Callender's view is similar to Brueggemann and others who believe that the Eden narrative belongs to J tradition or theologians, and it reflects that monarchy times of David and Solomon, and so dates in the 10th century. Brueggemann says: "Likely, this narrative reflects the influence of wisdom teachers who are preoccupied with understanding life and probing its mysteries . . . It may be that this text reflects concern for the Solomonic effort to overcome every mystery and to manufacture new knowledge, because knowledge is power.." W. Brueggemann, *Genesis: Interpretation: A Bible Commentary for Teaching and Preaching* (Atlanta: John Knox Press, 1982), 51. I will argue below that a later tradition, in particular that of the Exile, is more probable at least as a date of the final form of the text. In the same time it will not do any good to limit the background to one tradition. The story reflects salvation history in its entirety.

good and evil is something man is prevented from possessing, David is praised for possessing such qualities. Furthermore, as Cassuto has pointed out, the issue in Genesis 2–3 is not discerning but knowing good and evil.[54]

There are indeed signs in the text that the Wisdom tradition lies behind the Eden narrative, and they are well summarized by Schökel.[55] And if one holds to a general universal framework of reference in the first eleven chapters of Genesis, then this view is even more attractive.[56] It is easier to see themes of good, evil, life, and divine test in a text that speaks about the origin of the universe. But as Schökel himself argues, it would be wrong to imagine either that all Wisdom themes are present in Genesis 2–3, or that the ones that are present explain the narrative. After all, the creation account is a narrative, not a collection of maxims. Schökel thus argues from literary analysis that salvation history, not the abstract nature of man (a Wisdom motif), should be our point of departure in understanding the Eden narrative.[57]

It has already been mentioned that there are scholars who see in the tree of knowledge of good and evil a symbol of the Torah. There is a feature in the text that links it with the theme of Torah, namely the use of the verb צוה in piel (to command) in Genesis 2:16. From the same root צוה comes the word מצוה, which means "commandment" and which is "the classical lexeme for the promulgation of the law, especially in Deuteronomy and in the Priestly Code."[58] Therefore, we could argue that the prohibition not to eat from the tree is the real "commandment" or מצוה in the narrative. The remarks of Cassuto on this verse are important:

---

54. U. Cassuto, *A Commentary on the Book of Genesis I* (Jerusalem: Magnes Press, Hebrew University, 1961), 112.
55. L. Alonso-Schökel, "Sapiential and Covenant Themes in Genesis 2–3," in *Studies in Ancient Israelite Wisdom*, ed. J. L. Crenshaw (New York: KTAV, 1976), 472–479.
56. See for example: B. C. Birch, W. Brueggeman, T. E. Fretheim, & D. L. Petersen, eds., *A Theological Introduction to the Old Testament* (Nashville: Abingdon Press, 2005) 29–60.
57. Alonso-Schökel, "Sapiential and Covenant Themes," 473.
58. E. Otto, Die Paradieserzahlung Genesis 2–3: Eine nachpriesterschriftliche Lehrerzahlung in ihrem religionshistorischen Kontex, *BZAW*, 241, (1996): 178. See also for example Exod 15:26, 16:28; 20:6; 24:12; Lev 4:2, 13, 22, 27; 22:31; 26:3, 14, 15; Deut 4:2, 40; 5:10, 29, 31; 8:1, 2, 6, 11; 26:13, 17, 18; 27:1, 10; 28:1, 19, 13, 15, 45.

> This is the first time that the verb to command appears in the Torah; the first commandment in connection with forbidden food is enjoined here, serving as a symbol of, and introduction to, similar injunctions that were to be given to Israel in the future.[59]

The commandments of "YHWH Elohim" in Israel's salvation history mirror the commandment of "YHWH Elohim" in the garden. In both cases, keeping the commandment is a precondition to dwelling in the land. For example:

> You shall diligently keep *the commandments of the LORD your God* (מצות יהוה אלהים), and his testimonies and his statutes, which he has *commanded you* . . . that it may go well with you, and that you may go in and take possession of the good land that the LORD swore to give to your fathers. (Deut 6:17–18)

This observation meshes well with the literary shape of Genesis 2–3. The narrative climaxes in the exile from Eden. Mettinger sees that overall Genesis 2–3 is a story about "divine commandment, human disobedience, and the consequences of insurrection," and so the motif of divine commandment "has a central role and pervades the text as a whole."[60] We can thus conclude that the role of the commandment in Genesis 2–3 is central to the Eden narrative, just as the Torah and commandments of YHWH are of central importance in the salvation history of Israel.

2.2. The Covenant of Eden

There is a suggestion of the presence of the covenant motif in the Eden narrative in the name used for God. Whereas Genesis 1 uses the generic word for God "Elohim," starting from Genesis 2:4b he is "YHWH Elohim."[61] This combination is significant, as it introduces the covenantal name of

---

59. Cassuto, *A Commentary*, 124.
60. Mettinger, *The Eden Narrative*, 5, 51.
61. See L'Hour, "Yahweh Elohim."

God. This intentional feature aims to make the reader read Genesis 1 and 2–3 together in a binocular fashion.[62] L'Hour argued that this comes from a Yahwistic conviction that YHWH is both Israel's covenant partner and the God (Elohim) of all creation,[63] which is a view that is common in almost all commentaries.[64] The point here is that the narrator of Genesis 2–3 forces the reader to think in terms of the covenant when reading the Eden narrative.

The general structure of ANE and biblical covenants is evident in the narrative. Covenants in general included: a historical introduction, border delineations, stipulations, witnesses, blessings, and curses.[65] The Eden narrative begins with the creation of the universe and of man and the planting of Eden, both of which can be seen as gracious acts by God.[66] The garden was after all – to a certain degree – a place of bliss and delight. The word Eden עדן could well mean "a place of pleasure and delight," or a "well-watered place."[67] This is based on associating עדן with its homonym in Hebrew "delight, pleasure or abundance."[68] Genesis 13:10 suggests that Eden could mean a well-watered place. In these cases, we can view Eden as a gift or an act of grace from God towards man.

But the tree of knowledge of good and evil and the commandment to work and keep the garden underline another vital feature, namely that of conditionality. Brueggemann thus says that whereas the garden is an act of utter graciousness, the trees disclose the character of that graciousness,

---

62. B. T. Arnold, *Genesis. New Cambridge Bible Commentary* (Cambridge University Press, Cambridge, 2009), 56.
63. L'Hour, "Yahweh Elohim," 525.
64. See G. J. Wenham, *Genesis 1-15. Word Biblical Commentary*, (Waco: Word Books, 1987), .55–58.
65. Weinfeld, *Promise of the Land*, 225; G. Von Rad, *Old Testament Theology (Vol. 1): The Theology of Israel's Historical Traditions,* Trans. D.M.G. Stalker (Edinburgh and London: Oliver & Boyd, 1962), 132. Biblical covenant will be studied in detail in chapter 3.
66. For Bruggemann, "the gracious action of Yahweh" is the real point of each story in Genesis 1–11. W. Brueggemann, "David and his Theologian," *Catholic Biblical Quarterly* 30 (1968): 161.
67. Wenham, *Genesis 1-15*, 61. Another suggestion for the meaning of Eden is that it is an Akkadian word that is borrowed from Sumerian that means "steppe or plain." See Millard, "The Etymology of Eden," 103–106.
68. 2 Sam 1:24; Jer 51:34; Ps 36:9.

and so "there is no cheap grace here."[69] The commandment in Eden is also expressed positively, in the commissioning of "working and keeping" Eden. The two terms used, עבד and שׁמר, are "technical terms used frequently for the service of God and observance of the commandments."[70] As such, the commandment in 2:15 could be viewed in the light of the covenant tradition.

So God acted graciously (Eden), set the conditions (to work and keep and the garden, not to eat from the tree), and then he set the sanctions in case Adam broke the commandment: "For in the day that you eat of it you shall surely die" (Gen 2:17). This sure death came of course in the form of the expulsion from Eden. But this is not the end of the story. A promise of ultimate victory over the serpent is made in Genesis 3:15. The offspring of the woman will bruise the head of the serpent. Adam and Eve are spared and they begin a new life outside Eden.

Grace, the making of conditions, punishment and redemption (or a promise of redemption) are the skeleton of the story of Eden. This is very similar to, and in a sense a microcosm of, Israel's salvation history and the grant of land. Covenant theology is the key to the narrative sequence in Genesis 2–3.[71] Schökel summarizes the Eden narrative in a very precise manner:

> In bare skeleton the narrative of the two chapters is: God creates Adam, brings him to a garden, presents him with animals, a wife, and some trees; then lays upon him a command under sanction. Adam and his wife rebel. After a brief trial, God condemns them, but does not break with them totally. More concisely: God gives benefits and imposes a precept; man rebels; God punishes, then reconciles. What is the source of this narrative pattern? Derivation from myths has failed. The

---

69. Brueggemann, *Genesis: Interpretation*, 45.
70. Alonso-Schökel, "Sapiential and Covenant Themes," 474.
71. See N. Lohfink, *Das Siegeslied am Schilfmeer: Christliche Auseinandersetzungen mit dem Alten Testament* (Frankfurt am Main: Josef Knecht Verlag, 1965), 91; Mettinger, *The Eden Narrative*, 49–50.

narrative of Gen 2–3 is simply the classic outline of salvation history. There is a minor pattern, that of the covenant.[72]

2.3. Eden and Deuteronomistic Theology

The above reading of Genesis 2–3 argues for salvation history as the appropriate framework for understanding the narrative. We can even argue that it is the Deuteronomistic theology in particular that gives the Eden narrative its shape. This is based on the retribution theology of blessing and curse that is found in Eden. There is a stress on obedience and divine testing in Genesis 2–3, similar to what we find in the Deuteronomistic theology. Moreover, choice between blessing and curse, death and life, is given in both cases.[73] The question is: to which voice will Adam/Israel listen?

A comparison between Deuteronomy 8 and Genesis 2–3 is sufficient to show the similarities:

8:7–9 For the LORD your God is bringing you into a good land, a land of brooks of water, of fountains and springs, flowing out in the valleys and hills, a land of wheat and barley, of vines and fig trees and pomegranates, a land of olive trees and honey, a land in which you will eat bread without scarcity, in which you will lack nothing, a land whose stones are iron, and out of whose hills you can dig copper.	2:8–9 And the LORD God planted a garden in Eden, in the east, and there he put the man whom he had formed. And out of the ground the LORD God made to spring up every tree that is pleasant to the sight and good for food.
8:11 Take care lest you forget the LORD your God by not keeping his commandments and his rules and his statutes, which I command you today.	2:16–17a You may surely eat of every tree of the garden, but of the tree of the knowledge of good and evil you shall not eat.

---

72. Alonso-Schökel, "Sapiential and Covenant Themes," 474.
73. Gen 2:15–17; Deut 11:26–28; 30:15–20.

8:19 And if you forget the LORD your God and go after other gods and serve them and worship them, I solemnly warn you today that you shall surely perish.	2:17b For in the day that you eat of it you shall surely die.

Mettinger can therefore argue:

> The disobedience of Israel in the Deuteronomistic History is transformed into the disobedience of the first human couple. The consequences of this primeval act of disobedience by the first humans are understood to affect all human life . . . In this, they are representative of the whole human race. Thus, *while the [Deuteronomistic History] supplies an etiology for the loss of the land, the Eden Narrative serves as an etiology for the loss of the Garden of Bliss.*[74]

This association between Eden and Deuteronomistic history is an important one, as it sets the whole of the history of Israel as the background to the Eden narrative. This view goes beyond traditional scholarship, which reads the narrative through the lens of the documentary hypothesis, and associates Genesis 2–11 with the "J" tradition.[75] The framework of the Eden narrative goes beyond the times of the southern kingdom. It speaks of salvation history in its entirety up to the exile. The exile from Eden mirrors

---

74. Mettinger, *The Eden Narrative*, 59 (emphasis in the original).

75. Brueggemann, for example, says that the Yahwist "generalizes about David for Adam, the Israelite kings for all men. He sees in the Davids what is in every man, i.e., loved by God and rebellious against that love and therefore in exile." W. Brueggemann, "David and his Theologian," 176. Haag also argues for 1 Sam 4–6 and 2 Sam 6:1–8:24 as the more relevant context or framework for Gen 2–3 is and that the Eden story is in fact an expression of common ancient Yahwistic theology. E. Haag, *Der Mensch am Anfang. Die Alttestamentliche Paradiesvorstellung Nach Gn 2-3. (Trierer Theologische Studien vol. 24)*, (Trier: Paulinus, 1970). See also J. Van Seters, *Prologue to History: The Yahwist as Historian in Genesis* (Louisville: Westminster John Knox Pr, 1992), 105–134. For an analysis and critique of reading the Gen 2–3 with the lens of the Documentary hypothesis, see Stordalen, *Echoes of Eden*, 187–198. In page194, he says: "The high level of unverified presumptions in the traditional exegesis of Genesis 2–3 must account for the fact that it is impossible to reach agreement on the issue of sources and redactions in that story." See also Wenham, *Genesis 1-15*, xxxiv–xxxv.

the exile to Babylon, and limiting the Judean kingdom as the background to the Eden narrative will fail to see this relationship between the two exiles. It is better to adhere to a general agenda of covenant or Deuteronomistic theology in Genesis 2–3.

2.4. Conclusion

It has been shown how the commandment of YHWH Elohim is a central motif in the Eden narrative, and how our understanding of the covenant with Israel further enriches this idea. Major covenantal themes are evident in the narrative. The Deuteronomistic history in particular provides the most likely framework for the narrative.

This suggests that the garden of Eden should not be understood in an abstract mythical framework. Instead, our framework should be salvation history, and this will open the door for fresh interpretations of Genesis 2–3. On this basis, we can suggest that in the Eden narrative: Adam mirrors Israel, the commandments of YHWH mirror the Torah, Eden mirrors the land of promise, the expulsion from Eden mirrors the exile, and the promise of redemption in Genesis 3:15 mirrors the prophetic promises of restoration.[76] The Eden narrative is, among many other things, Israel's story. It mirrors the history of the OT in many aspects. In particular, the notion of Eden as the first Promised Land is a logical and natural conclusion, and the theological ramifications of this will be considered below.

---

76. We must be careful in how far can we push the correlation between Eden and salvation history? Schökel for example attempts to read the entire Eden narrative in comparison with the salvation history of Israel, arguing in the process that even Eve fits in this pattern as a symbol to the temptations of the promise land: "the gifts of companionship and love become mortal danger – symbolic of the temptations of the promised land." He also parallels the questioning of God to Adam to Moses' questioning Aaron after the sin of Sinai, and Joshua's questioning of Achan. Alonso-Schökel, "Sapiential and Covenant Themes," 475–477. Though I believe that we should read the covenantal tradition and salvation history as a legitimate framework for understanding Gen 2–3, it will be a stretch to read every detail in the story in this manner. The point is that the general framework of the narrative is a covenantal one. Moreover, the narrative does more than echo the salvation history of Israel, and speaks about issues of gender relationship and free will for example.

3. Eden as a Kingdom

Symbolism of the garden theme in general, and in particular the theme of the garden in Eden as a royal garden, has not received enough attention in recent scholarship.[77] Careful examination however will show that the Eden narrative is described in a way that reflects a theocracy – with God as the ultimate ruler, Adam as his vicegerent, and the garden as the sphere of this rule. This section will therefore explore two things: Eden as royal garden and the nature of this theocracy, and Adam as a royal figure.

3.1. Eden as a Royal Garden

The theme of royal gardens is very common in ANE literature. "One emphatically symbolic type of gardens appears in ancient Near Eastern royal gardens."[78] Kings in the East had a custom of building great gardens outside the palace from which they ruled their empires, and there are many stories and legends describing this phenomenon.[79] There are also examples in the OT of this custom. King Manasseh was buried in the garden of his house, the garden of Uzza – בגן־ביתו בגן עזא, and so was Amon.[80] Zedekiah the king of Judah had a garden – גן המלך.[81] There is also the famous proph-

---

[77]. For Stordalen, the fact that gardens as symbols received so little attention among biblical scholars is "conspicuous." He suggests that this silence was generated "in order to avoid pre-critical exuberance on the 'paradise' topic" which was indebted to the LXX translation παραδεισος for גן. However, he believes that "there should be every reason for exploring the symbolic significance of a garden to a biblical Hebrew audience." Stordalen, *Echoes of Eden*, 84.

[78]. Ibid., 94.

[79]. Dumbrell, "Genesis 2:1-3," 221–222. A good summary of these stories can be found in Stordalen, who gives multiple examples of this custom from Mesopotamia and Syria-Canaan, showing the symbolism of these royal gardens. Stordalen, *Echoes of Eden*, 94–102. Bremmer argues that Hellenistic features of royal gardens influence the description of Eden. Bremmer, "Paradise," 1–20.

[80]. 2 Kgs 21:18, 26.

[81]. 2 Kgs 25:4, Jer 39:4, 52:7; see also Neh 3:15. Despite this Stordalen still remarks that "as compared to palace gardens of Assyria and Babylonia, biblical tradition is disappointingly silent." He is right in that there is no clear description of these gardens or their function or symbol. Stordalen, *Echoes of Eden*, 101.

ecy in Ezekiel 28 against the King of Tyre who was in "Eden, the Garden of God" and was cast to the ground because of "his pride."[82]

The word used in the LXX for garden, παραδεισος, is a Persian loan word, and means "park," or "orchard," or "royal garden."[83] Noort observes that this word fits with the tradition of the ANE "royal gardens."[84] Bremmer noted that the translators could have chosen another word, κηπος, but did not do so because it would hardly have conjured up the image of a royal park worthy of YHWH.[85]

The evidence from ANE literature on royal gardens and the meaning of παραδεισος is hardly enough in itself to establish Eden as a royal garden. But it needs to be taken in consideration with the following discussion of Adam as a vicegerent or intermediary figure.

3.2. Adam as a Vicegerent

Modern scholarship has spoken a lot about the vicegerency of Adam, especially in relation to Genesis 1 and the creation formula (1:27–28), more than in connection with Genesis 2. By vicegerent we mean someone exercising delegated power on behalf of a king or a magistrate. The creation formula in Genesis 1 will be discussed separately below and this part will focus mainly on the vicegerency of Adam in Genesis 2–3.

3.2.1. The King as Gardener

Contrary to the popular view that Eden was only a place of paradisiacal rest, there was work to be done in Eden. God placed Adam in the garden in

---

82. Neiman considers this prophecy foundational in understating Gen 2–3. He concludes that Eden is a royal garden – the dwelling of the divine king. He then argues that the same was evident in Gen 2–3, which has fewer mythological elements in it. Neiman depends heavily in his analysis on ANE stories of gardens and on the general theme of God as King in the entire OT. Neiman, "Eden, the Garden of God," 123.

83. Lewis, "Localization of the Garden of Eden," 171.

84. Noort, "Gan-Eden," 21.

85. Bremmer, "Paradise," 17. The two Greek words are found in Ecc. 2:4–5: "I made great works. I built houses and planted vineyards for myself. I made gardens and parks (εποιησα μοι κηπους και παραδεισους) and planted all kinds of fruit trees in them." This also suggests that παραδεισους is used describe a royal park.

order for him to work it and keep it (Gen 2:15). This was Adam's vocation, or mandate. Eden was a place of work, and not just rest.[86]

In particular, Adam was a gardener. He served God the creator in maintaining the very best of his creation – the garden of Eden. He was God's servant or representative in Eden. Callender looks at Adam as a "divine servant."[87] Having already established that the primal human is presented as an intermediary figure and as a king, for him, then, when Genesis 2:15 presents Adam as a gardener, it makes sense because the idea of kings as gardeners is not foreign to the ANE. "The Mesopotamian king as gardener has clear cultic overtones, and the cultic involvement of the king in Mesopotamia has been well documented, as is true in Israel."[88]

Stordalen on the other hand sees that, although "there is no explicit biblical reference to the king as gardener," some OT passages (like Ps 72:16) portray the ruler as "pivotal for the distribution of blessing upon the nation," and that royal gardens symbolize "the favorable effect of the ruler on his empire."[89] He then concludes:

> Given the symbolism of royal gardens in neighboring culture, it seems reasonable to assume a similar symbolic Hebrew royal ideology. Positive evidence for this assumption remains weak.[90]

So it is possible that, by portraying Adam as a gardener, the text was implying that Adam is to be seen as a royal figure.[91]

---

86. The cultic tone of the phrase – לעבדה ולשמרה has been discussed above.
87. Callender, *Adam in Myth and History*, 65.
88. Ibid., 65. Dumbrell also observed that "the notion of the monarch as a gardener for the deity is also found in the ancient Near East." Dumbrell, "Genesis 2:1-3," 222.
89. Stordalen, *Echoes of Eden*, 102.
90. Ibid., 102.
91. Wyatt also argues that the idea of the king as a gardener is found in Mesopotamian royal ideology, and so the Adam of of Gen 2–3 is to be interpreted as the paradigm of the king. However, he seems to take this argument too far when he makes an interesting observation concerning the meaning of Gen 3:23, which speaks of Adam's expulsion from Eden. For him Adam was also expelled "from tilling the soil from which he had been taken" (and not to till the soil from which he had been taken as commonly translated), implying that the punishment included the stripping of some royal responsibilities, mainly being the gardener. Wyatt also suggests that the common OT royal title עבד יהוה "undoubtedly carries with it the overtone of cultivation, so that it is in effect the

3.2.2. Name Giving

In Genesis 2:20 Adam gives names (ויקרא האדם שמות) to all the animals of the garden, symbolizing his rule and authority over them. "Name giving in the ancient Orient was primarily an exercise of sovereignty, of command."[92] It was God first who gave things names in the creation. He called (ויקרא) the light day, and the darkness night . . . etc. God could also change the names of people (e.g. Abram to Abraham). We also see this with other ANE kings. Joseph received an Egyptian name from the king of Egypt (Gen 41:45), and so did Eliakim and Mattaniah from the kings of Egypt and Babylon (2 Kgs 23:34; 24:17). By giving the animals names, therefore, mankind is given a share in YHWH's dominion over creation.[93]

The degree to which Adam had authority over animals (and even Eve, since he called her by her name) is disputed. Ramsey, who despite observing that in the OT "the act of bestowing a name on a person or a place is a demonstration of authority over that person or place," says this should not be taken to mean that Adam "controlled and subordinated" the things named.[94] For Westermann, name giving simply symbolizes "that man is autonomous within a certain limited area." Therefore:

> The meaning is not, as most interpreters think, that the man acquires power over the animals by naming them . . . But rather that man gives the animals their names and thereby puts them into a place in his world.[95]

The degree to which Adam had authority in Eden may be disputed, but it remains that the text portrays him as having some sort of authority. By giving the animals names, Adam acts in a way comparable with other kings

---

equivalent of 'Yahweh's gardener'." N. Wyatt, "When Adam Delved: The Meaning of Genesis III 23," *Vetus Testamentum* 38, no. 1 (1988): 118–119.

92. Von Rad, *Genesis*, 83.

93. D. T. Asselin, "The Notion of Dominion in Genesis 1–3," *The Catholic Biblical Quarterly* 16 (1954): 293.

94. G. W. Ramsey, "Is Name-Giving an Act of Domination in Genesis 2: 23 and Elsewhere?," *The Catholic Biblical quarterly* 50, no. 1 (1988): 25–30.

95. Westermann, *Genesis 1-11*, 228.

in the ANE. His exercise of authority in Eden was similar to – but surely less than – the authority that God had over creation.

3.2.3. The Royal Formula in Genesis 2:7

There is other evidence of the royal status of Adam in Eden:

> Then the LORD God *formed the man of dust* from the ground and *breathed into his nostrils the breath of life*, and the man became a living creature. (Gen 2:7) (emphasis added)

For Brueggemann, this verse "speaks of the process whereby a nobody is entrusted with the powers and responsibilities of kingship." And so, behind the creation formula lies a royal formula of enthronement. "To be taken from dust means to be accepted as a covenant-partner and treated graciously."[96] There are similar stories in the ANE of kings being raised from dust by the gods. Egyptian myths, for example, portray the creator god *Khnum* as fashioning the king's son, Amenhotep, on the potter's wheel.[97]

Wifall approves Brueggemann's commentary on the first part of the verse and argues that the second part of the same verse makes the very same point, modeling a kingship prototype. He compares the mention of the breath of life in Genesis 2:7b with myths about ancient Mesopotamian kings and argues that it "appears to have its ultimate origin in connection with ancient Near Eastern kingship."[98] When God breathed into Adam's nostrils the breath of life, Adam was enthroned as king.[99]

---

96. Brueggemann gives three examples besides Gen 2:7 that speak of being raised or enthroned from dust to power: 1 Sam 2:6–8, 1 Kgs 16:2–3 and Ps 113:7–8. For him therefore, Gen 2 (a J document) speaks of David in the first place, and the text speaks "quite clearly a theology for the monarchy." W. Brueggemann, "From Dust to Kingship," *Zeitschrift für die Alttestamentliche Wissenschaft* 84, no. 1 (1972): 2–4. He also reaffirms this elsewhere, arguing that Gen 2–11 speaks about the life of David all the way to Solomon. Gen 3 for example is about David and Bathsheba. Gen 12:1–3 "confronts Israel and especially Solomon with a prophetic demand that he decides what his reign is about." Brueggemann, "David and his Theologian," 179. See also n. 66.
97. Westermann, *Genesis 1-11*, 203.
98. W. Wifall, "The Breath of His Nostrils: Gen. 2: 7b," *CBQ* 36 (1974): 240.
99. Ibid., 239. Like Brueggemann, Wifall considers this part of Genesis to be authored by the Yahwist (a J document), and is a text for the monarchy. Adam therefore is the prototype for David. Eden is a prototype for the kingdom of Israel. "The Yahwist has

3.3. The Image of God: Genesis 1:26–28

Modern scholarship has for long treated Genesis 1 and 2 as two different documents, coming from two different sources. Genesis 1 is a P document, and Genesis 2 is a J document.[100] As a result, the two stories are generally studied separately as two creation accounts. In addition, since J has long been considered as earlier than P, Genesis 2 has generally been read in isolation and without connecting it to Genesis 1, which came later in the tradition.

Whereas this is not the time to argue for or against the documentary hypothesis,[101] we will argue for the validity of reading Genesis 1–2 as *two complementary stories*, based at least on their final shape and place in the canon. Rendtorff argues:

> [It] would be a real canonical reading to follow the final canonical author who wants us to read and to think together the two chapters of the biblical text that have different origins, styles and ideas but belong together according to the intentions of those who delivered the Hebrew Bible to us.[102]

Furthermore, it will be suggested below that Genesis 2 seems to be a later document than Genesis 1 and that it cannot be simply taken for granted that Genesis 2 is older than Genesis 1.

When the creation of Adam in Genesis 2 is read in the context of the creation of humankind in Genesis 1,[103] more light will be shed on the vocation of Adam as a gardener in Eden. In particular, Genesis 1:26–28 is of great importance:

'demythologized' the royal mythology in line with Israel's covenant faith. He has done this without compromising Yahweh's unique position as Israel's sole King and God by portraying the relation of David to Israel as the prototype for the relation of Adam to mankind" (p. 239).

100. See Wenham, *Genesis 1-15*, xxv–xxxv.

101. See no. 109.

102. R. Rendtorff, "Canonical Interpretation: A New Approach to Biblical Texts," *Pro Ecclesia* 3, no. 2 (1994): 143.

103. I will follow most commentators and translations here in that Genesis 1 speaks of the creation of humanity, and Genesis 2 speaks in particular of the first man Adam.

> Then God said, "Let *us make man in our image*, after our likeness. And let them have *dominion* over the fish of the sea and over the birds of the heavens and over the livestock and over all the earth and over every creeping thing that creeps on the earth." So God created man in his own image, in the image of God he created him; male and female he created them. And God blessed them. And God said to them, "Be fruitful and multiply and fill the earth and *subdue it and have dominion* over the fish of the sea and over the birds of the heavens and over every living thing that moves on the earth." (emphasis added)

The language used to describe the first humans in these verses is "royal."[104] The unavoidable conclusion of this creation formula is that being created in God's image entails having some sort of dominion.[105] To have dominion and to subdue the earth are connected to being made in God's image. Middleton is right in proposing that the image of God is "the royal function or office of human beings as God's representatives and agents in the world, given authorized power to share in God's rule over the earth's resources and creatures."[106] And as Asselin has observed: "Man is God's image not because of what he is, but because of what he is given: a share in the divine sovereignty over creation."[107] In fact Genesis 1:26 could be translated as, "Let us make man in our image, after our likeness, *in order that they have dominion*."[108] Psalm 8:5–6 supports the link between the creation and crowning of man: "Yet you have made [man] a little lower than the heavenly beings and *crowned him* with glory and honor. You have

---

104. Callender, *Adam in Myth and History*, 206.

105. For the different interpretations of the image of God, see: Wenham, *Genesis 1-15*, 26–32; Westermann, *Genesis 1-11*, 142–165. For a comprehensive study, see J. R. Middleton, *The Liberating Image: The Imago Dei in Genesis 1* (Grand Rapids: Brazos Press, 2005).

106. J. R. Middleton, "The Liberating Image? Interpreting the Imago Dei in Context," *Christian Scholars Review* 24, no. 1 (1994): 12.

107. Asselin, "Notion of Dominion in Genesis 1–3," 293.

108. W. J. Dumbrell, *The Search for Order: Biblical Eschatology in Focus* (Grand Rapids: Baker Book House, 1994), 19.

given him *dominion* over the works of your hands; you have put all things under his feet."

Moreover, McCartney observes from Genesis 5:3 that being made in someone's image conveys the relationship of a father to a son. He also notes that in the ANE the king was considered as the son of God. He then argues:

> Man as image means man as son, and the son of God is a king. Consequently, included as one function of this imageness was man's *dominion* (Gen 1:28). God's rule of earth was, in the original order of creation, accomplished through the agency of man's vicegerency.[109]

Adam was created as the image of YHWH, the ultimate and divine king and ruler, to indicate that the earth was ruled over by YHWH.[110] This is clear not only from the text of Genesis itself, but also from external ANE evidence. Wenham observes that it was common in the ANE to view the king as God's image and thus representative on earth, and that both Egyptian and Assyrian texts describe the king as the image of God.[111] Alexander also remarks that the commandment to Adam and Eve as image bearers to multiply and fill the earth recalls ANE rulers setting their images in distant places in order to indicate that their authority had reached that far.[112] In short, to have God's image means to rule on his behalf.

The first humans are to have dominion over creation (Gen 1:26) and are also to subdue the earth (Gen 1:28). The word used in Genesis 1:28 (כבש) is familiar in connection with the Israelite conquest of Canaan and David's subduing of the nations.[113] It is a strong word, stronger than the more common רדה, which was used in Genesis 1:26. But the meaning of both words in this context is clear and amounts to the same thing. Westermann

---

109. D. G. McCartney, "Ecce Homo: The Coming of the Kingdom as the Restoration of Human Vicegerency," *The Westminster Theological Journal* 56, no. 1 (1994): 2 (emphasis in the original).
110. G. K. Beale, *The Temple and the Church's Mission* (Downers Grove: InterVarsity Press, 2004), 82.
111. Wenham, *Genesis 1-15*, 30.
112. Alexander, *Eden to The New Jerusalem*, 76–78.
113. Num 32:22, 29; Josh 18:1; 1 Chr 22:18; 2 Sam 8:11.

reckons that both words bring to mind ANE royal ideologies. The expression רדה is "derived from the court language of the great empires," and כבש "derives from the rule of the king."[114]

When we read the account of Adam's creation in Genesis 2 in the context of the creation of the first man in Genesis 1, the suggestion that Adam functioned as a vicegerent is reinforced. The use of the same word אדם in these stories to designate both humankind and one man is purposeful, and not merely an accident of the Hebrew language.[115] In Genesis 1, האדם means humanity (or "adam"). Genesis 2 is talking about the one particular man Adam (or "Adam"). We can argue that the "Adam" of Genesis 2 represents the "adam" of Genesis 1 and is supposed to fulfill what "adam" was created and made for. One "Adam" was chosen and appointed from among the "adam" as a representative. In other words, the Adam of Eden *represents* all humankind.

Moreover, when we read Genesis 1:26–28 into Eden, we can interpret Adam's actions as the beginning of the fulfillment of the commission in 1:28.[116] It will not be an overstatement to say that working and keeping Eden is the fulfillment of subduing the earth, and that naming the animals is the fulfillment of having dominion over the animals.

3.4. Conclusion

Adam is portrayed in Genesis 2 as a royal figure, and the garden as his royal domain. He rules for the ultimate creator King. He represents God on this earth, and the garden is the place from which he exercises his rule. The garden itself can be viewed as a royal garden and Adam is the gardener/king. We have already seen that Adam was also portrayed as a priestly figure and the garden as a sanctuary. It is no surprise that the Hebrew word for temple היכל can also mean palace.[117] The king as priest is also not foreign to ANE traditions.

---

114. Westermann, *Genesis 1-11*, 161.
115. P. Enns, *The Evolution of Adam: What the Bible Does and Doesn't Say About Human Origins* (Grand Rapids: Brazos Press, 2012), 68.
116. Beale, *Temple and the Church's Mission*, 82.
117. 1 Kgs 21:1; 2 Kgs 20:18.

We may also conclude that order outside the garden of Eden depends on Adam as a vicegerent. It is noticeable how Genesis 2 starts with a problem (2:5) that is arguably resolved in the creation of both Adam and the garden (2:7–8). For Stordalen, Genesis 2:5 is the key to understanding the plot of the Eden narrative. He observes:

> The qualitative deficiency of 2:5 is "over-solved" in the garden, which enjoys both water and a working gardener. The spatial task, however, is "under-solved" as long as the solution occurs only in the garden, and not in the "land."[118]

Therefore, for the problem of 2:5 to be fully solved, the task of Adam inside Eden must extend beyond Eden. In other words, the blessing of the land outside Eden depends on Adam and Eve. Eden is the source of blessing, order, and life for the land outside, as evident from the reference to the four rivers.[119] Beale and others have suggested that the boundaries of Eden were eventually supposed to extend in order for this fully to take place:

> As [Adam] was to begin to rule over and subdue the earth, he was to extend the geographical boundaries to the Garden of Eden until Eden extended throughout and covered the whole earth. This meant the presence of God which was limited to Eden was to be extended throughout the whole earth. God's presence was to "fill" the entire earth.[120]

We can thus argue that the kingdom of Eden was supposed to extend via the rule of Adam until the blessing and order of Eden covered the rest of the earth.

---

118. T. Stordalen, "Man, Soil, Garden: Basic Plot in Genesis 2–3 Reconsidered," *Journal for the Study of the Old Testament* 17, no. 53 (1992): 17.
119. Ibid., 17.
120. Beale, "Eden," 10–11. Elsewhere, Beale observes similar patterns to this idea in Babylonian and Egyptian traditions. Beale, "Eden," 82. Other scholars who suggested that Eden was supposed to ultimately extend or expand until it covered the whole earth include Dumbrell, "Genesis 2:1-3"; Walton, "Eden, Garden of"; Kline, *Kingdom Prologue*; and Alexander, *Eden to The New Jerusalem*.

However, "when man fell, he spoiled his vicegerency; man was cast out of the garden, and the earth was no longer compliant in its subjection to him."[121] The sin of Adam and Eve can be viewed as an act of treason: by betraying God and giving their allegiance to Satan they in a sense dethroned him.[122] The result is a world in chaos, without the rule of God. This is what Genesis 4–11 is about. Eden lost its potential to bless the world outside.

4. Eden and Biblical Theology

We will next see that Genesis 2–3 has an important role to play for the rest of the unfolding drama of biblical theology – as more than just a general introduction to Israel's history. As such, we will be able to argue that Adam can be seen as proto-Israel, and the garden of Eden as a proto-Land or the first Promised Land.

4.1. Genesis 2–3 and Salvation History

According to traditional scholarship, Genesis 2–3 plays a minimal role the biblical narrative for many different reasons. Brueggemann for example believes that this is an "exceedingly marginal text,"[123] while von Rad has commented that the contents of Genesis 2–3 are "conspicuously isolated" in the OT.[124]

Stordalen says that scholars who regard Genesis 2–3 as marginal do so in part because of the view that Genesis 1–11 is a foreign and universal preface to the national history of Israel, and that the cosmology of Genesis 1–11 is not really Hebrew, and its primary context remains the corpus of ANE cosmological material.[125] The conventional view on the authorship and date of Genesis 2–3 has also led some scholars to consider it a marginal text in biblical theology. According to traditional scholarship, Genesis 2–3 is a ninth- or even tenth-century BCE document that comes from the J

---

121. McCartney, "Ecce Homo," 3.
122. Alexander, *Eden to The New Jerusalem*, 78.
123. Brueggemann, *Genesis: Interpretation*, 41.
124. Von Rad, *Genesis*, 102.
125. Stordalen, *Echoes of Eden*, 25–26.

source, and it reflects the Yahwist's theology of the kingdom.[126] It is an early text, and so when interpreting it, we should not compare it to later passages from the Prophets or the Writings. The primary context for Genesis 2–3 therefore is ANE myths and epic passages.

But the discussion above has offered a different perspective, namely that Genesis 2–3 is in fact rooted in the salvation history of Israel, and that it is more than a general preface. Themes like covenant, retribution, kingdom, and temple are evident in that narrative. Enns thus argues that Adam's story is not really a story of human origins but of Israel's origins.[127] It has also already been noted how Haag had argued that the paradise theme in the OT originates from the experience of the *Heilsgeschichte* of Israel, and how Lohfink and Schökel had argued that the theme of the covenant lies behind the garden of Eden narrative. Furthermore, as Stordalen comments, "it is plainly inconceivable that the religious community behind the Pentateuch would preface its national history with a 'foreign' cosmology."[128]

Moreover, there are serious challenges that have arisen recently to the conventional view regarding the authorship and date of Genesis 2–3, and many have noted how there are conflicting theories within traditional scholarship on this matter.[129] In fact, recently more scholars are arguing for a later postexilic date for Genesis 2–3. Mettinger for example argues:

> The Eden Narrative probably presupposes the Priestly creation account in Genesis 1. It is also clear that it presupposes the main tenets of Deuteronomistic theology . . . it presupposes a development of ideas about YHWH and death that was not complete until postexilic times. A late date for the Eden

---

126. Brueggemann for example, says: "The narrative is commonly assigned to Israel's early theological traditions. It perhaps is concerned with the new emergence in Israel of a royal consciousness of human destiny, for which the main issues are power and freedom." Brueggemann, *Genesis: Interpretation*, 40.
127. Enns, *Evolution of Adam*, 66.
128. Stordalen, *Echoes of Eden*, 28.
129. J. Goldingay, *Old Testament Theology: Israel's Gospel (Vol. 1)*, (Downers Grove: InterVarsity Press, 2003), 867. Stordalen also concludes that the high level of unverified presumptions in the traditional exegesis of Gen 2–3 must account for the fact that "it is impossible to reach agreement on the issue of sources and redactions in that story." Stordalen, *Echoes of Eden*, 194.

Narrative explains why there are no allusions to it whatsoever in the literature prior to the very late period.[130]

Schökel has also argued for a later date from the silence of the rest of the OT on the Eden narrative. "The literary enigma and silence of other books is better explained by accepting a later composition."[131] Stordalen also argued for a later date, and observed from a study of vocabulary and themes that "in Ezekiel, late parts of Isaiah, in Job, Sirach, Wisdom and onwards, however, there is great interest in the subject."[132] For him, therefore, the context for reading Genesis 2–3 is early and late sapiential literature and late Babylonian and especially early Persian priestly and prophetic literature.[133]

We can also add that if the exile of Adam and Eve from Eden in Genesis 3 mirrors Israel's own exile, then this could be another indication of a later date for the narrative. Moreover, the promise of the restorative seed of the woman could be seen as reflecting the later exilic promises of restoration.[134]

It follows that we can no longer treat Genesis 2–3 as simply an isolated or marginal general preface that only interacts with ANE myths, though it may also fulfill this function. Instead, Genesis 2–3, in its final form, presupposes salvation history, reflects on it, and even interprets it. And by virtue of its place in the canon and the fact that it is talking about the first

---

130. Mettinger, *The Eden Narrative*, 134.

131. Alonso-Schökel, "Sapiential and Covenant Themes," 480.

132. See for example Ezek 28:11–26; 36:35; 47:1–12; Isa 51:3. Stordalen, *Echoes of Eden*, 210.

133. Ibid., p. 212.

134. The original Eden story could be very ancient. As Cassuto suggests, "there existed among the Israelites, before even the Torah was written, a poetic tradition concerning the garden of Eden." Cassuto, *A Commentary*, 72. I am suggesting a later date for the final form of the narrative based on the striking similarities between the story of Israel in the land and the story of Adam in Eden. The transition and process of editing the texts of the OT from generation to generation is well known, and Gen 2–3 should be no exception. Brueggemann, commenting on Gen 1–11 and textual criticism, says: "The key issue in reading these texts . . . is to see that the canonization process of editing and traditioning has taken old materials and transposed them by their arrangement into something of a theological coherence that is able to state theological affirmations and claims that were not intrinsic to the antecedent materials themselves." W. Brueggemann, *An Introduction to the Old Testament: The Canon and Christian Imagination* (Louisville: Westminster John Knox Press, 2003), 31.

humans, Genesis 2–3 must be regarded as a vital introduction to salvation history, and in our case, to the theology of the land in the OT.[135] *The fact that Israel is prefigured in Genesis 2–3 by the first human, Adam, and that the Promised Land is prefigured by an ideal garden, Eden, is intended to communicate vital truths which should play a crucial role in the biblical theology of the land.*

This carries with it at least two implications for our study. The first is that Adam is proto-Israel, and the second is that Eden is proto-Promised Land. These two conclusions carry in themselves important implications for the theology of the land. "The story indicates for us what it means for human beings to be holy people and dwell in a holy land. The holy land is Eden, and the holy people are Adam and Eve."[136]

4.2. Adam Is Israel

The first important implication from the above discussion is that Adam is proto-Israel.[137] Adam and Eve are not only the first humans, but also the first people of God. The genealogies in Genesis 5, 11 connect Abraham and Noah *to Adam*, and this has theological implications, namely that Adam is the first Israelite. What the narrative is telling about Adam, it is in fact telling about Israel. As the first created human, Adam represents humanity. His actions have universal consequences. The narrative therefore is communicating something to Israel about her role, responsibilities and the consequences of her actions.

Adam was created outside of Eden, and he was then taken up and brought into it (Gen 2:15). This movement, described using the two

---

135. Although the themes of salvation history can be traced in Genesis 2–3, the technical terms are not present. But this does not affect our conclusion. Mettinger says this is due to the universalization tendency of the author. The fact that none of the Deuteronomistic terms for the law are used in the Eden narrative has to do with a universalization tendency. "The law is for Israel; the commandment in the primeval garden is for humanity. This universalization tendency could explain why the divine designation used in the narrative is YHWH Elohim. Of the two combined elements, the first refers to the God of Israel's covenant partner and the second to God as universal Creator." Mettinger, *The Eden Narrative*, 57–58.
136. M. Dauphinais and M. Levering, *Holy People, Holy Land: A Theological Introduction to the Bible* (Grand Rapids: Brazos Press, 2005), 29.
137. For Adam as proto-Israel, see Enns, *The Evolution of Adam*, 65–70.

Hebrew verbs לקח and נוח (hiphil), "reflects the two-fold movement with which the Israelites expressed redemption."[138] The second verb is especially important, as it draws attention to the notion of rest. The same verb is commonly used when describing the giving of the land to Israel so that they would experience rest.[139] Genesis 2:15 could be in fact translated as: "And YHWH God took Adam *and brought him to rest* in the garden of Eden."

Adam was placed in Eden for a reason, namely to work and keep it (Gen 2:17). We have already argued for his priestly and kingly role, as a vicegerent on behalf of God the creator. God ruled through Adam. Adam as vicegerent must exercise his royal authority and bring order out of chaos.

The role of Adam in Eden is thus transferred to Israel. To do so she must be obedient first. Adam's obedience was the condition to his staying in Eden. So "the placement of both Adam and Israel in divine space was conditional."[140] In this sense Adam was the first covenant breaker. Israel must learn from Adam that breaking the covenant has universal implications and that it affects the rest of humanity and indeed the rest of creation. As Dumbrell says:

> Israel was created, as was Adam, outside the divine space to be occupied . . . Both Israel and Adam were placed in divine space: Israel in Canaan and Adam in Eden. Israel was given, as was Adam, law by which the divine space could be retained. Israel transgressed the law, as did Adam. Israel was expelled, as was Adam, from the divine space . . . Clearly the creation account indicates to Israel the nature and purpose of her special status and role, which once belonged to the man. After Adam, the priest-king, failed to exercise his dominion over the world, the mantle passed to national Israel, a corporate royal priest.[141]

---

138. Alonso-Schökel, "Sapiential and Covenant Themes," 474.
139. See for example Deut 3:20; 12:10; 25:19; Josh 1:13, 15; 21:44; 22:4; 23:1; 1 Chr 22:9, 18; 23:25; Jer 27:11; Ezek 5:13; 37:14.
140. Dumbrell, "Genesis 2:1-3," 225.
141. Dumbrell, *The Search for Order*, 29.

Adam was expelled from Eden just as Israel was expelled from the Promised Land. His expulsion is an indication that he is not the actual owner of the earth or the garden,[142] and this should serve to remind Israel that she too was not the owner of the land. Furthermore, Adam's expulsion signifies the end of his vicegerency. He has lost his special status in Eden. The land suffers as a result of this loss of vicegerency. The ground is cursed (Gen 3:17), and the land is left in a state of chaos, groaning in search for redemption.

Finally, there is in God's words to the serpent a hint of an element of hope that this loss of status would be restored: "I will put enmity between you and the woman, and between your offspring and her offspring; he shall bruise your head, and you shall bruise his heel" (Gen 3:15). This statement, often dubbed the *protoeuangelion*, carries within it a notion of hope that is to be found in the "offspring" of the woman.[143] As the genealogies in Genesis 4–11 make clear, Abraham comes from the offspring of Adam and Eve, and this link is very important for the theology of Israel. Furthermore, the word used for "offspring" (זרע) is a very common word in Genesis, and it often speaks about the line running from Adam, to Abraham, to the twelve tribes of Israel. The offspring of the woman is Israel.[144] The main task of the זרע of the woman, Israel, is to "bruise the head of the serpent." Thus, Genesis 3:15 could be seen as a hint towards Israel being restored into her original vocation. This element of hope echoes the prophetic hope of restoration for Israel after the exile.

---

142. Tarazi, *Land and Covenant*, 32.

143. Yet Westermann comments that the explanation of 3:15 as a promise has been abandoned almost without exception among most biblical scholars. Westermann, *Genesis 1-11*, 260.

144. Most commentaries interpret the "offspring" of the woman as speaking of humanity collectively. The interpretation of the "offspring" as Israel is not to deny that it could also be interpreted as referring to humanity, just as interpreting Adam as proto-Israel does not mean that the story does not have universal implications. This interpretation highlights Adam/Israel representative role in the theology of the OT.

4.3. Eden Is the Land

The second implication of the importance of Genesis 2–3 for salvation history is that Eden is proto-land or the first Promised Land. This is a crucial point for any theology of the land. As Robertson stresses:

> Land did not begin to be theologically significant with the promise given to Abraham. Instead, the patriarch's hope of possessing a land arose out of the concept of restoration to the original state from which man had fallen . . . This simple fact, so often overlooked, plays a critical role in evaluating the significance of the land throughout redemptive history and its consummate fulfillment.[145]

Many land theologians, as already noted, fail to see this and therefore do not apply the themes in Eden to the theology of the land, and instead start their analysis of the theme of land in the promises to Abraham.[146] However, the promise to Abraham in Israel's history of salvation echoes the giving of Eden to Adam, and so our understating of Eden can shape how we understand the land promises in the rest of Scripture. "The garden of Eden is the gateway to understanding the land of Canaan."[147]

Some scholars have attempted to show a correlation between descriptions of Eden and the Promised Land in the OT.[148] Ottosson, for example, argues that the traditions of the OT used the conception of Eden in Genesis 2 "not only metaphorically and symbolically but also geographically" to describe the primary phase of the land of promise and also its final restoration.[149] Ottosson builds his conclusion on two observations: the identity of the four rivers, and the fact that the themes and motifs occurring in Eden were used when the salvation history of Israel was written.

---

145. O. P. Robertson, *The Israel of God: Yesterday, Today, and Tomorrow* (Phillipsburg: P&R, 2000), 4.
146. See no. 35 above.
147. A. Smith, "The Fifth Gospel," in *Eyes to See, Ears to Hear. Essays in Memory of J. Alan Groves*, ed. P. Enns, D. Green & M. Kelly (Phillipsburg: P&R, 2010), 79.
148. See for example W. Berg, "Israel's Land, Der Garten Gottes. Der Garten als Bild des Heiles im Alten Testament," *Biblische Zeitschrift* 32 (1988): 35–51.
149. Ottosson, "Eden and the Land of Promise," 177.

Ottosson's observation concerning the themes and motifs of Eden is valid. The Promised Land echoes Eden in Scripture. But his conclusion about the location of Eden is not without challenges. For him, the geography of Eden covered the area originally promised to Abraham and later described by the prophets "from the river to the river." Noting that the east rivers are Tigris and Euphrates, he then looked for two parallel rivers in the west and concluded that Pishon is the Nile, and that Gihon, necessarily a river parallel to the Nile, is a small stream south of Gaza called Nahal Besor. So the geography of Eden covers the area in between, which is the land promised to Abraham in Genesis 15:18–21.

There are at least two challenges to this intriguing theory. First, it is highly unlikely that the narrator would talk about three large and well-known rivers, while the fourth is a small unknown one. Second, not everyone today agrees that Pishon is the Nile. In fact, many think that Gihon is the Nile (cf. LXX).[150] Cassuto tries to resolve this by saying that Pishon and Gihon jointly form the Nile.[151] This would not affect Ottosson's theory about the location of Eden.

The location of Eden is a very complicated and much debated issue, and many solutions and theories have been advanced. Among the common suggested locations are Mesopotamia, Armenia (or the north) and Arabia. Some have concluded that the location is inaccessible,[152] and many believe that according to Genesis 2–3 Eden does not belong in our world.[153]

---

150. Those who believe Gihon is the Nile do so for two reasons: First, when the big rivers of the ANE are mentioned, the Nile cannot be missed. Second, the land of Cush means in the great majority of Old Testament texts the land south of Egypt (Isa 11; 20:3,5; Jer 13:23; 46:9).

151. Cassuto, *A Commentary*, 116.

152. Noort for example says that "the narrator wants to offer a mystified location for Paradise. Through geography he wants to demonstrate the reality of Paradise. Well-known, famous rivers derive from the universal river starting in Eden. Later versions and explanations go in the same direction, now covering the whole known world of their day. On the other hand, he does not want to locate Paradise in an accessible and locatable place. He transforms Paradise into reality by ending with the well-known Mesopotamian rivers. But this paradise is inaccessible." Noort, "Gan-Eden," 33. Wenham also observes: "The insoluble geography is a way of saying that it is now inaccessible to, even unlocatable by, later man." Wenham, *Genesis 1-15*, 66–67.

153. Stordalen for example says: "The luxurious land of Eden with its river and garden is part of the cosmic installations in temporal קדם. As such they locate somewhere in the divine realm." Stordalen, *Echoes of Eden*, 286. Cassuto also concluded: "The garden of

The question, however, is: should we try to locate Eden in the first place? It seems that Genesis 2:10–14 is not trying to describe geography (where Eden was), but theology (i.e. what and how the geography functioned). It is making a theological statement, namely that Eden is the source of blessing for the entire creation. Besides, it is highly unlikely that Genesis 2–3 was trying to describe the exact location in a literal geographical sense in a narrative that is full of symbols and metaphorical elements (e.g. the two trees, the serpent).[154] The language of Genesis 2–3 is mythic.[155] Myth is a "theologically serious way of expressing theological truth or giving account of the significance of events for later readers."[156] Looking at the Eden narrative as "myth" is not to say that the place itself is not real or that the story is entirely non-factual, or that the story belongs to the heavenly realm rather than the present world. This would run counter to the nature of God in the OT, who intervenes in history, time, and space. What we have in Genesis 2–3 is a theological way of narrating something that actually happened in our real world, while using metaphorical or symbolic language to express ideas beyond the realm of our senses.

Concerning Eden, Goldingay observes:

> Perhaps the names suggest that the river in Eden is the source of water to the north/northeast (Mesopotamia), to the south (Africa/Arabia) and to Jerusalem itself. The geography is imaginary, but it makes a realistic point. God's creation is the source of life for the entire world.[157]

Eden according to the Torah was not situated in our world." Cassuto, *A Commentary*, 118. And Mettinger argues: "What is important for us is that we are not justified in placing the events of Gen 2:10–14 in a real-world geographical context." Mettinger, *The Eden Narrative*, 16.

154. For Spero, "refusal to recognize the metaphoric nature of certain texts such as the Gan Eden story is to deprive oneself of one of the main sources of the wisdom of the Torah." S. Spero, "Paradise Lost or Outgrown?," *Tradition* 41, no. 2 (2008): 257.

155. Although the language is mythic, the story itself does not belong to ANE myths that occurred outside time and space. I stand with Alonso-Schökel who argued that the source of this narrative pattern does not derive from myths but from the salvation history of Israel. Alonso-Schökel, "Sapiential and Covenant Themes."

156. Goldingay, *Old Testament Theology*, 878.

157. Similarly, Tuell observed in his study on Ezek 47 and Gen 2–3 (where he equated Jerusalem of Ezek 47 with Eden of Gen 2–3) that the idea that "the great rivers of Assyria

Goldingay says that the river is the source of water *to* Jerusalem based on 2 Chronicles 32:30, which mentions a small spring by the name of Gihon in Jerusalem. But it is unlikely that Genesis 2:13 is talking about a small stream in Jerusalem, since this river flowed around the whole land of Cush.[158] Rather, Psalm 46:5, Ezekiel 47:1–12 and Zechariah. 14:8 say, in a highly symbolic context, that the river flows *from* Jerusalem into the outside world. These passages that associate Jerusalem or Zion with Eden do so symbolically and theologically and not literally or geographically. This might explain why Jerusalem in not mentioned directly in Genesis 2–3. This primeval story took place in the temporal קדם,[159] and as such it did not speak about contemporary places or geographies. As Gordon argues, the silence of Genesis 1–11 on Jerusalem arises in the first place from a "recognition of the claims of historical veracity." Jerusalem is not mentioned because "it was not believed to have played a part in the world's earliest history." However, the theological themes associated with Jerusalem are there, but not the actual city itself.[160]

Going back to the geography of Eden, Genesis 2:10–14 refers through famous rivers to well-known ANE nations – such as Babylon and Assyria (and probably Egypt) – that had a long historical interaction with Israel. By doing this, the text is implying that the garden of Eden is at the center of the world as Israel perceived it. The description of Eden and the four rivers elevates Eden over other nations and places. The fact that the

---

and Babylon flow from Zion makes no sense geographically. However, it makes abundant sense theologically. As creator of the whole earth, Yahweh's mountain is the source of life and fertility in all the world, not just Israel." S. Tuell, "The Rivers of Paradise: Ezekiel 47:1–12 and Genesis 2:10–14," in *God Who Creates: Essays in Honor of W. Sibley Towner*, ed. W. P. Brown and S. D. McBride (Grand Rapids: Eerdmans, 2000), 180.

158. Regardless of whether Cush refers to Ethiopia, as generally believed, or to the land of the Cassites in Western Iran. See E. A. Speiser, "The Rivers of Paradise," in *Oriental and Biblical Studies,* ed. J. J. Finkelstein and M. Greenberg (Philadelphia: University of Pennsylvania, 1967), 25–26.

159. For Stordalen, קדם in Genesis 2:8 is better understood temporally (from the old), not geographically (in the East). Stordalen, *Echoes of Eden*, 263–270.

160. Gordon therefore says: "Although there is no writing of Jerusalem/Zion back into Genesis 1–11 . . . the 'Protohistory' does make use of the concepts of sanctuary and holy land in its accounts of the first humans." Gordon, *Holy Land, Holy City*, 16.

rivers flow from Eden could imply that Eden was on a mountain,[161] and Ezekiel's identification of Eden as a holy mountain of God supports this (Ezek 28:14, 16).[162] This elevation, if maintained, is meant to be understood symbolically and theologically, in the same way in which Isaiah 2 elevates Zion on a mountain.

Similarly, the number "four" should be understood symbolically to indicate totality,[163] as, for example, the four winds, the four corners of the earth, the four beasts and the four horns as the kingdoms of the world (Dan 7; Zech 2:1). "The author projects a picture of the great river system that surrounded the world he knew, for the number 'four' circumscribes the entire world."[164] And so the garden of Eden was like the capital of the universe, and it could be argued that Adam was supposed to extend the boundaries of Eden, or the realm of God's reign, over the entire world.

Israel, therefore, must learn from Eden that the Promised Land must be a land of blessing to the nations outside. The theology of the land in Eden has universal implications, and the theology of the land in the rest of the OT must have the same universal implications. The land is a source of blessing to the world.

Eden, as the capital of the world, was an ideal place of rest,[165] as is evident from the description of the water and trees in it, and from the use of the verb נוח. The superior qualities of Eden are made even more special by the fact that Eden was a sacred place that mediated the presence of God in a special way. However, this feature was lost as a result of the disobedience of Adam. The good gift of the garden of Eden was lost. Covenant breakers cannot live in Eden. This is an important reminder to Israel that her land, just like the garden, "is something to be protected more than it is

---

161. Mettinger, *The Eden Narrative*, 27; Levenson, *Sinai & Zion*, 129; Neiman, "Eden, the Garden of God," 123.

162. Dumbrell, "Genesis 2:1-3," 224. See also R. J. Clifford, *The Cosmic Mountain in Canaan and the Old Testament* (Cambridge: Harvard University Press, 1972), 100.

163. Clifford believes that Gihon and Pishon were artificially formed to bring the number of rivers to four. Clifford, *Cosmic Mountain in Canaan*, 101.

164. Von Rad, *Genesis*, 79.

165. Some have called Eden a utopian place. See Y. Amit, "Biblical Utopianism: A Mapmakers Guide to Eden," *Union Seminary Quarterly Review* 44 (1990): 11–17. See also Stordalen, *Echoes of Eden*, 14. It is better to use the term "ideal," since "utopia" refers to an imagined place in which everything is perfect, and as imagined it could be unreal.

something to be possessed."[166] Moreover, Adam's exile from Eden was his death. There is no true life out of Eden. Eden teaches Israel that holiness and obedience are required for any holy land to mediate the presence of God and to be a place of rest.

The land apart from covenant faithfulness loses its capacity to bless the world outside it. In fact, the ground suffers as a result of the disobedience of Adam:

> Cursed is the ground (אדמה) because of you; in pain you shall eat of it all the days of your life; thorns and thistles it shall bring forth for you; and you shall eat the plants of the field. By the sweat of your face you shall eat bread, till you return to the ground, for out of it you were taken; for you are dust, and to dust you shall return. (Gen 3:17–19)

These verses describe the status of the land as a result of the curse. Such a ground is no longer capable of blessing the world. The ideal reality in Eden is reversed. The cursing of the ground affects every aspect of life. The new reality is described using words such as: curse, thorns, thistles, turmoil, sweat, and death. This dark reality can also be attributed to the abuse of vicegerency by Adam. Adam's sin had universal and cosmic consequences, and the land post the fall suffers from this fallen vicegerency. Eden and the earth around it suffer and are in need of restoration and healing. Perhaps this healing is hinted at in God's words to the serpent (Gen 3:15).

5. Conclusion: The Theology of Land in Eden

The Eden narrative in its final form was shaped, we have argued, in such a way as to echo and reflect the preceding story of Israel. With the land being a central theme in the theology of Israel, the Eden narrative therefore contains the first canonical version of the theology of the land. By virtue

---

166. V. P. Hamilton, *The Book of Genesis. Chapters 1-17* (Grand Rapids: Eerdmans, 1990), 171.

of being placed as an introduction to the Pentateuch, it should thus receive special attention as it sets the course for the rest of the biblical narrative. In other words, Eden paradoxically both reflects and sets the course for the story of Israel.

Land (the garden of Eden) was given as a gift from the good creator God. The whole creation was good, but one particular piece of land stood out – the garden of Eden. This land was a place of delight and rest, and as such it was a good and blessed place. Compared to the world surrounding it, it was an ideal place.

This land was also intended to be the source of blessing to the rest of the creation outside its borders. Life and fertility proceeded from this land into the entire creation, symbolizing the superiority of this land over against other lands, and symbolizing also the dependence of the entire creation on this land for life and blessing.

Man was created outside this land and then brought into it, in a movement of grace and salvation. He was placed in it to take care of it and to rule on behalf of God from it, so as to extend the realm of the divine rule beyond the borders of this land. In this sense the land was supposed to expand. Humanity enjoyed there a kingly and priestly status.

God and humanity enjoyed a special relationship in this land. It mediated the presence of God in a special way, and therefore God was present in a special way in it. It was the first holy land, and its holiness derived from God's presence in it.

Disobedience to the commandments of the sovereign creator God led to the loss of the royal and priestly status of man, and more importantly, results in the loss of the land. The loss of Adam's vicegerency and the loss of land go hand in hand. The land does not tolerate covenant breakers. After all, man did not possess it. It could be taken away from him just as it was given to him. The land also loses its capacity to bless as a result of disobedience.

The loss of Adam's vicegerency had universal consequences, and so the loss of the land affected the rest of creation that depended on it for blessing and life. The theology of the land in Eden has universal implications. As a result, there is no real life outside this land. Disobedience has consequences – death. Death according to the theology of the land is exile from the land.

The theology of the land in Eden reflects God's desire and intention to dwell among humanity and to treat them as co-workers with him in his creation. God wants humanity to be *"landed."* Biblical redemption will therefore be the restoration to the realities that the land had first embodied. These realities are realities of *shalom* between God and man, man and man, and man and creation. To be *"landed"* is to live as a community in a land in which God dwells, man works, and creation rests.

The Bible starts in a place, a place that was tragically lost. Thus, the history of Israel (and accordingly of all humanity) starts in the exile, with a longing for the return to the state of blessedness and enjoyment of being in a Promised Land – Eden. The dialectic in Israel's fortunes between landlessness and landedness, described by Brueggemann, started in the exile from Eden.[167] Genesis 4 starts in a state of landlessness, and the theology of the land from this point forward is a theology of anticipation – longing for restoration from exile. The statement in Genesis 3:15 thus gives hope that the landless will receive the gift of land again, the exiled will be restored, and the land will be healed.

---

167. Brueggemann, *The Land*, xi.

CHAPTER 2

The Land and Holiness

Introduction

This chapter focuses on the land as sacred place, and it argues that the Promised Land in the OT is portrayed as a special sacred place that is different or set apart from other lands in the wider creation. It is, in this sense, a "holy land." It will be further argued that the holiness of the land is a result of three factors. First, the presence of God in the midst of the land makes it holy. Second, holiness is directly related to the holiness of the people living in it. Third, the land itself demands holiness. Furthermore, the land in the OT has centers of holiness, which function as social centers for the nation as well. Jerusalem, and in particular Zion, becomes at a certain time the focal point in the land, and functions as the center of holiness.

1. Holy God, Holy People, Holy Land

For something to be called "holy" means that it is set apart. Sacred place is a "place where God is encountered in a special or direct way, by virtue of which the very nature of the place becomes holy and set apart from ordinary space."[1] The holiness of the land in the OT, as will be shown next,

---

1. L. Ryken, J. Wilhoit, T. Longman, C. Duriez, D. Penney, and D. G. Reid, eds., *Dictionary of Biblical Imagery* (Downers Grove: InterVarsity Press, 1998), 784.

depends on three factors: the presence of God, the holiness of the people, and the land itself.

1.1. Holy God – Derivative Holiness

In the times of the patriarchs, the designation of a particular piece of geography as a special or distinct place was linked to the phenomenon of theophany. This began with Abraham when he entered Canaan and built an altar in the place in which God appeared to him (Gen 12:7). When Jacob saw a dream of a ladder reaching to heaven, and heard the voice of God promising him the land, in fear he declared, "How awesome is *this place*! This is none other than the house of God, and this is the gate of heaven" (Gen 28:17). He then called that place *Bethel*, which means "house of God." And when he encountered the man who wrestled with him and changed his name to Israel, Jacob called the place *Peniel* (Gen 32:30), believing that he met God "face to face."

The same experience continues in the Mosaic tradition. When Moses met God for the first time in the wilderness, God told him to take his sandals off his feet, for he was standing on "holy ground" (אדמת־קדש) (Exod 3:5). Mount Sinai was considered a holy place, and the people were warned not to approach it when God descended there to encounter Moses (Exod 19:12). And when God instructed Moses to build the tabernacle, the place where God would dwell in the tabernacle was designated as the "holy of holies" (Exod 26:33).

In all these cases, a place was declared "holy" as a result of a special appearance of God in it. It was the presence of God that made the place holy. Similarly, the Promised Land is said to be holy because YHWH the God of Israel is present in it in a special way. It is God's land and is like no other land:

> You will bring them in and plant them on *your own* mountain, the place, O LORD, which *you have made for your abode*, the sanctuary (מקדש), O Lord, which your hands have established. (Exod 15:17)[2]

---

2. See also Ps 78:54.

You shall not defile the land in which you live, in the midst of which I dwell, for I the LORD dwell (שכן) in the midst of the people of Israel. (Num 35:34)

In Davies' comprehensive work on the land, he observes that:

> Yahweh's possession of the land was expressed in terms of "holiness," a conception which in its origin had little, if anything, to do with morality, but rather denoted a relationship of separation for or consecration to a god. Since the land was Yahweh's possession, it enjoyed a certain degree of closeness to him; for Yahweh dwelt in the midst of Israel.[3]

Joosten argues in his study on the land in the Holiness Code in Leviticus (Lev 17–26) that the camp of Israel in the wilderness on the way to the land is presented as a temporary arrangement with a view to a definitive establishment in the land.[4] In other words, what applied there in the camp should apply on the land. Joosten observes two qualities that qualify the land as holy: (1) Within the camp/land the word of YHWH has force, and (2) the presence of YHWH is within it.[5]

YHWH is not only present in the land, but the land is also said to be his: "For the land is mine" (Lev 25:23). The land is the "patrimony of YHWH," and this makes it a "holy land," or YHWH's "personal property."[6] For Joosten, the underlying concept behind the phrase the "land is mine" is a cultic one: the land belongs to YHWH because he dwells there.[7]

But was the land the place of God's constant dwelling? There are different positions that can be illustrated in von Rad and Joosten. For von Rad, the desert sanctuary is the one and only place of *meeting* between YHWH

---

3. Davies, *The Gospel and the Land*, 29.
4. J. Joosten, *People and Land in the Holiness Code: An Exegetical Study of the Ideational Framework of the Law in Leviticus 17-26* (Leiden: E. J. Brill, 1996), 137.
5. Ibid., 139–141.
6. W. Zimmerli, *Old Testament Theology in Outline* (Edinburgh: T&T Clark, 2000), 66.
7. Joosten, *People and Land*, 169.

and Israel – something that was a constantly recurring event.[8] If it were the dwelling place of God, then it would be meaningless for God to tell Moses that he will *meet* him there.[9]

Joosten, on the other hand, argues that the land was a divine dwelling place. He notes verses that speak about a constant presence of the glory and the cloud,[10] the frequent statement that ritual acts are performed before YHWH, and explicit statements in a number of passages that it is YHWH's intention to dwell among the Israelites.[11]

This discussion is an important yet complicated one, because, as will be shown below, the presence of God in any place depends on multiple factors. Moreover, even if we speak about a dwelling or presence of God in the land, this presence or dwelling is by no means unconditional or constant, as illustrated by the exile and the destruction of the temple.

Furthermore, the presence of God in the land does not mean that the land itself is "hallowed" by this presence. "Nowhere in [the Holiness Code], nor in other priestly texts, do we find the idea of the holiness of the land."[12] Davies, along these lines, speaks of *derivative holiness* as it pertains to the land in the Pentateuch:

> Because Yahweh was near to it, his own holiness radiated throughout its boundaries. Note that the term "holy land," which suggests that the land itself was inherently "holy" seldom occurs in the Old Testament; that is, the holiness of the land is entirely *derivative*.[13]

In other words, the holiness of the land is entirely dependent on the presence of God. If God were to leave this land, as in the case of the exile, the

---

8. See Exod 16:10; 40:34; Lev 9:6; 23; Num 14:10; 16:19; 17:7; 20:6.
9. Von Rad, *Old Testament Theology*, 239.
10. See Exod 40:34–38; Num 9:15–23.
11. See Lev 25:8; 29:45; Num 5:3; 35:34. Joosten, *People and Land*, 142–143.
12. Joosten, *People and Land*, 179. For Joosten, the difference maintained in (the Holiness Code) between the land and the sanctuary is one of degree: whereas the sanctuary is holy, and therefore in danger of being profaned, the land is merely pure and in danger of being defiled.
13. Davies, *The Gospel and the Land*, 29 (emphasis added).

land ceases to be holy.[14] In fact, the term "holy land" (הקדש אדמת) occurs only in Zechariah 2:12, and there too it is directly and unequivocally related to the presence of God in its midst:[15]

> Sing and rejoice, O daughter of Zion, for behold, I come and *I will dwell in your midst*, declares the LORD . . . And the LORD will inherit Judah as his portion in the holy land, and will again choose Jerusalem.[16]

The presence of God in a special way in the land and the fact that it is described as "his land" demand holy living, as manifested in the different laws that pertained to being in the land. Because it is God's land, Israel must pay extra attention, lest it pollute the land and evoke the anger of God: "And I brought you into a plentiful land to enjoy its fruits and its good things. But when you came in, you *defiled my land* and made *my heritage an abomination*" (Jer 2:7). And so Weinfeld observes: "Holiness of the Land involves purity which all the inhabitants of the land were commanded to observe, based on the belief that the entire land belongs to the God of Israel."[17]

The holiness code often repeats the phrase "when you come into the land,"[18] indicating a special status that the land enjoys. There was an "inside" and there was an "outside" the land, and there were certain laws that only applied in the land.[19] In addition, any sin committed in the land was more serious since it was committed in a land that belonged to YHWH.[20]

---

14. Waltke, *An Old Testament Theology*, 542.
15. In addition, the word used in Zech 2:12 is not the common word for land - הארץ, but אדמה, which is better translated as "ground."
16. Weinfeld believes that the term "holy land" here does not refer to the land as a whole, but only to Jerusalem: "The expression . . . should therefore be understood as referring to the area surrounding the Temple, namely, Jerusalem . . . In these verses, the expression 'the holy territory' . . . is parallel to that for Jerusalem, 'the holy city.' The actual meaning of this expression is the territory/earth of the holy – in other words, the ground belonging to the holy area (the Temple and Temple city); it does not mean 'holy land,' since such a concept does not appear in the Old Testament." Weinfeld, *Promise of the Land*, 204.
17. Ibid., 220.
18. Lev 19:23; 23:10; 25:2.
19. Lev 19:9–10; 23:22–23; 19:33–34; 22:24; 22:45; 26:2; 25:24.
20. G. Kwakkel, "The Land in the Book of Hosea," in *The Land of Israel in Bible, History, and Theology: Studies in Honour of Ed Noort*, ed. J. Van Ruiten and J. C. De Vos (Leiden:

And so, when Israel was in exile, she lived in an impure land.[21] The boundaries as such play a role in determining where is "holy" and "not holy." This can be seen with the tribes who decided to stay east of the river. East of the river is different from west of the river. Israel is stepping into a special territory.[22] As von Rad argues:

> The tribes living to the east of Jordan express the fears that they or their children might be denied their "portion in Yahweh" ... on the grounds that they live beyond the Jordan. It is even held to be debatable whether this land may not be unclean, in contradistinction to the land west of the Jordan which is in this context expressly designated "Yahweh's land."[23]

In short, the land is a distinct land from all other lands – a holy land. The distinction mark of the land is the presence of God in it. God chose the land as a medium for his encounter with his people. The presence of God further demands holiness from the people who dwell in his land.

1.2. Holy People – Mandated Holiness

The presence of God in the land depends to a certain degree on the presence of the Israelites in the land, for he dwells not merely in the land, but also in the midst of his people: "For I the LORD dwell in the midst of the people of Israel" (Num 35:34). Joosten even argues that if the Israelites are not living in the land, YHWH's ownership and lordship over it "are rendered problematic," because God's dwelling in the land is "inseparably connected to the fact that he dwells in the midst of the Israelites."[24] We can thus argue that the holiness of the land is related to the people of the land.

Brill, 2009), 181.
21. H. D. Preuss, *Old Testament Theology. Volume I* (Louisville: Westminster John Knox Press, 1995), 121. See also Amos 7:17; cf. Ps 137:4; Ezek 4:3.
22. See also S. Spero, "Who Authorized Israelite Settlement East of the Jordan?," *Jewish Bible Quarterly* 35, no. 1 (2007): 11–15.
23. Von Rad, "The Promised Land," 87.
24. Joosten, *People and Land*, 192.

Moreover, the OT warns consistently that the sins of the people of the land pollute the land and defile it.[25] The Israelites were directly commanded not to defile the land, but they failed, and as a result the land was polluted (Jer 2:7). This clearly shows that the actions of the people are determining factors when it comes to the holiness of the land. Holy living matters. *The land ceases to be holy as a result of the sin of its dwellers.*

We can therefore argue that the determining factor for the holiness of the land is not only the presence of God, but *also the holiness of the people living in it*. The holiness of the people is emphasized in God's calling to Israel in Exodus 19:6: "And you shall be to me a kingdom of priests and a holy nation (קדוש גוי)." The holiness required of the people of Israel is in three areas: (1) in the priestly literature, as ritual cleanness; (2) in the prophets, as the cleanness of social justice; and (3) in the Wisdom tradition, as the cleanness of individual morality.[26] These holiness requirements, manifested in the religious, social, and political spheres, are directly related to polluting the land.[27]

It is important to note that the requirements of holiness apply to all the inhabitants of the land equally – the Israelites, and the stranger living among them. This also applied to the nations that were in the land before Israel. If anything, Israel must be held to a higher standard:

> But you shall keep my statutes and my rules and do none of these abominations, *either the native or the stranger who sojourns* among you, for the people of the land, who were before you, did all of these abominations, so that the *land became unclean*. (Lev 18:26–27)

One important conclusion from this perspective is that God is not bound to the land. In other words, *Israel must learn that her actions are more important than her location*. It is here that we can understand one of the most puzzling dilemmas in OT theology of the land: the tribes that were

---

25. Lev 18:24–27; Num 35:33–34; Ps 106:38.
26. Ryken et al., *Dictionary of Biblical Imagery*, 390.
27. See Habel, *The Land is Mine*, 80.

allowed to live in Transjordan. This arrangement is puzzling since the OT makes it clear that Israel enters the Promised Land by crossing the river. Yet two and a half tribes are allowed to stay in Jordan. They are allowed to stay there *as long as* they obeyed the commandment of God:

> Only be very careful to observe the commandment and the law that Moses the servant of the LORD commanded you, to love the LORD your God, and to walk in all his ways and to keep his commandments and to cling to him and to serve him with all your heart and with all your soul. (Josh 22:5)

Obedience is more important than location. This is the lesson Israel had to learn in exile. They wrongly assumed that by being away from the land, they were away from the presence of God (Ps 137:1–4). But God in Ezekiel 11:16 declares that he can be present with the Israelites even in exile:

> Thus says the Lord God: Though I removed them far off among the nations, and though I scattered them among the countries, *yet I have been a sanctuary to them for a while in the countries where they have gone.*

The perspective of the exilic prophets is important, as we see that God manifests himself to the prophets who are with Israel in exile. Loss of the land is not accompanied by the loss of God or revelation.[28] As Clements concludes:

> Ezekiel in his vision saw the very presence of Yahweh in all its majesty coming to him in his distant place of exile. There is no suggestion, therefore, that Yahweh was simply the God of Israel, or only of Palestine, but his power was shown to extend throughout the entire universe.[29]

---

28. Preuss, *Old Testament Theology Vol 1*, 127.
29. R. E. Clements, *God and Temple* (Oxford: Basil Blackwell, 1965), 103.

In summary, just as the land could become holy by the presence of God in it, it could become unholy by the actions of its inhabitants. At the same time, living a holy life, even outside the land, is more important than being in the land. God can reveal himself to his people anywhere and is not bound by any land.

1.3. Holy Land: The Land Personified Demands Holiness

The OT offers a third dimension to the holiness of the land, namely that the *land itself* demands holiness. This is evident in texts where the land itself is personified.[30] The land falls into prostitution, vomits, is polluted and defiled, is sinned against, is judged, and is ultimately healed.[31] The land is also *responsible* before God to keep the Sabbath (Lev 25:2). Somehow, the land owes worship to YHWH, which signifies the special relationship it enjoys with him.[32] In all these examples, the land is more than just turf. It is indeed portrayed as a person.[33]

We cannot then tell the biblical story without reference to the land. It is a major player in the plot, and as a player it makes demands and is itself affected and polluted by the sins of its inhabitants. Israel's disobedience not only offends YHWH, but it also affects the land. The land has its own life and its own meaning. It is the land that is finally abused.[34] This perspective about the land reminds us that land in the OT is not merely soil, or a piece of real estate in the ANE. Land is a theological concept that is loaded with meaning and implications.[35] It also emphasizes that the land itself demands holiness, as explicitly indicated in Leviticus 18:24–25:

---

30. For Cohn, the land in the OT is commonly addressed "anthropomorphically." R. Cohn, "From Homeland to the Holy Land: The Territoriality of Torah," *Continuum* 1, no. 1 (1990): 9.

31. See Lev 18:25; 19:9; 20:22; 26:35; Num 13:32; 35:33–34; Deut 21:23; 24:4; 2 Chr 7:14; Isa 24:5; Jer 2:7; Ezek 7:2–4.

32. Davies, *The Gospel and the Land*, 29.

33. A. Neher, "The Land as Locus of the Sacred," in *Voices from Jerusalem. Jews and Christians Reflect on the Holy Land*, ed. D. Burrell and Y. Landau (New York : Paulist Press, 1992), 19. Joosten similarly argues that in a few passages in the Holiness Code, the land was not considered in its practical, geographic sense, but was represented as a living being with its own personality. Joosten, *People and Land*, 152.

34. Brueggemann, *The Land*, 112.

35. Ibid., 2.

> Do not make yourselves unclean by any of these things, for by all these the nations I am driving out before you have become unclean, and the *land became unclean*, so that I punished its iniquity, and *the land vomited* out its inhabitants.[36]

Two things are evident from this verse. First, Israel is responsible for the land just as were the nations before her. Second, and more important for this discussion, it was because the land became unholy that it vomited out its inhabitants. It was not God who drove the nations out, but the land. In fact, if we only relate holiness to the presence of God in the land, then these verses pose a problem for us, because they are talking about the land *before* Israel settled in it. Davies thus concludes that the land vomited them "because of its holiness."[37]

What caused this land to be holy? Davies suggests that the land was already characterized by holiness *before* Israel entered it and brought the Torah to it because YHWH owned it and dwelled in the midst of it.[38] Davies builds his argument on Numbers 35:34: "You shall not defile the land in which you live, in the midst of which I dwell, for I the LORD dwell in the midst of the people of Israel." However, the second phrase in the verse clearly speaks of God as dwelling in the *midst of the people*. It seems then that the verse links the presence of God in the land with the presence of the people of Israel in the land, whereas Leviticus 18:24–25 is speaking about the land before Israel entered it. In other words, Leviticus 18 seems to treat Canaan differently from other lands.

The land must therefore – according to this perspective at least – be *inherently holy*. This holy land demands holiness. It does not tolerate unholiness, and vomits those who pollute her. Cohn then rightly speaks of a tension in the biblical drama, manifest in the question: "Can Israel be truly at home in a land that can 'vomit out' its inhabitants?"[39]

---

36. See also Lev 18:27–30; 20:22.
37. Davies, *The Gospel and the Land*, 31.
38. Ibid., p. 31.
39. Cohn, "Homeland to the Holy Land," 5.

Furthermore, it is important to observe that the land not only demands holiness from its inhabitants; it also depends for its own fertility on the holiness of the people so that it can be in reality a land "flowing with milk and honey." This is highlighted in the climatology of the land of Canaan, which depends on rain to be fertile:

> For the land that you are entering to take possession of it is not like the land of Egypt, from which you have come, where you sowed your seed and irrigated it, like a garden of vegetables. But the land that you are going over to possess is a land of hills and valleys, which drinks water by the rain from heaven, a land that the LORD your God cares for. The eyes of the LORD your God are always upon it, from the beginning of the year to the end of the year. (Deut 11:10–12)

Canaan, in contrast to Egypt and even Mesopotamia, depends on rain to be fertile. In other words, the obedience of the Israelite will be the key for their survival in the land, because the land needs rain, and rain depends on obedience:

> *The Promised Land is not an easy land – it is not paradise . . .* when God brought his people to this land, he built into it those elements that would provide a framework for his people to understand life with him . . . This would be a land that made demands. It must wait for God to open the heavens. It must wait for rain . . . *this is a land that will demand faith.*[40]

In summary, the land that Israel received as a gift and was about to enter was a special and different land – it demands holiness. This perspective highlights the role of the land in the biblical drama as an independent player. Moreover, Canaan is a land that makes demands from its inhabitants. These demands are a precondition to dwelling in the land, and for the

---

40. G. M. Burge, *The Bible and the Land* (Grand Rapids: Zondervan, 2009), 25–26 (emphasis added).

health of the land itself. In the case of unholiness, the land will vomit its inhabitants. For the land to be a "holy land," its inhabitants must live a life characterized by holiness.

1.4. Conclusion

There are three different dimensions to the holiness of the land that complement each other. Any balanced theology of the land must take into account all three dimensions together or holistically. Holding these three views together prevents us from absolutizing the position of land over against other considerations. Therefore, we should maintain equally and at the same time that:
- God's presence in the land makes the land holy
- Land depends on the holiness of the people for its status as holy
- Land independently demands holiness

These three points are interrelated and must be held together. The triangle of God, people, and land provides a holistic lens with which we can approach the biblical drama as it pertains to the theology of the land. There can be no holy land without the presence of God, just as there can be no holy land without the inhabitants of the land being holy, and just as there can be no holy land without meeting the demands of the land itself.

2. Sanctuaries

2.1. From Land to Zion

Holiness in the history of OT Israel always had a geographical center or a sanctuary. This can be seen in Eden, the tabernacle and then the temple. These sanctuaries, and in particular the temple, are important for the theology of the land. Many scholars have observed that the focus on land in the OT narrows progressively from land into Jerusalem, Zion and then temple.[41] This shift started with the elevation of Jerusalem as the capital of

---

41. See for example D. E. Gowan, *Eschatology in the Old Testament* (Edinburgh: T. & T. Clark Publishers, 2000), 9–20; Weinfeld, *The Promise of the Land*, 202–220; J. G. McConville, "Jerusalem in the Old Testament," in *Jerusalem Past and Present in the Purposes of God*, ed. P. W. L Walker (Carlisle: Paternoster Press, 1992), 21–51.

the Davidic kingdom, and with the building of the temple, which became the center of the religious life of Israel. Yet it was only after the exile, according to Weinfeld, that Jerusalem assumed the place of the land in the theology of Israel:

> After the fall of the kingdoms of Israel and Judea, the returning Israelites concentrated around the Temple and the city of Jerusalem. Due to the concentration, the religious and national emphasis, as reflected in Second Temple period sources, shifted from "the land" to "the city" and "the Temple."[42]

The temple was a special sacred space like no other:

> And the LORD said to him (Solomon), "I have heard your prayer and your plea, which you have made before me. I have *consecrated* (הקדשתי) this house that you have built, by putting my name there forever. My eyes and my heart will be there for all time." (1 Kgs 9:3)

There are many similarities as regards holiness between the land and the sanctuaries; so what was said about the land above applies to the temple. God manifests himself in a special way in the temple (2 Chr 7:2), special holiness is required for the priests who ministered there (2 Chr 7:7–11), and the obedience of the people is what guarantees the continuation of the blessings that proceeded from the temple (1 Kgs 6:11–13; 9:4–5).

Mount Zion, the geographical location of the temple, is also considered a special and distinct place in the OT.[43] According to the Psalms, it is God's holy hill (2:6) and he sits enthroned there (9:11) and shines forth from there (50:2). Special holiness is required for people to dwell there (15:1). Zion is the city of God (87:3), his holy habitation and mountain, and he

---

42. Weinfeld, *The Promise of the Land*, 202.
43. For a good and brief summary of the major theological themes associated with Zion, see H. D. Preuss, *Old Testament Theology. Volume II* (Louisville: Westminster John Knox Press, 1996), 39–50; R. B. Dillard, 1988, "Zion," in *Baker Encyclopaedia of the Bible*, ed. W. A. Elwell and B. J. Beitzel (Grand Rapids: Baker Book House, 1988), 2199–2203.

is in the midst of her and she will not be moved (46:4–5; 48:1; 99:9). She is beautiful in elevation, the joy of all the earth, the city of the great King (48:2) and the perfection of beauty (50:2). God loves Zion more than any other place (78:68; 87:1–2). It is therefore no wonder that in addition to being called the "city of God," it is also called his "dwelling place" (74:2; 76:2; see also Joel 3:17, 21).

Many scholars have found similarities between the conception of Zion in the OT and ANE myths, in particular the concept of the cosmic mountain as the dwelling place of the gods.[44] Clifford's comprehensive study on cosmic mountains in Canaan shows that heaven and earth when united were seen together as a mountain.[45] The mountain was the axis of the universe and was the connecting point between the different spheres. Clifford then argues that elements of the Canaanite traditions of the mountain of El had influenced Israelite traditions of Sinai, and that Baal's mountain, Zaphon, had come "nominatim" into Israelite religion. He also argued that the idea of the navel of the earth, or the *omphalos*, known among the Greeks, is used of Jerusalem.[46] Zimmerli made similar observations, namely that the idea that YHWH has his dwelling place at the source of the rivers that water the world parallels the Canaanite depiction of El (Ps 46:5); that Zion as a world mountain recalls what the Ugaritic texts say of the dwelling place of Baal (Ps 48:3); and that even the term "city of God" is probably based on a Canaanite model.[47]

What seem to distinguish the Israelite religion from the surrounding ANE religions are the ethical and moral elements that are attached to the presence of the deity in the sanctuary. The community life in Israel centered around these circles of holiness, stressing visibly the importance of holiness as the mark or sign of the community. It was as if holiness started from the holy of holies in the tabernacle/temple and then progressively went outward, demanding holiness as a way of living. "God's holy presence

---

44. Levenson, *Sinai & Zion*, 137.

45. Clifford, *Cosmic Mountain in Canaan*, 190.

46. Ibid., 190–192. Gordon completely rejects the *omphalos* theory, arguing that in Ezek 5:5 the point is that God has made Jerusalem the center of attention because of his own interest in her. Gordon, *Holy Land, Holy City*, 30.

47. Zimmerli, *Old Testament Theology*, 77.

radiates outward from the sanctuary throughout the entire land and imposes its demands on all the inhabitants."[48] The consequences of the lack of holiness were devastating in the case of the temple, as it could mean its destruction (1 Kgs 9:6–9), and the departure of the glory of God from Jerusalem (Ezek 11:22).

2.2. The Legitimacy of Zion

Zion in the OT, as we have just noted, is more than a place, and we can talk of a theology that is associated with Zion. Von Rad, for example, speaks of a "Zion tradition," based primarily on Psalm 2. He summarizes the tradition as: (1) YHWH takes up his abode on Mount Zion, (2) Zion thus becomes the throne of YHWH and his chosen king, and (3) YHWH wins a victory over an alliance of nations opposed to him and his king, with the battle and victory being couched in mythological terms.[49]

One of the most puzzling things when it comes to the Zion theology is the question of the temple and its legitimacy. In the OT, God did not ask for a temple, and even when David offered to build the temple, the writer of the book of Samuel portrays God as not so enthusiastic about building it, asking rhetorically: "Did I ever ask for a house?" (2 Sam 7:6–7; 1 Chr 17:6). God in the OT, up until the building of the temple, has been a mobile God, and he says to David that he preferred it so:

> I have not lived in a house since the day I brought up the people of Israel from Egypt to this day, but I have been moving about in a tent for my dwelling. (2 Sam 7:6)[50]

Even Solomon himself wondered when he built the temple:

---

48. Joosten, *People and Land*, 177.
49. Von Rad, *Old Testament Theology*, 46.
50. Levenson has already observed the same theme in the Sinai event. He observes that God manifested himself outside the camp, and commented: "YHWH's self-disclosure takes place in remote parts rather than within the established and settled cult of the city . . . in other words, the deity is like his worshipers: mobile, rootless and unpredictable." That is why, for Levenson, Sinai is an event and not a place. Levenson, *Sinai & Zion*, 22–24.

> But will God indeed dwell on the earth? Behold, heaven and the highest heaven cannot contain you; how much less this house that I have built! (1 Kgs 8:27; see also 2 Chr 2:6; 6:18; Isa 66:1–2)

In the midst of the strong Zion theology in the OT, these verses stand out in a surprising way. They are present even after the first and second temples were built, and were probably preserved as a reminder and a safeguard for the Israelite religion after the temple was destroyed. God does not need the temple, and he did not ask for it. Moreover, the people can do without the temple. This is one of the most important lessons learned by the people in exile, namely that God is there in exile with his people.

These verses that hold a conflicting view of the temple and Zion challenge the legitimacy of the Zion tradition. Furthermore, the history of the monarchy reflects a negative side of the Zion tradition, highlighted by the failure of Solomon in his last days, when other gods were worshipped in Zion (1 Kgs 11:6) and the Israelites lived as slaves (1 Kgs 12:4). Brueggemann expresses the point quite starkly:

> The temple serves to give theological legitimacy and visible religiosity to the entire program of the regime. The evidence is beyond dispute that he [Solomon] so manipulates Israel's public worship that it becomes a cult for a static God, lacking in the power, vigor, and freedom of the God of the old traditions. . . . Yahweh is now cornered in the temple. His business is support of regime; to grant legitimacy to it and to effect forgiveness for it as is necessary . . . In the Solomonic period even God now apparently has no claim on the land. He is guest and not host.[51]

After Solomon's death and the division of the kingdom, the temple became a cause of the conflict and the division, and so Jeroboam decided to build other sanctuaries in the newly established Northern kingdom (1 Kgs

---

51. Brueggemann, *The Land*, 80–81.

12:25–33). The temple became an idol in itself, and God was left out of the picture.

McConville challenges the notion that there is a "Zion tradition" in the OT, and refused to tie this tradition to the historical Jerusalem.[52] He argues that a comprehensive and canonical reading of the OT, that takes the perspective of the exile into consideration, cannot support a strong and permanent Zion theology. He alludes to different key passages, like the hesitation in supporting the monarchy, the hesitation in building the temple, and the criticism of the monarchy as proof that the OT seems to reject the Zion tradition.[53] As for the Psalms, McConville argues that we cannot take certain individual Psalms in isolation from the wider OT context and the final canonical form of the book of Psalms. For example, Psalm 89, which ends book three of Psalms, concludes with a very negative tone towards Zion, due to Israel's historical exile experience.[54] He also argues that other Psalms contradict the common Zion tradition. Psalm 87 is inclusive in nature, and book four of the Psalms seems to promote the kingship of God without a reference to Zion.[55] He concludes that the Zion tradition in the Psalms is shaped by the locus of the Psalter's formation, which is not the cult of the first temple, but the setting after the exile. The Zion tradition has been changed and modified as a result of the destruction of the temple and monarchy.[56]

As for prophetic literature, McConville again argues that, when read from the perspective of the exile, it becomes apparent that the prophets were not talking about historical Jerusalem, but about a futuristic faithful and eschatological Jerusalem.[57] The prophecies cannot be speaking about the actual return from exile, for the reality of the returned community was far from ideal.[58]

---

52. McConville, "Jerusalem in the Old Testament," 21–51.
53. Ibid., 29–30.
54. Ibid., 32.
55. Ibid., 30.
56. Ibid., 32.
57. Ibid., 34–43.
58. Ibid., 45.

McConville's perspective is important, as it at least reveals that the OT does not speak in one voice about a distinct and permanent place in which God will forever dwell, and which he will protect against all circumstances. As we have already shown, the designation of any place as holy does not mean that it will always be holy, for its holiness is closely tied to the holiness of the people. In addition, God is not confined to one place. If there is then a Zion tradition in the OT, it must be read symbolically as referring to an ideal situation in which, in the event of faithfulness, God dwells with his people. *Zion is a theological concept more than it is a geographical place.* There is no doubt that this theological concept was merged in history with the historical city of Jerusalem, but this does not make the Jerusalem of history the source of and ultimate local of this tradition. The significance of Jerusalem is in the fact that it pointed to this higher reality of a Zion tradition.

It is important to note that the temple in the biblical tradition pointed beyond itself towards the dwelling of God in heaven and to the fact that God fills the whole world with his glory (Isa 6:3). Psalm 78:69 declares that God built his sanctuary "like the high heavens," and "like the earth, which he has founded forever." Beale comments on this verse by pointing out that the temple, and indeed any sanctuary in the OT, was only temporal and not meant to last, because it pointed beyond itself:

> God never intended that Israel's little localized temple last forever, since, like the Eden Temple, Israel's temple was a small model of something which was much bigger: God and his universal presence, which could never eternally be contained by any localized earthly structure.[59]

Levenson emphasizes the same point. Speaking about the temple, he sees that there is no contradiction between the concept of the God who dwells in a temple, and the God who fills heaven and earth because "the temple is the epitome of the world, a concentrated form of its essence, a

---

59. Beale, "Eden," 15–16.

miniature of the cosmos."[60] Quoting Psalm 11:4 "The LORD is in his holy temple; the LORD's throne is in heaven," he comments:

> It is for this reason that the Hebrew Bible is capable of affirming God's heavenly and his earthly presence without the slightest hint of tension between the two . . . What we see on earth in Jerusalem is simply the earthly manifestation of the heavenly Temple, which is beyond localization. The Temple of Zion is the antitype of the cosmic archetype . . . The world is God's temple, and in it he finds rest, just as in the miniature man makes of it, the earthly Temple atop Mount Zion.[61]

In other words, the temple in Jerusalem was there as a pointer to higher reality. The legitimacy of the Zion tradition is maintained as long as it is seen as pointing towards a higher reality. The earthly historical Zion during the time of the monarchy is the antitype, and what matters ultimately is the archetype or the real thing. Any reference to the theology of Zion must be understood in this framework. It is a reference not to the earthly historical Zion during the time of David, but to the faithful and idealized Zion – the real Zion. This Zion will be the focus of the prophets and will be at the heart of many eschatological prophecies.[62]

3. Conclusion

The holiness of the land in the OT, and that of Zion, is a historical phenomenon that depends on different historical variables. Once a place is designated as holy, there is no guarantee that it will remain so forever. It is ultimately the presence of God that designates any geography as holy. In addition, there is an interrelation between the sanctifying presence

---

60. Levenson, *Sinai & Zion*, 138.
61. Ibid., 140.
62. A more detailed analysis of the prophetic literature and how it portrays Zion will come in chapter 5 of this study.

of God in any geographical place and the holiness of the inhabitants of that geography.

The presence of God is not a fixed entity. It cannot be fixed or locked into one physical place. The glory of God is in one sense always "on the move" in the history of Israel, and in another it fills the whole earth. The earthly temple points towards this reality and cannnot by definition be the ultimate dwelling place of God.

Therefore, and in conclusion, it is against the outlook of the OT generally to elevate the land or Zion to the position of a permanent holy place – a place *always* favored by God, or as an *eternal* dwelling place of God. This should warn against absolutizing the land or any sacred geography. The land and Zion are not ultimate objects in the faith of the OT. Faithfulness to God is more important than location. If any characteristic of the land is to be highlighted, it is that it is a land that demands holiness. This is the only fixed entity. In this regard, the lessons learned from Eden are still valid. If even Eden, the first sanctuary, could lose its holiness, then no land is immune. The land demands holiness, just as Eden demanded holiness.

CHAPTER 3

The Covenanted Land

Introduction

Israel's land in the OT was part of the covenant between God and Israel, and as such it cannot be understood in a vacuum, but always in its covenantal context.[1] The covenants between God and Noah, Abraham, Israel, David, and postexilic Israel are *the Sitz im Leben* for the theology of the land in the OT.[2]

This chapter will look first at the concept of covenant in the OT in general, before examining how it helps our understanding of the theology of the land. We will examine the nature of the land as covenanted both conditionally and unconditionally, and we will consider what it means for the land to be an eternal inheritance. We will see that with the gift of land comes a set of commandments that regulate life in the land, and these

---

1. Brueggemann, *The Land*, 62.
2. The major covenants in the OT between God and man are (1) the covenant with Noah (2) Abraham and the Patriarchs (3) Israel in Sinai and then Moab (4) David and Solomon and (5) the new covenant in the prophets. In addition, the relation between God and Adam in Eden can be viewed as a covenant, as already argued for in chapter 1 of this study. For a detailed study of the biblical covenants, see W. J. Dumbrell, *Covenant and Creation: An Old Testament Covenantal Theology* (Carlisle: Paternoster, 1984), M. Weinfeld, "ברית," in *Theological Dictionary of the Old Testament (Vol. 2)*, ed. H. Ringgren and G. H. Botterweck (Grand Rapids: Eerdmans, 1975), 253–278; J. Goldingay, "Covenant," in *The New Interpreter's Dictionary of the Bible (Vol. 1)*, ed. Abingdon Press (Nashville: Abingdon Press, 2006), 767–778; B. K. Waltke, "The Phenomenon of Conditionality within Unconditional Covenants," in *Israel's Apostasy and Restoration: Essays in Honor of Roland K. Harrison*, ed. A. Gileadi (Grand Rapids: Baker Book House, 1988), 123–140.

commandments are the condition upon which Israel could keep the land. The ethical tasks assigned to Israel will be highlighted before drawing final conclusions.

1. Covenants in the Old Testament: Two Main Types

It is very common in OT scholarship to speak of two kinds of covenant within the larger context of ANE covenants.[3] The first is the Covenant of Grant, also known as a promissory covenant. The "grant" constitutes a promise from the master to his servant, which puts an obligation on the master. The second is the Treaty Covenant. The "treaty" constitutes an obligation of the vassal to his master, the *suzerain*.[4] Both these covenants are between a master and his servant. The structure is also similar, as both preserve the same elements: a historical introduction, border delineations, stipulations, witnesses, blessings, and curses.[5]

1.1. Covenants of Grant

In the OT, the covenants with Abraham and David are typically considered covenants of grant. "Like the royal grant in the ancient Near East so the covenants with Abraham and David are *gifts* bestowed upon individuals

---

[3]. The Hebrew word for covenant is ברית. The etymology of this word is not clear, and different derivations were suggested and are summarized by Weinfeld. Weinfeld, "ברית," 253–255. The meaning of the term, commonly translated "covenant," is also a matter of debate. Most acknowledge that a covenant is agreement between two parties in which one or both makes a promise to the other, and the promise is strengthened by an oath and by stipulations. See for example Goldingay, "Covenant"; G. A. Herion and G. E. Mendenhall, "Covenant," in *The Anchor Bible Dictionary (Vol. 1)*, ed. D. N. Freedman (New York: Doubleday, 1992), 1179–1202. Weinfeld on the other hand says that ברית in Hebrew does not mean an agreement or a settlement between two parties, but that it implies the notion of imposition, liability, or obligation. Weinfeld, "ברית," 255. Similarly, von Rad says that covenant is an agreement imposed by a superior on an inferior. Von Rad, *Old Testament Theology*, 129. For a survey of recent scholarship on the meaning and concept of covenant in the OT and NT, see S. Hahn, "Covenant in the Old and New Testaments: Some Current Research (1994–2004)," *Currents in Biblical Research* 3, no. 2 (2005): 263–292.

[4]. Weinfeld, *Promise of the Land*, 225.

[5]. Ibid., 225; von Rad, *Old Testament Theology*, 132.

who excelled in serving loyally their masters."[6] An important passage here is Genesis 15:17–18:[7]

> Behold, a smoking fire pot and a flaming torch passed between these pieces. On that day the LORD made a covenant (כרת ברית) with Abram, saying: "To your offspring I give this land (נתתי את־הארץ), from the river of Egypt to the great river, the river Euphrates." (Gen 15:17–18)

In this ceremony, God "cuts a covenant" with Abraham, and pledges to "give" his descendants "this land." By passing between the two pieces of the animals, God as the suzerain commits himself and swears to keep the promise. It is as if he is invoking a curse upon himself.[8] Weinfeld links the gifts bestowed on Abraham (the land included) and David to their loyalty. He alludes to terminologies such as "he kept my charge," "walked before me in truth," "his heart was whole to his master," "walked in perfection."[9]

1.2. Treaty Covenants

The covenant with Israel in Sinai, together with the covenantal framework in the book of Deuteronomy, is widely compared with Treaty Covenants.[10] In this type of covenant, there is an obligation or stipulation (condition) imposed on the servant or vassal from his master or suzerain. In the case of Israel, the stipulation is the Law given to Moses on Sinai, with its wider

---

6. M. Weinfeld, "The Covenant of Grant in the Old Testament and the Ancient Near East," *Journal of the American Oriental Society* 90, no. 2 (1970): 184 (emphasis added).

7. See also Genesis 12:1–3; 15:12–21; 17:1–14.

8. Weinfeld, *Promise of the Land*, 252. This interpretation of this incident is very common among OT scholars, and depends on the wider context of ANE treaties. Wenham, however, does not accept it, and instead suggests that the pieces represent Israel, and that the action portrays God as walking with his people. He believes that it is unusual in the OT to God to invoke a curse upon himself. Wenham, *Genesis 1-15*, 333.

9. Weinfeld, *Promise of the Land*, 184.

10. Dumbrell, *Covenant and Creation*, 115. For a discussion on the relationship between the covenant between God and Israel in Sinai and the Suzerain treaty in the ANE, see A. Hill, "The Ebal Ceremony as Hebrew Land Grant?" *JETS* 31 (1988): 399–406; M. G. Kline, *Treaty of the Great Kings: The Covenant Structure of Deuteronomy* (Eugene: Wipf & Stock Publishers, 2012).

implications. In the book of Deuteronomy in particular, the possession of the land is conditional on obedience:

> And now, O Israel, listen to the statutes and the rules that I am teaching you, and do them, *that you may live*, and go in and take possession of the land that the LORD, the God of your fathers, is giving you. (Deut 4:1)[11]

2. Land and Covenant

2.1. The Land as a Gift within the Covenant

Israel had a land to live in because, quite simply, God had given it to her.[12] The land was God's good gift to Israel, and she did nothing to merit this gift.[13] Yet at the same time:

> It is insufficient simply to say that the LORD "gave the land to Israel," without taking into consideration the context of the gift, which was the covenant relationship and its reciprocal commitments. The land was an integral part not only of the LORD's faithfulness to Israel, but also of Israel's covenantal obligation to the LORD.[14]

The land, to begin with, is a *promised* land.[15] Canaan is first mentioned in the Abrahamic narrative and is a significant part of the covenant between God and Abraham. The initial call to Abraham (Gen 12:1–3), however, does not include a promise of a possession of land, but the later encounters

---

11. See also for example Deut 6:1–3; 8:19–20; 11:13–17; 16:20; 28:15–68.
12. Wright, *Old Testament Ethics*, 85.
13. Zimmerli, *Old Testament Theology*, 64.
14. Wright, *Old Testament Ethics*, 92.
15. For a good summary of all the promises of the land in the Pentateuch, see D. J. A. Clines, *The Theme of the Pentateuch*, JSOT Press (England: Sheffield, 1997), 37–47.

do.[16] The land is promised to Abraham's seed, and these promises are later reaffirmed to Isaac (Gen 26:3) and Jacob (Gen 28:13).[17]

For the Israelite community entering the land after the exodus, the land is a feature of the covenant in Sinai (Deut 4–6). The receiving of the land by Israel is based on the initial promises to Abraham and the patriarchs (Deut 9:5–6), but at the same time, it is conditional on obedience (e.g. Deut 4:1).

In the covenants with David and Solomon, prosperity and long life in the land are part of these covenants as well (2 Sam 7; 1 Kgs 9:1–7). And after the exile and loss of land (because of the breaking of the covenant by Israel), God initiates yet another covenant, a new covenant, which is a futuristic or unrealized one. The restoration to the land naturally is included in the new covenant as well (e.g. Jer 32:39–44; Amos 9:11–15).

In all these episodes of Israel's history, land and covenant are always linked. Land cannot be understood or studied apart from covenant.

2.2. Conditional or Unconditional Gift?

One way to look at the question of land and promise would be to simplify it and categorize it into the two types discussed in the previous section: grant and treaty. However, it is not really this simple. The land promises in the OT are multifaceted in nature, and there is a tension between two seemingly contradictory themes: the unconditional promise or gift versus the conditional stipulations. Was the land a grant, or was it under treaty? How are we to resolve the tension between these two ideas?

For some scholars, the issue is a matter of *development* within the biblical narrative, which is the result of a reinterpretation of history by the succeeding generations of Israel. Weinfeld, relying on textual criticism, argued

---

16. Gen 12:7; 13:15; 15:18; 17:8; 24:7.

17. Von Rad considers this theme of promise-fulfillment as the main theme in the first six books of the OT, which he groups together as the Hexateuch. The fulfillment of land promises in the book of Joshua (Josh 21:41, 43; 23:14–16) is central to the first part of the narrative of Israel. Von Rad, *Old Testament Theology*, 129–135. The same view is held by Davies, who argues: "It is the linking together of the promise to the patriarchs with the fulfillment of it in the settlement that gives to the Hexateuch its distinctive theological character. For the Hexateuch the land is a promised land, and that inviolably." Davies, *The Gospel and the Land*, 24.

that what started as an unconditional covenant, was interpreted and edited by later generations (after the exile) into a conditional covenant:

> The exile of Northern Israel, the destruction of Jerusalem, and the disruption of the dynasty refuted, of course, the claim of the eternity of the Abrahamic and Davidic covenants, thereby necessitating a reinterpretation of the covenants. This was done by making them conditional, i.e. by asserting that the covenant is eternal only if the donee keeps his loyalty to the donor.[18]

Von Rad speaks as well of a shift from unconditional to conditional, or as he put it, from grace to law. He called this shift "striking":

> It is nevertheless striking that alongside this presentation of the commandments there is another one, in which the commandments are not seen as the norm of the new life in settled territory, but in which compliance with the commandments is the condition on which the land may be received and possessed. Israel is to observe the commandments in order that he may enter the good land, or may have long life in the land which Yahweh is going to give him. Does not the promise of the land in this conditional form pave the way for a declension from grace into law?[19]

---

18. Weinfeld, *Promise of the Land*, 250. Weinfeld explains this argument with the support of the documentary hypothesis. He says (p. 186): "One has to admit that the conditionality of the inheritance of the Land, which is attested primarily in Deuteronomy and the Deuteronomic school, in editorial layers of JE (Gen 15:16; 18:19), and in the priestly code (Lev 18:26–28; 20:23–24; chap. 26), is not explicit in the old traditions themselves. Indeed, it seems that the fall of Samaria and the northern exile triggered the development of the idea of conditionality. Although the idea itself might be old, albeit not expressed explicitly, the prevailing notion before the fall of Samaria was that the Land was given to the Israelites forever (Gen 13:15; 17:8; Exod 32:13). Only after the loss of the northern territories was the covenant of God with the Patriarchs interpreted as based on condition."

19. Von Rad, "Promised Land and Yahweh's Land," 91 (emphasis in the original). Keulen similarly says: "A shift in the theology of the land can be observed between Deuteronomic and Deuteronomistic passages. Was the gift of the land unconditional, it becomes

Kaiser strongly objects to this interpretation, arguing that the stipulations referred only to any future generation's *participation* in the benefits of the covenant, and did not affect the transmission of the promise to future generations. For him, the *ownership* of the land as a gift from God is eternal, but the occupation of it by any given generation is conditional.[20] Miller also sees the stipulations in a similar manner. Commenting on the land in Deuteronomy, he says:

> Israel cannot justify her *original* possession of the land on the basis of her behavior; she must, however, justify or preserve her *continuing* and *future* possession on the basis of her behavior both in terms of the worship of God and a proper use of the possession which is her salvation gift.[21]

Other scholars have opted to reinterpret the covenants in an unconventional manner. Orlinsky defines the covenant as a "contract" that "God and Israel entered into, *voluntarily and as equals.*"[22] He argues against the suzerain theory,[23] and emphasizes that Abraham and Israel are not to be viewed as vassals who received a gift or a grant. He further rejects any notion of a free gift:

> This solemn agreement on the part of God and Israel was no gift, with no strings attached – no more on the part of God than on the part of the patriarchs or Israel; on the contrary, it

---

conditional." E. J. Keulen, "Reversal of a Motif: The Land Is Given into the Hand of the Wicked. The Gift of Land in Some Wisdom Texts," in *The Land of Israel in Bible, History, and Theology: Studies in Honour of Ed Noort*, ed. J. Van Ruiten and J. C. De Vos (Leiden: Brill 2009), 198. See also Zimmerli, *Old Testament Theology*, 69.
20. W. C. Kaiser, "The Promised Land: A Biblical-Historical View," *Bibliotheca Sacra* 138, no. 552 (1981): 307.
21. P. D. Miller, "The Gift of God: the Deuteronomic Theology of the Land," *Interpretation* 23 (1969): 461 (emphasis in the original).
22. H. M. Orlinsky, "The Biblical Concept of the Land of Israel: Cornerstone of the Covenant between God and Israel," in *The Land of Israel: Jewish Perspectives*, ed. L. A. Hoffman (Notre Dame: University of Notre Dame Press, 1986), 28 (emphasis in the original).
23. Ibid., 56.

was a normal and valid care of *give and take* common to every kind of contract into which two parties voluntarily enter, with strings very much attached thereto.[24]

For Orlinsky, Abraham and Israel fulfilled what was required of them to enter this contract. When they broke the legal contract, they were punished. But the promises are forever, because the conditions were already met. However, Orlinsky's definition of the covenant as a contract between two equals cannot be supported from biblical evidence. To the contrary, in the Abrahamic narrative God changes Abraham's name from Abram to Abraham, which is a sign of lordship. The covenant of Sinai resembles the ANE treaties in a remarkable fashion, so it becomes very difficult to argue for this theory of "two equals."[25]

On the other hand, vander Hart believes that a grant was always conditional.[26] He builds on the work of Szubin and Porten on the meaning of the *"dashna"* concept in Egypt, who argued that a *dashna* was not a grant to be held in perpetuity by the father and his estate but a gift *subject to revocation* by the sovereign benefactor.[27] Vander Hart thus says that it is only in the way of faithfulness to the Torah and humility before YHWH that the promise of possession of the land is received.[28]

Katanacho also sees no unconditionality in the Abrahamic covenant, but he relies on internal biblical evidence.[29] He goes to the Hebrew text of Genesis 12:1–3, and challenges the common translation of 12:2b (והיה ברכה), which is usually translated as "you will be a blessing."[30] For

---

24. Ibid. 42–43 (emphasis in the original).
25. For Orlinsky, the land is more central than the covenant. "Were it not for the Land that God promised on oath to Abraham and Isaac and to Jacob and to their heirs forever, there would be no covenant." In other words, the covenant was cut in order to preserve the land. Orlinsky, "Biblical Concept," 34.
26. M. D. Vander Hart, "Possessing the Land: As Command and Promise," *Mid-America Journal of Theology* 4, no. 2 (1988): 139–155.
27. H. Z. Szubin and B. Porten, "Royal Grants in Egypt: A New Interpretation of Driver 2," *Journal of Near Eastern Studies* 46, no. 1 (1987): 39–48.
28. Vander Hart, "Possessing the Land," 150.
29. Katanacho, *The Land of Christ*.
30. See for example the ESV, RSV: "So that you will be a blessing;" the KJV: "And thou shalt be a blessing;" and the NIV: "And you will be a blessing."

Katanacho, the phrase should be translated as: "Be a blessing so that I can bless those who bless you."[31] He then says:

> The text does not claim an unconditional grant of land to Abram, let alone his descendants. The imperative force at the beginning of the second set followed by a *waw* consecutive and an imperfect requires a conditional interpretation of verses 2–3.[32]

In other words, there is an element of conditionality in the first call to Abraham. The evidence from the translation of the Hebrew text of Genesis 12:2b is indeed a strong one, and is supported by the larger Abrahamic narrative. In the initial call to Abraham, there was first the command to leave a land for another land, and then, depending on our translation of Genesis 12:2b, there is the imperative to "be a blessing." The covenant of Genesis 15:17–18 is preceded by a reference to Abraham's faith (15:6): "And he (Abraham) believed the LORD, and he counted it to him as righteousness." The narrative in Genesis 17 starts with a call for Abraham to walk before God and be perfect (17:1), and ends with a commandment of circumcision (17:9–10). The Hebrew of Genesis 17:1 "be blameless" is in the imperative (והיה תמים), similar to 12:2b, "be a blessing." Genesis 18:19

---

31. Ibid., 78. The translation of this unusual construction has been an issue of debate, and different options were offered. Wenham translates it: "And you shall be a blessing." Wenham, *Genesis 1-15*, 277. Wolff translates it: "So that you will effect blessing," making the blessing of Abraham to the nations the result or the fruit of the blessing of God to Abraham. H. W. Wolff, "The Kerygma of the Yahwist," *Interpretation* 20 (1986): 137. Baden, writing a whole lengthy article on the translation of Gen 12:1–3, argues that translating 12:2b as a purpose clause is possible, but not the only way. He then says that the decision by some scholars to translate it as a purpose clause is based not in the morpho-syntax of the verbal sequence but rather on the scholar's interpretation of the passage as a whole and its meaning for the rest of the biblical narrative, directing toward the establishment of Abraham as a source or example of blessing for the rest of the world. For Baden, the more correct translation, the one based on the morpho-syntax of the verbal sequence, is: "And you be a blessing." J. S. Baden, "The Morpho-Syntax of Genesis 12: 1–3: Translation and Interpretation," *The Catholic Biblical quarterly* 72, no. 2 (2010): 223–237. The ASV captures the imperative and translates it: "And be thou a blessing."
32. Katanacho, *The Land of Christ*, 79. See also Essex, who also believes that the Abrahamic covenant was conditional. K. H. Essex, "The Abrahamic Covenant," *Masters Seminary Journal* 10, no. 2 (1999): 191–212.

makes justice a condition to the fulfillment of the promise, and Genesis 22 makes the point that it is *because* Abraham obeyed he will receive the blessing, including the land:

> By myself I have sworn, declares the LORD, *because you have done this* and have not withheld your son, your only son, I will surely bless you . . . *because you have obeyed my voice.* (Gen 22:16–18)[33]

The same pattern can be viewed in the Davidic covenant. Gordon, for example, observed that the seemingly unconditional covenant of Davidic kingship (2 Sam 7) was qualified and restrained in other texts:[34]

> Keep the charge of the LORD your God, walking in his ways and keeping his statutes, his commandments, his rules, and his testimonies, as it is written in the Law of Moses, *that you may* prosper in all that you do and wherever you turn. (1 Kgs 2:3–4)

The land was indeed a gift. God initiated the call to Abraham. The relationship is that of master to his servant. But it is hard to argue for total "unconditionality" in the Abrahamic or the Davidic covenants. More recently, Hahn has observed that, in recent OT scholarship, the idea that covenant means obligation and is essentially one-sided has been largely abandoned in favor of the view that covenants establish kinship bonds (relations and obligations) between covenanting parties.[35]

Waltke captures this phenomenon of conditionality within the unconditional covenants in the OT. In his seminal article on the theme of

---

33. Von Rad commented on the first call to Abraham in Gen 12:1–3 by observing that the land promise is missing. For him, "the promise of the land is thus to some extent kept apart from the great pronouncement in which God declares his purpose." He then argued that only after God tested Abraham in blind obedience does he give the promise that he will possess the land. Von Rad, "Promised Land and Yahweh's Land," 84.
34. Gordon, *Holy Land, Holy City*, 106.
35. Hahn, "Covenant," 264. Hahn surveyed the major works on the concept of covenant from the years 1994 to 2004.

conditionality within unconditional covenants, he argues from different texts that there are not only conditional elements in the grants, but also unconditional elements in the treaties, and concludes that YHWH's "grants and treaty do not rival or exclude, but complement one another."[36] Similarly, Dumbrell speaks of the phenomenon of unconditionality in the Sinaitic covenant, which he argued is seen in the golden calf narrative. There, Israel failed, but when Moses prayed and reminded God of the promises to Abraham, God allowed the story to continue.[37] Brueggemann in this context reminds us as well that the rhetoric at the boundary in Deuteronomy is that of pure gift and that there is no hint of achievement or merit or even planning. The land is given by the giver of good gifts and the speaker of faithful words.[38]

Perhaps, in conclusion, it is not adequate to simplify the land question into a debate between "grant" versus "treaty" or "conditional" versus "unconditional." In the OT, gift and commandment "represent two sides of the same coin."[39] OT covenants seem to be unique and it is not an easy task to standardize them with ANE covenants or with each other. The tension between the promise and the condition, the indicative and the imperative, is part of the narrative and it is there for a reason. The OT introduces us to the concept of a gift that comes with conditions. On the one hand, it wants to underscore the sovereignty of God and his gracious nature, evident by his giving of the land. On the other, it wants at the same time to underscore the ethical and moral nature of God, and to show how this demands nothing but total allegiance from the people of God.

---

36. Waltke, "Phenomenon of Conditionality," 125. Waltke rejects the notion that the Deuteronomist reinterpreted the grants to Abraham and David by putting conditions on them and mentions Weinfeld as an example of someone who had argued for this.

37. W. J. Dumbrell, "The Prospect of Unconditionality in the Sinaitic Covenant," in *Israel's Apostasy and Restoration. Essays in Honor of Roland K. Harrison*, ed. A. Gileadi (Grand Rapids: Baker, 1988), 141–155. See also Lev 26:41–45; Deut 9:5.

38. Brueggemann, *The Land*, 46.

39. Zimmerli, *Old Testament Theology*, 66.

3. Land as a Mandate

We can shed more light on this relationship between gift and commandment when we consider the meaning of terms such as "give," "inheritance," and "forever," within the OT framework. What does it mean for God to give (נתן) the land to Israel as an inheritance (נחלה)? Does that mean that Israel can claim eternal (עד־עולם) ownership of the land?

One way to look at these terms is to view them as legal terms that speak of ownership and entitlement. *Nahalah* is commonly defined as inheritance.[40] Preuss defines it as a "*continually owned* piece of earth that one has acquired through inheritance, allotment, or allocation."[41] Inheritance, he continues, designates the land as the gift of God that comes "without merit or effort."[42] For Orlinsky, inheritance is a legal term that denotes not a gift but the legal transfer of property.[43] Similarly, he defines the verb נתן as a "legal, real estate term to indicate transfer of ownership of or title to a piece of property."[44]

These definitions might work within a familial land property context. However, they fail to take into consideration the many verses in the OT that speak of God as the ultimate owner of the land – *even after it was given*. Leviticus 25:23 is a clear example: "The land is mine. For you are strangers and sojourners with me."[45] In addition, these definitions fail to deal with the many statements that speak of the possession of the land as conditional upon obedience,[46] and that speak of God plucking the people up off *his* land in the case of disobedience (2 Chr 7:20).

---

40. For a comprehensive analysis of the use of the term in the ANE and the OT, see M. Lipinski, "נחל," in *Theological Dictionary of the Old Testament (Vol. 9)*, ed. H. Ringgren and G. H. Botterweck (Grand Rapids: Eerdmans, 1998), 319–335.
41. Preuss, *Old Testament Theology*. 123 (emphasis added).
42. Ibid.
43. Orlinsky, "Biblical Concept," 44 (emphasis added).
44. Ibid., 31.
45. See also Exod 15:13, 17; Deut 32:43; 2 Chr 7:20; Ps 85:1; Joel 2:18; 3:2. In addition, building altars in the land was another sign that the land belongs to God. When Abraham entered Canaan, one of the first things he did is build an altar to God (e.g. Gen 12:9). This is a sign that the land belongs to God. Goldingay, *Old Testament Theology*, 209.
46. See for example Gen 18:9; Lev 18:24–28; Deut 4:40; 6:13–18; 8:11–20; 11:16.

One must, therefore, seek a different interpretation of these terms – one that is in line with the wider OT narrative. We noted above Szubin and Porten's work on the *dashna* concept. In their study, they show that the ANE knew of two kinds of grant: (1) *dashna*, which was a gift subject to revocation by the sovereign giver, and (2) *paradashna*, which, once given, could not be recalled by the giver.[47] Vander Hart argues that the land was more of a *dashna* than a *paradashna*. His argument is supported by the OT narrative, and in particular the exile.[48]

Gordon has also observed that the term עַד־עוֹלָם, translated "forever," should also be considered along these lines.[49] "Forever" does not always indicate unconditionality, as evident for example in 1 Samuel 2:30:

> Therefore the LORD, the God of Israel, declares [to Eli]: "I promised that your house and the house of your father should go in and out before me forever (עַד־עוֹלָם)," but now the LORD declares: "Far be it from me, for those who honor me I will honor, and those who despise me shall be lightly esteemed."

In this verse, God makes a promise of eternal priesthood to Eli, using the term "forever" (עַד־עוֹלָם), but then surprisingly revokes this eternal promise almost immediately. This verse and other promises in the OT show that eternal promises can be "revoked" by God.[50] Chris Wright suggests therefore that the expression "forever" in the OT "needs to be seen, not so much in terms of 'everlastingness' in linear time, but rather as an intensive expression within the terms, conditions and context of the promise concerned."[51]

---

47. Szubin and Porten, "Royal Grants in Egypt," 44–45.
48. Vander Hart, "Possessing the Land," 141–142.
49. Gordon, *Holy Land, Holy City*, 104–106.
50. Other examples that Gordon uses to illustrate the use of forever are Exod 29:9; Jer 35:19; Num 25:10–13; 1 Sam 2:30; 1 Chr 23:13.
51. C. J. H. Wright, "A Christian Approach To Old Testament Prophecy Concerning Israel," in *Jerusalem Past and Present in the Purposes of God*, ed. P. W. L. Walker (Cambridge: Tyndale House, 1992), 6.

It is therefore imperative that we employ a more comprehensive definition for the term *nahalah*. Rendtorff suggests that we read it as a theological legal term.[52] For him, *nahalah* is "God's possession, which is handed over and left to Israel as a possession given *on trust*, as it were as a 'fief.'"[53] Along the same lines, Habel argues:

> Nahala . . . is not something simply handed down from generation to generation, but the entitlement or rightful property of a party that is legitimated by a recognized social custom, legal process, or divine character.[54]

This is an important definition and concept. A custom or a treaty constantly regulates land. The land is territory under treaty. It is important, therefore, to emphasize in OT study that the gifted land is always a covenanted land under treaty. It is therefore better, and more in line with the biblical narrative, to define *nahalah* as a mandated land. In the words of Brueggemann:

> Land with Yahweh brings responsibility. The same land that is gift freely given is task sharply put. Landed Israel is under mandate.[55]

Chris Wright uses a very helpful analogy to describe Israel's relationship with God and the land, and he derives it from Leviticus 25:23. For him, God is the divine "landlord," and the Israelites are his tenants. They "possess" the land. They "occupy" and use it. But God "owns" the land. He concludes:

---

52. R. Rendtorff, *The Canonical Hebrew Bible: A Theology of the Old Testament* (Leiden: Deo, 2005), 458.
53. Ibid., 460 (emphasis added).
54. Habel, *The Land is Mine*, 35.
55. Brueggemann, *The Land*, 94.

Like all tenants, therefore, Israelites were *accountable* to their divine landlord for proper treatment of what was ultimately his property.[56]

The land is given to Israel as a gift, but that does not make it Israel's property. Israel does not own the land, for with the land Israel is given a task. The land is not simply an arbitrary gift for Israel's enjoyment, but rather a mandate that comes with responsibility. This is the reason why Israel was brought into a land in the first place. Tarazi thus reads the allotment of the land not as an allocation of land to each of the tribes, as though each would become owner. Rather, the allotment was an assigning of the tribes to certain parts of the land.[57] In other words, in the land, Israel is given a mandate – a responsibility and a task. It is not the other way around. Israel is assigned to the land, and not the land to Israel. This may then explain why the Levites were not assigned land, because they already had a task or mandate:

> Therefore Levi has no portion or inheritance (נחלה) with his brothers. The LORD is his inheritance (נחלה), as the LORD your God said to him. (Deut 10:9)

The inheritance of the tribe of Levi is God and this means that serving him is their assignment. Similarly, the rest of the tribes have a different portion and a different assignment. The tribe of Levi serves the Lord in the sanctuary, just as the Israelites serve the Lord in the land. It is not so much about territory. It is about service. This is also probably why the two and a half tribes were allowed to stay in Jordan, for after all, "any land could have been chosen."[58] The bond Israel has is with God through service, and not with land. "Let my people go, that they may serve me" (Exod 8:1).

In conclusion, it is in this manner that we must view the conditions of the covenant. Keeping the covenant (or serving God) was not merely the

---

56. Wright, *Old Testament Ethics*, 94 (emphasis added). Cohn also uses the same terminology of Israel as tenants. Cohn, "Homeland to the Holy Land," 6.
57. Tarazi, *Land and Covenant*, 130.
58. Habel, *The Land is Mine*, 64.

condition to stay in the land, but the *goal* and *reason* why Israel was brought into the land at the outset. Israel was not chosen for her sake and luxury. The purpose of arriving at the land is to keep the commandments of God:

> And he gave them the lands of the nations, and they took possession of the fruit of the peoples' toil, *that* (בעבור) *they might keep his statutes and observe his laws.* (Ps 105: 44–45)[59]

And so as Marchadour and Neuhaus remind us:

> Land is not an absolute or an isolated gift. The Land is given to Israel for a distinct purpose: to provide a space in which it can embody faithfulness to the Torah. To live according to the Torah is to live in a place of rest.

We must not lose sight of this purposefulness behind the promises of the land. Keeping Torah and being faithful to God take precedence over any claim of entitlement. This is why Israel was given a land as an inheritance. Furthermore, the obedience of Israel and her keeping of the covenant mark Israel as a distinct covenant community – God's chosen people.

4. Stipulations of Keeping the Covenant – Ethics in the Land

God brought Israel to the land so that they model a different and distinct community, set apart from the other nations. Israel is supposed to be an ideal community:

> Now therefore, if you will indeed obey my voice *and keep my covenant,* you shall be my treasured possession *among all peoples,* for all *the earth* (הארץ) is mine; and you shall be to

---

[59]. The BDB defines (בעבור): "for the sake of, on account of, in order that." F. Brown, S. Driver, and C. Briggs, *The Brown-Driver-Briggs Hebrew and English Lexicon* (Peabody: Hendrickson Publishers, 1996).

me a kingdom of priests and a holy nation. (Exod 19:5–6) (emphasis added)

These verses come immediately before the giving of the Ten Commandments and the Law. Keeping the covenant here is not merely the means of keeping the land, but the way in which Israel is to be a witness for God to all the other nations in other lands. All the *earth* belongs to God (and not just Canaan), and as such he is interested not only in Canaan, but in the whole earth. God wanted Israel to live a life distinct from the other nations, and that is why he gave these commandments and the Law. If the Israelites were to copy the lifestyle of the other nations, they would be forced out of the land, just as the other nations had been forced out of it.[60] The exile is directly related to the concept of the covenant and the land as mandated.[61]

In the OT, God gives different commandments and laws in connection with covenant obedience. Certain sins were highlighted as directly leading to exile. These sins can be categorized in three categories: idolatry, Sabbath, and social justice.[62]

4.1. Idolatry

Worshipping multiple gods was common in the ANE, but the God of Israel is different in this matter. The first commandment is clear: "You shall have no other gods before me" (Exod 20:1). There are various OT texts that associate polytheism with loss of the land. For example:

---

60. See Lev 20:22–23; 18:24–28.
61. According to Weinfeld, the idea that breaking the covenant will lead to punishment is not foreign to the ANE: "The idea that exile and desolation are the punishment for failing to observe God's commandments is based, therefore, in the typology of violating a covenant. One who violates a covenant with his sovereign can anticipate exile and the desolation of his land. This is the case with Israel, the vassal, who breaks the covenant with its sovereign, the God of Israel. The same pattern can also be seen in the Assyrian treaty between Esarhaddon and his vassals." Weinfeld, *Promise of the Land*, 193.
62. A good summary of the sins in the OT that can lead to exile can be found in Weinfeld's work on the land. Weinfeld sees that each source or tradition in the biblical history focused on one sin. Weinfeld, *Promise of the Land*, 181–224. See also Brueggemann, who prefers to use the term "tasks" to describe what will lead to exile from the land. The tasks, according to him, are: Prohibition of Images, Sabbath, and care for brother and sister. Brueggemann, *The Land*, 58–62.

> Take care lest your heart be deceived, and you turn aside and serve other gods and worship them; then the anger of the LORD will be kindled against you, and he will shut up the heavens, so that there will be no rain, *and the land will yield no fruit*, and you will *perish quickly off the good land that the LORD is giving you*. (Deut 11:16–17)[63]

Weinfeld believes that the sin of idol worship is particularly emphasized in the "Deuteronomic sources," where it is considered "the determining factor" that will lead to exile from the land.[64] Mixed marriages in the OT are in many cases forbidden and are considered a direct cause for forfeiting the right to the land, and the rationale behind this is that intermarriage leads to unfaithfulness to God and to worshipping other gods.[65]

4.2. Sabbath, Land Sabbath, and Jubilee

In Leviticus 25 God explains to Israel the laws of land Sabbath and the Jubilee.[66] In verse 18 he sets these laws as a condition for living securely in the land. In the next chapter, God declares that in the event of unfaithfulness:

> Then the land shall enjoy its Sabbaths as long as it lies desolate, while you are in your enemies' land; then the land shall rest, and enjoy its Sabbaths. As long as it lies desolate it shall have rest, the rest that it did not have on your Sabbaths when you were dwelling in it. (Lev 26:34–35)

And 2 Chronicles 36:21 declares that the exile lasted seventy years "until the land had enjoyed its Sabbaths," and that "all the days that it lay desolate

---

63. See also Deut 4:25–26; 8:19–20; 30:17–18. Ps 106 narrates the history of Israel, and it makes the point that unfaithfulness to God is what led Israel to exile.
64. Weinfeld, *Promise of the Land*, 195.
65. Ibid., 196. See for example Josh 23:12–16; Ezra 9:11–12, 14.
66. For more on the topic of the Jubilee, see Wright, *The Mission of God*, 289–300; J. Goldingay, "Jubilee Tithe," *Transformation* 19, no. 3 (2002): 198–205; Habel, *The Land is Mine*, 104–108.

it kept Sabbath, to fulfill seventy years." Weinfeld refers this tradition to the "priestly source," which connects the laws of the Sabbatical and Jubilee years with the covenant at Sinai and the declaration of freedom and views the transgression of these laws as the primary reason for the exile of Israel from its land.[67]

The importance of these laws in Leviticus 25 is that they are a reminder to Israel that she does not own the land, for the land belongs ultimately to God (25:23). Israel is not free to do with the land whatever she wants, or to claim eternal possession of it. Land Sabbath is a reminder that land is not *from* Israel but is a gift *to* Israel, and that land is not fully given over to Israel's self-indulgence.[68]

Breaking the Sabbath day will also lead to forfeiting the right to the land.[69] The prophets spoke about this, and this was one of the points of emphasis for Nehemiah when he returned from Babylon to help the new community.[70]

4.3. Social Justice

No other sin in the OT was tied more directly with being expelled from the land than the sin of socio-economic injustice.[71] Justice is emphasized in almost all the traditions. In Genesis 18:19, God says about Abraham:

> For I have chosen him, that he may command his children and his household after him to keep the way of the LORD by doing *righteousness and justice* (צדקה ומשפט), *so that* (למען) the LORD may bring to Abraham what he has promised him.

---

67. Weinfeld, *Promise of the Land*, 194.
68. Brueggemann, *The Land*, 59.
69. Levenson made a very interesting point regarding the relationship between the land and the Sabbath. He says: "The Sabbatical experience and the Temple experience are one. The first represents sanctity in time, the second, sanctity in space, and yet they are somehow the same." Levenson, *Sinai & Zion* 145.
70. See for example Ezek 20:12–13, 20–21; Isa 56:1–8; 58:13–14; Neh 13:17–18.
71. For more on socio-economical justice in the OT, see Wright, *Old Testament Ethics*, 146–180, 253–279; A. Hartropp, *What Is Economic Justice?: Biblical And Secular Perspectives Contrasted* (Milton Keynes: Paternoster, 2007).

Abraham was chosen for this reason – doing righteousness and justice – and this would bring the promise to fulfillment. In Deuteronomy 16:19–20, justice is again portrayed as a prerequisite to staying in the land:

> You shall not pervert justice (משׁפט)... Justice, and only justice (צדקצדק), you shall follow, that (למען) you may live and inherit the land that the LORD your God is giving you.[72]

Miller comments on this verse:

> The mode of living demanded of those who would receive the divine gift and enjoy it is characterized by the enduring effort to insure that all who live in the land shall be treated justly.[73]

The Torah in general has a lot to say about the poor, the stranger, the sojourner, the widow, and orphan.[74] They are redefined, according to Brueggemann, as "brothers and sisters." "It is one of the tasks that goes with covenanted land and keeps the land as covenanted reality: those who seem to have no claim must be honored and cared for."[75] This is because land is not "for self-security but for the brother and sister."[76]

Yet it was the "classical" prophets who elevated this issue above probably all other considerations and related it directly to the exile. As Chris Wright says: "The prophets simply would not allow Israel to get away with claiming the blessing and protection of the covenant relationship for their society while trampling on the socio-economic demands of that relationship."[77]

---

72. McConville says that the pair משׁפט and צדק express both the basis and practice of law. משׁפט, he says, refers to the individual case, a just decision, and צדק is the more abstract quality that underpins such decisions, namely justice. J. G. McConville, *Deuteronomy* (Downers Grove: InterVarsity Press, 2002), 287.
73. Miller, "The Gift of God," 461.
74. See for example Exod 22:21–24, 23:6, 9; Deut 10:19; 15:7–11; 24:19–22. See also R. B. Herron, "The Land, the Law, and the Poor," *Word & World* 6, no. 1 (1986): 76–84. In addition, Lev 20 links sexual morality with inheriting the land. See in particular Lev 20: 23–24.
75. Brueggemann, *The Land*, 61.
76. Ibid., 73.
77. Wright, *Old Testament Ethics*, 98

Amos is conspicuous for his emphasizing social justice. His call to "let justice roll down like waters" (5:24) is followed by a warning of exile; "and I will send you into exile beyond Damascus" (5:27).[78] Jeremiah makes a similar point:

> For if you truly amend your ways and your deeds, if you truly execute justice one with another, if you do not oppress the sojourner, the fatherless, or the widow, or shed innocent blood in this place, and if you do not go after other gods to your own harm, *then I will let you dwell in this place, in the land that I gave of old to your fathers forever.* (Jer 7:5–7)[79]

Micah had a similar warning against the false security of the rulers of Israel who took the land promises for granted or as a license for land grab and control:

> Hear this, you heads of the house of Jacob and rulers of the house of Israel, who detest justice and make crooked all that is straight, who build Zion with blood and Jerusalem with iniquity. Its heads give judgment for a bribe; its priests teach for a price; its prophets practice divination for money; yet they lean on the LORD and say, "Is not the LORD in the midst of us? No disaster shall come upon us." Therefore because of you Zion shall be plowed as a field; Jerusalem shall become a heap of ruins, and the mountain of the house a wooded height. (Mic 3:9–12)[80]

The Psalms also highlight this theme. Psalm 37 is particularly interesting, where the term "inherit the land" is mentioned five times. But who inherits the land? It is those "who wait for the Lord" (v. 9), "the meek" (v. 11), "those blessed by the Lord" (v. 22), "the righteous" (v. 29), and "those

---

78. See also Amos 6:6–7.
79. See also Jer 7:8–15; 21:12–14; 22:3–5; Isa 5:12–13; Ezek 16:49.
80. See also Mic 2:1–2.

who keep his way" (v. 34). In contrast, the evil ones will fade away. Justice, righteousness and care for the poor are emphasized as good qualities all over the Psalm (vv. 6, 7, 14, 21, 28, 30). The conclusion of Psalm 37 is that "the dwellers on the land are the poor and the weak."[81]

5. Conclusion

The land in the OT is a covenanted land. It is a gift that comes with a condition – a mandated land. Israel's lifestyle in the land is supposed to make Israel distinct from other nations. This is the goal and reason behind the choosing of Israel and the land. With election comes responsibility. Israel is called to a particular land so that she will model and embody (1) faithfulness to God, (2) a system of land management that emphasizes that God is the ultimate owner of the land, and (3) a system of social justice where no one is left out. These are the conditions of keeping the gift of the land. Failure to keep these commandments had led to the "exile" of the nations that preceded Israel's arrival in the land, and would ultimately lead to Israel herself forfeiting the right to the land.

The comparisons here with the Eden narrative are unmistakable. Israel, like Adam, is chosen for a mission and a task, and is gifted a good land, but this gift is regulated by stipulations. The gift of land, like the gift of Eden, is really more of a mandate than a free gift. Both Israel and Adam knew the consequences of their disobedience beforehand. Both are representatives of God, and both represent humanity before God. So when Israel, like Adam, breaks the covenant, she loses the special land. In this regard, Canaan is "Eden – 'take two'!"

---

81. P. D. Miller, "The Land in the Psalms," in *The Land of Israel in Bible, History, and Theology: Studies in Honour of Ed Noort,* ed. J. Van Ruiten and J. C. De Vos (Leiden: Brill, 2009), 191. Miller's article on the theology of the land in the Psalms argues that the voices of the psalmists do not offer a different perspective on the land from what one finds elsewhere in Scripture. On the contrary, he said, they echo Deuteronomy and the Deuteronomistic History and many other parts of the Old Testament.

CHAPTER 4

Kingship, Vicegerency and Universal Dominion

Introduction

This chapter focuses on the land in relation to the theme of kingship. It will be argued that Israel and her king in the OT played the role of God's vicegerent on earth. As such, they were responsible for the land before God; they also represented God before the nations of the earth, and they represented the nations before God. In the first part, we will look briefly at the vicegerency of Abraham. The second part will deal with Israel as a nation and its royal status. The bulk of the chapter will be devoted to the vocation of kingship in relation to Israel, the role and status of the king, and the theology of the monarchy in general. The chapter concludes with a discussion about the boundaries of the land in the OT, and argues that the promise of the land is a promise that God will use Israel to implement his universal dominion and kingly rule throughout the world.

1. Abraham as a Royal Figure

The biblical narratives seem to portray Abraham as a royal figure, even though he was never called a king and did not live in one fixed land or have dominion over a territory. We can start by looking at the first call to Abraham in Genesis 12 and the covenant that God established with him from that point onward. In particular, he is to bless the nations of the world (Gen 12:3b) – a point that is repeated many times in Genesis 12–22. We should comprehend the calling of Abraham against the backdrop of the scattering of the nations in Genesis 11. The nations that were scattered will now be blessed (or cursed, depending on their relationship with Abraham's seed). God would make Abraham's name great, in contrast with the people of Babylon who had sought to make a name for themselves (Gen 11:1–9). More importantly, God was the one here taking the initiative. He was starting a new history and a new civilization, and he chose a new humanity to represent him, promising them a land. Abraham and his seed would be the focal point of a new era in history. They would be the new rulers who would bring order into the chaos of the world.

In chapter 3 we noted Weinfeld's argument that when God made a promise to Abraham to give him the land, he was motivated by Abraham's loyal service. These promises are typologically parallel to the "royal covenantal grants" of the Hittites and Assyrians.[1] According to McCartney, "the idea of covenant as vassal treaty implies that God is suzerain king and that those with whom he makes covenant are subordinate kings."[2] Furthermore, in Genesis 17:6 God promises Abraham, after changing his name from Abram to Abraham, that kings shall come from him. This is a promise of a royal dynasty, and it emphasizes the royal flavor of the covenant. Abraham's seed that will be a blessing to the families of the world is now identified as a "royal line."[3] Moreover, Kline observes that ancient suzerains used to assign their rulers dynastic names, and argues that the giving of new names to Abram and Sarai (Gen 17:5) when presenting to them a promissory grant of royalty is in accord with this custom.[4]

When we read the promise to Abraham in this manner, the fact that the land is part of the promise becomes a logical concept, since kings need a territory to rule over. In Genesis 22:17, Abraham is promised that his "offspring shall possess (ירש) the gate of his enemies." The Hebrew ירש has

---

[1]. Weinfeld, *Promise of the Land*, 229.
[2]. McCartney, "Ecce Homo," 3.
[3]. T. D. Alexander, *The Servant King: The Bible's Portrait of the Messiah* (Vancouver: Regent College, 2003), 30.
[4]. Kline, *Kingdom Prologue*, 333.

the notion of possessing by force or dispossession and is commonly linked with the land as its object. Wenham comments that in these statements Abraham is "portrayed not merely as the archetypal Israelite who has faith in God, but as a conquering king who has been promised victory over his foes and a great territory."[5]

In conclusion, a "dynasty" with "royal" overtones is established in the Abrahamic narrative – a dynasty that will function as a point of reference in the history of the world. The fate of the nations will depend on their relationship to this new dynasty, whether for blessing or curse (Gen 12:2). Further hints are given about this dynasty in Jacob's blessing on his sons (Gen 49). There, it is declared that the line of royalty will go through Judah and that "to him shall be the obedience of the peoples" (49:10–11). Finally, Abraham, the nomad, is promised a land that will be the sphere of his seed's dominion.

2. The Royal Status of Israel

The perception of the royal Abrahamic dynasty is confirmed and advanced in the way the Pentateuch describes Israel as a nation. In Exodus 4:22–23, Israel is declared to be the firstborn son of God and is compared with the son of Pharaoh.[6] We have already seen in chapter 1 how kings in the ANE were portrayed as sons of the gods (Ps 2:6). By comparing Israel with the son of the Pharaoh, the text elevates Israel as a nation to the status of royalty. We can see another indication of the royalty of Israel in her calling in Exodus 19:6: "And you shall be to me a *kingdom* of priests and a holy nation." The Hebrew text takes two very common OT terms and

---

5. Wenham, *Genesis 1–15*, 335.
6. The declaration of Israel as the son of God was repeated over and over in the OT. See, for example, Deut 8:5; 14:1; 32:5–6, 18–19; Isa 1:2; 30:1, 9; 43:6; 63:16; 64:8; Jer 3:14, 19, 22; 31:9, 20; Hos 11:1; Mal 1:6; 20:10. Wright speaks of two levels in Israel's sonship: the national and individual ones. The national level has to do with the election of Israel, and is unconditional in nature. The individual level, on the other hand, requires faithfulness from the individual to be properly called son/daughter of God. C. J. H. Wright, *God's People in God's Land: Family, Land, and Property in the Old Testament* (Grand Rapids: Eerdmans, 1990), 15–22.

combines them in an uncommon way: ממלכת כהנים.⁷ Wells comments on this phrase:

> If YHWH is king, then it follows that the people over whom he exercises his kingship will be his kingdom. Because of YHWH, Israel has royal associations.[8]

Whether it is a royal priesthood or a priestly kingdom, the two concepts – kingdom and priesthood – carry within them the notion of representation. Moreover, it was not strange in the ANE or ancient Israel to have the two positions united in one figure (e.g. David, Ps 110). The uniqueness of this verse is that it applies the two concepts to Israel *as a nation*. Levenson, perhaps with an element of overstatement, confirms:

> All of Israel is endowed with sovereignty, for the nation as a whole has become royal in character. . . . Both Israel as a nation and the Israelite as an individual stand in the position of royal vassals of the divine suzerain.[9]

Levenson observes that such an endowment of sovereignty could be compared to an ANE suzerain conferring sovereignty upon his vassal. This is important for understanding the role of Israel as a vicegerent or representative of God on earth. In the land, Israel represented God before the other nations of the earth. The goal was to establish a different kingdom in the midst of other kingdoms: "You shall be my treasured possession *among all peoples, for all the earth is mine*" (Exod 19:5).

The book of Joshua describes how, to a certain degree, Israel was able to establish this kingdom under the leadership of Joshua. Israel entered the land and took possession (ירש) of the land of other nations (Josh 1:15;

---

7. For the different options of translating this phrase, see J. B. Wells, *God's Holy People: A Theme In Biblical Theology* (Sheffield: Sheffield Academic Press, 2000), 50–52; J. Durham, *Exodus. Word Biblical Commentary* (Waco: Word Books, 1987), 263. The LXX translates the phrase as "royal priesthood," whereas the Vulgate translates it "priestly kingdom." The most literal translation, according to Wells, is "kingdom of priests."

8. Wells, *God's Holy People*, 51.

9. Levenson, *Sinai & Zion*, 71–72.

18:1–3; 23:4). There was a sense of newness in this regard. Something old had gone (the original inhabitants of the land with their religions, gods, and governing systems); something new came to replace it (new people, new religion, YHWH as the only God, and a new governing system). Joshua and the Israelites were replacing the old monarchs with a new "kingdom," in which God will be king, and the land is "subdued" before the Israelites (Josh 18:1).

The Hebrew term used for subdued in Joshua 18:1 is כבש in the Niphal, and it calls to mind Genesis 1:28, where the same verb is also coupled with the land (הארץ) as its object.[10] In Genesis, the verse describes the mandate of Adam, having just been created in God's image, to subdue הארץ. We have already seen in chapter 1 that being created in the image of God can be interpreted as a sign of royalty. Ute Neumann-Gorsolke sees priestly influence at work in the text of Joshua 18:1, connecting it to Genesis 1:28.[11] The goal of this, according to Neumann-Gorsolke, is to link the gift of land with the creation narrative and to give the land a "theological foundation."[12] One can also look at the repeated statements in the conclusion of the book of Joshua that God had "given rest" to the Israelites in the land (21:44; 22:4; 23:1); this too links the land with the creation narratives.

In conclusion, Israel in the OT has features of a kingdom *even before the time of the monarchy*.[13] In the land, Israel establishes an alternative society, one that is ruled by the laws of God given at Sinai and at the Jordan boundary. In other words, the status of Israel as a kingdom does not depend on a king, a capital, or an army. Rather, it is the result of the people as individuals and as a society being faithful to God and subduing the land and its kings under the authority of the real creator King. This was a kingdom

---

10. See also Num 32:22, 29; 1 Chr 22:18.
11. U. Neumann-Gosolke, "'And the Land Was Subdued Before Them . . .'? Some Remarks On The Meaning of כבש in Joshua 18:1 and Related Texts," in *The Land of Israel in Bible, History, and Theology: Studies in Honour of Ed Noort*, ed. J. Van Ruiten and J. C. De Vos (Leiden: Brill, 2009), 73–86. For Neumann-Gorsolke, the root כבש is not of a violent or military action, but a of movement of the feet: to step upon or move feet upon land, which was a symbolic act in the ANE of taking possession (p. 84).
12. Ibid., 85.
13. Levenson, *Sinai & Zion*, 75.

of a different kind, for it was based on God's kingship over the nation and the land.

It is important to point out at this stage that there is nevertheless a tension between the idealized expressions of faith on this matter and the actual reality. Israel never lived up to this ideal of being a kingdom of priests and a blessing to the nations; neither was the land fully subdued before them. The book of Joshua, for example, makes two points regarding the conquest. On the one hand, there are the statements that the land was fully conquered and Israel enjoyed rest.[14] On the other hand, there are statements in Joshua and Judges that state the opposite; namely that the land was not fully conquered.[15] In fact, Joshua 13:1 claims that "there remains yet very much land to possess," and surprisingly, Judges 2:22 claims that it was God who left the inhabitants, in order to "test" Israel. Japhet comments pertinently:

> The generally accepted view is that the actual historical situation is more accurately reflected in the statements about the incompleteness of the conquest than in those about the complete fulfillment of the promises; the latter are regarded as *expressions of faith and religious conviction* rather than of historical facts.[16]

We must distinguish therefore between what took place in Israel's history and what was projected in Israel's faith. These two seem to be in dialogue throughout the biblical narrative, and this reflects the fact that the ideal was never realized in OT biblical history. The portrayal of Israel as a "kingdom of priests" is thus more of an expression of faith and hope than a historical reality. "Kingdom of priests" is what Israel is ideally supposed to be, and is what precisely she failed to achieve.

---

14. Josh 10:42; 11:23; 18:1; 21:43.
15. Josh 13:1–7; 23:12; Judg 2:21.
16. S. Japhet, "Conquest and Settlement in Chronicles," *Journal of Biblical Literature* (1979): 207 (emphasis added).

3. The Theology of Kingship in Israel

3.1. The Deuteronomic Account

The monarchy is anticipated by the Deuteronomic history (at least canonically), which speaks with some specificity about the position of kingship in Israel and what should make it distinct. Deuteronomy 17:14–20 speaks about the king, and anticipates what, ideally, he should look like. Precisely, he must be an Israelite who is chosen by God (17:15). He should not indulge in riches and marry many wives (17:16–17). He must also keep the law (17:18) and live humbly (17:20).

This passage sets very high standards for kingship in Israel, and seems to reflect closely Solomon's reign and even to be criticizing it.[17] This has led to many views regarding its date of origin. These views range from just before the monarchy, to Solomon's time, to Josiah's reform, and to the exile.[18] In all cases, these verses represent the Deuteronomic requirement of kingship. At the same time, it is important to note that, according to the Deuteronomic tradition, the concept of a king and a kingdom can be redeemed. This is important to remember when we look at the actual establishment of kingship in Israel during the time of Samuel, for there it seems that God is opposed to the concept of the monarchy.

Staying with Deuteronomy 17, the limitations placed on the king in this passage are radical when compared with kingship in the ANE, and with the actual behavior of Israelite kings.[19] Brueggemann believes that the key to understanding this passage is found in the term "from among your brethren," which he understands to be a "covenantal phrase." For him, what is really taking place in this passage is a redefinition of the concept of kingship. Instead of being mainly about the interests of the king, kingship here is mainly about serving others. He further explains:

> "One from the brethren" means one in the context of covenant, one whose discernment of power concerns gifts and

---

17. See for example 1 Kgs 4:26–28; 10:14–29; 11:1–8.
18. For a good summary of these views, see McConville, *Deuteronomy*, 283–284.
19. Ibid., 283.

tasks, one who will not reduce society to coercion and people to slaves. This teaching thus calls for a radical redefinition of what kingship is all about. It is not to control the land, but to enhance the land for the sake of the covenant partners to whom the king is bound by common loyalties and memories.[20]

In short, the vision for the king of Israel is not much different from what was expected from Israel as a nation and as a kingdom of priests. God chooses both Israel and the king, and in both situations, the laws of God should have the central role in the structure of the kingdom. If anything, the king is to advance the vision of Israel as an ideal society and as a kingdom of priests. In addition, Israel must aspire to seek a different kind of kingship – one that is distinct from the nations around her.

3.2. A King, or No King?

The establishment of the Israelite kingship in 1 Samuel 8 is one of the most intriguing passages in the OT. The account gives a very negative view of the monarchy and describes it as a rejection of God himself (1 Sam 8:4–7). The king in 1 Samuel 8:11–18 is described as a tyrant who will be the exact opposite of Deuteronomy 17. In fact, the image is that of slavery, similar to what Israel endured in Egypt. There would be no equality and no social or economic justice, and the land would not be distributed fairly. We can also observe that this account of kingship "is explicit and accurate, both as a description of contemporary non-Israelite monarchy and as a prediction of what Israelite monarchy actually became from the reign of Solomon and increasingly thereafter."[21]

Interestingly, the human rationale behind accepting this structure of governing is simple: "That we also may be *like all the nations*" (1 Sam 8:20). Israel wants to be like the other nations. They no longer want to be distinct. This is at the core of the negative image given to the monarchy in 1 Samuel 8, and is precisely what the law warns Israel against doing: copying other

---

20. Brueggemann, *The Land*, 71.
21. Wright, *Old Testament Ethics*, 59.

nations' lifestyle.[22] This description of the establishment of the monarchy, coupled with the accounts of David's and Solomon's sins, has caused some scholars to interpret the presentation of the monarchy in the OT in a very negative way. Tarazi for example says:

> Man being king is the epitome of disobedience because it challenges God's kingship, that is, his sole proprietorship of the earth and all that lives on it. Thus it is the king, *per se*, who is the real source of all troubles.[23]

So what do we make of this image of kingship in the OT, especially in the light of other images that celebrate the king of Israel (e.g. Ps 2)? How do we reconcile Deuteronomy 17 with 1 Samuel 8? The proposal, laid out in Deuteronomy 17, is of a different style of kingship, a "distinction" from the norm. The reality, described in 1 Samuel 8, is "assimilation" or compromise to the world. The OT therefore presents a tension between the proposed ideal and the actual reality. The proposed ideal is in fact an expression of the *faith of Israel*, whereas the actual reality is the *history of Israel*, and often these two are not in harmony. We have already seen such tension in the reality of Israel, which was far from being a kingdom of priests and which failed fully to conquer the land. This tension will be further intensified when we compare the dark side of the Davidic and Solomonic reigns with the glorious songs of Israel that celebrated the king of Israel.

3.3. The Vicegerency of the King of Israel

According to the faith of Israel, as celebrated in the hymns and statements about the king and Davidic dynasty, the king of Israel is God's vicegerent. As such, he is God's representative on earth, and is responsible for the

---

22. See for example Lev 20:22–26.
23. Tarazi, *Land and Covenant*, 141. Brueggemann, on the other hand, believes that the problem with Israel does not lie in the office of kingship *per se*. The problem is that Israel chose the wrong land management method, one not in line with Deut 17. In other words, the problem was in the job description of the king, and the fact that he would be similar to other kings in other nations and other lands. The king's task should have been "not to control the land, but to enhance the land for the sake of the covenant partners." Brueggemann, *The Land*, 72.

land of his dominion before God. He is also a representative of the people before God.

The Psalms declare that the king is chosen and anointed by God (Pss 45:7; 110:1).[24] In 2 Samuel 7:12–14, God declares to David:

> *I will raise up your offspring after you*, who shall come from your body, and I will establish his kingdom. He shall build a house for my name, and I will establish the throne of his kingdom forever. *I will be to him a father, and he shall be to me a son.* (emphasis added)

According to this ideology, the king of Israel is not only chosen by God, God also adopts him and declares him to be his son.[25] This is confirmed in Psalm 2:6–7: "As for me, *I have set my King on Zion*, my holy hill. I will tell of the decree: The Lord said to me, '*You are my Son*; today I have begotten you.'"

Many scholars argue that, according to this ideology, the monarch as son of God is the representative on earth of YHWH – the universal ruler whose throne was in heaven.[26] "When the Son of David rules on Zion, the reign of God is properly upon the earth."[27] Or as Levenson puts it:

> Davidic kingship is an earthly manifestation of divine kingship. . . . The scenario of Psalm 2 takes place upon a split set. God is "enthroned in heaven"; the Davidic king is enthroned

---

24. We must consider the royal psalms first in their historical context, without ascribing to them Messianic expectation and before treating them as prophecies. For more, see S. Gillingham, *Psalms Through The Centuries* (Oxford: Blackwell Pub, 2008). She remarks (p. 5): "It seems fairly certain that many psalms were composed in the *pre-exilic period – psalms for the king to use in the Temple (for example, Pss 2, 72, 89, 110 and 132), psalms which ratified the conviction that God would protect the city of Zion from invasion (such as Pss 46, 48), and psalms which would be used in times of national distress (for example, Pss 74, 77, 79, 80, 82)." Gillingham further says, "The so-called 'royal psalms' and 'Zion hymns' would have been used with an eye to the future, to encourage the community whose present experience would have made them question the confident faith expressed within them."

25. See also 1 Chr 17:13; 28:5.

26. Habel, *The Land is Mine*, 26. See also Zimmerli, *Old Testament Theology*, 92.

27. McCartney, "Ecce Homo," 3.

on earth (vv. 4, 6). But the two realms are linked. The lower is simply the human manifestation of the higher, Mount Zion being the common side of the two tiers of reality.[28]

This is further advanced in Israelite theology by declaring the throne of David as the throne of YHWH himself. The Chronicler called the throne of the king "the throne of the kingdom of the Lord" (1 Chr 28:5), or simply "the throne of the Lord" (1 Chr 29:23; 2 Chr 9:8), and he called the kingdom of David the "kingdom of the LORD" (1 Chr 17:14; 28:5). Psalm 132:12–13 also declares that God has specifically chosen Zion as a dwelling place, in relation to the kingship of David.

Furthermore, the king of Israel plays the role of a "mediator," and it is no wonder therefore that he is said to have brought rest and security to the land. Peace prevails for Israel when the king subdues the land:

> Solomon ruled over all the kingdoms from the Euphrates to the land of the Philistines and to the border of Egypt . . . And *Judah and Israel lived in safety,* from Dan even to Beersheba, every man under his vine and under his fig tree, all the days of Solomon. (1 Kgs 4:21, 25)

The king brings not only peace and security to the land, but also social justice and care for the poor and the oppressed in Israel. By doing this, he is a source of blessing to the nation. Psalm 72 is very important in this regard:

> Give the king your justice (משפט), O God, and your righteousness (צדק) to the royal son [literally, son of the king]! *May he judge your people with righteousness, and your poor with justice!* Let the mountains bear prosperity [literally שלום, or peace] for the people, and the hills, in righteousness! *May he defend the cause of the poor of the people,* give deliverance to the

---

28. Levenson, *Sinai & Zion*, 155.

children of the needy, and crush the oppressor. (Ps 72:1–4; see also vv. 12–13)[29]

One interesting feature of these Psalms is that they link the role of the monarch in bringing divine justice with cosmic order.[30] And so as Miller observes:

> There is a clear connection between the king's righteous reign and the flourishing of the land. This is expressed both in terms of the king's active care of the poor and the needy and with regard to his resistance to the wicked in the land . . . Psalm 72 hangs all the blessings of the land and life on the land upon the activity of the king to "save the lives of the needy."[31]

In conclusion, the king of Israel is called the "son of God" in the OT, in a similar fashion to Israel's being called the "son of God." This means that, according to this ideology, the king represents on earth the God who is in heaven. In addition, the shift from the sonship of Israel as a nation to the sonship of the king means that the king now represents Israel, and as such plays a crucial role when it comes to securing blessing and rest for the land and for the people of the land. The land, to a certain degree, depends on the king for spiritual and physical fertility.

We can observe once again that there is a tension between the reality on the ground and these statements of faith about the king and his role. David and Solomon (not to mention the divided kings after them) failed to live up to these ideals, despite some measure of success in certain periods, and this, according to Zimmerli, paved the way for the messianic expectations.[32] The failure of the kings of Israel to live up to these ideals will be dealt with

---

29. See also Ps 45.
30. Habel, *The Land is Mine*, 28.
31. Miller, "The Land in the Psalms," 195–196. See also Zimmerli who asserts that "Psalm 72 is revealing in its linking of a righteous kingship . . . and the universal sovereignty of the king with the notion of prosperity in the natural world under his rule." Zimmerli, *Old Testament Theology*, 91.
32. Zimmerli, *Old Testament Theology*, 92.

4. The Failure of the Monarchy

The reality of the monarchy is a disappointing one. One needs only to look at the accounts of the kings of Israel in the books of Samuel and Kings. Starting from Saul, the kings of Israel (and later the divided kingdom) broke the law and disobeyed God. David, the most celebrated king in Israel, lived a life that included many dark episodes. He was thirsty for revenge (1 Sam 25:13), shed much blood, waged great wars (1 Chr 22:8; 28:3), and had a troubled family, which ultimately led to a civil war in his kingdom (2 Sam 13–19). Most infamously, he abused his power by committing adultery and murder (2 Sam 11). The manner in which David abused his royal authority is startling. As Brueggemann explains in relation to David's adultery:

> David had presumed himself immune from Torah, as kings always are tempted to presume. The story in subtle fashion raises the question of the relation of king, Torah, and land. Is the king free to do what he will with his extensive turf?[33]

The life of David draws near its conclusion with the tragic account of the census (2 Sam 24). Though the reason behind the census is not mentioned in the story, one could guess that it was concerned with military purposes, or that it might have been linked with taxation or forced labor service.[34] As such, it typifies what went wrong with the monarchy: it became an opportunity for power and control.

The reign of Solomon further intensified the mentality of power. As already mentioned, he did the opposite of what is commanded in

---
33. Brueggemann, *The Land*, 75.
34. A. A. Anderson, *2 Samuel. Word Biblical Commentary* (Dallas: Word Books, 1989), 284.

Deuteronomy 17 by acquiring horses, marrying many wives, and turning Israel into slaves.[35] He also built altars to other gods in the land (1 Kgs 11:7), denying in essence YHWH's ultimate ownership of the land. Solomon went as far as giving portions of the land to king Hiram, presuming that the land was his to give (1 Kgs 9:11). Rehoboam, son of Solomon and first king of Judah, expresses the nature of his father and of his own reign: "My father made your yoke heavy, but I will add to your yoke. My father disciplined you with whips, but I will discipline you with scorpions" (1 Kgs 12:14).

The situation in the divided monarchy was no better. Perhaps no other story in the accounts of the kings of Judah and Israel illustrates the abuse of power by kings with regard to the land than the story of King Ahab and the vineyard of Naboth (1 Kgs 21). The relatively large space this narrative receives in the book of Kings is an indication that the narrative demands special attention. Ahab, king of the Northern kingdom, sees the vineyard of Naboth the Jezreelite, covets it, and presumes that he has entitlement to ask Naboth to sell it to him (21:2). Naboth, on the other hand, rejects this, based on his belief that this is a land entrusted to him by God as an inheritance and therefore he cannot sell it (21:3). In the words of Brueggemann: "Naboth is responsible for the land, but is not in control over it. It is the case not that the land belongs to him but that he belongs to the land."[36]

The infamous queen Jezebel intervenes in the story, and reminds Ahab that, as king of Israel, he is entitled to take the vineyard (21:7). A plot is made, Naboth is killed, and Ahab receives the vineyard (21:16). Power and manipulation are in play here. Ahab and Jezebel act in a way that presumes that simply because they are king and queen, they have entitlement to any land. The victim in this narrative is Naboth, who represents powerless Israel. The way in which Naboth and Ahab relate to the land manifests a startling contrast. One treats it as a gift, the other as an entitlement. One believed that it belonged to the community; the other wanted it for self-indulgence.

---

35. See 1 Kgs 4:26–28; 10:14–29; 11:1–8; 12:4.
36. Brueggemann, *The Land*, 88.

The story concludes with judgment on Ahab. He was found guilty of murder and "taking possession": "Thus says the Lord, Have you killed and also *taken possession? . . . In the place* where dogs licked up the blood of Naboth shall dogs lick your own blood" (1 Kgs 21:19).

The king, who is supposed to be the guardian of justice in the land (as seen in Ps 72), instead is responsible for inflicting injustice on the people of the land. God intervenes and brings justice, for he is concerned for justice. Interestingly, justice is enacted in the same place where Naboth is killed, hinting perhaps that the land is involved in the avenging of his death.

The Israelite monarchy project failed; and the king as the main figure in this system holds the main responsibility for this failure. Instead of being a source of blessing and fertility for the land, he was the cause of the tragedy for the people and the land. King after king abused their power and presumed ownership of the land and its inhabitants, worshipped foreign gods in the land, and produced a kingship system that copied that of the previous inhabitants of the land – even that of Egypt, the place of slavery.

5. Universal Dominion

Israel and her king are celebrated in the OT for reigning over more than just the land – there are indications that Israel is given universal dominion. The notion of universal dominion goes back to the early traditions of Abraham. It is therefore important at this stage, and before considering the theme of universal dominion in the faith of Israel, to look at the issue of the boundaries of the land and simply ask: What are the boundaries of the Promised Land? The issue is controversial, because of the different descriptions that we find in the OT of these boundaries.[37]

The boundaries of the land in the OT roughly make two maps: (1) the land of Canaan, (see map 1) and (2) a wider territory (from the river to the river) that includes most of the ANE (see map 2). We can speak of "micro borders" – Canaan; and "macro borders" – the Euphrates. In

---

37. Gen 12:5; 17:8; 15:18–21; Exod 23:31; Num 34:1–12; Deut 1:7; 11:24; Josh 1:3–4; Judg 20:1; 1 Sam 3:20; 2 Sam 3:10; 17:11; 24:2, 15; 1 Kgs 4:25m; 10:23–24.

addition, in the different periods, the land had different shapes. The allotted land, for example, is different from the land during David's and then Solomon's reigns.[38]

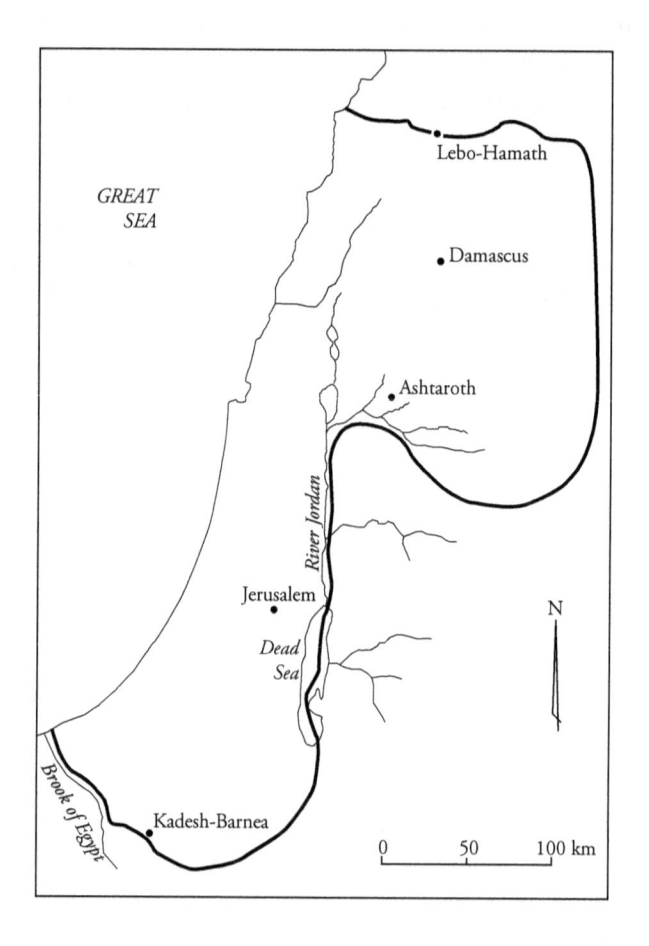

Map 1: Numbers 34:3–12

Maps adapted from M. Weinfeld, *The Promise of the Land: The Inheritance of the Land of Canaan by the Israelites* (Berkeley: University of California Press, 2003), 57–58.

---

38. For detailed maps of the conquest and the reigns of David and Solomon, see Z. Ridling, *The Bible Atlas* (The Access Foundation, 2000), maps 38, 39, and 53.

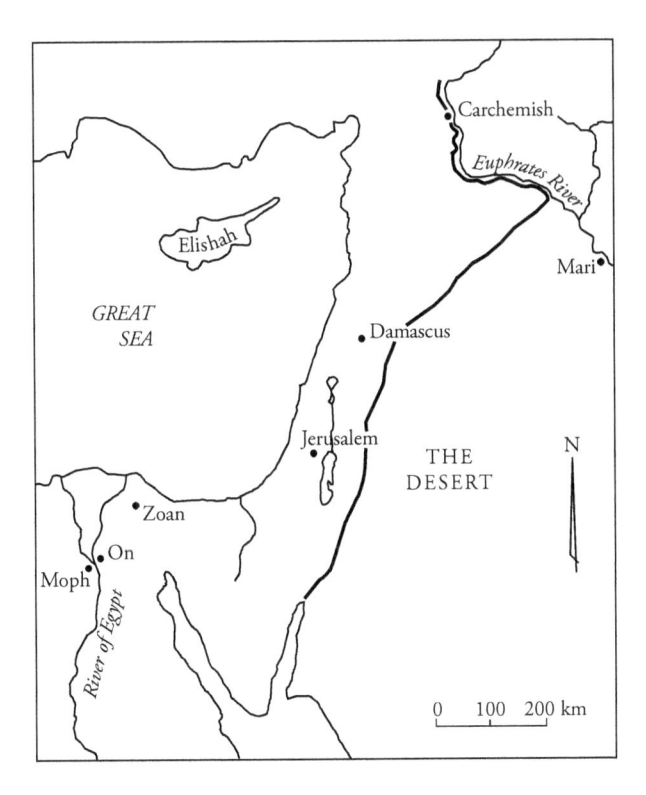

Map 2: Genesis 15:18–2

Scholars have offered different interpretations of this problem. For some, the issue can be resolved through textual criticism. Weinfeld, for example, spoke of two sources for these two maps: Priestly (P) and Deuteronomic (D).[39] The land in the P sources is Canaan and does not include the territory east of the river Jordan. After the conquest and expansion during David's time, however, there was a need for expanding the territory. Therefore, the D sources, according to Weinfeld, spoke of "imperial boundaries" which included the territory east of the river and which are described as reaching up to the Euphrates.[40] Kallai, on the other hand, believes that there are not

---

39. Weinfeld, *Promise of the Land*, 55–76.
40. Similarly, von Waldow says that "the descriptions of boundaries reflect the situation of different periods." H. E. von Waldow, "Israel and Her Land: Some Theological Considerations," in *A Light unto My Path: Old Testament Studies in Memory of Jacob M.*

two but three different "lands" in the OT: (1) the patriarchal land, (2) the land of Canaan, and (3) the land of Israel. He explains:

> Of these three, Canaan is the Promised Land, while the land of Israel, despite its partial territorial divergence, is the realization of this promise. The patriarchal boundaries, however, although closely linked with the promise of the land, patently differ from the other two delineations.[41]

These explanations are insufficient and fail to appreciate fully the theological dimension behind these variations. Katanacho is probably right in rejecting both of these explanations. He argues that Weinfeld ignored the "present *textus receptus*, underestimating the intelligentsia of ancient Israel," and that Kallai lacked "sufficient textual support for his tripartite division of the land."[42]

Other scholars tried to reconcile the two maps into one map. Townsend argues that the OT speaks of the land in two ways: general and specific. The wider boundaries are general descriptions and are variable and do not actually fix borders, whereas the descriptions of Canaan (e.g. Num 34) are specific descriptions and make for exact boundary. Therefore, he argues, the general descriptions should be understood as approximations which locate the land between familiar geographic points.[43]

Meanwhile, Kaiser tried to reconcile the two maps by arguing that they are in fact one.[44] For him, the phrase in Genesis 15:18 "from the river of Egypt to the great river, the river Euphrates" does not mean from the Nile to the Euphrates. The river of Egypt is a small river placed at the "Wadi

---

Myers, ed. H. N. Bream, R. D. Heim and C. A. Moore (Philadelphia: Temple University Press, 1974), 498.
41. Z. Kallai, "The Patriarchal Boundaries, Canaan and the Land of Israel: Patterns and Application in Biblical Historiography," *Israel Exploration Journal* 47, no. 1–2 (1997): 70.
42. Katanacho, *The Land of Christ*, 38.
43. J. L. Townsend, "Fulfillment of the Land Promise in the Old Testament," *Bibliotheca Sacra* 142, no. 568 (1985): 328.
44. Kaiser, "The Promised Land," 303–305.

el-'Arish," which reaches the Mediterranean Sea at the town of El-'Arish.[45] As for the great river, he argues:

> But is the Euphrates River to be equated with the Great River? Could it not be that these are the two extremities of the northern boundary? This suggestion proves to have some weight in that the other topographical notices given along with these two river names would appear to be more ideally located in the valley which currently serves as the boundary between Lebanon and Syria. The river running through this valley is called in modern Arabic Nahr el-Kebir, "the great river."[46]

Both Townsend and Kaiser are trying to harmonize the variations in the maps, and by doing so they downplay the differences in them. These are insufficient explanations. The general area Townsend refers to is much larger than the specific one.[47] Kaiser's explanation stretches the evidence too much. It is hard to argue that the OT describes two relatively unknown rivers, Wadi el-'Arish and Nahr el-Kabir, as boundary markers and calls them the river of Egypt and the great river.

More recently, two scholars offered more convincing explanations for the variations. Rachel Havrelock offers a fresh explanation for the existence of two maps – a socio-religious one that alludes to biblical criticism.[48] Believing that maps in Israel displayed how spatial representation of the nation relied on intersecting mythic and political standards,[49] she argues that both sets of maps have one thing in common: they both run from water to water. This portrait of the land, she argues, resonates with cosmological

---

45. Ibid., 303.
46. Ibid., 304.
47. This would be the equivalent to saying today that modern-day Palestine/Israel corresponds to the Middle East: Palestine/Israel is the specific description and the Middle East is the general.
48. R. Havrelock, "The Two Maps of Israel's Land," *Journal of Biblical Literature* 126, no. 4 (2007): 649–667.
49. Ibid., 649.

descriptions.⁵⁰ This has intentional motifs, and will at the same time explain the variation in the two maps:

> The designation of seas and rivers as boundaries conveys a sense that the order of the land reflects the structure of the cosmos… Therefore, even when the borders of the land are construed differently, the east-west axis must span from sea to river in order that the land appear as a microcosm of the cosmos itself. These borders offer geographic proof of the enveloping character of God and state alike. The flexibility concerning which river forms the eastern boundary results from the fact that the mythic morphology prevails over cartographic specifics. The two sets of maps can coexist because their configurations of the land do not conflict, both corresponding to the authorizing cosmological system.⁵¹

As to how the different resources contributed to the shaping of these two sets of maps, Havrelock argues that the Canaan maps do not exalt kings but sideline them in order to promote priestly ideologies, whereas the Euphrates maps enunciate more support for the kings, but only for the kind of whom the Deuteronomists approve. In addition, the Jordan maps correspond to ancient Egyptian maps of Canaan, but replace the rule of the Pharaoh with that of Israel, whereas the Euphrates maps imagine an Israel mirroring Babylonia, hence the reference to the Euphrates.⁵²

The remarks of Havrelock are very helpful in that they point to the cosmological dimension of the boundaries. For, as will be argued more extensively below, Israel *did* speak of her land with such universal language. However, although it is helpful to relate the OT texts to the wider ANE context, it seems that Havrelock assumes too much about the background of each text describing the boundaries and about the influence that the background had on the authors of these texts.

---

50. Ibid., 656.
51. Ibid., 657–658.
52. Ibid., 659–660.

Nili Wazana offers probably the most important interpretation when it comes to the two maps.[53] She asserts that the images of the land in the OT are literary descriptions and, therefore, the basis for examining them must begin with literary analysis.[54] Building on that, she observes that there are two land *concepts* in the OT (but not two land maps). The first deals with the land of Canaan, which, she argues, was a conventional well-known geographical unit.[55] The Euphrates boundaries, however, are not about new or different boundaries. Rather, it is about a different conception. Wazana mentions here five important texts, the ones that go beyond Canaan in their description: Genesis 15:18–21; Exodus 23:31; Deuteronomy 1:7; 11:24; and Joshua 1:3–4. These texts, she argues, describe the land using literary spatial merism in the form of "from . . . to."[56] Wazana then explains why it is wrong to treat these passages as boundary descriptions, since it will conflict with other statements and incidents from within the traditions to which these passages individually belong.[57] She then says:

> Merism expressions utilize the prepositions "from" and "to" to denote generalizations, presenting a whole (usually abstract) concept, rather than its components . . . These merism expressions are not intended to define the extremities of the structure, but to denote its entire magnitude, its extremities determining the whole and characterizing it.[58]

---

53. N. Wazana, "From Dan to Beer-Sheba and from the Wilderness to the Sea: Literal and Literary Images of the Promised Land in the Bible," in *Experiences of place,* ed. M. N. MacDonald (Cambridge: Harvard University Press, 2003), 45–85. See also her Hebrew book: N. Wazana, *All the Boundaries of the Land: The Promised Land in Biblical Thought in Light of the Ancient Near East* (Jerusalem: Bialik Institute, 2007).
54. Ibid., 45.
55. Ibid., 50. Wazana adds: "Though the exact extent of the political-geographical unit may have fluctuated over the ages as a result of political and historical changes, the general designation is an accepted standard term [Canaan] referring to a known core area and adjacent peripheral zones."
56. Merism is a figure of speech by which totality is expressed by means of polarity. Examples of merism in the OT include expressions like "from Dan to Beersheba," and "from the river to the river," "heavens and earth," and "rich and poor."
57. Wazana, "From Dan to Beer-Sheba," 54–55.
58. Ibid., 56.

Wazana analyses the aforementioned texts, and argues that terms like "wilderness," "the great river," and "the great sea" should be understood in their literary and ANE context:

> The terms figuring in the spatial merisms depicting the Promised Land are larger bodies of water, such as seas and rivers, or remote, extreme regions, such as the wilderness or mountain territories. In ancient Near Eastern traditions these are the areas *depicting the very ends of the earth.*[59]

Wazana's conclusion is of extreme importance to the theology of the land:

> The promise reflected in spatial merisms is not to be understood literally, nor should it be translated and transformed into border lines on maps. It is a promise of *world dominion* . . . In the Bible there is only one map of the borders of the Promised Land, and it refers to an entitled, specific political entity: "the land of Canaan" . . . The spatial merisms in promise terminology reflect a land that has no borders at all, only ever-expanding frontiers; they are referring to *universal rule.*[60]

The resolution of the universal dimension of the promises of the land that both Havrelock and Wazana allude to seems to be the best explanation of the variation in the maps. It can also be confirmed when we look at the bigger picture in the OT. The universal extension of the land can be seen in many passages and expressions related to the land, starting from Abraham's time. In Genesis 13:14–17, the land is also delimited and not defined:[61]

> The Lord said to Abram . . . Lift up your eyes and look from the place where you are, northward and southward and eastward and westward, for all the land (הארץ) that you see I will

---

59. Ibid., 64 (emphasis added). Wazana gives numerous examples of this phenomenon from the ANE (pp. 64–70).
60. Ibid., 71 (emphasis added).
61. Tarazi, *Land and Covenant*, 56.

give to you and to your offspring forever. I will make your offspring as the dust of the earth, so that if one can count the dust of the earth, your offspring also can be counted. Arise, walk through the length and the breadth of the land (הארץ), for I will give it to you.

It is no wonder that the land is not specified in the first call to Abraham (Gen 12:1–3). Instead, as Alexander observes:

> The climax of the speech comes in the statement that "through you all the families of the earth will find blessing" . . . The promise that Abraham will become a great nation, *implying both numerous seed and land*, must be understood as being subservient to God's principal desire to bless all the families of the earth.[62]

Katanacho, commenting on God's blessing to Abraham in Genesis 22:17, rightly emphasizes:

> It seems that the land of Abraham is not going to have fixed borders. It will continue to expand as it conquers the gates of the enemies, thus increasing in size both territorially and demographically. The land of Abraham will continue to extend until it is equal to the whole earth.[63]

It therefore follows that we can speak of two concepts of the Promised Land in the OT: the one realized – Canaan, and the one anticipated – the earth. Canaan, the land of promise, is the first stage in the realization of the universal promise. The fact that the OT continually speaks of these universal dimensions of the land makes Israel look forward and anticipate

---

62. T. D. Alexander, *From Paradise to the Promised Land: An Introduction to the Pentateuch* (Carlisle, Cumbria: Paternoster Press, 2002), 146 (emphasis added).
63. Katanacho, *The Land of Christ*, 80.

further expansions of the land, and this explains why Israel conceives of her kingship as ultimately or ideally universal.

The Psalms have glorified images – even mythical ones – of the king and the scope of his reign. According to Psalm 2:8, God will give the king the nations as his inheritance (נחלה) and *the ends of the earth* as his possession (אחזה). The use of נחלה and אחזה is important, as it reminds us of Israel receiving the land as נחלה and אחזה. In the same manner, Psalm 45:16 declares that the king will make his children *princes in all the earth*. In Psalm 72, the psalmist prays: "May he have dominion from sea to sea, and from the River to *the ends of the earth* . . . May all kings fall down before him, *all nations serve him*" (72:8, 11).[64]

The universal reign will be also an inclusive one, as is evident in Psalm 87, which speaks of Jerusalem, the city of God, that has different nations as citizens. These nations are said to be born in Jerusalem.[65] The psalm assumes that Jerusalem has extended its boundaries to include all these nations and regions. This shows that Jerusalem still plays a central role in this universal formula.[66]

The blessing that the king of Israel is supposed to bring surpasses Israel and extends outwards to other nations and kings. Therefore, the blessing of Abraham to the nations is fulfilled in the king of Israel. Through the king of Israel, the nations of the earth shall be blessed. There is a parallel, if we

---

64. This ideology can be also seen in some of the statements in the historical books about Solomon: For example, "Solomon ruled over all the kingdoms from the Euphrates to the land of the Philistines and to the border of Egypt. They brought tribute and served Solomon all the days of his life . . . And people of all nations came to hear the wisdom of Solomon, and from all the kings of the earth, who had heard of his wisdom" (1 Kgs 4:21, 34). See also 1 Kgs 10:1 and 2 Chr 9:26.

65. For a detailed analysis of Psalm 87, see Y. Katanacho, "Jerusalem is the City of God: A Palestinian Reading of Psalm 87," in *The Land Cries Out. Theology of the Land in the Israeli-Palestinian Context*, ed. S. Munayer and L. Loden (Eugene: Wipf and Stock, 2012), 181–199. About the inclusive nature of the Psalm, Katanacho says (p. 196): "Psalm 87 puts a vision of equality and an absence of subordination before us. There are no second-class citizens in Zion. This equality is not just civic but is also covenantal. They all share the same God, are born in the same city, and registered by the same hands. Their linguistic, historical, and military differences are not important. What unites them is God himself. Geography is no longer a point of tension because Zion belongs to God, not Israel. It is the city of God, and he alone can grant citizenship in his city. Citizenship comes by divine declaration, not by biological rights."

66. Habel, *The Land is Mine*, 27.

work backwards, between the king of Israel, Israel in Sinai, and Abraham. In addition to being of the same Abrahamic royal dynasty, the king, like Israel, is to rule, subdue, and bring rest and blessing to the land and to the ends of the earth.

6. Conclusion

The theology of the land has a universal thrust. The reign of God through his appointed "son" – whether Adam, Israel or the monarch – must go beyond the land and reach to the ends of the earth. The land (הארץ), according to this OT belief, is indeed the whole earth (הארץ). This teleological linkage is aided by the fact that the Hebrew (and Greek for that matter, γῆ) has the same word for both.[67] The theology of the land is ultimately the theology of the earth, and this, in turn, will take us back to the creation (Ps 24:1).

Abraham, Israel, and the king of Israel are sequential episodes that was intended to bring about a "governed world."[68] The first episode was in Eden, where Adam was the first vicegerent who was given the task of governing the world. The sphere of dominion of Israel was also intended by God to expand gradually. The vicegerency of Israel and her kings, like that of Adam, carried within it a responsibility to represent and rule for God on earth. The land depends on the God's vicegerent for prosperity and order. Israel and her kings failed to keep this responsibility, but because of the faithfulness of God there is always a renewed hope of a new Israelite kingdom and an ideal future king.

---

67. Based on this, Paul Tarazi, in his book *Land and Covenant*, intentionally decided to use earth for הארץ and not land, arguing that is it the most proper theological translation.
68. Dumbrell, *Covenant and Creation*, 66.

CHAPTER 5

The Land in the New History

Introduction

This chapter focuses on the prophetic tradition and its vision for the future in the context of the destruction of the monarchy and the exile. The three themes of holiness, covenant, and vicegerency, outlined in the three previous chapters, will now be considered as they relate to the future of the land as portrayed in the eschatological visions of the prophets. It will be seen how these visions redeemed all the failures within Israel's actual history into glorious and ideal images in the future – what can be termed "a new history." These visions created a new sense of hope in Israel and included a redefinition of holiness, covenant, vicegerency, but ultimately of the land.

1. From Crisis to New History

The destruction of Jerusalem and the exile created a moment of crisis for Israel. It is impossible to overstate the psychological, emotional, and theological effect of the exile on the community. The loss was theological, and it was perceived to indicate YHWH's abandonment of Israel and the nullification of all the old promises of divine presence.[1] Even after Israel returned from exile, the situation did not dramatically change. The overall situation

---
1. W. Brueggemann, "The Hope of Heaven . . . on Earth," *Biblical Theology Bulletin: A Journal of Bible and Theology* 29, no. 3 (1999): 106.

of the postexilic community was different from life as it was depicted for the times of David and Solomon, and far from the ideals preached by the prophets: the Davidic kingship was not re-established, not everyone returned from Babylon, there was no real independence in the land, and the new temple was modest in size. In addition, there was no real repentance and transformation in Israel. The situation can be summed up in the prayers of the Levites upon returning from exile that *"we are slaves this day; in the land* that you gave to our fathers to enjoy its fruit and its good gifts" (Neh 9:36).

Brueggemann divides biblical history in the OT into three parts. The first history is the one started in Adam; the second is that started in Abraham; and the third history is the one hoped-for and imagined by the prophets. He refers to the third history as the "new history."[2] It can be argued that this hoped-for new history developed in the theology of Israel as both the result of the failures of Israel,[3] and as a response to the exile. In this part of biblical history, which we will call the eschatological era for Israel, the God of Israel intervenes in this world to bring about a new order.

A very helpful study of this eschatology is that of Gowan.[4] He notes how eschatology deals with transformation of (1) human society, (2) the human person, and (3) nature (or land). Gowan provides a very important insight regarding the promises of this eschatological era:

> They [the promises] speak of circumstances that scarcely could be expected to arrive as the result of normal, or even extraordinary, human progress . . . One of the distinctive features of these hopes is their sense of the radical wrongness of the present world and the conviction that the radical changes, to make

---

2. Brueggemann, *The Land*, 124.

3. Preuss for example says about the messianic hopes in the OT: "The tensions between the ideal and the real within the monarchy on the one hand and between its presentation and evaluation on the other, the particular features of royal ideology that led to the creation of a present messianism, even more the courtly style that enriched this ideology, possibly even the increasing influence of the promise of Nathan that developed, and the retrospectives on the great period of David are, taken together in their complex and multilayered form, the factors that led to the development of a messianic hope in ancient Israel." Preuss, *Old Testament Theology, Vol. II*, 34.

4. Gowan, *Eschatology in the Old Testament*.

things right, will indeed occur "in that day," that is, at some time known only to God. The OT vision of the future deals throughout with the world in which we now live.[5]

This is important when it comes to studying eschatology. Eschatology in the OT is about divine acts which correct the wrongness of this world. It is not *merely* about the future, but it is more about what *God does* in the future, to establish a new and better reality within this present world.

The eschatological age, as already noted, is an imagined or hoped-for one, but not in the sense of being unreal. Rather, it is about a new reality that the prophets created in the imagination of their listeners, which in turn led to a renewed hope that was based on these promises. At the same time, the prophets necessarily continued to use old models to communicate the new reality. This led to a paradoxical sense, both of continuity and discontinuity. In other words, the eschatological reality, though described in old terminologies and images, would far exceed the original realities. Many of the themes of the Zion theology are found in the eschatological Jerusalem, but now they are idealized and even universalized, as Chris Wright notes:

> When prophets spoke about the future, they could only do so meaningfully by using terms and realities that existed in their past or present experience. The realities associated with being Israel in their day included their specific history and such things as the land, the law, Jerusalem, the temple, sacrifices and priesthood . . . To speak of restoration without recourse to such concrete features of being Israel would have been meaningless, even if it had been possible . . . Moreover, even in the Old Testament itself, there was an awareness that the fulfillment of prophecies that were made in terms of the concrete realities of Israel's life and faith would actually go beyond them . . . In other words, there seems to be an awareness that although the future has to be described in concepts drawn

---
5. Ibid., 1–2.

from Israel's historical nationhood, it will in fact ultimately transcend them.[6]

In other words, the prophets had to draw on the past to project into the future a vision of hope. They had to go back into old history to cast a vision for a new one. The prophets could only speak of the new history in terms of the old history, for they had no other images or models. But the use of such images "inevitably suggested that the old history really continues in some way, when surely it does not."[7]

This new history is colorfully and poetically described. The prophets viewed this history through the different theological lenses that represented their own setting. As Brueggemann explains:

> Jeremiah, *rooted in the categories of Deuteronomy*, anticipates the new land as a place where Torah is known and embraced (Jeremiah 31:33–34). Ezekiel, *rooted in priestly tradition*, imagines and expects a well-ordered holy precinct, so that all of the land is reconfigured as a sanctuary for YHWH's holiness. And Isaiah, *rooted in royal tradition*, can appeal to the image of a great royal procession of homecoming, evoked by royal decree that is received as "gospel."[8]

The three themes that Brueggemann highlights neatly match with the major three themes which we already highlighted: holiness, covenant, and kingdom. As we now trace these three themes in this new history portrayed in the eschatological visions of the prophets, we will find that holiness appears through the "priestly tradition" of Ezekiel, covenant through the "Deuteronomic categories" of Jeremiah, and vicegerency through the "royal tradition" of Isaiah. Prophecies from other prophetic books will also be considered as they relate to the discussion. Statements in these prophecies about Zion and Jerusalem will be deemed as relevant for our discussion

---

6. Wright, "A Christian Approach," 4–5.

7. Brueggemann, *The Land*, 124.

8. W. Brueggemann, *Old Testament Theology: An Introduction* (Nashville: Abingdon Press, 2008), 295 (emphasis in the original).

2. Eschatological Holiness in the Land's New History

2.1. The Sanctifying Presence of God

Ezekiel is famous for his prophecy of the valley of the dry bones, where Israel is given life again and is restored to her land. The prophecy concludes with a promise that God will dwell in the land, in the midst of Israel, and this in turn will effect sanctification of the people. Holiness is then guaranteed:

> They shall dwell *in the land* that I gave to my servant Jacob, where your fathers lived . . . And I will set them *in their land* and multiply them, and will *set my sanctuary* (את־מקדשי ונתתי) *in their midst forevermore. My dwelling place shall be with them*, and I will be their God, and they shall be my people. Then the nations will know that I am the LORD who *sanctifies* Israel (את־ישראל מקדש), *when my sanctuary is in their midst forevermore.* (Ezek 37:25–28)[10]

In Ezekiel's final vision, the theology of the land focuses on the concept of the new Jerusalem with its new temple. The book concludes with a long description of the new and glorious city with its new mega-size temple (Ezek 40–48).[11] There, the restoration of Jerusalem would find its climax

---

9. In the post-exilic eschatological prophecies in the OT, Zion/Jerusalem takes a prominent place, and one can argue that Zion/Temple theology replaces land theology. See Gowan, *Eschatology in the Old Testament*, 9–21; Brueggemann, *The Land*, 131.

10. See also Ezek 36:25 where God promises to cleanse Israel: "I will sprinkle clean water on you, and *you shall be clean from all your uncleannesses*, and from all your idols I will cleanse you."

11. For more on the size and architecture of Ezekiel's Temple, see M. S. Odell, *Ezekiel* (Macon: Smyth & Helwys, 2005), 481–495. It is highly doubtful that Ezekiel was referring to real geographical dimensions, as Curtis observes: "The clear theological significance of Ezekiel's presentation of a restored Israel raises the fact that there are a

in the return of YHWH to dwell *permanently* in his rebuilt temple-city.[12] Ezekiel 43:1–5 is important in this regard:

> Then he led me to the gate, the gate facing east. And behold, *the glory of the God of Israel was coming from the east*. And the sound of his coming was like the sound of many waters, and the earth shone with his glory . . . And I fell on my face. *As the glory of the LORD entered the temple by the gate facing east*, the Spirit lifted me up and brought me into the inner court; and behold, *the glory of the LORD filled the temple*.

The fact that God himself will dwell in the city is a major development, since earlier in the same book God departed from Jerusalem (Ezek 11:23). Tuell believes that something significant is taking place in the theology of Ezekiel: whereas the earthly Zion has ceased to be a place of divine presence, it is the heavenly Zion (the one he visits in his final vision) that is now the place of the divine presence.[13] There is a strong sense of newness. The new city now takes the place of the old and is a permanent dwelling place of God. Interestingly, the only name of "the city" in Ezekiel 40–48 is "The Lord is there" (שמה יהוה) (Ezek 48:35).

The same reality of newness and God's divine presence in Jerusalem is echoed in Zechariah:

> Thus says the Lord: I have returned to Zion and *will dwell in the midst of Jerusalem*, and Jerusalem shall be called *the faithful city*, and the mountain of the Lord of hosts, the *holy mountain*. (Zech 8:3)

God now dwells in Jerusalem, and the city is here called "the faithful city," which shows that a radical transformation has taken place in Jerusalem. It is

---

number of biblical statements and descriptions which purport to be geographical but whose primary purpose is theological." A. Curtis, *Oxford Bible Atlas* (Oxford: Oxford University Press, 2007), 7.

12. Clements, *God and Temple*, 105.
13. Tuell, "The Rivers of Paradise," 188.

also called "the holy mountain." This may explain the use of the term "holy land/ground" in Zechariah 2:12:[14] "And the Lord will inherit Judah as his portion in the 'holy land/ground' (הקדש אדמת)." This is the only time in the Hebrew Bible that the land is called "holy land/ground."[15] Zechariah is speaking about an eschatological reality here.

There is in Haggai also a strong sense of criticism of the old system with its symbols, and, at the same time, there is also a sense of a newness that is about to arrive as a result of God's divine presence. Haggai speaks of how, one day, the Second Temple will be renewed in a way that would exceed the first one in glory and splendor:

> I will fill this house with glory, says the LORD of hosts . . .
> The latter glory of this house shall be greater than the former, says the LORD of hosts. And in this place I will give peace, declares the LORD of hosts. (Hag 2:3, 7–9)[16]

The tension in the history of Israel involving the triangle of holy God, holy people, and holy land is finally resolved in a new reality in which God himself will take the initiative and will intervene in history. In this newness, there is a "supersession of literal, physical geography by 'Sacred Geography.'"[17]

2.2. An Inclusive Zion

There seems to be an inclination in the prophetic literature towards making space for non-Israelites to benefit from the new reality of sacred geography. It is true that Ezekiel's vision in 40–48 focuses entirely on Israel and Jerusalem, and Ezekiel 44:5–9 shows a strongly exclusive mentality towards

---

14. Zech 2:16 in the Hebrew text.
15. "אדמת" is better translated as ground.
16. Haggai's first statement reveals how the return from exile in the sixth century BC was not viewed as the fulfillment of the eschatological prophecies. Not only was the new temple very modest in size (2:3), the overall situation of the post-exilic community was far from the ideals preached by the prophets. The re-emergence of the messianic prophecies in Chronicles also reveals that Israel continued to hope and look forward even after they returned from exile.
17. Gordon, *Holy Land, Holy City*, 66.

non-Israelites: "No foreigner, uncircumcised in heart and flesh, of all the foreigners who are among the people of Israel, shall enter my sanctuary" (44:9). This led Katheryn Darr to argue that Ezekiel's depiction of marvelous future conditions is exclusive of peoples and lands outside the land of Israel, and that the transformation of Israel's barren land and deadly water is not a foretaste of a universal return to Edenic conditions, but a manifestation of blessing poured out upon Israel and her land.[18]

Yet though the text in Ezekiel 40–48 does not say that the transformation goes beyond the land, a universal dimension is evident in the section.[19] This is seen in particular in chapter 47, where sojourners who live among the Israelites will receive an inheritance just like the Israelites (47:22–23) (in an apparent contradiction of 44:5–9). The territory of Israel also seems to expand, as it reaches beyond Jerusalem, all the way to Damascus (47:13–23). In addition, there is in the chapter the mythic use of rivers and waters, which brings to mind images of creation. Ezekiel is called – as in the entire book – "son of Adam" (47:6). The comprehensive language in 47:9 is unmistakable: "every living creature."

In other words, Ezekiel seems to reflect a tension in postexilic Israel as it pertains to attitudes towards foreigners. Ezekiel 44:5–9, in a manner similar to what we find in Ezra-Nehemiah, advocates an exclusive theology, in an attempt to preserve the identity and purity of Israel. Ezekiel 47:20–23, on the other hand, anticipates a time – in the eschaton – in which a transformed and secure Israel will incorporate non-Israelites and allow them to have even an inheritance in the land.

The universal and inclusive nature of the restoration is confirmed when we consider the evidence of other prophetic passages.[20] The book of Isaiah in particular seems to have a strong positive and inclusive attitude towards the nations. The Zion we find there will be inclusive of other ethnicities

---

18. K.P. Darr, "The Wall around Paradise: Ezekielian Ideas about the Future," *Vetus Testamentum*, (1987): 278–279.
19. Tarazi, commenting on the vision of Ezekiel 40–48, observes that the Hebrew term used to describe the land in Ezekiel is אדמה and not ארץ, and believes this is significant, because אדמה is more comprehensive than ארץ. Tarazi, *Land and Covenant,* 165–166.
20. Darr admits that other prophets speak of the universal nature of the restoration, and cites Isa 19:19–22 as an example. However, she refuses to apply this on Ezekiel. Ibid., 274.

and nationalities, and the words of God will guide all the nations (Isa 2:2–3).[21] Holiness now "would extend beyond its normal confines."[22]

One of the clearest statements in Isaiah that shows a remarkably positive attitude towards the nations as it pertains to the temple is found in Isaiah 56. There, Isaiah claims that one day the temple will be a "house of prayer for all peoples." In the new temple, everybody will be equal, reminiscent of the original state of humanity:

> Let not the foreigner who has joined himself to the LORD say, "The LORD will surely separate me from his people" and let not the eunuch say, "Behold, I am a dry tree." For thus says the LORD . . . I will give them an everlasting name that shall not be cut off. And the foreigners who join themselves to the LORD, to minister to him, to love the name of the LORD, and to be his servants . . . these I will bring to my holy mountain, and make them joyful in my house of prayer; their burnt offerings and their sacrifices will be accepted on my altar; *for my house shall be called a house of prayer for all peoples.*" (Isa 56:3–7)

We can also refer here to Joel's prophecy about the day of the Lord. There, the sanctifying of the people will not be limited to just one people, as Joel prophesies:

---

21. The origin and date of Isa 2:2–5 have been the subject of intense debate. The different views are summarized in H. G. M. Williamson, *A Critical and Exegetical Commentary on Isaiah 1-27 (Vol. 1)*, (London: T&T Clark, 2006), 174–178. According to Williamson, the strongest evidence points to a late exilic period as the most likely date for its composition (p. 178). If this is so, then the passage belongs to the more-inclusive post-exilic tradition that we see, for example, in Isa 56:7 and Ezek 47:22. However, the dating or origin of the passage does not affect our interpretation. The fact remains that the Hebrew Scriptures include a strong inclusive and universal vision for the future.

22. Gordon, *Holy Land, Holy City*, 71. Gordon also cites Zech 14:20–21: "And on that day there shall be inscribed on the bells of the horses, 'Holy to the Lord.' And the pots in the house of the Lord shall be as the bowls before the altar. And every pot in Jerusalem and Judah shall be holy to the Lord of hosts, so that all who sacrifice may come and take of them and boil the meat of the sacrifice in them. And there shall no longer be a trader in the house of the Lord of hosts on that day."

> And it shall come to pass afterward, that I will pour out my Spirit on *all flesh* . . . And it shall come to pass that *everyone who calls* on the name of the Lord shall be saved. For *in Mount Zion* and in Jerusalem there shall be those who escape. (Joel 2:28, 32)

Isaiah's remarkable vision of a universal Zion and his statement that the temple will be called a house of prayer for all peoples, Ezekiel's words about the equal status of the sojourners and their sharing of the inheritance, and Joel's prophecy that all flesh will receive the Spirit – all reveal a voice within the OT tradition that hopes for a future in which Jerusalem, the temple, and the land will be inclusive and open to all. There will be no pure and impure. In this sacred geography, all are sanctified.

2.3. The Healing of the Land

The healing of the land is a necessary part of the new order, since the land has already been defiled. This defilement of the land is not merely a metaphorical thing, and the land itself needs redemption.[23] The restoration will therefore include the restoration of the land as a fertile land with Edenic features.[24] Moreover, this renewal or healing of the land would extend so as to be "not only of the land, but of creation itself, to a new heaven and a new earth."[25] Ezekiel describes how the renewal will begin in Jerusalem and in the new temple in particular:

> This water flows toward the eastern region and goes down into the Arabah, and enters the sea; when the water flows into the sea, the water will become fresh. And wherever the river goes, every living creature that swarms will live, and there will be very many fish. For this water goes there, that the waters of the sea may become fresh; so everything will live where the river goes. (Ezek 47:8–9)

---

23. Gen 3:17–18; Isa 24:5–6; Jer 2:7; 16:18; Ezek 5:11.
24. Isa 4:2; Joel 2:23; 3:17–18; Amos 9:13.
25. Dumbrell, *Covenant and Creation*, 184–185. See also Isa 11:6–9, 35:1–10; 65:17–18, 25.

The healing power of the water coming out of the temple is emphasized in that it will even heal the waters of the Dead Sea. The new city-temple is a place that gives life. It is described in Edenic terms. One of the most important aspects of Ezekiel 47:1–12 is that it depicts the new Zion as a new garden of Eden.[26] In this passage we read of a river that flows with healing water, and of different trees – right in the middle of the new sanctuary. All this is a clear sign that what is at issue here is the restoration of Eden.[27] The sanctuary is a place that heals and gives life beyond its confines. The expansion of holiness is an expansion of life and healing.

2.4. Conclusion: An Ideal Zion

The holiness of the land is directly related to the presence of the holy God in the midst of his holy separated people. The triangle of God-Land-People created one of the biggest problems in OT history, exemplified in these two biblical verses:

> Do not make yourselves unclean . . . lest the land vomit you out when you make it unclean, as it vomited out the nation that was before you. (Lev 18:18, 24)

> You are not able to serve the LORD, for he is a holy God. (Josh 24:19)

Israel failed to worship the holy God in a land that demanded holiness, just as Adam and Eve failed by their sin of disobedience in the Eden sanctuary. This tension is finally resolved when God, in a dramatic fashion, takes the initiative and intervenes in history. This is the point towards which OT history is moving. Zion will be the epicenter of the new history, a new garden

---

26. Tuell, "The Rivers of Paradise," 189.
27. The same can be said about the vision of Zech 14 regarding the living water coming out of Jerusalem. The healing of the land is announced in very poetic language: "The whole land shall be turned into a plain from Geba to Rimmon south of Jerusalem. But Jerusalem shall remain aloft on its site from the Gate of Benjamin to the place of the former gate, to the Corner Gate, and from the Tower of Hananel to the king's winepresses. And it shall be inhabited, *for there shall never again be a decree of utter destruction.* Jerusalem shall dwell in security" (Zech 14:10–11).

of Eden. The future Zion will be an inclusive one, and there is thus a hint that "holy land" will become, at a certain point, "holy earth" (Isa 65:17). The Hebrew ארץ means both land and earth, and this linguistic resemblance reminds us of the common theological and teleological foundation for both land and earth.

3. New Covenant in the Land's New History

3.1. The Gift of a New Heart and Guaranteed Obedience

The history of Israel up until the exile can be summed up in the following words of Waltke:

> Israel's history, always torn between what had been projected for Israel's history and what had been realized, provoked an acute tension between the two kinds of unilateral covenants. On the one hand, YHWH's oaths committed him to bless Israel irrevocably. On the other hand, Israel's inability to keep his treaty . . . disqualified the nation from participating in these blessings. Only an elect remnant within the nation kept the treaty. As a result, contrary to YHWH's desires, the nation was cursed, not blessed. A new arrangement had to be sought.[28]

It is to this new arrangement, or new covenant, that the prophets will point, especially after the exile. The tension between God's insistence on moving forward with the story and Israel's failure to be a partner produced an impasse, which only a new initiative from God could resolve. The prophets, therefore, imagined a new history with a new covenant. The most important prophecy in the OT that specifically speaks of a "new covenant" is that of Jeremiah, chapters 30–33. In particular:[29]

---

28. Waltke, The Phenomenon of Conditionality," 136.
29. For more on the interpretation of this passage in modern scholarship, see H. D. Potter, "The New Covenant in Jeremiah XXXI 31–34," *Vetus Testamentum* (1983): 347–357.

> Behold, the days are coming, declares the LORD, when I will make a new covenant with the house of Israel and the house of Judah, not like the covenant that I made with their fathers on the day when I took them by the hand to bring them out of the land of Egypt . . . I will put my law within them, and I will write it on their hearts. And I will be their God, and they shall be my people. And no longer shall each one teach his neighbor and each his brother, saying, "Know the LORD," for they shall all know me, from the least of them to the greatest, declares the LORD. For I will forgive their iniquity, and I will remember their sin no more. (Jer 31:31–34)[30]

God guarantees the obedience of the people of God in the new era, by the giving of the new heart. Since obedience was a condition for lasting presence in the land, this is a significant development. There will be no more calls to repentance. As Brueggemann comments:

> It is no longer thought by Yahweh that obedience will yield a new existence in the land. Thus the motif of repentance is transformed to the gift of new heart and new spirit. Now the possibility of land is exclusively Yahweh's initiative.[31]

The new covenant replaces the old one, because the old one is broken. It simply did not work, and a new arrangement is needed. Jeremiah's vision is thus "either a direct attack on the limitations of the Deuteronomic procedure, or a considerable development from it."[32] In the new covenant, God will take full control – even over the desires and actions of Israel. This time, the law will be written in the hearts of the people, guaranteeing that Israel will fulfill her part.

With covenants, two parties are involved. Yet this time, God will take the roles of both parties. "The new covenant successfully resolves the tension

---

30. See also Jer 32:39; Ezek 11:19; 36:26, which are all in line with the theology of the Deuteronomist who spoke of a circumcised heart (Deut 30:6).
31. Brueggemann, *The Land*, 132.
32. Potter, "New Covenant in Jeremiah XXXI 31-34," 351.

between God's oath and Israel's obligations."[33] This is the most important feature of the new covenant, and the feature that radically distinguishes it from the old one. Now the future of this history rests more totally with YHWH. He takes new responsibility for history.[34]

3.2. The Land in the New Covenant: An Inclusive Inheritance

The land is interestingly absent from the main passage about the new covenant in Jeremiah (Jer 31:31–34). The thrust of the new covenant seems to be the change God is effecting in Israel as his people, and this does not depend on Israel's location. It is the people of Israel that need renewal. This does not mean, however, that Jeremiah does not speak of a future restoration to the land. Like the other prophets, he speaks about God's gathering of Israel from the nations:

> Behold, I will gather them from all the countries to which I drove them in my anger and my wrath and in great indignation. I will bring them back *to this place*, and I will make them dwell in safety... I will make with them an everlasting covenant... and I will plant them in this land in faithfulness (Jer 32:37, 40–41).[35]

Israel will receive the land again, yet it will continue to be a covenanted land. The fact that this was a new and a better covenant does not negate the idea that the land is still covenanted. This time, however, God himself will be the guarantor of the covenant's obligations. The result of writing the law in the people's hearts and of knowing the Lord is the creation of a new community centered on the law – a community that will keep the covenant.

When we consider other prophets, we will see again that the benefits of the new covenant will not be limited to Israel. Isaiah, for example,

---

33. Waltke, "The Phenomenon of Conditionality," 139.
34. Brueggemann, *The Land*, 121.
35. See also for example Isa 11:11–12; Ezek 20:34; 36:24–28; Amos 9:9–14; Zech 10:6.

envisions nations coming to Zion, wishing to learn the ways of the God of Israel and to walk in his paths (2:3). The same book speaks of the "Servant of YHWH" as a witness and a leader for new peoples and nations that did not know him before (55:3–5). Foreigners will no longer be separated from the people of God (56:3), and the eunuchs will keep the Sabbath and the covenant and receive a name better than sons and daughters. They then would come to the house of God, which will be called a "house of prayer for all peoples" (56:3–7).

It was Ezekiel, as we have seen, who produced the most striking statement on this issue. Having already prophesied about the new history, where he spoke about the spiritual restoration of Israel (36:25–26), her reception of new life (37:9–10), and restoration of her land (36:24; 37:25) under the banner of the one shepherd (37:24) in what he called a "covenant of peace" (37:26), he concludes his book with a picture of a new conquest, allotment, and division of the land. What is particularly striking is that, this time, the sojourners will receive an inheritance as well, just like the native-born Israelites (47:21–23).

This inclusive feature of the new covenant appears elsewhere in the OT, and this should not be a cause for astonishment or puzzlement.[36] The circumcision of the heart in the new covenant brings to mind the covenant with Abraham, in which circumcision is the sign of the covenant. In the Abrahamic covenant, it is not only Abraham and Isaac who are circumcised; Ishmael and the "strangers bought with money" are also circumcised (Gen 17:23–27). This can be interpreted as an early anticipation of the inclusive nature of God's covenants.[37]

The promises of restoration included a promise that Israel will be gathered in her land again. God will ensure that Israel keeps the covenant. Once this takes place, the prophets hint that non-Israelites will benefit and participate in this new arrangement, even sharing in the inheritance of the land.

---

36. Tarazi, *Land and Covenant*, 183.

37. Moreover, the first call to Abraham in Gen 12:1–3 reaches its climax in the phrase: "through you all the families of the earth shall be blessed." In Gen 17, in the same passage when God promised the land to Abraham, he changed Abraham's name from Abram to Abraham, because he will make him the "father of a multitude of nations" (Gen 17:5).

3.3. Ideal Covenantal Society

The covenantal obligations, as examined above in chapter 3, were threefold: faithfulness to God, Sabbath and Jubilee, and social justice. For the new covenant to endure, God will guarantee that these obligations are met. First, the gift of the new heart will lead Israel to fear God and never to turn away from him (Jer 32:39–40). They will be cleansed from their idols (Ezek 36:25) and the Lord will be their God (Ezek 36:28).

Second, and with regard to the Sabbath and Jubilee laws, the postexilic tradition reemphasizes the continual relevance of these laws. Ezekiel, for example, spoke regularly about the Sabbath in the new Jerusalem (e.g. Ezek 46:1, 3, 4, 12), while the Chronicler portrayed the seventy years of exile as due to Israel's breaking the Jubilee laws (2 Chr 36:21). More importantly, the eschatological age in Isaiah 61 was defined as a Jubilee year, the year of the Lord's favor:[38]

> The Spirit of the Lord God is upon me, because the LORD has anointed me to bring good news to the poor; he has sent me to bind up the broken hearted, *to proclaim liberty* (דרור) to the captives, and the opening of the prison to those who are bound; *to proclaim the year of the LORD's favor*, and the day of vengeance of our God; to comfort all who mourn. (Isa 61:1–2)

By using the term דרור, which is connected with the Jubilee practice,[39] the prophet reinterprets the Jubilee year eschatologically.[40] The proclamation

---

38. C. R. Bruno, "'Jesus is Our Jubilee' . . . But How? The OT Background and Lukan Fulfillment of the Ethics of the Jubilee," *JETS* 53, no. 1 (2010): 94. For more on the relationship between Isaiah 61 and the Jubilee law, see D. L. Baker, "The Jubilee and the Millennium. Holy Years in the Bible and Their Relevance Today," *Themelios* 24, no. 1 (1998): 44–69; B. C. Gregory, "The Postexilic Exile in Third Isaiah: Isaiah 61:1–3 in Light of Second Temple Hermeneutics," *JBL* 126, no. 3 (2007): 475–496.
39. The term דרור in the sense of liberty is a rare word in the Hebrew Bible, appearing only in Lev 25, Jer 34, Ezek 46, and here in Isa 61 – all passages related to the Jubilee. Gregory, "Postexilic Exile in Third Isaiah," 484.
40. Baker, "The Jubilee and the Millennium," 52.

of דרור for the captives in Isaiah 61 is, like Leviticus 25, "a proclamation of release or liberty for the oppressed members of the covenant community."[41]

The new age, or the new Jubilee, will be an age of restoration and rebuilding not only for the people, but also for the land: "They shall build up the ancient ruins; they shall raise up the former devastations; they shall repair the ruined cities" (Isa 61:4). In addition, one could argue that the paradisiacal "rest" described in Micah 4:4 is reminiscent of the creation "rest" in Genesis: "But they shall sit every man under his vine and under his fig tree, and no one shall make them afraid."

Third, when it comes to social justice, in the new age and under the new covenant justice and equity will be the norm in the land. There will be no more slaves and no more poor and oppressed. It will be an ideal situation (e.g. Isa 32:16–18). Psalm 85, a postexilic psalm, describes life in the land in the era of restoration, and speaks not only of the new nature, but also of the sociological new realities in the land, using idealistic language:

> Surely his salvation is near to those who fear him, that glory may *dwell in our land*. Steadfast love and faithfulness meet; righteousness and peace kiss each other. Faithfulness springs up from *the ground*, and righteousness looks down from the sky. Yes, the LORD will give what is good, *and our land will yield its increase*. Righteousness will go before him and make his footsteps a way. (Ps 85:9–13)

Miller comments on this psalm:

> It is in some sense a picture of the peaceable kingdom, an idyllic description of a place where truth, justice, and prosperity endure . . . The psalm is a powerful description, ultimately eschatological in its force, of a place where God's salvation

---

41. Bruno, "Jesus is Our Jubilee," 93.

is enacted and where all the virtues of love and faithfulness, justice and righteousness are manifest.[42]

In short, under the administration of the new covenant, the land becomes a place where the covenantal obligations are met – resulting in an ideal reality. God alone is worshipped and the whole land rests. Faithfulness, justice, and peace are the marks of this land. This is the point towards which the biblical narrative has been moving all along.

Finally, the result of this new "everlasting covenant" (Isa 61:8) is that the nations of the world will recognize Israel as a nation blessed by God: "Their offspring shall be known *among the nations*, and their descendants in the midst of the peoples; all who see them shall acknowledge them, that they are an offspring the LORD has blessed" (Isa 61:9). This again underlines Israel's mission and calling in relation to the rest of the nations, and shows that keeping the covenant will have influence beyond Israel. Israel's covenantal arrangements in the land serve as a model and a sign to the other nations of the world.

3.4. Conclusion: An Ideal Covenant

The land in the OT is always a covenanted land, and this highlights the ethical and moral responsibility of the inhabitants of the land. Canaan was lost because of disobedience, just as Eden was lost because of disobedience. In exile, the prophets speak of a new vision for a better land. Yet for this to become a reality, God will have to circumcise the hearts of the people, and bring about obedience to the covenant obligations. Only then will hope become reality. The land in the new covenant is marked by worship of God, total obedience, justice, righteousness, and equality for all. The land will not be lost again, because God will guarantee that the requirements of the covenant are met. At least in this regard, the land in the new covenant surpasses Eden.

---

42. P. D. Miller, "The Land in the Psalms," in *The Land of Israel in Bible, History, and Theology: Studies in Honour of Ed Noort,* ed. J. Van Ruiten and J. C. De Vos (Leiden: Brill, 2009), 194.

4. The Royal Vicegerent in the Land's New History

4.1. A Future Davidic Kingship

The third mark of the new history is the establishment of a new ideal Davidic kingdom in the land and the rise of a new vicegerent – the Messiah. The prophets, from all the different periods, spoke of the revival of this kingdom.[43] These messianic prophecies are not only a product of the crisis of faith in Israel that happened after the exile. Some of these prophecies may actually have emerged during the era of the monarchy.[44]

The messianic figure is at the heart of these future prophecies. He is an ideal king, is glorified, and is celebrated and even given divine attributes – in a fashion similar to what we have already seen in the previous chapter about the glorified image of the king in the theology and hymnology of Israel. Yet this time, the prophets are clearly pointing to a future reality that is the result of – and can only be the result of – divine intervention in the course of history.

The future king as vicegerent would bring the dominion of God on earth. He is celebrated and given divine attributes. In Isaiah 9:6 he is called "a mighty God" and is also given "everlasting dominion." In Micah 5:2 he is described as "coming forth from of old, from ancient days." In Jeremiah 23:6 he is called "YHWH is our righteousness." This elevation of the vicegerent is in line with the theology of kingship in Israel, where the king is described for example as sitting at the right hand of God and is addressed as lord (Ps 110:1).

At the same time, this future king remains an Israelite who comes from the line of David. As the story of Israel reached moments of crisis, whether it is the failures of the individual kings or the exile, the prophets of Israel created a sense of hope by reminding the people that God in his faithfulness would not abandon Israel. They did so by creating ideal images of a

---

43. See Isa 11:1; Jer 23:5; Ezek 34:23; Hos 3:5; Amos 9:11.
44. Thompson argues that prophecies in the first part of Isaiah (chs 1–39) were intended as a critique to the monarch when the prophet "was so concerned about the lack of justice and righteousness among his countrymen and on the part of their leaders." M. E. W. Thompson, "Israel's Ideal King," *JSOT* 24 (1982): 86. For more on the rise of the Messianic hope in Israel, see Preuss, *Old Testament Theology*, 34.

future Davidic king, as this was the only possible way of giving hope to Israel in the midst of such crises.

4.2. The Servant of YHWH and the Kingship of YHWH

The messianic figure will be the one who would bring the sovereignty and rule of God in its full realization. As McCartney observes, "the hope of restoration of God's kingship is tied to the restoration of God's vicegerent as king."[45] This can be shown in the prophetic descriptions of the role of the future king. In Micah, for example, the promise that the Lord would reign in Zion (4:7) is followed by the prophecy of the ruler from Bethlehem (5:2). Similarly, the great promise of Isaiah 40–55 is that God will return to Jerusalem as a conquering king:

> How beautiful upon the mountains are the feet of him who brings good news, who publishes peace, who brings good news of happiness, who publishes salvation, who says to Zion, "Your God reigns." (Isa 52:7)[46]

Stuhlmueller argues that in these chapters of Isaiah, the kingship of the Lord summarizes the essentials of Israel's newly created salvation.[47] The kingship of the Lord and the return to the land are connected together in this theology. Selman also observes:

> Yahweh's kingship is demonstrated in historical events, most notably the return from exile. Indeed, in Isaiah 40–55, the cry "Yahweh reigns" sums up the prophetic call for God's people to return to their land, and especially to Zion itself.[48]

---

45. McCartney, "Ecce Homo," 6.
46. See also Isa 40:9–10; 41:21; 43:15; 44:6.
47. C. Stuhlmueller, "Yahweh-King and Deutero-Isaiah," *Chicago Society of Biblical Research* 15 (1970): 34.
48. M. Selman, "The Kingdom of God in the Old Testament," *Tyndale Bulletin* 40, no. 2 (1989): 178.

McCartney argues that the promises of divine kingship in Isaiah 40–55 are closely tied to the ministry of the servant of the Lord figure (יהוה עבד) in these chapters. For him, the servant stands in place of the anointed king prior to the exile.[49] As a result, the return of the Lord as king in Zion (52:7) is bound up with the humiliation and exaltation of his "servant" (52:13).[50]

The identity of the servant of the Lord in Isaiah 40–55 has been a subject of intense debate.[51] Lessing says that the history of interpretation has produced at least four types of suggestion: the servant is an individual, a collective group of people, a mythological/cultic figure, or Isaiah deliberately left the identity of the servant ambiguous.[52] The confusion arises from the fact that the servant is addressed as "Jacob"/"Israel" in 41:8, yet in 49:5–6 he himself is distinguished from "Jacob"/"Israel" because he is the one who restores the fortunes of "Jacob"/"Israel."[53] In 53:4–8 there is also a clear distinction between the servant and Israel. There, the servant suffers

---

49. McCartney, "Ecce Homo," 5.
50. Ibid., 6.
51. The Servant of the Lord appears in what is commonly known as the four Servant Songs: Isa 42:1–4; 49:1–6; 50:4–9; 52:13–53:12. The interpretation of these songs as a distinct special group of texts within Isa 40–55 has been challenge by many scholars. See for example Mettinger, who argues that the Servant of the Lord should be interpreted on the basis of the context provided by Isa 40–55 as a whole, and not simply in the passages where the Servant is mentioned (the Songs). T. N. D. Mettinger, *A Farewell to the Servant Songs: A Critical Examination of an Exegetical Axiom* (Lund: CWK Gleerup, 1983).
52. R. R. Lessing, "Isaiah's Servant in Chapters 40–55. Clearing up the Confusion," *Concordia Journal* (Spring 2011): 130. In addition to these views, Wilshire argues that the Servant is not actually a figure, but the cultic-center and city of Zion-Jerusalem. L. E. Wilshire, "The Servant-City: A New Interpretation of the "Servant of the Lord" in the Servant Songs of Deutero-Isaiah," *JBL* 94, no. 3 (1975): 356–367. Hugenberger, on the other hand, argues that Isaiah was referring to the second Moses, namely to the prophet of Deuteronomy 18. G. P. Hugenberger, "The Servant of the Lord in the 'Servant Songs' of Isaiah: a Second Moses," in *The Lord's Anointed. Interpretation of Old Testament Messianic Texts,* ed. P. E. Satterthwaite, R. S. Hess and G. J. Wenham (Grand Rapids: Baker, 1995), 105–140. For Orlinksy, who challenges to begin with any notion that the term "Servant of the Lord" was employed as a technical term in Isa 40–55, the central personage in all the passages in which the term appears is the prophet himself (Second Isaiah). H. M. Orlinsky, "The So-Called 'Servant of the Lord' and 'Suffering Servant' in Second Isaiah," *Vestus Testamentum Supplements* 14 (1967): 118.
53. Some scholars interpret the Servant to be corporate Israel based on statements in Isa 40–55 that the servant is Israel. See for example Mettinger, *Farewell to the Servant Songs*, 45. For Snaith, the Servant is primarily the "597 exiles, but gradually it tends to widen in conception to include all the Babylonian exiles." N. H. Snaith, "Isaiah 40–66: A Study of the Teaching of the Second Isaiah and its Consequences," *Vestus Testamentum Supplements* 14 (1967): 174.

for the sake of Israel and acts on her behalf (e.g. 53:6). In addition, and as Bruce observes, the afflictions of Israel, according to the prophet, were due to Israel's transgression, whereas the afflictions of the servant, according to the same prophet, were due to the transgression of others.[54]

Yet is the identity of the servant at this stage the important issue? The focus in Isaiah seems to be more on the *role* of the servant than on his identity, or, as Walton puts it, "the imagery of the Servant is more important than the identity of the Servant."[55] Furthermore, we should seek to identify the intentionality behind the double usage of the term "Israel" in these sections. Isaiah could be using the term with a dual sense. This is similar, for example, to the use of the word אדם in Genesis 1 and 2. In one sense, אדם is humanity, in another, אדם is an individual who represents humanity. In Isaiah, an individual Israelite (ישראל) from Israel will redeem corporate Israel (ישראל). In other words, the Israelite of the songs in Isaiah 49–53 represents the corporate Israel of Isaiah 42. But is there such a figure who can represent Israel? And if yes, then who? Bruce argues that there is such a figure, and it can only be *the king*:

> There is one man who could be closely identified with his nation and yet be distinct from it, who by virtue of his special relation to it could bear its sin, even, if necessary, sacrificing his life for it, who could at the same time be taken note of by nations and their rules; that is the king. In ancient societies

---

54. F. F. Bruce, *This is That. The New Testament Development of Some Old Testament Themes* (London: Paternoster, 1968), 88. The concept of suffering on behalf of others in Isa 53:10–12 makes Orlinsky's thesis that the main figure in Isa 53 is the prophet himself (Second Isaiah) doubtful. It is highly unlikely that the prophet would claim about himself that "he bore the sin of many, and makes intercession for the transgressors" (53:12). Furthermore, Orlinsky's argument that the concept of "Vicarious Suffering" is post-biblical in origin, and cannot be found in the Jewish interpretation of Isa 53, is not entirely accurate. For as N. T. Wright has shown, there was in Second Temple Judaism something "which literally dozens of texts attest: a large-scale and widespread belief, to which Isaiah 40–55 made a substantial contribution, that Israel's present state of suffering was somehow held within the ongoing divine purpose." Orlinsky, "The So-Called 'Servant of the Lord'," 118; N. T. Wright, *Jesus and the Victory of God* (Minneapolis: Fortress, 1996), 591.
55. J. H. Walton, "The Imagery of the Substitute King Ritual in Isaiah's Fourth Servant Song," *JBL* 122, no. 4 (2003): 742.

with a sacral kingship this was specially true; the king was not only his people's representative before God and men but was a representative of God to his people – in Israel, Yahweh's anointed one.[56]

Bruce bases his interpretation of the servant in royal terms on a number of factors. He observes that in Isaiah 55:3–5, the one who is portrayed as a "witness to the peoples, a leader and commander for the peoples" (55:4) is the fulfillment of God's "steadfast, sure love for *David*" (55:3), and at the same time "may with high probability be identified with the Servant of the Songs."[57] Moreover, the description of the one who is a shoot from the stump of Jesse in Isaiah 11:1–11 has many similarities with the description of the Servant of the Lord in Isaiah 42:1–4, and one could argue that they are describing the same figure. Both, for example, have the Spirit resting upon them (11:2; 42:1), bring justice (11:4; 42:3), and impact the nations (11:11; 42:1).[58] Bruce also compares Isaiah 61:1–6 with these passages and suggests that it represents the "earliest interpretation of the Servant." Isaiah 61:1–6 speaks of the Spirit of the Lord dwelling upon a figure who will in return bring restoration to Zion, and Bruce suggests that the passage is reading the Davidic Messiah into the Servant of the Lord.[59]

In Isaiah 40–55 the servant is never addressed as king (מלך), because the term king is exclusively reserved for the Lord.[60] This probably explains why

---

56. Bruce, *This is That*, 89.
57. Ibid., 83.
58. Walton and Alexander also speak of similarities between the Servant of the Lord in Isa 40–55 and the Messianic figure of Isa 1–40. Walton, "Eden, Garden of," 742; Alexander, *The Servant King*, 109. Moreover, Rowley observes that the passages dealing with Davidic Messiah in the OT and those treating of the Suffering Servant are "eschatological in their reference, in that they deal with the bringing of the age when God's will should prevail within Israel and beyond." Therefore, there is merit in interpreting the Servant of the Lord in royal terms. H. H. Rowley, *The Servant of the Lord and other Essays on the Old Testament* (Oxford: Basil Blackwell, 1952), 90.
59. Bruce, *This is That*, 90. For more on the Servant of the Lord as a royal representative of Israel, see Walton's article on The Imagery of the Substitute King Ritual in Isaiah's Fourth Servant Song. Walton, "Eden, Garden of."
60. For YHWH as king in Isaiah 40–55, see Stuhlmueller, "Yahweh-King and Deutero-Isaiah."

some scholars hesitate to ascribe royalty to the servant figure.[61] Alexander suggests that Isaiah uses the term "servant" to describe the coming king because he is trying to contrast him with the unfaithful contemporary kings of Israel (in the first part of the book), while at the same time contrasting him with Israel the unfaithful servant (in the second part of the book).[62] In addition, Alexander suggests that it is particularly because the term king (מלך) is exclusive to the Lord in the second part of Isaiah that the servant is not called king; this then serves as an "important reminder of the Davidic king's position in relation to God himself."[63]

The Servant in Isaiah 40–55 is, therefore, an Israelite royal figure who would represent his people and contribute to bringing the rule of YHWH back to Jerusalem. In portraying the servant in such a manner, Isaiah is offering a transformed theology of kingship, portraying the ideal king as a servant who functions as a humble instrument of God's will and plan.[64] In this new vision, the king's path to exaltation (52:13) will be so radically different that it will be hard to comprehend and believe it (Isa 53:1). The king is "despised and rejected by men; a man of sorrows, and acquainted with grief" (Isa 53:3). The path to Jerusalem's glorious future (Isa 54) is through the suffering of this Servant-king (Isa 53). The important new perspective of Isaiah 53 for the theology of the land is that *the land will be restored through the "service" and "suffering" of this Servant-king.*

4.3. Restoration, Justice and Peace in the Land

Whether one agrees with this royal image of the servant or not, it is still the case that the servant, like the messianic figure, is chosen by God for a specific role. He will be instrumental in restoring the fortunes of Israel (Isa 49:5, 8–10). His ministry would bring justice and righteousness to the land, and he would care for the oppressed:

---

61. See, for example Preuss: "The so-called Servant Songs in Deutero-Isaiah are not messianic, for the songs possess their own content and literary form that do not conform to messianic texts." Preuss, *Old Testament Theology, Vol. II*, 50. See also Zimmerli, *Old Testament Theology*, 215–227.
62. Alexander, *The Servant King*, 110–111.
63. Ibid., 111. Alexander also suggests that the Servant is not called king so as to distinguish him from the Persian king Cyrus.
64. Walton, "Eden, Garden of," 742.

> Behold my servant, whom I uphold, my chosen, in whom my soul delights; I have put my Spirit upon him; he will bring forth *justice to the nations*. He will not cry aloud or lift up his voice, or make it heard in the street; *a bruised reed he will not break*, and a faintly burning wick he will not quench; he will faithfully *bring forth justice*. He will not grow faint or be discouraged, *till he has established justice in the earth* (הארץ); and the coastlands wait for his law. (Isa 42:1–4)

As already observed, this is precisely what the first part of the book of Isaiah had said regarding the ministry of the Davidic Messiah. The shoot from the stump of Jesse will judge the poor with righteousness, and decide for the meek of the land/earth with equity (Isa 11:1–4). "*Righteousness* shall be the belt of his waist, and *faithfulness* the belt of his loins" (Isa 11:5). The reign of this new king will be thus characterized by peace and prosperity. One of his names is "prince of peace," because there will be no end of the increase of his government and *of peace*" (Isa 9:6–7). In Isaiah 11, after the stump of Jesse establishes a rule of justice, the result will be universal and cosmic peace:

> The wolf shall dwell with the lamb, and the leopard shall lie down with the young goat, and the calf and the lion and the fattened calf together; and a little child shall lead them. The cow and the bear shall graze; their young shall lie down together; and the lion shall eat straw like the ox. The nursing child shall play over the hole of the cobra, and the weaned child shall put his hand on the adder's den. They shall not hurt or destroy in all my holy mountain; for the earth shall be full of the knowledge of the LORD as the waters cover the sea. (11:6–9)

Such descriptions of the Messiah as an agent of justice in the land and of his kingdom as one of peace and prosperity are not limited to Isaiah. Jeremiah, for example, speaks of a day when David's righteous branch will reign as king and deal wisely, and execute justice and righteousness in the land (Jer 23:5).[65] Zechariah speaks of the coming king of Zion as a king of peace who will end war and speak peace even to the nations (Zech 9:9–10).

Justice and truth thus characterize the ministry of the Messiah. The result of his ministry is that the reign of God in the eschatological era will be a reign of peace. In the eschatological visions of the prophets, all the failures of David, Solomon, and the kings of Israel are redeemed in this ideal figure. The vocation of the vicegerent will be redeemed, and the land, as a result, will enjoy peace and rest.

4.4. A Kingdom of No Limits

The prophets' vision of the future reign of God is universal in its scope. The ministry of the Messiah goes beyond the land in its influence: there is no end to the increase of his governance (Isa 9:7); his ministry has cosmic effects (Isa 11:6–9); he rules from sea to sea, and from the river to the ends of the earth (Zech 9:10); he shall be great to the ends of the earth (Mic 5:2). In addition to having a dominion that extends to the "ends of the earth," the king's dominion will also incorporate the nations of the world:

> The earth shall be full of the knowledge of the LORD *as the waters cover the sea.* In that day the root of Jesse, who shall stand as a *signal for the peoples–of him shall the nations inquire,* and his resting place shall be glorious. (Isa 11:9–10)

Thus, in Isaiah God declares that the Servant of the Lord would be his agent of salvation to the nations of the world.

> It is too light a thing that you should be my servant to raise up the tribes of Jacob and to bring back the preserved of Israel; I will make you as a light for the nations, that my salvation may reach *to the end of the earth.*" (Isa 49:6)[66]

---

65. See also Jer 33:15–16.
66. See also Isa 42:1–2, 55:3–5.

The realization of the reign of God on earth will not happen at once, but instead will be gradual. Isaiah, immediately after the "Suffering Servant" song, calls on Jerusalem to fulfill her destiny:

> *Enlarge the place of your tent*, and let the curtains of your habitations be *stretched out*; do not hold back; lengthen your cords and strengthen your stakes. For you will *spread abroad to the right and to the left*, and your offspring will possess the nations and will people the desolate cities… For your Maker is your husband, the LORD of hosts is his name; and the Holy One of Israel is your Redeemer, the God of the *whole earth* he is called. (Isa 54:2–3, 5)

The biblical hope is of a universal kingdom that implements the reign of YHWH, the creator and king of the earth, through his vicegerent – the Messiah. Yet this hope is also a challenge and a mandate to Israel. These verses in Isaiah contain a challenge for Israel to expand her territory, and this challenge is based on what God is doing in history, and on the fact that he is the God of the whole earth. The eschatological vision of Jerusalem includes its expansion until it embraces the whole earth.

The universality of the reign of God is also advanced in the book of Daniel. Daniel speaks of a kingdom that will never be destroyed, will trump all the other kingdoms of this world, and will also be eternal (Dan 2:44). This kingdom will feature a messianic-type of figure, called the "Son of Man," who has divine attributes. He stands in the court and presence of God, and has authority and power delegated to him (7:13). People from every nation will serve him and he is given an everlasting dominion (7:14). As to the extent of his reign:

> And to him was given dominion and glory and a kingdom, that all peoples, nations, and languages should serve him; his dominion is an everlasting dominion, which shall not pass away, and his kingdom one that shall not be destroyed. (Dan 7:13–14)

In short, the kingdom that the OT prophets point towards has no limits. It extends to the ends of the earth, rules over all the nations, subdues all other kingdoms, and is eternal. This overall universal emphasis reflects the belief that the God of Israel – the creator God – is ultimately the sovereign king over the universe and the God who controls the destiny of all the nations of the earth.[67]

4.5. Conclusion: An Ideal Kingdom

The OT portrays God as intending since the beginning to bring his reign on earth through a selected vicegerent. This was expressed in the successive episodes in the history of Israel, from Adam, through Abraham and Israel, to the monarchy. Adam, Israel and the monarchs all failed to actualize the reign of God on earth and to extend it. This prepared the way for the messianic theology articulated in the prophetic literature. The prophets speak of a future Davidic ideal king, with divine attributes, who will establish a universal kingdom in Jerusalem, a kingdom that will ultimately realize the reign of YHWH over all the earth.

This theology of universal messianic dominion is in line with the theology of Israel that we have already established in the previous chapters. In OT biblical theology God's vicegerent has always had a universal mission, whether he is Adam, Israel, the king, or the future Messiah. It is still a "particular" Israelite mission, yet this particular mission relates directly to the universal. The king of Israel is ultimately the king of the world; the land over which he reigns is the whole earth (Ps 2:8). This is all because YHWH, the God of *Israel*, is himself the sovereign ruler and creator of the *entire earth*. As a result, the future kingdom is described in universal and creational categories – which in biblical theology requires the use of Edenic language. It is an ideal place, the kingdom *par excellence*!

---

67. Isa 6:3; 40:21–26; 54:5; Jer 1:10; 10:12; 23:23–24; 25:15–29.

5. Conclusion

The prophetic vision for the future of Israel is one of restoration. In this new reality, the land will be restored to its original divine intention as a *holy* and *covenanted* land where God reigns supremely through his vicegerent. The imperfections in the realization of these themes in the history of Israel, starting with Adam, are rectified through a divine initiative. Hence the prophets' emphasis that it is God who guarantees this reality: "The zeal of the LORD of hosts will do this" (Isa 9:7).

This eschatology that is developed by the prophets generates hope for Israel. This hope, however, goes far beyond a mere going back to the physical land, the return of a Davidic human king, or the rebuilding of the temple. Instead, it is a hope for a new renewed and glorified reality. God would dwell in the land with his people. Hearts would be changed. Nature would be healed. The king would be just. The temple would be "a house of prayer for all the nations." Zion would be a universal capital. Peace and prosperity would prevail. Strangers would share in the inheritance. The borders of the land would disappear and the land would expand. In short, the land would become an ideal expression of God's original intent for humanity – in other words, a new garden of Eden.

CHAPTER 6

The Theology of the Land in the Old Testament

Introduction

The first part of this chapter, which concludes the OT part of this dissertation, argues that the OT repeatedly portrays the Promised Land as Eden restored. This is done through numerous literary and thematic means, and has very important theological ramifications for the theology of the land – especially as it relates to the theology of creation and God's ultimate plan for the universe. The second part of the chapter looks at the role the land plays in the overall biblical narrative and in the resultant biblical theology of the OT. Some final conclusions about the theology of the land in the OT will be presented at the end.

1. The Land as Eden Regained

We have argued in chapter 1 that the Eden narrative in its final canonical form is edited or retold so as to re-enact the story of Israel from creation to exile. It is a retelling of the story of Israel in universal terms, with the intention of highlighting Israel's universal vocation. We will next see that the land in biblical narrative was often idealized and described in a language that portrays a supreme state of perfection; so it could be argued that the image in mind is that of Eden regained. The idea of Eden, however, was not created after the exile. This may seem like a circular argument, but it is perfectly possible that an essential idea of Eden went way back into Israel's history and was not suddenly created *de novo* after the exile. To argue that Genesis 2–3 in its final form is a late text is not to argue that Israel in its early stages did not know of such a tradition. There seems to be an image, as we will now see, in the consciousness of Israel of an ideal place, which is behind her yearning for rootedness, and behind the portraying of the Promised Land in Edenic language.

1.1. Canaan and Eden Parallelism

There are striking similarities between the narrative of Israel in the land and the narrative of Adam in Eden, as discussed in detail in chapter 1. The subsequent study of the land in the OT has revealed more details about the similarities between the land and Eden. We can briefly summarize these similarities as follows:[1]

- The land, like Eden, is a distinct place that has a special role in God's plan.
- The land, like Eden, is described as a holy sanctuary and the place of the dwelling presence of God.
- The land, like Eden, demands holiness as a condition for those who live in it.
- The land, like Eden, is defiled and cursed as a result of ungodliness.
- The land, like Eden, is under treaty. The punishment for breaking this treaty is forfeiting the right to live in the land, and exile.
- The land, like Eden, is the sphere of the reign of God; this reign is supposed to extend until it ultimately reaches the ends of the earth.

---

1. Scholars who have observed some parallelism between Adam in Eden and Israel in the land include Dumbrell, *Covenant and Creation*; M. Ottosson, "Eden and the Land of Promise," in *Congress Volume, Jerusalem 1986*, ed. J. A. Emerton (Leiden: Brill, 1986), 177–188; W. Berg, "Israel's Land, der Garten Gottes. Der Garten als Bild des Heiles im Alten Testament," *Biblische Zeitschrift* 32 (1988): 35–51; L. E. Cooper, *Vol. 17: Ezekiel*. The New American Commentary (Nashville: Broadman & Holman Publishers, 1994); Kline, *Kingdom Prologue*; Marchadour and Neuhaus, *The Land, the Bible, and History*; Enns, *The Evolution of Adam*; S. D. Postell, *Adam as Israel: Genesis 1-3 as the Introduction to the Torah and Tanakh* (Eugene: Pickwick Publications, 2011).

- The land, like Eden, is supposed to be the setting for an ideal society and for authentic humanity.

In addition, the following parallels between Israel and Adam have been suggested in this study:
- Israel, like Adam, is supposed to multiply and fill the earth.
- Israel, like Adam, is endowed with a royal and priestly vocation.
- Israel, like Adam, plays the role of a vicegerent: representing God on earth, and representing humanity in the presence of God.
- Israel, like Adam, has a universal mission.
- Israel, like Adam, loses the right to the land, and her priestly and royal vocation, due to disobedience.
- Israel, like Adam, loses her capacity to be a blessing to the nations.

The similarities between the narratives of Israel and Eden do suggest that the OT portrays the land as Eden regained. In other words, Israel in the land is the first step towards the restoration of Eden.

1.2. Edenic Descriptions of Canaan

The Promised Land, Canaan, is often described in the OT using Edenic language. The journey from Egypt into Canaan is described as entering a blissful place with water and fertile gardens:[2]

> If you walk in my statutes and observe my commandments and do them, then I will give you your rains in their season, and *the land shall yield its increase,* and *the trees of the field shall yield their fruit.* Your threshing shall last to the time of the grape harvest, and the grape harvest shall last to the time for sowing. And you shall eat your bread to the full and dwell in your land securely. *I will give peace in the land,* and you shall lie down, and none shall make you afraid. And I will

---

2. For the description of the land in the OT as a garden, see Berg, "Israel's Land, der Garten Gottes." Von Rad believes that these almost paradise-like descriptions "would surely seem to have been composed under the influence of Canaanite nature-religion." Von Rad, "The Promised Land," 89.

> remove harmful beasts from the land, and the sword shall not go through your land. (Lev 26:3–6)

> For the LORD your God is bringing you into a *good* land, a land of *brooks of water*, of fountains and springs, flowing out in the valleys and hills, a land of wheat and barley, of vines and fig trees and pomegranates, a land of olive trees and honey, a land in which you will eat bread without scarcity, in which *you will lack nothing*, a land whose stones are iron, and out of whose hills you can dig copper. (Deut 8:7–9)[3]

> I gave you a land on which you had not labored and cities that you had not built, and you dwell in them. You eat the fruit of vineyards and olive orchards that you did not plant. (Josh 24:13)

> And I brought you into a *plentiful land* to enjoy its fruits and its good things. (Jer 2:7)

It is hard to read such passages without connecting this idealistic image with the garden of Eden, which crowns the good creation, has rivers and trees, and is a place in which mankind lacks nothing. "One can hardly escape the impression that what is being depicted through such references is Eden recaptured, paradise recovered."[4]

We can find many allusions to Genesis 1–3 in the descriptions of the land in the OT. The land is described as *an exceedingly good land* (Num 14:7–8), which suggests a reference to the goodness of the creation in Genesis 1. Leviticus 26:12 says that God will "walk among" the Israelites in the land, using the same verb form (יתהלך) which echoes the "walk" of God with Adam and Eve in Eden in Genesis 3:8.[5] Similarly, the phrase "land flowing with milk and honey," which was used to describe the new

---
3. See also Deut 3:20; 6:10–11; 12:10–11; 28:3–6; 33:28.
4. Dumbrell, *Covenant and Creation*, 120. See also Marchadour and Neuhaus, *The Land, the Bible, and History*, 28.
5. Wright, *Old Testament Ethics*, 185.

land of Israel,[6] evokes images of blissfulness and fertility. In a sense, the milk and honey stand in sharp contrast to the thorns and thistles of the cursed ground (Gen 3:18), and, as Anderson observes, according to the ancient view, milk and honey in abundance were blessings of paradise. To wanderers who were used to life in the barren wilderness, Canaan was a veritable paradise.[7]

The exodus out of Egypt and into the Promised Land has parallels with the creation narrative in Genesis,[8] where God made the universe out of formless waste:[9]

> God's acts of redemption for the people – their deliverance from the control of the Egyptians, the guidance to the promised land, and establishment there – typically viewed as "historical" acts, are presented according to the paradigm of creation. These events are given cosmological significance. Israel's redemption is part of God's new act of creation.[10]

---

6. Exod 3:8, 17; 13:5; 33:3; Lev 20:24; Num 13:27; 14:8; 16:13, 14; Deut 6:3; 11:9; 26:9, 15; 27:3; 31:20; Josh 5:6; Jer 11:5; 32:22; Ezek 20:6, 15.

7. B. W. Anderson, *The Living World of the Old Testament* (Harlow: Longman), 111. Levine, on the other hand, disagrees with the notion that milk and honey refer to the fertility of the land. Rather, it is a meliorative expression signifying uncultivated land. He argues that such topography is well suited for pasturing, but not for agriculture. The description is supposed to convey that Israel depends for its survival on obedience to God, for the land needs rain for vegetation. E. Levine, "The Land of Milk and Honey," *Journal for the Study of the Old Testament* 25, no. 87 (2000): 43–57. Levine is correct in observing that land in reality lacked fertility and depended on rain. Yet these descriptions of the land must be viewed as statements of faith, as will be argued below. The verse in Num 14:7–8 clearly and directly makes the connection that because it is an exceedingly good land it flows with milk and honey. For more on this phrase and its relationship to the religions of the ANE, see P. D. Stern, "The Origin and Significance of 'The Land Flowing with Milk and Honey'," *Vetus Testamentum* 42, no. 4 (1992): 554–557.

8. Wright, *Old Testament Ethics*, 139; Enns also argues that the in the OT creation and redemption are not two separate acts. Enns, *The Evolution of Adam*, 65.

9. For the translation of תהו and בהו in Gen 1:2 and the rest of the OT, see T. D. Tsumura, "The Doctrine of Creation ex nihilo and the Translation of *tōhû wābōhû*," in *Pentateuchal Traditions in the Late Second Temple Period. Proceedings of the International Workshop in Tokyo, August 28-31, 2007.* (Supplements to the Journal for the Study of Judaism 158), (Leiden: Brill, 2012), 3–22.

10. R. Simkins, *Creator & Creation: Nature in the Worldview of Ancient Israel* (Peabody: Hendrickson Publishers, 1994), 111.

Israel's desert experience is linked with the "howling waste of the wilderness" (Deut 32:10), using the term תהו which describes the state of the earth before creation.[11] Israel's experience is one of coming out of "formless waste" (Gen 1:2) into the "goodness" of creation (Gen 1:31). The land was naturally described as a good land (הארץ טובה),[12] echoing the description of the creation, and implying restoration to the original state. In addition, arrival at the land was described as "arrival at a Sabbath-rest,"[13] evoking the Sabbath-rest of creation:[14]

> *And the LORD gave them rest* on every side just as he had sworn to their fathers. Not one of all their enemies had withstood them, for the LORD had given all their enemies into their hands. (Josh 21:44)[15]

Moreover, Solomon's reign in its idealized state is presented as a period of paradisial rest (1 Kgs 4:25; 8:56). Von Rad, however, thinks that we should see the rest here in its historical context as referring to the peace granted to a nation plagued by enemies and weary wandering.[16] He also argues that it has nothing in common with the "rest" mentioned in the creation narrative in Genesis 2.[17] Von Rad is correct in stressing the original historical context and the rest Israel enjoyed from her enemies (e.g. Josh 21:44b). Yet we cannot but observe that in addition to the thematic similarities between the two episodes, the verb נוח in the *Hiphil*, used in Joshua 21:44a (also Deut 3:20), is the same one used about God "placing" Adam in Eden. Moreover, the Psalms speak of the land as God's resting place,

---

11. Marchadour and Neuhaus, *The Land, the Bible, and History*, 28.
12. See also Exod 3:8; Deut 1:25, 35; 3:25; 4:21; 6:18; 8:7, 10; 9:6; 11:17; 28:12; Josh 23:15–16; Judg 18:9; 1 Kgs 14:15.
13. Kline, *Kingdom Prologue*, 338.
14. Dumbrell, *Covenant and Creation*, 122.
15. See also Deut 3:20; 12:9; 25:19; 28:65; 1 Kgs 8:56.
16. G. Von Rad, "There Remains Still a Rest for the People of God: An Investigation of a Biblical Conception," in *The Problem of the Hexateuch and Other Essays*, ed. G. Von Rad (Edinburgh and London: Oliver & Boyd, 1966), 95.
17. Ibid., 101.

which evokes the image of God resting after creation (Gen 2:2).[18] Psalm 95:11 speaks of the land as God's resting place, and Psalm 132 celebrates Zion as the place of God's rest (Ps 132:13–14).

Some of the Eden-like descriptions should not be understood in a literal fashion. The geographical reality of Canaan differs considerably from these descriptions.[19] In fact:

> Other lands might well have served as better places for God to forge a people: places where rainfall was more abundant, where wars were less frequent, where crops grew richly and wildlife could be easily found.[20]

In reality, Egypt and Mesopotamia were more fertile lands than Canaan, mainly because of the big rivers in these areas. Canaan depended completely on rainwater (Deut 11:10–12), and when rain was scarce, it was hard to find food in Canaan (Ruth 1:1). There is clearly a measure of exaggeration in these Eden-like descriptions of Canaan. The land is "is extravagantly idealized."[21] As Zimmerli observes:

> If you have had the opportunity to compare with your own eyes the actual possibilities offered by the fertile valley of the Nile with those offered by the sterile mountain landscape of Palestine, you will see at once how much this land, the pledge of divine favor, is here viewed in the light of a faith in divine splendor and a glory that far transcends reality.[22]

---

18. Gen 2:2 speaks of God "resting" after creating the world, using the word שבת. Despite that, the author of the New Testament book of Hebrews (which has a strong Jewish flavour) finds it acceptable to link the rest in Gen 2:2 with that of Israel in the land (Heb 4:1–5). See R. C. Gleason, "The Old Testament Background of Rest in Hebrews 3: 7–4: 11," *Bibliotheca Sacra* 157 (2000): 281–303; H. W. Attridge, "'Let Us Strive to Enter That Rest': the Logic of Hebrews 4: 1–11," *The Harvard Theological Review* (1980): 279–288.
19. See Levine, "The Land of Milk and Honey."
20. Burge, *The Bible and the Land*, 25.
21. Dumbrell, *Covenant and Creation*, 120.
22. Zimmerli, *Old Testament Theology*, 65.

For Von Waldow, these descriptions expressed the *gratitude* of Israel towards God for the gift of land:

> In such language, the land of Israel becomes almost a kind of paradise. It did not bother the Israelites that the reality fell considerably short of that. Canaan appeared to them a paradise not because of its character as a land but because it was a gift of Yahweh. For that the Israelites expressed their gratitude by exuberantly praising the land.[23]

Yet there is probably more than simple gratitude for a gift in these descriptions. Instead, these are theological expressions of faith and hope. For, as Curtis reminds us, "there are a number of biblical statements and descriptions which purport to be geographical but whose primary purpose is theological."[24] We can then understand these descriptions in a theological and symbolical manner, and as faith expressions. Ottosson is correct in saying that the traditions of the OT used the conception of Eden *metaphorically, symbolically, and geographically* to describe the land.[25] It is not strange for the OT to use geography to communicate theology. The description of Zion in Psalm 46:4, where "there is a river whose streams make glad the city of God," is a clear example of this phenomenon. This river in Zion, accompanied with the statement in the same verse that Zion is the holy habitation of God, makes the parallels between Zion and Eden more evident.[26]

In short, Israel celebrates the gift of land by painting glorious images of this gift. The canonical descriptions of Canaan resemble a land that is more like a garden-land. It is a place of fertility and blessing. It is Eden in a sense restored. In the words of the Hebrew poet:

> How lovely are your tents, O Jacob, your encampments, O Israel! Like palm groves that stretch afar, like *gardens beside a*

---

23. Von Waldow, "Israel and Her Land," 499.
24. Curtis, *Oxford Bible Atlas*, 7.
25. Ottosson, "Eden and the Land of Promise," 177.
26. Gordon, *Holy Land, Holy City*, 70.

river, like aloes that the LORD has planted, like cedar trees beside the waters. Water shall flow from his buckets, and his seed shall be in many waters. (Num 24:5–7)

1.3. The Restoration as Eden Regained

The restoration of Israel from exile is described by the prophets in poetic language, as a return to Eden:

> For the LORD comforts Zion; he comforts all her waste places and makes her wilderness *like Eden*, her desert like *the garden of the LORD*; joy and gladness will be found in her, thanksgiving and the voice of song. (Isa 51:3)

> Thus says the Lord God: On the day that I cleanse you from all your iniquities, I will cause the cities to be inhabited, and the *waste places* shall be rebuilt. And *the land that was desolate* shall be tilled, instead of being the desolation that it was in the sight of all who passed by. And they will say, This land that was desolate has become *like the garden of Eden*, and the waste and desolate and ruined cities are now fortified and inhabited. (Ezek 36:33–35)

Isaiah and Ezekiel are speaking of the day in which Zion would be comforted, referring to the end of exile. Both of them use the word Eden to describe the restoration. The restoration of the land is presented as a return to Eden. The use of creational language in these prophecies is deliberate. Just like creation out of formless waste (Gen 1:2), the waste places, the wilderness, and the desert will turn into Eden, the garden of God.[27]

Ezekiel's vision of the new history as Eden restored is confirmed in his final vision of Jerusalem (40–48), and in particular of the temple (47:1–12).

---

27. Brueggemann, in fact, believes that the use of the chaos language in Gen 1:2 deliberately reflects the situation in exile: "While chaos is a term that may refer in an ontological sense to formlessness, here [Gen 1:2] it describes the historical formlessness of exile. The text contrasts Israel's land of future, characterized by all Yahweh's blessings, with the land of the present, described as formless and void, dark, surely the experience of the faithful in Babylon."Brueggemann, *The Land*, 135.

One of the most important aspects of Ezekiel's vision is that it depicts the new Zion as a new garden of Eden. In Ezekiel 47:1–12 we read of a river that flows with healing water (v. 8), and of a variety of trees – located right in the middle of the new sanctuary (v. 7). As in the entire book, Ezekiel is addressed as "son of Adam" (v. 6), a title which imbues a creational atmosphere to the book in general, and to this passage in particular. Tuell suggests that these verses should not be taken literally about real streams in Jerusalem. Instead, he suggests:

> As the connections between Ezekiel 47:1–12 and Genesis 2:10–14 reveal, Ezekiel understood the symbol of Zion in a new way . . . For Ezekiel, the earthly Zion, with its city and temple, was a bitter disappointment. It was the mythic, heavenly reality – Zion as YHWH's home and, specifically, *Zion as Eden – that proved a more worthy ground for hope.*[28]

In addition to these references, which portray the restoration to the land as a return to an Edenic state of affairs, other prophetic passages describe the reality in the new history in idealistic Edenic language. Zechariah echoes Ezekiel's vision of water coming out of the temple (Zech 14:8). Micah describes the restoration as a place of peace and rest, in which people sit under vine and fig trees, evoking Edenic images (Mic 4:4). Amos 9:14 describes the restoration of the tent of David using Edenic language:

> I will restore the fortunes of my people Israel, and they shall rebuild the ruined cities and inhabit them; they shall plant vineyards and drink their wine, and they shall make gardens and eat their fruit.

So does Joel 3:18:

> And in that day the mountains shall drip sweet wine, and the hills shall flow with milk, and all the streambeds of Judah shall

---

28. S. Tuell, "The Rivers of Paradise," 189 (emphasis added).

flow with water; and a fountain shall come forth from the house of the LORD and water the Valley of Shittim.

So how are we to understand these statements that mention Eden (Isa 51:3; Ezek 36:33–35), or the ones that elude to it (Ezek 47:1–12; Amos 9:14; Joel 3:18)? Surely not literally, since it is highly unlikely that the prophets were envisioning a literal return to a particular place called Eden. The prophets were envisioning a new reality that transcends description. They used metaphors that were known to their audiences in description of this new reality. The language of Eden, with all that was associated with it, was chosen as the ideal and only fitting language. Eden, as a place and as a language, evokes memories of ultimate perfection, joy, peace and harmony.

In addition, and as Chris Wright explains:

> As Israel's eschatology sought to express its conception of God's *ultimate* purposes, it found its most helpful resource in God's *original* purposes; namely, a good and perfect earth available for human enjoyment and blessing.[29]

In other words, there seems to be a link in OT theology between the origins and the culmination of the creation. The OT prophets anchored their eschatological visions in the concept of an ideal original *place* and the good creation of God. Israel's way of imagining the future is directly tied to her understanding of her origins. The past, just like the present, is thus a source of hope for Israel. Israel's hope for the future is, in a sense, a return to her past – only this time it is a past that has been transformed by God's new action along the timeline of history.

1.4. The Eschatological Restoration as a New Creation

In Ezekiel's prophecy of the valley of the dry bones (Ezek 37), the prophet uses the image of God's original creation to describe the resurrection of Israel from the dead. The Spirit gives life to Israel, just as he gave life to Adam the first man:

---

29. Wright, *Old Testament Ethics*, 138 (emphasis in the original).

> Then the LORD God formed the man of dust from the ground and breathed into his nostrils the breath of life, and the man became a living creature. (Gen 2:7)

> Thus says the Lord God to these bones: Behold, I will cause breath to enter you, and you shall live. (Ezek 37:5)

The vision speaks of the transformation of death into life – all in connection with the restoration to the land, which has just been described as a new garden of Eden (Ezek 36:35). Ezekiel 37 is thus a re-creation of the creation narrative, with the regenerated Israel as the new Adam, and the land as the new garden of Eden. In addition, the curse of death in Eden is reversed here into the gift of life.

If the land is the new garden of Eden, this would demand that there be a new heaven and new earth, in order to parallel the creation narrative. It is no surprise therefore that the transformation of the land will ultimately be a transformation of the whole earth, as Isaiah describes it:

> For behold, *I create new heavens and a new earth*, and the former things shall not be remembered or come into mind . . . For behold, I create Jerusalem to be a joy, and her people to be a gladness. I will rejoice in Jerusalem and be glad in my people; no more shall be heard in it the sound of weeping and the cry of distress . . . They shall build houses and inhabit them; they shall plant vineyards and eat their fruit . . . My chosen shall long enjoy the work of their hands. They shall not labor in vain or bear children for calamity . . . The wolf and the lamb shall graze together; the lion shall eat straw like the ox, and dust shall be the serpent's food. They shall not hurt or destroy *in all my holy mountain*. (Isa 65:17–25)

There are numerous symbols in this poem that come directly from the first three chapters of Genesis. In addition to the theme of creation, this passage reflects the Edenic state of affairs before the fall and the restoration of many of the things that went wrong as a result of the fall. Interestingly, the serpent's punishment of eating dust from Genesis 3:14 is upheld, which confirms the link between this passage in Isaiah and the first three chapters of Genesis. The vision of Isaiah thus comes across as a reversal of the Adamic curse. It is worth recalling the effects of the sin of Adam, God's first vicegerent: the ground is cursed, pain, thorns and thistles, sweat, and death (Gen 3:17–19). Just as Adam's transgression had cosmic effects, so the restoration of Israel will have cosmic effects. The whole of creation will be renewed and restored. As Marchadour and Neuhaus conclude:

> The Land will be restored in an outpouring of grace. But which Land? And under what circumstances? The dynamics involved in the gift, its loss and its return, ultimately concern not just Israel but all of humanity, of which Israel is the representative. The Land of Israel typifies the entire face of the earth. Restoration of the Land signifies the restoration of all creation and the eradication of the traces of sin.[30]

In Isaiah 65, the creation of a new Jerusalem is equated with the creation of new heavens and a new earth. The prophet is not speaking here of two separate themes. The land and creation are inseparably intertwined. The restoration of Jerusalem brings the restoration of the whole world. God's holy mountain will be the center of the new creation. Only a renewed Jerusalem can function as a center of blessing to the rest of the world (Isa 2:2–4).

The renewal of creation highlights God's commitment to it. This commitment is apparent in the OT in the goodness of the creation to begin with (Gen 1:31), and in the covenant God made with the creation in the Noah narrative (Gen 9:8–17). It is quite possible that Ezekiel had the covenant of Noah in mind when he spoke of a "covenant of peace" in the eschatological era (34:25; 37:26). If so, then once again the renewal of Israel and that of creation are being linked.

In the new history, the renewed land as Eden restored will recapture its role as a center of blessing for the good creation. Only then can we speak of new heavens and a new earth. The state of affairs according to the prophetic

---

30. Marchadour and Neuhaus, *The Land, the Bible, and History*, 62.

vision will be translated into cosmic peace and universal prosperity. This is a vision of a new humanity in a perfect world.

2. The Land and Old Testament Biblical Theology

2.1. The Land in the Biblical Narrative

The study of the theology of the land, we therefore contend, should have its starting point in the theology of creation and the garden of Eden narrative. It will be hard to understand the role the land plays, both within OT biblical theology and within the story of Israel, if we fail to appreciate the relationship between the land and the garden of Eden.[31] Starting in the garden of Eden ensures that due explanation is given to the universality of Israel's mission, and the global dimension of the theology of the land. In addition, it helps interpreters to underscore the ethical and moral responsibility that is attached to God's gift of land, and to comprehend the scope of Israel's covenantal obligations and the consequences of breaking this covenant.

The election of Abraham and the assignment of land to his seed occur in a context of restoring humanity back to Eden.[32] As Hamilton observes:

> The blessing of Abraham promised seed, land, and blessing. The promise of seed overcomes the cursed difficulty of childbearing and the loss of harmony between the man and the woman. The promise of land hints at a place where God will once again dwell with his people. The promise of blessing heralds the triumph of the seed of the woman over the seed of the serpent.[33]

Consonantly with the pattern in Eden, God created Israel outside of the land, and brought her into the land, and gave her a task. Abraham's call is simultaneously not merely a response to Eden, but also a response to the

---

31. Robertson, *The Israel of God*, 4.
32. Munayer, "From Land of Strife to Land of Reconciliation," 250.
33. J. Hamilton, "The Seed of the Woman and The Blessings of Abraham," *Tyndale Bulletin* 58, no. 2 (2007): 272.

entire primeval biblical history.[34] Genesis 4–11 describes a world that has gone wrong and is in need of redemption. In this context, the land promise can be viewed as a response to the scattering of the nations in Genesis 11. God now takes the initiative (compare Gen 11:4 with 12:1a) to bring together all the scattered families of the earth under the banner of one family, and so "with the promise of a homeland for Abraham's descendants, the centrifugal direction of human homelessness is checked, and a geophysical center for human blessing offered."[35]

Looking at the land from this perspective, we can conclude that *the land promise is not an end in itself, but rather the first step of an answer to a universal and human problem.* Israel is not promised and given the land for her sake or for the sake of receiving a land. Israel is chosen and given a land so that she becomes "the vehicle by which the blessing of redemption would eventually embrace the rest of humanity."[36] Through Abraham and the newly established community, and from this newly Promised Land, the families of the earth are to be blessed, and Abraham will eventually become the "father of many nations." As a successor to Adam, Abraham is chosen to take on the role of *representative humanity.*[37] Thus, within biblical theology, God's solution for the scattering of humanity and everything that went wrong in Genesis 3–11 comes in progressive stages through a person chosen by God and through this person's seed (echoing Gen 3:15).

Israel, as Abraham's seed, is called to be a "kingdom of priests" and a "light to the nations," and her king is entrusted with a universal mission. Israel is therefore a second Adam raised by God,[38] with both Israel and her

---

34. Brueggemann, *The Land*, 19. Estes explains: "The land promise in 12:7 is a reversal of the pattern of expulsion that dominates Genesis 3–11. Dispersion or homelessness is manifested in Adam and Eve's removal from Eden (3:23–24), the curse on Cain (4:16), and the scattering of Babel (11:8), but it is strikingly reversed in the divine call of Abram . . .Though Eden could not be regained by human means, divine grace to Abram gives the prospect of the restoration of the land, fertility, and blessing lost by the human parents." D. J. Estes, "Looking for Abraham's City," *Bibliotheca Sacra* 147, no. 588 (1990): 409.
35. Cohn, "From Homeland to the Holy Land," 6.
36. Wright, *Old Testament Ethics*, 49.
37. I am indebted in using this term to my professor at Westminster Theological Seminary, Douglas Green.
38. Beale, "Eden," 12.

king being called the "son of God," in a way which echoes the role of Adam as God's son.

We should also notice the pattern that is echoed in OT biblical theology – that of a blessed humanity filling the earth. According to the biblical canon, God's first communication with humanity included a blessing followed by a commandment: "And God blessed them. And God said to them, 'Be fruitful and multiply and fill the earth (הארץ) and subdue it, and have dominion . . .'" (Gen 1:28).

The same calling is repeated to Noah in the fresh start granted to humanity (Gen 9:1–7). This calling is precisely what is echoed in God's calling of Abraham[39] – something which we might fail to see if we start the biblical theology of the land in Genesis 12. To be sure, Israel may have started in Genesis 12, but she remains only one ingredient of the Bible's overarching story. The biblical story starts before Israel, and will go on after and beyond Israel. The driving force in biblical theology is God's original intention to bless all humanity, and his delegating to a representative human, in the first instance, the responsibility of extending his cosmic rule.

God's original purposes are naturally his ultimate purposes. Therefore, Israel's eschatology, as seen in later parts of the OT, inevitably reflects God's desire to bless all humanity, and to redeem not just the land of Israel, but all creation as well. Old Testament prophecies concerning the future of Israel and her land are thus bound up with the future of the nations and the world. *The biblical hope for the redemption of Israel and her land is ultimately a biblical hope for the redemption of the world and its nations.*

All of this then pushes us to the conclusion that the theology of the land, following the pattern of Eden, is not about a small piece of real estate in the ANE or about the small ethnic group that inherited it. The land is part of a larger scheme that is about redeeming and restoring the whole of creation. The restoration of the whole earth starts with one particular land and one family. The particularity of Israel is not a hindrance to the universal mission, but rather the necessary and divinely ordained means towards fulfilling it. This movement from the particular to the universal is integral to the biblical pattern of redemption.

---

39. Ibid., 13.

2.2. The Land as a Prototype for Eschatological Cosmic Restoration

Land as הארץ is strongly linked with the creation and earth as הארץ. The purpose and destiny of the land and that of the earth are inseparable. The land in this capacity functions as a prototype, pointing forward to the eschatological destiny of the earth. The restoration of the land as a new garden of Eden and a place of an ideal society is the "first fruits" of the restoration of the earth. What God will do to Israel, he will do to the nations. Similarly, what God will do to the land, he will do to the earth. God's commitment to the land is a guarantee that he will renew the earth. We have seen this theme repeatedly in the prophetic literature, which proclaims that the restoration of Israel culminates in the creation of new heavens and a new earth (Isa 65).

The theology of the land, therefore, reminds us of the goodness of the creation, and as God's good creation, the land/earth/הארץ will be redeemed. God will not just abandon his creation, but will redeem it. The land functions as a prototype of the redeemed earth.[40] The land in the biblical history of Israel points forward to a better reality – a reality that can only be described by going back to the original intention of the good creation. The biblical hope is creation redeemed.

2.3. The Land as a Paradigm for Other Societies

Israel was supposed to be an ideal community in the midst of the nations (Exod 19:5). As such, the regulations and laws about the land in Israelite society can be viewed as a model for the ideal in ancient times. Chris Wright calls this "a *paradigmatic* understanding" of the relevance of OT Israel to other nations in other lands.[41] Wright's book *Old Testament Ethics for the People of God* explores some of the land laws in the OT in detail, and their relevance for today's world. He argues:

---

40. Wright, *Old Testament Ethics*, 185.
41. C. Wright, *Old Testament Ethics*, 183. See also C. J. H. Wright, "Biblical Reflections on Land," *Evangelical Review of Theology* 17 (1993): 161.

> Many of the Old Testament laws and institutions of land use indicate an overriding concern to preserve this comparative equality of families on the land. So the economic system also was geared institutionally and in principle towards the preservation of a broadly based equality and self-sufficiency of families on the land, and to the protection of the weakest, the poorest and the threatened – and not to interests of wealthy, landowning elite minority.[42]

Wright also emphasizes that it was Israel as a *society* that functioned as a paradigm or a model for the world, and he calls this "the social dimension of redemption."[43] Collectively, Israel "constituted a concrete model, a practical, culturally specific, experimental exemplar of the beliefs and values they embodied."[44] The role of the land in the theology of Israel emphasizes this social dimension of Israel's calling and mission. The OT is not mainly about redeeming individuals, but about redeeming societies. It is concerned with life on earth and with organizing and structuring it in a manner that is pleasing to God the creator.

2.4. Conclusion: From Land to Earth

The land is an important theme in OT biblical theology. Israel in her land is the *means, prototype* and *paradigm* for the redemption of other nations in their lands and ultimately the earth. The land was part of a plot that ultimately concerned the restoration of all creation. The restoration of the land is linked with the restoration of the earth, and serves as a divine pledge that

---

42. Wright, *Old Testament Ethics*, 56. Wright observes for example how in the Canaanite society the king owned all the land and there were feudal arrangements with those who lived and worked on it as tax-paying tenant peasants. Meanwhile, the land in Israel was divided up as widely as possible into multiple-ownership by extended families (p. 55). He also observes that the division of the land recorded in the book of Joshua intends that the possession and use of the land should be distributed as widely as possible throughout the whole kinship system, noting that the land could not simply be bought or sold commercially, but had to be retained within the kinship groups, in order to preserve this system (p. 56).
43. Ibid., 49–51.
44. Ibid., 68.

God will restore all things. The land laws of Israel served as an ideal model for other societies in the ANE.

3. The Land and Old Testament Theology – Concluding Remarks

3.1. *Why* a Land?

The theology of the land must ask the question: why a land? Why did God promise Abraham a land to begin with?

> Why is a particular geography critical in God's plan for history? The significant role of this local geography is counterintuitive, since the covenantal God of Abraham is the Creator of both heaven and earth who proclaims, "For all the earth is mine."[45]

Our study has aimed to answer this critical and foundational question. By starting in Eden, we have argued that the particularity of the story of Israel is supposed to be *a paradigm* for all the nations on earth, *the means* towards the restoration and redemption of the rest of God's creation, and the *prototype* of this redemption. Israel is set apart and assigned a land for a purpose. We cannot and should not assess the OT's portrayal of Israel without this larger picture. The election of Israel and the promise of the land are purposeful in nature. They point outward towards a more universal and encompassing fulfillment. The land is one part of a bigger project.

In addition, the giving of a land as part of this project of redemption highlights that God is committed to his created order and to the redemption of human society. Redemption in the OT is not merely about individuals, personal piety, or spiritual existential experiences. It is about redeeming whole societies on earth, and ultimately the whole of humanity. It is an "earthly" phenomenon.

---

45. E. B. Korn, "Jewish Reflections on Richard Lux's' The Land of Israel (Eretz Yisrael) in Jewish and Christian Understanding," *Studies in Christian-Jewish Relations* 3, no. 1 (2009): 4.

The biblical storyline could have been different: God could have given Abraham moral commandments for himself and his family. He could have instructed him to wander around in the world proclaiming the worship of the one true God. Instead, he chooses to bring Abraham to a place, to engage in human history and geography, and to create from Abraham's descendants a unique and distinct society – one that would reflect his image on earth in the midst of the nations. This is the biblical pattern of redemption.

Finally, this pattern of choosing a nation and a land and dwelling in the midst of people underscores God's desire for fellowship with humanity. The OT portrays God as a God who seeks to dwell among humanity. This is evident throughout the OT biblical history, whether in the garden of Eden, the tabernacle, or the temple. It is in this sense that we could describe the faith of Israel as "incarnational."[46]

3.2. From the Particular to the Universal

Transformation in the OT moves from a center outward. We have seen this in the callings of Adam, Abraham and Israel. This movement from the center affects change and transformation in other places and lands. This does not negate or undermine the importance and particularity of the center, nor should it affect the unique cultural particularities of other places or lands. The center remains the paradigm or prototype after which other lands are shaped. The particularity of Israel and the universal application of her ministry go hand in hand.

The universal and international dimensions are by no means foreign to the theology of the OT, as has already been illustrated in the previous chapters. The OT starts with the creation of the universe. The calling of Abraham is a response to a universal problem. Abraham is called to be a blessing to the nations. The ideal king of Israel is called to reign over "the ends of the earth." Throughout the biblical history of Israel, non-Israelites join Israel and become part of the narrative, with Ruth as the obvious example. The prophets celebrate the God who rules over all the nations.

---

46. See N. T. Wright, "Jerusalem in the New Testament," in *Jerusalem Past and Present in the Purposes of God*, ed. P. W. L. Walker (Grand Rapids: Baker, 1994), 58.

In fact, many oracles are addressed to the nations, and whole books in the OT, like Jonah and Nahum, deal with other nations. The eschatological promises are thus a climax of this universalizing theology of the OT. These promises are inclusive to the extent that strangers will also inherit the land with Israel.

The universal framework is important for the theology of the land. It reminds us that God is ultimately concerned "not only with one piece of land but with all the land of the earth," and that Israel's experience in her land is but a "microcosm of the world's experience with the earth and its land."[47] With this in mind, we can now apprehend the land-related ethics in the OT in a new manner. The OT commandments of how to live in the land and how to keep it can be applied to all peoples in all lands. Statements in the Wisdom literature are relevant here. For example, Psalm 37 declares:

> For the evildoers shall be cut off, but those who wait for the LORD shall inherit the land. (v. 9)

> But the meek shall inherit the land and delight themselves in abundant peace. (v. 11)

> For those blessed by the LORD shall inherit the land, but those cursed by him shall be cut off. (v. 22)

> The righteous shall inherit the land and dwell upon it forever. (v. 29)

> Wait for the LORD and keep his way, and he will exalt you to inherit the land. (v. 34)

Yet which land is the psalm speaking about? And to whom can it be addressed? Are we bound to say that such statements, by virtue of being Israelite, only apply to Israel? Or instead, by virtue of being part of biblical theology (and by being part of the Wisdom literature), should we apply

---

47. D. T. Olson, "Biblical Perspectives on the Land," *Word & World* 6, no. 1 (1986): 21.

them to all peoples in all lands? Similarly, we can apprehend statements in Proverbs about the land in the same manner:

> So you will walk in the way of the good and keep to the paths of the righteous. For the upright will inhabit the land, and those with integrity will remain in it, but the wicked will be cut off from the land, and the treacherous will be rooted out of it. (Prov 2:20–22)

We can interpret these statements as universal in application because they are part of the Hebrew Bible, whose main plotline is universal in scope. Israel's mission and distinctiveness are by divine intention supposed to be a paradigm for all. God's ideals for humanity are the same everywhere. The meek will always and everywhere inherit the land. The wicked will always and everywhere be cut from the land. The holiness of the land – indeed any land – depends after all on the moral standards of its inhabitants.

This inevitably necessitates for a shift in OT biblical theology from the theology of the land to the theology of הארץ, or *ha'artez*. The theology of ha'aretz is about the land, every land, and ultimately the earth. The theology of the land in the OT is not merely about a particular nation in the ANE and her relationship to her land (though it includes this), but is much more than that. The movement from the particular to the universal is part of the fabric of the OT theology. The theology of the land of Israel is ultimately the theology of every land and every nation. It is the theology of land as "earth." The fact the Hebrew language uses the same word, הארץ, for both "land" and "earth" aids our theological and teleological linkage between the two themes.

3.3. Theologies of the Land

The theology of the land in the OT is not static or dogmatic. It is not a once-and-for-all fixed teaching. Rather, it is a developing theology that interacts with the context and the movement of the history of Israel. This is evident, for example, in the "back and forth" relationship between the promise and the condition. Land laws develop throughout the history, and the emphasis in each period varies. The theology of the land is part of the developing journey of Israel. As the story of Israel progresses, it becomes apparent that moral values trump any theology of entitlement.

Meanwhile, what is projected or promised differs from what was actually realized in many areas. The Promised Land has cosmic boundaries, and is described in Edenic language; but the historic realization in Canaan was different. Similarly, the promised vicegerent is an ideal, just Israelite, but the reality differed. The promised return from exile is projected as a glorious era, but the reality after the exile differed considerably from what is prophesied. All of this shows that we must avoid simplistic and absolute definitions and resolutions when it comes to the theology of the land in the OT; at the same time we must acknowledge the existing tension between the projected and the actualized.

In addition, we must also acknowledge that there are multiple voices and players in the OT that seem to be in conversation with each other and sometimes appear to disagree. In the theology of the land, the OT does not offer a monologue but a dialogue. This inner dialogue is seen, for example, in the voices in favor of kingship and those that oppose it. There are voices that promote a strong Zion theology, and others that seem to critique this theology. There is a dialogue also when it comes to the building of the temple. There is also a tension between the conditional and the unconditional nature of the land promises. There are also the two poles of exclusiveness and inclusiveness within the history of Israel. These debates depend largely on the historical context, and can often present us with two seemingly contradictory arguments. All these different threads are an essential part of the OT fabric. We must appreciate these multiple layers and voices and listen carefully to the dialogue, and even the tension, that takes place in the biblical history.

As the history of Israel progresses, most of these debates are not fully resolved; arguably their resolution is postponed for the future in Israel's new history. Whereas Ezra and Nehemiah, for example, advocate an exclusive Jewish ideology, the eschatological visions of the prophets by and large advocate a more inclusive one. The kingship debate is resolved in the form of a messianic ideal figure, who ensures that YHWH will remain the ultimate king, and who exercises authority with justice and righteousness. The temple debate is also resolved in the form of a mythical and glorified temple. The theology of the land therefore is a complex of multiple voices within the one tradition, and the ideal theology of the land is mainly found in the prophetic visions.

3.4. The Limited Importance of the Land: Ethics Trumps Location

We began this study by quoting Brueggemann and Weinfeld, two influential theologians from two faith traditions. Both stressed the importance of the land in OT theology. For Brueggemann, "land is a central, if not *the central theme* of biblical faith."[48] And for Weinfeld, "the fate of the land is the focal point of biblical historiography."[49]

The land is indeed a central theme in the theology of the OT and Israel. The story of Israel is that of moving into, out of, and back to the land. The land is a central element in the historical periods of Israel. The land, as has also been shown, features as an integral part in the major themes of the OT theology.

Yet is the land central to the *faith* of Israel? In other words, would Israel's faith and religion survive if ever she were to leave her land? Would Israel's calling be compromised if Israel were not present in this distinct geographical area in the ANE? Could Israel be Israel in Babylon?

One of the most striking implications of the exile is that God is present with Israel in the exile and that his presence is not limited to the Promised Land.[50] Israel remained the people of God even in exile. We can arrive at the same conclusion from other periods in the history of Israel. Israel as a nation was not born in the land. Thus, Levenson argues that since Israel was called and given her mission in the wilderness, her identity does not depend on her being a sovereign political state in her land.[51]

Conversely, being present in the land physically does not always guarantee God's favor upon Israel, nor does it guarantee that Israel will live in security and peace. The period of the monarchy was often far from ideal.

---

48. Brueggemann, *The Land*, 3.
49. Weinfeld, *Promise of the Land*, xvi.
50. Clements, *God and Temple*, 103.
51. Levenson, *Sinai & Zion*, 75.

David's rule is marred by a civil war that divided the nation, and Solomon's rule is described by some Israelites as a period of harsh slavery. The divided monarchy period witnessed an increase in wars and unrest, and much injustice and a lack of compassion for the marginalized of society, as is evident from the prophetic literature. Even after Israel returned from exile, being in the land physically did not mean that Israel prospered, as is evident from the prayer of Nehemiah: "We are slaves this day in the land that you gave to our fathers to enjoy its fruit and its good gifts" (Neh 9:36–37).

Ezekiel criticizes the voices that are obsessed with the land during the exile. Granted that he did prophesy about a glorious return to the land, he never pushed for this to happen in his time, instead sending a strong warning:

> Son of man, the inhabitants of these waste places in the land of Israel keep saying, "Abraham was only one man, yet he got possession of the land; but we are many; the land is surely given us to possess." Therefore say to them, "Thus says the Lord God: You eat flesh with the blood and lift up your eyes to your idols and shed blood; *shall you then possess the land?*" (Ezek 33:24–25)

One more time, *the moral and ethical demands of God trump all claims of entitlement to the land*. It is not about being in the land, but what people do in the land. In other words, being in the land physically does not equal being in the land theologically. Israel could be in the land and have the temple, and still feel as slaves with no temple. Being in the land is more than just being physically present in the land. In fact, one could be in the land theologically, by obeying the commandments of God, without having to be in the land physically. For God, in the end, "is near to all who call on him, to all who call on him in truth" (Ps 145:18). The psalmist here "appears to be saying that the presence of YHWH does not depend upon one's location, but upon one's willingness to call him from a stance of truth."[52]

---

52. Ibid., 131.

One could argue, therefore, that someone like Daniel was in the land theologically – by living as an example of the ideal Israelite in the midst of the Babylonians – without being in the land physically. The book of Daniel never mentions that Daniel considered returning to the land, nor does it advocate such a return. Indeed, if anything, the book seemingly celebrates Daniel for living as an ideal Israelite in the state of exile. Daniel is presented as an example to follow, even though he lived in exile. It is no surprise therefore that postexilic Israel survived the loss of land and adapted in whatever context she found herself – whether the rule of Persians or the Greeks, or the Diaspora.

This perhaps explains why the vision of a new covenant in Jeremiah 31:31–37 does not include a promise of a return to the land.[53] The focus is on the people and the transformation that will take place in them and cause them to know and keep the Law. The ideal image of Israel, according to Jeremiah 31:31–37, is that of a nation that knows the Law and that is forgiven of her sins. Israel's restoration to the land is not a determining factor in her transformation and new identity.

The movement between loss of land and settling in the land is *not* about losing and settling in a particular geographical place. The theology of the land is ultimately about restoring the whole earth to God. It is about how to live in any given place in any given time as the people of God in a way that pleases him. Biblical faith according to the first testament can survive without being present in Canaan. It cannot survive, however, if loving God and loving one's neighbor do not define the lifestyle of the people of God.

---

53. Jer 31:31–37 is commonly acknowledged as the central passage in Jer 30–33. These chapters are collectively known as the book of consolation or the book of comfort. The land is mentioned though in other passages in Jer 30–33. See Jer 32:36–44; 33:23–26.

First-Century Jewish Theology of the Land

Land Theology in First-Century Judaism

Dunn observes that Second Temple Judaism stood on what he calls "four pillars of Judaism": (1) monotheism, (2) election: a covenant people, a Promised Land, (3) covenant focused in Torah, and (4) land focused in temple.[54] Evidently, the land continued to play a central role in Jewish thinking during Jesus' time. Davies similarly remarks that, although in the written sources of Second Temple Judaism the land is mentioned less frequently, there is still continuity between these sources and the OT when it comes to the main themes of the theology of the land.[55] He adds that Pharisaism "so cherished the view that there was an unseverable connection between Israel and Yahweh and the land that this view has been referred to as a 'dogma' of the Pharisees."[56] Burge similarly confirms that the land was still central to Jewish identity, that the promise of the land was still anchored to the covenant, and that life in the land was still contingent on upholding the righteousness expected by God.[57]

The return from exile in Babylon, together with the new realities which the returnees faced, did not change the importance of the land, but simply resulted in altering the borders of the land to suit the new reality. As Weinfeld explains:

---

54. J. D. G. Dunn, *The Partings of the Ways: Between Christianity and Judaism and their Significance for the Character of Christianity* (London: SCM Press, 2006), 24–48.
55. Davies, *The Gospel and the Land*, 49–55.
56. Ibid., 55.
57. Burge, *Jesus and The Land*, 11.

> In the Second Temple period, the area that was subject to the laws of purity and impurity, as well as the other laws that were binding upon the Land of Israel, was the region within the borders of those who went up from the Babylonian exile . . . and no longer the previous borders of those who came from Egypt . . . All territory settled by those who returned from the Babylonian exile was holy . . . but areas inhabited by Gentiles or Samaritans were not considered holy.[58]

This observation from Weinfeld also shows that purity laws *within the land* were very important among Palestinian Jews in Second Temple Judaism. Discussions about "what is pure," "who is pure," and "where is pure" were very common among the Jews in this period, and for some, like the Pharisees, the lack of purity explained why the restoration of the land had not fully taken place yet. By contrast, for a smaller minority, like the Qumran community, the land was completely impure, so there was a need to separate from the communities in the land, and to practice a stricter form of purity, waiting for the time of cleansing and restoration.

In addition, there was a theological and a functional link in Second Temple Judaism between the land and Eden on the one hand, and Adam and Israel on the other:

> If we are to understand first-century Judaism we me must rank Land, along with Temple and Torah, as one of the major symbols. It was YHWH's Land, given inalienably to Israel . . . The Land was, of course, not only a symbol: it was the source of bread and wine, the place to graze sheep and goats, grow olives and figs. It was the place where, and the means through which, YHWH gave his

---

58. Weinfeld, *The Promise of the Land*, 75.

covenant people the blessings he had promised them, which were all summed up in the many-sided and evocative word *shalom*, peace. It was the new Eden, the garden of YHWH, the home of the true humanity.

Israel's covenantal vocation caused her to think of herself as the creator's true humanity. If Abraham and his family are understood as the creator's means of dealing with the sin of Adam, and hence with the evil in the world, Israel herself becomes the true Adamic humanity.[59]

This observation confirms our findings and argument in the first chapters of this study that the OT does indeed portrays the land as Eden restored and Israel as a second "restorative" Adam. What we have observed was itself observed by first-century Jews, and it penetrated their thought and practice.

Expectations of Restoration

However, the reality on the ground – no less in Jesus' time than it was during the previous four hundred years after the return of some Jews from exile – was very dim and difficult. There was a sequence of oppressive empires and foreign occupations. With the exception of the Hasmanian dynasty, there was no Jewish kingdom and no Jewish sovereignty over the land or Jerusalem, and most Jews still lived outside of the land. This explains the many Jewish revolts that took place in these years – like the Maccabean revolt, which successfully established Jewish sovereignty in the land for a short time, the revolt of the death of Herod the great (4 BC), the great revolt in (AD 66–70), and the Bar Kokhba revolt (AD 132–135).

---

59. N. T. Wright, *The New Testament and the People of God* (Minneapolis: Fortress Press,1992), 226, 262.

In addition, no biblical or Second Temple sources claimed that the temple itself had been truly re-occupied by the presence of God after the exile. Therefore, as N. T. Wright argues, most Palestinian Jews in the first century described their situation as one of being *still in exile:* they were expecting and yearning for restoration.[60] This restoration, according to Wright, would include three main elements: (1) the return from exile, (2) the defeat of evil, and (3) the return of YHWH to Zion.[61] History was thus divided, in many first-century Jewish resources, into two ages: "this age" and "the age to come" (the age of restoration); or, in Hebrew, *ha-'olam hazeh and ha-'olam haba.*

We can see these expectations of restoration in many NT passages. Consider the prayer of Zachariah in the introduction of Luke's Gospel, which speaks of God visiting and "redeeming his people," "raising a horn of salvation from the house of David," "remembering the covenant with Abraham," and "delivering Israel from her enemies" (Luke 1:68–75). Walker rightly asserts, "the fact that these hopes of restoration existed in Jesus' day was itself an admission that *Israel was still effectively in a period of exile.*"[62] This is important for our understanding of what Jesus actually accomplished. If Luke is here claiming in the introduction of his Gospel that the time of the restoration and the end of exile has arrived, then this has very important implications for the theology of the land. This prayer comes from the mouth of someone who lived in the land, which again suggests that the exile we are talking about is not a literal political one, but more truly, a *theological one*: physically the Jews might be back in the land, but theologically Israel was still in exile.

---

60. Ibid., 268–269. Bryan believes that Wright takes the argument too far when it comes to Israel being still in exile. He says: "Inasmuch as Wright uses 'exile' to sum up this sense of bondage and hope of restoration, he often means by it little more than 'non-restoration'." Regardless of the definition of exile, the fact remains that first-century Jews were expecting some sort of divine intervention in history that would restore the fortunes of Israel. S. M. Bryan, *Jesus and Israel's Traditions of Judgement and Restoration* (Cambridge: Cambridge University Press, 2002), 13.
61. Wright, *Jesus and the Victory of God.*
62. Walker, *Jesus and the Holy City,* 43 (emphasis added).

A Different Perspective from the Diaspora

However, there seems to have been an alternative line of thought that emerged among some Jewish theologians in that period (especially, but not only, among diaspora Jews), which went some way to undermining the place of the actual land of promise and Jerusalem as defining elements in the Jewish faith and identity. Bailey observes how it is possible to observe two developments during the two centuries before the NT period: one is to *universalize* the promise of the land and the other is to *spiritualize* it. He mentions as examples for universalization:[63]

> And I will give to thy seed *all the earth which is under heaven*, and they shall judge *all the nations* according to their desires, and after that they shall get *possession of the whole earth and inherit it forever*. (Jub. 32:19)

> Therefore the Lord assured him by an oath that the nations would be blessed through his posterity; that he would multiply him like the dust of the earth, and exalt his posterity like the stars, and cause them *to inherit from sea to sea and from the River to the ends of the earth*. (Sir. 44:21)

Meanwhile, for spiritualization he gives examples from Enoch (40:9), which speaks of "inheriting eternal life," and from 2 Baruch (14:13; 51:13), which speaks of "inheriting the world to come."[64] Horbury similarly sees this spiritualization of the land promises in

---

63. K. E. Bailey, "St. Paul's Understanding of the Territorial Promise," *The Near East School of Theology Theological Review* XV, no. 1 (1994): 60. See also Beale: "Both the OT and Judaism viewed Israel's land promises as containing within themselves a notion that the boundaries of the promised land would be expanded to encompass the entire earth." Beale, *New Testament Biblical Theology*, 756.

64. We can also see this in the lawyer's and the ruler's questions to Jesus about "inheriting eternal life" (Luke 10:25; 18:18).

how the community could also be interpreted as a temple – especially, but not only, in the Qumran texts. In addition, he observes that in a great strand of rabbinic thought, "works of loving-kindness" form an effectual sacrifice, and that God was understood as not *requiring* any sacrifice, but simply *allowing* it as a concession (which in effect nullified the necessity of the temple).[65]

Amaru, who studied the theology of the land in two very important diaspora Jewish figures, Josephus and Philo, came to a similar conclusion: "Both [Philo and Josephus] read into the text an element of universalism."[66] Furthermore, for Josephus, "Judaism is a religion of law, of obedience, which is rewarded not by the classical messianic kingdom, but by a renewed existence and in the revolution (of the ages) by the gift of a better life."[67] In a different volume, which expands the scope of her study to include Jubilees and the Testament of Moses, she concludes that all of these four writers rewrote "biblical Land theory" and reconstructed the narratives "such that the Land no longer functions as the key signature of covenantal history."[68]

It is easy to write off these conceptions of the land as belonging to elite Jews in the Diaspora who were attempting to interact with their Hellenistic context. Yet as Burge observes,

> Early scholarship once described Diaspora Judaism as compromised by Hellenism and not normative. But abundant evidence now makes clear that these Diaspora

---

65. W. Horbury, "Land, Sanctuary and Worship," in *Early Christian Thought in its Jewish Context*, ed. J. M. G. Barclay and M. D. Hooker (Cambridge: Cambridge University Press, 1996), 214.
66. B. H. Amaru, "Land Theology in Philo and Josephus," in *The Land of Israel: Jewish Perspectives*, ed. L. A. Hoffman (Notre Dame: University of Notre Dame Press, 1986), 85.
67. Ibid., 86.
68. B. H. Amaru, *Rewriting the Bible: Land and Covenant in Post-Biblical Jewish Literature* (Valley Forge: Trinity Press International, 1994), 116.

communities saw themselves as fully Jewish, holding to their culture and faith with integrity.[69]

During the first century more Jews were living outside the Holy Land than within it – a fact which must have had major implications for Jewish thinking and perspective. We cannot therefore ignore these views about the land among some diaspora Jews in the first century. Those Jews, despite their affection for Jerusalem and yearly pilgrimage, had chosen *not* to live in Judea, and considered it perfectly acceptable to be living in diaspora as faithful Jews, as long as they kept Torah. The observance of Torah took three distinctive features for them: Sabbath observance, dietary laws, and circumcision. This contributed to establishing these as markers of Jewish identity and communal life.[70]

Amaru believes that these views about the land are not "true to their biblical source" and do not "fit well with the explicit particularism of biblical land theology."[71] However, it is important to notice that, in their own mind, both Josephus and Philo, and indeed other writers from that period, felt that they were in fact true to the biblical sources, and tried to argue for their theology using arguments from Scripture. This matches what we have argued for above – namely that the universalization of the land promises can indeed be found in the OT itself and was a legitimate ingredient of biblical hope and expectation. Moreover, biblical Judaism evidently adjusted in the Diaspora to surviving outside the boundaries of the land, but could not survive outside the boundaries of the Torah. In other words, it is not accurate to argue that this strand of theology is distinctively a development of Second Temple Judaism – as if the traces for it cannot be found in the OT. Nor is it fully correct to argue that the early church was shaped by

---

69. Burge, *Jesus and the Land*, 16.
70. Ibid., 19.
71. Amaru, "Land Theology in Philo," 85.

attitudes about the land formed in diaspora Judaism;[72] instead Paul and the NT writers argue for their position about the land promises by appealing to OT texts.

Conclusion

The land continued to constitute a major role in the theology of Israel; yet, as we have seen, the theme continued to develop and reshape. The most important development in the land theology in Second Temple Judaism was the tendency among some groups and intellectuals to speak about the land in symbolic and idealistic fashion, seeing it as pointing to a greater transcendental reality.

In Jesus' time, there was a complex diversity of views regarding the land. Not only did diaspora Jews think differently about the land from Palestinian Jews. There also existed within Palestinian Judaism some quite diverse approaches regarding the land, purity and restoration: the Pharisees believed that strict observance of the Torah was the solution; the Zealots tried to take initiative into their own hands; the Sadducees made political alliances; and the Essenes and those at Qumran chose separation from the "corrupt" Jerusalem and temple.[73]

What this brief survey tells us is that the land was one of the heated topics of the days – indeed, possibly, the most heated. It would be strange, then, if Jesus did not touch on this issue. Jesus' diverse actions (whether being baptized in the Jordan River, cleansing the temple, or riding a donkey) and his various teachings (whether about the kingdom, possessions, Caesar, purity, violence, David or Abraham) must always be understood as a part of an ongoing dialogue with his

---

72. See for example Burge and Dunn who both argue that Stephen in his speech in Acts 7 had Hellenistic influences. Burge, *Jesus and the Land*, 16; Dunn, *The Partings of the Ways*, 90.

73. See Wright, *The New Testament*, 167–213.

contemporaries and with the issues which were uppermost in their minds and worldview.

The same must apply to those occasions when he was silent over certain issues or chose not to emphasize particular topics. Since the Land was a "hot topic" for Jesus' contemporaries, Jesus' refusal to endorse the hope of the majority on this issue must be seen as intentional – pointing to a subtly alternative interpretation. It is therefore impossible for the Land to be a "non-issue" in the NT. Given that this was the major theme of the OT, there was no way that Jesus or the writers of the NT, who all saw their message as being the true and ultimate fulfillment of the OT, could have "turned a blind eye" to this theme. On the contrary, we must interpret their actions and words as deliberately pointing to a new and deeper fulfillment of that OT story. The Land therefore *cannot but be* an important theme in the NT.

CHAPTER 7

The Jesus-Event and the Land

Introduction

This chapter is an introduction to the study of the theology of the land in the NT. It argues that the life and teachings of Jesus provide the hermeneutical key to the understanding of biblical theology in general and of the biblical theology of the land in particular. Other theological developments that came as a result of the coming of Jesus will also play a key role in our understanding of the land in the NT. These developments include the arrival of a new era in history, the judgment on Israel, and the inclusion of Gentiles into the people of God. The overall argument is that since the NT authors claim that Jesus is the climax of Israel's story, and since the land is a major part of that story, therefore the land must be an important theme in the NT.

1. The Study of the Land in the NT

The study of the theology of the land in the NT is very challenging. Unlike the OT, a surface reading of the NT suggests that the land is not a major theme in biblical theology in the NT, let alone a central one.[1] Many theolo-

---

[1] Waltke for example says: "The trajectory of the Land motif into the New Testament, however, is the most difficult biblical motif to track. This is so because the New Testament rarely uses the term 'land' for salvation history after the death and resurrection of Jesus Christ." Waltke, *An Old Testament Theology*, 559.

gians struggle to find the theme of land in the NT and hence conclude that land is not an important theme in the NT. With the exception of Davies,[2] Wenell,[3] and Burge,[4] there are no major works devoted exclusively to theology of the land in the NT, and very few scholars devote a section to the land theme in NT theology books.[5]

However, the NT is not entirely silent about the land, and there are many signs that it does have something to say about the theology of the land. And even if such a silence, as we shall see, is maintained in certain places, it is in itself a silence that arguably is making a statement. The way to investigate the theme of the land in the NT is not therefore by searching for references in the NT that mention the "land" (γῆ in Greek, e.g. Matt 5:5; Eph 6:1–3). It is also not best done, we suggest, by contrasting the theme of the land in the NT with the theme in the OT, or even with Jewish theology in the first century AD. These two approaches will unavoidably conclude that the land is no longer important in biblical history. A different approach is needed. Our contention is that, if instead we recognize the Jesus-event as the starting point of the NT's theology, then a significant biblical theology of the land in the NT will emerge.

---

2. Davies, *The Gospel and the Land*.

3. K. J. Wenell, *Jesus and Land : Sacred and Social Space in Second Temple Judaism* (London: T & T Clark, 2007).

4. Burge, *Jesus and The Land*.

5. Notable exceptions to this include Waltke and Beale; both devote an entire chapter to this theme. Waltke, *An Old Testament Theology*, 558–587; Beale, *New Testament Biblical Theology*, 750–774. Bruggemann's book on the land includes one chapter about the land in the NT. Brueggemann, *The Land*, 157–172. Walker's book on Jesus and Jerusalem is very relevant to this discussion and many themes overlap. Walker, *Jesus and the Holy City*. In addition, see Walker's two articles on Jesus and the land and the Apostles and the land in Johnston and Walker, *The Land of Promise*, 81–99, 100–120. Inge observes that the lack of works of substance on the theology of the land in the NT is because "scholars do not seem to feel that 'place' is a category of sufficient importance in the New Testament to warrant their attention." J. Inge, *A Christian Theology of Place* (Burlington: Ashgate, 2003), 48.

2. The Jesus-Event as a Hermeneutical Key

In order for us to understand the NT, we must do what the NT authors themselves did: pick up the story of Israel from the exile onward and interpret that narrative in the light of Jesus' coming – what we might call the "Jesus-event." By the "Jesus-event" we mean both the life, ministry, teachings, death and resurrection, and ascension of Jesus, as well as how these events impacted the way in which the apostles understood the biblical narrative or the history of redemption. The Jesus-event according to the NT is *the* focal point in the biblical narrative, and all preceding and proceeding events in this narrative are relativized in relation to, or by comparison with, this focal point.

The place to start our investigation of the land theme in the NT, therefore, is the life of Jesus. "No biblical theology of the land is possible which bypasses Jesus on this issue."[6] The last thirty years have witnessed many studies on Jesus and the origins of Christianity, which have helpfully focused on the Jewish context in which the Christian message emerged, and argued that the Gospels and Epistles should be read in that context.[7] Yet one major implication of such studies, in particular those of Wright and Dunn, is that they have restored a confidence in discovering the historical Jesus – or at least have emphasized the importance of the historical Jesus for the theology of the evangelists and Paul.[8]

---

6. P. W. L. Walker, "The Land and Jesus Himself," in *The Land of Promise,* ed. P. Johnston and P. Walker (Downers Grove: InterVarsity Press, 2000), 115.

7. See for example E. P. Sanders, *Jesus and Judaism* (Philadelphia: Fortress Press, 1985); Wright, *The New Testament*; Wright, *Jesus and the Victory of God*; Dunn, *The Partings of the Ways*. These studies became to be known as the "third quest." For more, see B. Witherington, *The Jesus Quest: The Third Search for the Jew of Nazareth* (Downers Grove: InterVarsity Press, 1997); M. Wilkins and J. P. Moreland, eds., *Jesus Under Fire. Modern Scholarship Reinvents the Historical Jesus* (Grand Rapids: Zondervan, 1994).

8. It is true that what we have in the Gospels is a theological reflection or interpretation by the evangelists on the life of Jesus, yet this does not necessarily mean that the Gospels are not historical. As Wright argues, "it is a basic mistake of method to suppose that because the evangelist, like all writers that ever existed, had reasons for selecting and arranging what was written, the material is therefore non-historical." Wright, *Jesus and the Victory of God,* 333. In addition, Wright has argued how all synoptic Gospels portray Jesus and the continuation of the story of Israel, and therefore: "the fact that the evangelists believed themselves to be bringing the story of Israel to its great climax, the turning-point from which at last the long history of the world would change course, means inescapably that

It is of huge significance that all four Gospels start their narrative of Jesus by linking it with the OT narrative and by arguing that Jesus is in fact continuing this narrative. Matthew's genealogy (1:1–17), Mark's citation of Isaiah and Malachi (1:2–3), Luke's account of the words of the angel and the prayers of Mary and Zechariah (1:16–17, 46–55, 68–79), and John's claim that Jesus came to his "own" (1:11) – all point to the conclusion that the evangelists saw the Jesus-event that they are narrating as the continuation and the climax of the story of Israel. As Dunn confirms:

> Unless a NT theology both recognizes and brings out the degree to which the NT writers saw themselves as in continuity with the revelation of the OT and as at least in some measure continuing or completing that revelation, it can hardly provide a faithful representation of what they understood themselves to be about.[9]

We need at the same time to emphasize the importance of the resurrection of Jesus as the defining moment in the Jesus-event:

> We interpret Scripture rightly only when we read it in light of the resurrection, and we begin to comprehend the resurrection only when we see it as the climax of the scriptural story of God's gracious deliverance of Israel.[10]

The belief that the Jesus-event is the climax of the story of Israel is evident in Luke's account of Jesus' post-resurrection words to his disciples that everything written about him in "the Law of Moses and the Prophets and

---

they believed themselves to be writing (what we call) history, the history of Jesus." Wright, *The New Testament*, 397.

9. J. D. G. Dunn, *New Testament Theology: An Introduction* (Nashville: Abingdon Press, 2009), 23. Dunn further explains that the NT writers viewed their writings as "a valid addition to or even completion of the then not yet closed canon of the OT."

10. R. B. Hays, "Reading Scripture in Light of the Resurrection," in *The Art of Reading Scripture*, ed. R. B. Hays and E. F. Davis (Grand Rapids: Eerdmans, 2003), 216. As Dunn also confirms, "it is impossible realistically to envisage a form of Christianity which did not have this conviction at its heart and basis" (regardless of whether one believes that it happened or not). Dunn, *The Partings of the Ways*, 242.

the Psalms" must be fulfilled: his suffering, resurrection, and the proclamation of the gospel to the nations beginning from Jerusalem (Luke 24:44–47).[11] And as Enns comments:

> Jesus is not saying that there are some interesting Old Testament prophecies that speak of him . . . Rather, he is saying that *all* Scriptures speak of him in the sense that he is *the climax of Israel's story.* The Old Testament as *a whole* is about him, not a subliminal prophecy or a couple of lines tucked away in a minor prophet. Rather, Christ – who he is and what he did – is where the Old Testament has been leading all along.[12]

Enns argues for what he calls a "christotelic" reading of Scripture that the writers of the NT had: "The Old Testament as a whole, particularly in its grand themes, finds its *telos*, its completion, in Christ."[13] In addition, N. T. Wright points out that it was *Jesus himself*, and not simply the NT writers, who communicated this impression:

> Jesus . . . claimed in word and deed that the traditional expectation was now being fulfilled. The new exodus was under way: Israel was now at last returning from her long exile. All this was happening in and through his own work.[14]

One of the most importance statements of Paul in this regard is 2 Corinthians 1:20: "For *all the promises* of God find their Yes *in him.*" This is "one of the most theologically pregnant statements in all of Paul's writings."[15] Moreover, Walker argues that the phrase "all the promises"

---
11. The same belief is echoed by Paul, who claimed in 1 Cor 15:3–4 that the Gospel, namely Jesus' death and resurrection, was in "accordance with Scriptures."
12. P. Enns, 2005, *Inspiration and Incarnation: Evangelicals and the Problem of the Old Testament* (Grand Rapids: Baker Academic, 2005), 120 (emphasis in the original).
13. Ibid., 154.
14. Wright, *Jesus and the Victory of God*, 243.
15. Beale, *New Testament Biblical Theology*, 638.

would necessarily include those concerning the land.[16] In other words, the story of Israel, in its totality, including the part related to the land, must find its fulfillment – its Yes – in Jesus. *Therefore, the land cannot but be a major theme in the story the NT writers are telling – a story that is continuing on the story of the OT, in which the land was such a central theme.* Furthermore, some themes in the NT – like the selection of the twelve disciples, Jesus' interaction with the temple, and the covenant with Abraham – are strongly tied with the theme of the land. If the land is a major theme in the OT, then it is inherently and inevitably a major one in the NT.

3. The Jesus-Event Aftershocks

In addition to the Jesus-event, we should also notice the existence of three other major "aftershocks" that shaped the formation of NT biblical theology in general, including that of the land.[17] These will be unpacked in the course of this study, and are all consequences of the Jesus-event –hence they can be called "aftershocks." These aftershocks are not merely theological developments. Just like the Jesus-event, they are historical events that caused theological developments and rethinking. We will mention them briefly now, since they form key foundations behind the NT theology of the land.

3.1. The Arrival of the Age to Come

The first aftershock of the Jesus-event relates to the understanding of the "age" or "time." The NT authors assume that the Jesus-event brought about the "age to come" of which the OT prophets spoke – which is what we referred to, following Brueggemann, as the "new history."[18] This is the natural outcome of believing that Jesus is the climax of the story of Israel.

---

16. Walker, *Jesus and the Holy City*, 117.

17. The developments mentioned here are not the only ones that resulted from the Jesus-event, but are the ones that are related to the theology of the land. A comprehensive study of these developments is beyond this study, and must include the confession of the early Christians about the deity of Christ, which was a major historical development that increased the divide between the early Christians and Judaism. See Dunn, *The Partings of the Ways*, 215–300.

18. See above chapter 5, section 1. See also Brueggemann, *The Land*, 124.

Israel's story was suspended awaiting the new messianic age. By claiming that Jesus is the Messiah and that he is the climax of the story of Israel, the NT authors are implying that the age to come has begun.

A small example from the Gospels and another from Paul will suffice at this stage. When Jesus read the prophecy of Isaiah in the synagogue in Nazareth, he ended the reading with a very clear and conclusive statement: "*Today* this Scripture has been *fulfilled* in your hearing" (Luke 4:21). The original prophecy in Isaiah 61 spoke clearly about the time of the restoration and the end of exile. The message is clear: restoration has begun in and through the ministry of Jesus.

Meanwhile, Galatians 4:4 describes the time of the coming of Jesus as "the fullness of time," which means that in his understanding the old age is completed, and the new age has begun.[19] Paul here "reads the Bible in light of a central conviction that he and his readers are those upon whom the ends of the ages have come."[20]

It is important, however, to note that in the NT this new era in history has been inaugurated *but not yet consummated*. The NT speaks, as we will see, of a final future consummation, which will take place in the second coming of Christ. Yet much of the NT theology hinges on the notion that the new history has already begun, and that the NT writers assume that they are already living in the inaugurated eschaton. In addition, even when we talk about the consummation, it is a consummation that is based on the inauguration; it completes what has already begun.

3.2. Israel Rejects the Messiah

The second aftershock after the Jesus-event is the rejection of Jesus and the apostles by the Jewish leaders and the inhabitants of Jerusalem, and the consequent judgment on Israel because of this rejection – a judgment that culminated in the destruction of Jerusalem in AD 70. Though we cannot speak with certainty as to which NT books were written after AD 70, or whether for example the portrayals in Matthew 24 are *post-eventum* or not,

---

19. See also Mark 1:15: "the time is fulfilled."
20. R. B. Hays, *Echoes of Scripture in the letters of Paul* (New Haven: Yale University Press, 1989), 121.

we can still trace throughout the NT a progressive development of a negative attitude towards Israel, Jerusalem and the temple. This will climax in judgment on the Judaism of Jesus' time.

Again an example from the Gospels and another from Paul will suffice at this stage. The parable of the vineyard (Matt 21:33–46) narrates the continuous rejection of the tenants (Jewish leaders) to the messengers of the master (God), which culminated in their killing of the son (Jesus). The conclusion of the parable is decisive: "the kingdom of God will be *taken away from you* and *given to a people* producing its fruits" (Matt 21:43). Israel has failed in her mission, and lost her privileges, and *other people* have been given that mission.

In Romans 11, Paul reaches the same conclusion using a different image – that of an olive tree (11:16–24). Some branches (unbelieving Jews) were cut off because of unbelief, and "wild branches" were grafted it (believing Gentiles) because of their faith in Christ.

What is vitally important to observe here is that this negative attitude towards the Judaism of the first century and towards Jerusalem is not a rejection of the OT as such, nor indeed a negation of the promises of God to Israel. On the contrary, the NT authors, as will be argued, claim that the new Christian movement is the legitimate continuation to the story of Israel.

3.3. The Inclusion of Gentiles

The third aftershock is related to the second – the inclusion of Gentiles into the people of God. In both examples mentioned above, the Jewish people's rejection to Jesus led to the door being opened to new peoples; Gentiles from different nations and different lands.

In the book of Acts the conversion of Cornelius (Acts 10) and the Jerusalem council (Acts 15:6–29) – along with the persistent Jewish rejection of the gospel – led to the apostles mission to the Gentiles and the universalization of the Christian message. In its last chapter Paul meets with Jewish leaders in Rome in an attempt to persuade them to join the Christian faith. Their rejection prompts him to declare in a summative fashion: "therefore let it be known to you that this salvation of God has been sent *to the Gentiles*; they will listen" (Acts 28:28).

At the same time, we must underline that not all of the Jewish people rejected the Christian message. The first believers, after all, were Jews. As a result, much of Paul's theology is centered on the idea of the church as consisting of Jews and Gentiles, and how this is in fact consistent with God's purposes that were revealed in the OT. In Galatians 3 Paul declares that in Christ "there is no Jew or Gentile" (3:28) and that both are descendants of Abraham (3:29) – all based on the argument "that in Christ Jesus the blessing of Abraham might come to the Gentiles" (3:14). As Hays explains, Paul's interpretive strategies of the OT "refract Scripture in such a way that the church – composed of Jews and Gentiles together – comes into focus as the goal of God's redemptive action."[21]

This reveals what Walker calls a "mysterious paradox" in NT biblical theology. The NT affirms that the inclusion of the Gentiles came as a result of *both* the judgment on Israel *and* the outworking of God's economy of salvation declared in the OT. "Although this mysterious paradox is not easily explained, both these 'levels of causation' need to be affirmed if we are to be true to the New Testament witness."[22]

4. Conclusion

This brief introduction aimed to establish the centrality of the Jesus-event for the study of biblical theology in the NT. Jesus' ministry, death, and resurrection are presented in the NT as the climax of the story of Israel, and as such signify a focal point in the history of salvation. We also find elements in the Jesus-event that hint at and prepare the way for the three aftershocks mentioned above (the realization of the new history, the judgment on Israel, and the inclusion of the Gentiles). There is no doubt that each of these aftershocks, on in its own, is a major focal point in the development of the biblical narrative and the breakaway of Christianity from Judaism. Yet we must see these aftershocks in relation to and as a consequence to the Jesus-event.

---

21. Ibid., 84.
22. Walker, *Jesus and the Holy City*, 317.

In addition, the Jesus-event and the aftershocks that followed had severe consequences on the "parting of the ways" between the new Christian movement and Second Temple Judaism – to use Dunn's terminology.[23] This monumental cleavage cannot be explained historically or interpreted in isolation from the Jesus-event. It must have started with Jesus. As Dunn concludes in his masterful work on the "partings of the ways" between Christianity and Judaism:

> The breach was not immediate or sudden. It *began* with Jesus, but without Easter and the broadening out of the gospel to the Gentiles the two currents might have been contained within the same banks.[24]

The Jesus-event and the three aftershocks will turn out to have crucial consequences on the theology of the land in the NT. If the new history that the OT prophets had spoken about has indeed arrived, this will inevitably affect the way in which we understand the concept of restoration to the land, since the land was an integral part of the new history in the OT. If Israel was judged (and since the temple was destroyed), this will have a significant effect on how we understand the continuous role of the

---

23. Dunn, *The Partings of the Ways*.
24. Ibid., 301 (emphasis added). However, Dunn's other conclusions in this book should be challenged. Even though he says in this quote that it began with Jesus, he seems to give in the book more weight to Hellenistic influences, the inclusion of the Gentiles, and the destruction of Jerusalem – more than he gives credit to Jesus himself for beginning this breach. The breach was so radical that it cannot be explained simply on the basis of these factors. In addition, Jesus' disciples were Palestinian Jews, not Hellenist Jews. Paul described himself as a Pharisee (Phil 3:5), and his Jewish ideology was shaped in Jerusalem and not in the diaspora. The early Christians shifted dramatically from the Judaism of their time, and risked their lives, and they must have found the justification for such a radical move in the life and teachings of Jesus, and in particular to the resurrection of Christ. Finally, Dunn's final conclusion on the period of the final and conclusive parting of ways is questionable: "if there is one period in which the seams uniting the two main segments of the heritage of Second Temple Judaism finally pulled apart, that period is almost certainly the first thirty to thirty-five years of the second century. However many threads remained linking the sundered parts, however closely together they lay, and however much alike they were, *by the end of the second Jewish revolt, Christian and Jew were clearly distinct and separate*" (p. 318). In light of his earlier statement – that the breach "began in Jesus" – one wonders if it is logical that it took more than 100 years for the final breach to happen.

particularity of Israel and her land in the economy of salvation. And if Gentiles were actually included, then this will inevitably affect our understanding of the boundaries of the land. Moreover, since we have seen how the NT claims that the story of Israel continues in Jesus, it follows that the land *cannot but be an important theme in the NT theology.*

Finally, and before we conclude this chapter, it is important to note that the argument for the theology of the land in the NT does not stem only from the Jesus-event. For example, the land was a debated theological topic in the time of Jesus, and it is inconceivable that Jesus and Paul ignored the topic completely. There are also other theological factors that lead towards the same conclusion. Christianity is an incarnational faith. It is grounded in real events in history and the Bible claims that history will culminate in new heavens and new *earth*. Moreover, Christ rose *bodily*. Therefore, a theology that "spiritualizes" the land does not take adequate account of the biblical witness. These factors aid our conclusion that the land cannot but be a major theme in the NT.

CHAPTER 8

Jesus and Holy Space

Introduction

This chapter looks at the relationship between Jesus and the land as it pertains to its holiness. This will done by looking on how Jesus related to the most sacred of spaces in the Judaism of his time: Jerusalem and its temple.[1] The NT, we will argue, portrays Jesus as embodying in his person the realities related to the sanctuaries of the OT. Paul thus views the church as the new temple, deriving its holiness from Jesus and the Spirit. This resulted in a breaking down of the boundaries of spatial holiness, and a redefinition of the holiness that is required from the people of God. Inevitably, this also resulted in severe consequences for the place of Jerusalem and its temple – and by extension, the land – as a special holy territory. The overall conclusion is that the coming of Jesus has announced the arrival of the eschatological temple.

---

1. Waltke says: "Since the New Testament does not use the term 'Land,' we have to work with equivalent terms that imply Land, such as 'Jerusalem,' 'throne of David,' 'temple,' and 'Zion'." Waltke, *An Old Testament Theology*, 559. We have already observed how in post-exilic Judaism Jerusalem and the Temple took the place of land. See Weinfeld, *The Promise of the Land*, 202. In the time of Jesus, and because of the geopolitical reality of the Roman occupation, and the Gentile presence in the Galilee area, Jerusalem and its Temple took an even stronger position in the Jewish life and theology.

1. Background: The Temple in the Time of Jesus

The temple played a central role in Palestinian Judaism in the times of Jesus. The description of Judaism in this period as "Second Temple Judaism" testifies to the centrality of the temple.[2] Its significance was in three aspects: the presence of God, the sacrificial system, and the temple's political significance.[3] The temple had six degrees of holiness: (1) Holy of Holies, (2) Holy Place, (3) Court of Priests, (4) Court of Israel, (5) Court of Women, and (6) Court of Gentiles.[4] The Holy of Holies represented the center of holiness, and this holiness spread gradually: from the holy of holies, to the outer courts, to Jerusalem, and to the land. We have seen how the religious and national emphasis, as reflected in Second Temple period sources, "shifted from 'the land' to 'the city' and 'the temple.'"[5] It follows that – unless there are strong arguments to the contrary – we can argue that what applies to the temple and Jerusalem will by implication apply to the land.

We should read Jesus' interaction with Jerusalem and in particular the temple within this context. Anything Jesus said or did in Jerusalem and temple should be seen in dialogue with these contemporary views of the temple's relationship with the land. We cannot overemphasize the magnitude of Jesus' claim that he is "greater than the temple" (Matt 12:6), and how his audience would have received such a statement. Jesus' relationship with Jerusalem and the temple will prove to be very important for our understanding of the theology of the land in the NT.

---

2. Dunn, *The Partings of the Ways*, 42. For Dunn, the land in Second Temple Judaism was "focused in temple."

3. Wright, *Jesus and the Victory of God*, 407.

4. Dunn, *The Partings of the Ways*, 51. Dunn also notes how the Talmud speaks of 10 degrees of holiness, from the land inward to the holy of holies.

5. Weinfeld, *The Promise of the Land*, 202. See also chapter 2 above, section 2.1.

2. The Embodiment of God's Presence, and the Nullification of Holy Place

The NT speaks of Jesus' relationship with Jerusalem and its temple in two ways: It speaks positively of Jesus as the embodiment of divine presence of earth, and negatively in terms of the nullification of holy places. The two aspects are interrelated. The fact that Jesus embodies the divine presence nullifies the role of Jerusalem and the temple. We will look in the next section at these two aspects, focusing sometimes on one of them more than the other.

2.1. In the Synoptic Gospels

The encounter between Jesus and holy space in the NT is evident in the synoptic Gospels, and we will discover that it goes beyond Jesus' relationship with Jerusalem. Matthew proclaims that Jesus is "Immanuel" (1:23), that when the disciples meet in his name he will be "among them" (18:20),[6] and that he will be always present with his disciples (28:20). Matthew in essence asserts that Jesus as "God with us" is the embodiment in his own person of that "which previously had been signified by the *shekinah* in the Jerusalem Temple."[7] This is also evident in the transfiguration in the appearance of the "bright cloud" (Matt 17:5). The cloud recalls the divine presence in the OT.[8] The divine presence is now mediated through Jesus.

The public ministry of Jesus confirms this,[9] and in particular his acts of forgiveness of sins.[10] As Beale observes, Jesus' repeated claim that

---

6. Wright observes that this saying in Matt 18:20 echoes a statement from the Second Temple period – "Pirqe Aboth 3:2" – which says: "If two sit together and words of the Law are spoken between them, the Divine Presence rests between them." Wright, *Jesus and the Victory of God*, 297.
7. Walker, *Jesus and the Holy City*, 31.
8. Exod 13:21–22; 19:16; 24:15–18; 33:9–10; 40:34–38; 1 Kgs 8:10–11. See R. T. France, *The Gospel of Matthew* (Grand Rapids: Eerdmans, 2007), 649–650.
9. Holwerda say: "Jesus' entire public ministry is actually a fulfillment of what the temple symbolized." D. E. Holwerda, *Jesus and Israel: One Covenant or Two?* (Grand Rapids: Eerdmans, 1995), 69.
10. Matt 9:2; Mark 2:5; Luke 5:20; 7:48. For Dunn, the major issue when it comes to the forgiveness of sins is that Jesus took the place of the cult. Jesus "usurped the role of God which God had assigned to priest and cult . . . He who took upon himself the priestly task of pronouncing absolution, without the authorization of the Temple authorities and

forgiveness now comes through him "and no longer through the sacrificial system of the temple *suggests strongly that he was taking over the function of the temple.*"[11] The same could be said about Jesus' statement to Zacchaeus in Luke 19:9 that "salvation" had come into his house. The force of such a sentence, argues N. T. Wright, "is lost unless it is realized that, in making such pronouncements, Jesus was implicitly claiming to do and be what the temple was and did."[12]

The synoptic Gospels frame their narrative to include a climactic clash between Jesus and Jerusalem in the final week before the passion,[13] with the "cleansing of the temple" as a central incident.[14] The symbolic meaning of Jesus' action in the temple generated a lot of discussion.[15] Sanders famously proposed that Jesus' action in the temple was not simply a "cleansing," but a symbolic prophecy of the destruction of the temple.[16] Similarly, Wright argues that the cleansing of the temple should be viewed as an acted parable of judgment on Israel.[17] Bauckham, on the other hand, argues that Jesus' demonstration was a symbolic denunciation of the activities that he attacked. In other words, Jesus was judging the corruption in the temple system, but not necessarily symbolizing its destruction.[18] Yet, as Bauckham

---

without reference to the cult, might well be seen as putting a question mark against the importance and even the necessity of the cult, and, more threateningly, as undermining the authority of those whose power rested upon that system." Dunn, *The Partings of the Ways*, 62.

11. Beale, *New Testament Biblical Theology*, 632 (emphasis added).

12. Wright, "Jerusalem in the New Testament," 58.

13. Matt 21–25; Mark 11–13; Luke 19–21.

14. Matt 21:12–13; Mark 11:15–17; Luke 19:45–46.

15. For a brief survey on the different scholarly views on the significance of the cleansing incident, see Wright, *Jesus and the Victory of God*, 413–416; Dunn, *The Partings of the Ways*, 62–65.

16. Sanders, *Jesus and Judaism*, 61–76. For a critique of Sanders' argument, see C. A. Evans, "Jesus' Action in the Temple: Cleansing or Portent Destruction?" *The Catholic Biblical Quarterly* 51 (1989): 237–270.

17. Wright, *Jesus and the Victory of God*, 334.

18. R. J. Bauckham, "Jesus' Demonstration in the Temple," in *Law and Religion: Essays on the Place of the Law in Israel and Early Christianity*, ed. B. Lindars (Cambridge: James Clarke & Co, 1989),, 72–89. Similarly, for Dunn, Jesus' action should be viewed as a "symbolical representation of the 'cleansing' of the Temple which would be necessary if it was to serve its intended eschatological function, and possibly even a symbolical attempt to bring about these conditions." Dunn, *The Partings of the Ways*, 64.

himself observes, the destruction of the temple was implied in the saying with which Jesus interpreted the action itself – as a divine judgment on the abuses Jesus denounced.[19] The wider context of Jesus' action as presented in the synoptic Gospels thus seems to favor the notion that Jesus was indeed attacking the temple of his time and what it symbolized, and not merely reforming or cleansing it.

The synoptic Gospels include prophecies by Jesus predicting the destruction of the Jerusalem and its temple, in a manner similar to Jeremiah. For example, Jesus says in Luke 19:41–44 that Jerusalem's enemies "will not leave one stone upon another in you, because you did not know the time of your visitation."[20] Matthew 23:37–38, which speaks of the temple as "your house" and not "God's house," claims that Jerusalem and its temple will be left desolate:

> O Jerusalem, Jerusalem, the city that kills the prophets and stones those who are sent to it! How often would I have gathered your children together as a hen gathers her brood under her wings, and you were not willing! See, *your house is left to you desolate.*[21]

What is really significant is that, unlike Jeremiah, none of these prophecies speak of a future restoration or a reversal of fortunes. The judgment seems to be final and conclusive, and the incident with the cursing of the fig tree leaves no doubt as to the *finality* of the judgment.[22] The withering

---

19. Bauckham, "Jesus' Demonstration in the Temple," 86.
20. See also Luke 21:20–24; 23:27–31.
21. See also Luke 13:32–35.
22. Matt 21:18–22; Mark 11:12–14, 20. The context in which the cursing occurred is important. In both Matthew and Mark it takes place in the final week, and both evangelists associate it with the cleansing of the temple. In addition, Wright claims that Jesus' statement at the conclusion of the incident, that if his disciples had faith they could cause the mountain to be taken up and thrown into the sea – that this statement is actually about Mount Zion, and not any mountain, since when Jesus said this when he was in the Mount of Olives, which stands opposite to Mount Zion. If Wright is correct, then the cursing of the fig tree is a direct and explicit final judgment on Jerusalem and the Temple. Wright, *Jesus and the Victory of God*, 494.

of the fig tree is "an apocalyptic word of judgment that will find its analogue in the future destruction of Jerusalem and its temple."[23]

The Gospels interpret Jesus' death as a "ransom," suggesting that he offered his life as sacrifice (Matt 20:28; Mark 10:45).[24] In addition, and "as stated fairly explicitly at the last supper, Jesus on the cross was to become the place of sacrifice."[25] By offering himself as a sacrifice, Jesus established a new system that would counter the temple and render it unnecessary. The last supper is also important in that it signifies the establishment of a new pattern of worship. In the synoptic Gospels, the last supper follows the cleansing of the temple. The constitution of this new tradition could be then seen as a counter to the institution of the temple.

The death of Jesus *in* Jerusalem and *by* Jerusalem's leaders further intensified the negative attitude towards Jerusalem by the writers of the Synoptic Gospel. After Jesus died, the curtain of the temple was torn in two,[26] which could arguably be interpreted as a symbol that God had abandoned the territorial holy of holies of the temple.[27]

One way to explain the judgment on Jerusalem and the temple is to see it as a result of the positive claims of the Gospels about Jesus as the embodiment of God's presence. As we have seen, the synoptic Gospels claim that Jesus embodies in his person the presence of God on earth, and did in his ministry what the temple was supposed to do. As such, Jesus in his person

---

23. D. A. Hagner, *Matthew 14-28. Word Biblical Commentary* (Dallas: Word Books, 1995), 605.

24. The authenticity of the ransom saying as coming from Jesus has been disputed in modern scholarship. For a summary of the discussions and a defense of the authenticity of this saying, see C. A. Evans, *Mark 8:27-16:20. Word Biblical Commentary* (Nashville: Thomas Nelson, 2001), 120–125. See also V. Taylor, "The Origin of the Markan Passion Sayings," *New Testament Studies* 1, no. 3 (1955): 159–167.

25. Wright, "Jerusalem in the New Testament," 63. See Matt 26:26–28; Mark 14:22–24; Luke 22:19–20.

26. Matt 27:51; Mark 15:38; Luke 23:45. The veil should probably be understood as the veil that enshrouded the holy of holies (and not the outer veil). Evans, *Mark 8:27-16:20*, 510.

27. Hagner comments: "Clearly . . . the tearing of the veil is a type of apocalyptic sign pointing, on the one hand, to the wrath and judgment of God against the Jewish authorities, and, on the other, to the end of the temple, where God is no longer present." Hagner, *Matthew 14-28*, 849.

was a counter-temple movement.[28] Perhaps this is alluded to in Mark's record of Jesus' trial, where Jesus is said to have claimed that he would build a temple "not made with hands" (Mark 14:58).[29] The temple "not made with hands" refers to Jesus' body, and a contrast with the "temple built with hands" – the Jerusalem temple – is implied. Jesus is claiming here to be the *real* temple.[30]

Jesus and the temple were making the same claims. This sheds more light on the judgment motif in the synoptic Gospels towards Jerusalem and the temple. That is why for N. T. Wright the destruction of the temple is actually a vindication of Christ:

> Jesus had set his face, prophetically, against Jerusalem. He had staked his prophetic reputation upon the claim that the Temple would be destroyed. . . . In the light of this, those who claimed to be his followers were bound to see the continuing existence of Herod's Temple, and the city which housed it, as a paradox. Jesus would not be vindicated as a true prophet until it was destroyed by enemy action.[31]

---

28. Wright, "Jerusalem in the New Testament," 62.
29. Mark mentions the statement as coming from "false" witnesses. However, most scholars today believe that it represents something that Jesus actually said or at least something close to something that he said. Evans, *Mark 8:27–16:20*, 445. See also Wright, *Jesus and the Victory of God*, 493. It is possible that the false element in the false witnesses is that they claimed that Jesus said "I will destroy the Temple," and not simply "you destroy the Temple," as John records it (2:19). The witnesses might be referring to Jesus' prediction of the destruction of the temple (Mark 13:2) and falsely altering the predication into a claim that Jesus himself will destroy the temple.
30. Wenell makes an interesting observation about the use of the phrase "not made with hands." For her, the image implied by the phrase is from Israel's experience in the wilderness. Building on Exodus 15:17, she suggests that the temple "not made with hands" is connected to the model of the sanctuary in the camp in the wilderness. This, she suggest, recalls promises regarding the land as the goal of the period of wandering in the wilderness, and so "it is at least possible that Jesus and his group saw themselves as enacting a time before the entry into the land, in which case it might be entirely appropriate to speak of a temple not made by human hands if such might be seen as the goal of the exodus, and part of the new age. The calling of twelve disciples as tribal leaders would fit with this model." Wenell, *Jesus and Land*, 55–56.
31. Wright, *The New Testament*, 459.

Perhaps no other statement shows how Jesus relates to the temple more than Matthew 12:6. There, a discussion between Jesus and the Pharisees about purity rituals leads Jesus to declare climactically that he is superior to Israel's most sacred space: "I tell you, something *greater than the temple is here*" (Matt 12:6). In short, the coming of Jesus – the one who is greater than the temple – has rendered the temple unnecessary. Its time had come.

2.2. In the Fourth Gospel

John expressed the motif that Jesus embodied the presence of God perhaps more than any other NT writer. Writing most probably after the destruction of Jerusalem in AD 70,[32] he wanted to assert that the loss of Jerusalem and its temple could be endured.[33] From the outset of his Gospel, John declares that Jesus, the Word who is in fact God (1:1), "dwelt among us" (1:14). The Greek term σκηνόω could be literally translated as "tabernacled." John furthermore claims that we have "seen his glory" – a phrase reminiscent of the glory of YHWH in the tabernacle (Exod 40:34–35; Lev 9:23). This is clearly a confirmation that, in John's mind, Jesus embodies in his person the reality of the tabernacle in the experience of Israel. "What one hopes to find in the tabernacle one should find in Christ."[34]

In the conversation with Nathanael (1:47–51), Jesus mentions the story in Genesis 28 when Jacob saw the angels of God ascending and descending on a ladder. Jacob had called that place "Bethel," and had declared that this was the "house of God" and "the gate of heaven." Yet Jesus declares instead

---

32. For more on the date and authorship of the Gospel of John, and a summary of the different views, see D. A. Carson and D. J. Moo, *An Introduction to the New Testament* (Grand Rapids: Zondervan, 2005), 225–267. Even though they say, "almost any date between about 55 and 95 is possible," they seem to favour a date that is "nearer the end of that period than the beginning" (p. 264).

33. Walker's comments about the time and purpose behind John's writing are important: "If any of [John's] readers felt bereft of the Temple and of the spiritual focus provided by Jerusalem, John would have encouraged them not to mourn the loss of the city, but rather to see what God had done for them in Jesus." Walker, *Jesus and the Holy City*, 197. Davies also compares John's attachment to Jerusalem with that of Paul: "John has reached a position beyond Paul, where there is no longer even an emotional attachment to Jerusalem which according to some, as part of Judea, had become a city of his rejection, and where . . . there is a deliberate presentation of the replacement of 'holy place' by the Person of Jesus." Davies, *The Gospel and the Land*, 334.

34. Burge, *Jesus and The Land*, 50. See also John 1:18; 14:7–9.

that the angels of God are ascending and descending on the Son of Man – *himself*. As Davies confirms, "the point of John 1:51, in part at least, is that it is no longer the place, Bethel, that is important, but the Person of the Son of Man."[35] *Theophany is here associated with a person, not a place.*[36]

John then describes the cleansing of the temple incident at the beginning of Jesus' ministry (John 2:12–17), and follows it immediately with Jesus' declaration that he will raise a new temple, referring to the "temple of his body" (2:19–21). In other words, the new temple is nothing other than Jesus himself.[37] For Davies, John places the cleansing of the temple very early in his Gospel to signify that "a New Order had arrived," and that the holy place is to be displaced by "a new reality" – Jesus.[38] The statement of Jesus in 2:19, "destroy this temple, and in three days I will raise it up,"[39] reveals that it was Jesus himself, according to John, who claimed to be embodying the temple.[40]

John's comment that Jesus was talking about the temple of his body (2:21) reveals again that since Jesus and the temple were making the same claim, then one of them has to exclude the other. John's words thus imply that since Jesus replaced the temple, it will be destroyed and nullified. In order for Jesus to be raised as the new temple – the first existing temple

---

35. Davies, *The Gospel and the Land*, 289.
36. In addition, and according to Burge, since the purpose of the dream to Jacob in Gen 28 was to reaffirm God's promise of the land to him and his descendants, "Jesus is now the recipient of the promise of Holy Land held by Jacob." Burge, *Jesus and The Land*, 49.
37. For more on Jesus as the temple in John 2, see J. Chanikuzhy, *Jesus, the Eschatological Temple: An Exegetical Study of Jn 2,13-22 in the Light of the pre-70 C.E. Eschatological Temple Hopes and the Synoptic Temple Action* (Leuven: Peeters, 2012). See in particular p. 312–316. In particular, Chanikuzhy argues that John portrays Jesus as the *eschatological* temple.
38. Davies, *The Gospel and the Land*, 289.
39. The statement was recorded Mark 14:58 and Matt 26:61 as coming from false witnesses in Jesus' trial. However, as Wright argues, there is a good probability that Jesus was associated with a statement that is more or less equivalent: "Although Mark claims that the witnesses at the trial were 'false', the parallel tradition in John, the prophecy to the disciples on the Mount of Olives, and the mocking at the cross all reinforce the probability that a saying like this did indeed form part of his explanation of what he had done in the Temple courts." Wright, 1996, p. 493. It is possible that the false element in the false witnesses is that they claimed that Jesus "I will destroy the Temple," and not simply "you destroy the Temple," as John records it.
40. Walker, *Jesus and the Victory of God*, 281

must be nullified. This probably opens a new possibility on how to interpret the "cleansing of the temple":

> Here John gives the most valuable tool to interpret the temple action: Jesus is the temple. Through his death and resurrection, Jesus has become the eschatological temple . . . If Jesus is the real temple, then the other temples lose their reason of existence.[41]

The encounter between Jesus and the Samaritan woman in John applies the replacement motif on Zion as a place of worship. Jesus speaks of a coming hour in which Zion as a place of worship will be nullified (4:21) and of an hour that has already arrived in which true worshippers worship "in Spirit and truth" (4:23). "True worshippers do not emphasize the place of worship but the nature of worship."[42] The reference to truth (4:23) could be interpreted in John as a reference to Jesus himself (14:6). Jesus here "relativizes" all holy spaces, including Jerusalem, "by declaring the arrival of the age of the Holy Spirit – an age in which the presence of God is no longer focused in the temple."[43]

The following chapters in John focus on Jesus' ministry in Jerusalem. According to Davies, John deliberately relates a series of replacements associated with the different feasts of Judaism, and all of this then culminates in the statement in John 10:36 that God that Father has "consecrated" Jesus.[44] The word used here is ἁγιάζω, which is used in the LXX in Numbers 7:1 to describe Moses' consecrating the tabernacle. Therefore, "at the Feast of Dedication the old tabernacle and temple are replaced by the consecrated Christ."[45]

---

41. Chanikuzhy, *Jesus, the Eschatological Temple*, 405.
42. Y. Katanacho, "Reading the Gospel of John Through Palestinian Eyes," Paper presented at Institute of Biblical Research, Chicago, 16 November 2012.
43. A. Smith, "The Fifth Gospel," in *Eyes to See, Ears to Hear. Essays in Memory of J. Alan Groves*, ed. P. Enns, D. Green & M. Kelly (New Jersey: P&R, 2010), 88.
44. Davies, *The Gospel and the Land*, 294.
45. Ibid., 296.

In short, the fourth Gospel does not differ from the synoptic Gospels in the claim that Jesus is the new temple of God who replaced the old existing temple. If anything, John gives this claim more emphasis and clarity. Davies' conclusion of his study of John is conclusive: "The gospel is destined to personalize or Christify [holy] space, or, rather, holiness is no longer to be attached to space at all."[46]

2.3. In Stephen's Speech (Acts 7)

We can see the same pattern in the speech of Stephen in Acts 7. Stephen has been accused by the Jewish leaders, among many other things, of "speaking words against this holy place [the temple]" (Acts 6:13). His response was a lengthy speech in which he retold the story of Israel, de-emphasizing the role of the land, Jerusalem and the temple. In his selective approach to history, he recalls Abraham's calling outside of the land (7:2–3), and how Abraham did not receive the land as an inheritance (7:5). God then appeared and spoke to Moses also outside of the land (7:30), and Moses was with the "church" (ἐκκλησία) in the wilderness (7:38).[47] He then recalls the tabernacle (7:44), and more importantly, that despite the fact that Solomon built a temple, God does not dwell in man-made temples (7:48). At the end of the speech, Stephen locates Jesus, not in Jerusalem or the temple, but in heaven (7:56). For Burge, the selectivity in this speech communicates "the possibility that God's voice can be heard and holy land be found outside the Land of Promise."[48]

It is crucial to underline here that Stephen builds his argument from the OT tradition itself. Stephen here joins a discussion already existing in the OT about the validity of the temple. This is not a new question, and Stephen's arguments are not new. His rationale is basically a collection of OT verses:

---

46. Ibid., 290.
47. ἐκκλησία is the normal word used in the Septuagint for the gathered community of Israel. The term also is one Christians used for their own assembly, the church. J. B. Polhill, *Acts. The New American Commentary (Vol. 26)* (Nashville: Broadman & Holman Publishers, 1995), 199.
48. Burge, *Jesus and The Land*, 64. See also Davies, *The Gospel and the Land*, 272; Dunn, *The Partings of the Ways*, 88–89.

> Yet the Most High does not dwell in houses made by hands, as the prophet says, Heaven is my throne, and the earth is my footstool. What kind of house will you build for me, says the Lord, or what is the place of my rest? Did not my hand make all these things? (Acts 7:48–50)[49]

These are direct quotations from the OT.[50] They reflect the irony that Solomon expressed when he built a house for the One who cannot be contained in any house. They also reflect the initial dialogue between David and Nathan (2 Sam 7:5–7), when God simply declared that he did not request a temple. In other words, Stephen is not inventing a new tradition; he is joining an *already existing and long-standing conversation within the OT tradition.*

Dunn argues that Stephen here is shaped by Hellenistic influences, and that his views are those of Hellenist Christians: they are early signs of a breach between Hebrew Christians and Hellenist Christians.[51] We cannot speak conclusively about the extent to which Hellenism influenced Stephen, and whether Stephen's views are a reflection of Hellenist Christians *as opposed* to Hebrew Christians. Yet what we can say with certainty is that Stephen saw himself and his teaching as being in continuity with – or, at least, within the limits of – Israel and its Jewish tradition. His retelling of the story indicates that he was joining a discussion. Stephen, however, reaches a different conclusion to this discussion, and indeed to the story of Israel. Those associated with the Jerusalem temple are judged for betraying and murdering the "righteous one" and for not keeping the law (7:51–53). Jesus, on the other hand, the one who claimed to destroy this place (6:14), is now vindicated in heaven (7:56).

In conclusion, Stephen's speech outlines the conviction that "holy place" has been now relativized. Divine revelation is not narrowly tied to

---

49. According to Dunn, the adjective chosen, χειροποίητος (made with hands), would be a "horrifying word to use in this context" because it was the word used by Hellenistic Jews to condemn idolatry. In other words, Stephen was claiming that the Temple became an idol. Dunn, *The Partings of the Ways*, 89.
50. 1 Kgs 8:27; 2 Chr 2:6, 6:18; Isa 66:1–2.
51. Dunn, *The Partings of the Ways*, 95.

one place, and true faith is not concerned with one's location. Israel's hope is now to be found in "heaven," where the Son of Man is.

2.4. In the Writings of Paul

The appropriation of the divine presence to Jesus is not limited to the Gospels and Acts. We can mention Colossians, where Jesus is not only the "image of the invisible God" (1:15), but also the one in whom "all the fullness of God was pleased to dwell" (1:19) and the one in whom "the whole fullness of deity dwells bodily" (2:9). In other words, the locus of the divine presence is now found in the person of Jesus. Moreover, the church of Christ for Paul is *the* temple of God,[52] and this by implication "raises important questions about the status of the Jerusalem Temple."[53] Dunn concludes regarding these verses:

> The implication is clearly that the Temple no longer functioned for [Paul] as the focus of God's presence and as providing the means whereby a positive relation with him can be maintained.[54]

The fact that Jews and Gentiles are joined in the new temple (Eph 2:18–22) runs directly against the reality in the Jerusalem temple, which separated between Jews and Gentile, with a clearly placarded "dividing wall."[55] Moreover, if Christ were the ultimate sacrifice of atonement (Rom 3:25), then this would nullify the role of the temple. In Romans 12:1 Paul calls for a spiritual worship and the offering of living sacrifices, and not the offering of sacrifices in the Jerusalem temple.

---

52. 1 Cor 3:16–17; 2 Cor 6:16–18.
53. Walker, *Jesus and the Holy City*, 120.
54. Dunn, *The Partings of the Ways*, 100.
55. The term "dividing wall" in Eph 2:14 could be a reference to the Soreq Wall in the temple, which divided between Jews and Gentile in the temple. A pillar, presumably from the Jerusalem temple, was discovered in 1871, with the following inscription on it: "No man of another race is to enter within the fence and enclosure around the Temple. Whoever is caught will have only himself to thank for the death which follows." A. T. Lincoln, *Ephesus. Word Biblical Commentary* (Waco: Word Books, 1990), 141. The force of Paul's words can be even more appreciated when we consider that Paul almost lost his life because he was accused of escorting a Gentile into the temple. See Acts 21:27–29.

Finally, Paul's words in Galatians 4 reveal that Paul has developed a new paradigm through which he analyzes the significance of Jerusalem. The Jerusalem of Paul's day "is in slavery with her children" (Gal 4:25), and therefore what matters is the "Jerusalem above" (Gal 4:26). In Galatians 4:21–26, "Paul sees the Land, and its focal point Jerusalem, as both in theory and in practice relativized by the death and resurrection of the Messiah."[56]

In short, there is a new attitude in Paul towards Jerusalem and its temple. They are no longer the locus of divine presence – Jesus is. Moreover, and since Jesus is sacrifice, the temple now is rendered unnecessary. Jerusalem, and by implication the land, are no longer special places.

2.5. In the Epistle to the Hebrews

The book of Hebrews contains the strongest assertion that the place of Jerusalem and its temple, and by extension the land, has been nullified. The letter explicitly declares that Jesus is the high priest,[57] who ministers in the holy places, in the true tent that the Lord set up, and who offered himself as a sacrifice.[58] The new reality is accessible now through Christ (4:16; 10:19), the high priest over the house of God (10:19). The believers now have a new "altar" (13:10), which is clearly an alternative to the Jerusalem altar. The two altars are naturally "mutually exclusive."[59]

The inevitable result is that the old system is no longer needed. Jesus entered as high priest "once and for all" to the holy places, and secured by his own blood *eternal* redemption, and so no more sacrifices are needed (Heb 9:11–14). The sacrifices that the believers should offer in return, according to Hebrews, have also been altered. To give a sacrifice is to give praise to God, to do good, and to share what one has (13:15–16).[60]

The Jerusalem temple, as a result, is viewed as nothing but a shadow to the reality that has been revealed in Christ (8:5; 10:1). The author of Hebrews "explicitly teaches that the earthly sanctuary with its liturgy has

---

56. Wright, "Jerusalem in the New Testament," 69.
57. Heb 2:17; 3:1; 4:14; 5:5; 6:20; 8:1; 9:11; 10:21.
58. Heb 7:28; 8:2; 9:11–12, 28; 10:12.
59. Walker, *Jesus and the Holy City*, 206.
60. Similarly, see 1 Pet 2:5 which speaks of spiritual sacrifices.

been done away with forever, and he forbids the people of God from going back to that shadow."[61] It is true that Hebrews does not mention the temple, but always alludes to it indirectly. This does not mean, as Ellingworth suggests, that the author of Hebrews has no interest in the temple.[62] Rather, as Motyer asserts, "it is quite impossible that Hebrews could write about a heavenly sanctuary without connecting the earthly, even if the Jerusalem Temple had been destroyed by the time of writing."[63] Motyer then argues that the fact the temple does not appear in Hebrews is actually intentional:

> The Temple does *not* appear in Hebrews precisely so that the profound message of the letter *about the Temple* may actually be heard in its scriptural depth, and not be rejected out of hand.[64]

The same can be said about how the epistle treats Jerusalem as a city. At the conclusion of this homily, the author claims that his readers have already come to "Mount Zion" and to "the city of the living God," the heavenly Jerusalem – not the earthly one (Heb 12:22–24). We can appreciate the significance of such a statement when we consider that Jewish believers in those days were possibly tempted to continue the tradition of pilgrimage to Jerusalem, and the message of Hebrews speaks out against this. "If not an actual aim of the author, one possible effect of his argument in these verses was to minimize in the estimation of his readers the importance of the earthly Jerusalem as a place of pilgrimage."[65]

The strongest statement against the validity of Jerusalem is probably the one in the final chapter. Taking his cue from the example of Jesus, who was crucified outside the city, the author calls his readers symbolically – and maybe even literally – to leave behind them the city of Jerusalem and all that it represents:

---

61. Waltke, *An Old Testament Theology*, 574.
62. P. Ellingworth, *The Epistle to the Hebrews: A Commentary on the Greek Text. New International Greek Testament Commentary* (Grand Rapids/Carlisle: Eerdmans/Paternoster Press, 1993), 401.
63. S. Motyer, "The Temple in Hebrews: Is it There?" in *Heaven on Earth,* ed. S. Gathercole & T. D. Alexander (Carlisle: Paternoster Press, 2004), 178.
64. Ibid., p. 189.
65. R. P. Gordon, *Hebrews,* Second ed. (Sheffield: Sheffield Academic Press, 2008), 181.

> So Jesus also suffered outside the gate in order to sanctify the people through his own blood. Therefore *let us go to him outside the camp* and bear the reproach he endured. For here we have *no lasting city*, but we seek the city that is to come. (Heb 13:12–14)

The call to go to Jesus "outside of the camp" has different connotations, but must be understood in the first degree in the context of the author's argument against the cult of Jerusalem. This is an exhortation to sever the theological and social ties with the Jewish upbringing of the community, and this means a departure from dependence on the levitical priesthood with its feasts and sacrifices.[66] Since Jerusalem was at the heart of the Jewish cult of first-century Judaism, these words no doubt affect the way in which those who received the letter (a community of new Jewish believers) will view Jerusalem from now on. As Walker concludes, the author of Hebrews here "is challenging them to forego both a people and *a place*, both Judaism and *Jerusalem*."[67] We can thus conclude that, according to Hebrews, Jerusalem has lost its special status. It is no longer the glorious Zion, but simply a city that will not last (13:14).

2.6. The Jesus-Event and the Parting with Judaism

The NT evidence about the new attitude towards Jerusalem and its temple (and, by implication, the land) can only be written as a result of the powerful impact of the Jesus-event. This, then, sheds strong doubts on Dunn's argument about the parting of the ways between Christianity and Judaism with regards to the temple. Dunn seems to understate Jesus' attitude and position towards the temple when it comes to the NT theology of the temple. He believes that Jesus' actions in the temple should be viewed as "expressing the conviction that the temple had to be sanctified and made

---

66. P. E. Hughes, *A Commentary on the Epistle to the Hebrews* (Grand Rapids: Eerdmans, 1977), 580.
67. P. W. L. Walker, "Jerusalem in Hebrews 13:9–14 and the Dating of the Epistle," *Tyndale Bulletin* 45 (1994): 44 (emphasis added). The whole article argues convincingly that Heb 13:9–14 is talking about the earthly Jerusalem of his time.

ready for its eschatological function."[68] In other words, Jesus was not judging, but sanctifying the temple.

For Dunn, Jesus stands well within the diversity of Second Temple Judaism, and so there is nothing in Jesus' ministry and teaching which required or compelled a development out of, or a breach with, a Judaism focused on the temple of Jerusalem.[69] Dunn builds this conviction based on his argument that Jesus did not explicitly indicate that his death was "sacrificial" and that he was a substitute to the temple.[70] Moreover, it was Stephen and not Jesus who started the tradition of radical critique of the temple. Second or even third-generation Christians looked back to Stephen and the Hellenists as the beginning of the breach between Christianity and the predominant temple-centered Judaism of the mid-first century.[71]

Dunn's conclusions are questionable. Jesus' actions and statements about the temple are more than a critique. As we have already seen, the NT in all its traditions portrays Jesus as replacing the temple, not reforming it. No Second Temple Judaism group or book claimed that a person *replaced* or *embodied* the temple. In addition, the synoptic Gospels include very harsh words towards Jerusalem and the temple, and leave no room for a reformed temple or a restored Jerusalem. Moreover, it is also very doubtful that Paul, John and other NT writers based their strong convictions about the temple on a homily by Stephen, or were heavily indebted to Hellenistic influences. It is far more plausible that they would reach these conclusions based on the sheer drama of the Jesus-event itself.[72] More precisely, it seems more plausible that this new and radical perspective on Jerusalem and its temple owes its origin to Jesus himself.[73]

---

68. Dunn, *The Partings of the Ways*, 64.
69. Ibid., 75.
70. Ibid., 75–76.
71. Ibid., 90.
72. Interestingly, Dunn believes that in Paul (p. 100), John (p. 125), and the Hebrews (p. 121) the parting of the ways with regards to the Temple has already begun. Yet he argues that it was the Stephen Episode that began the breach, and not Jesus himself.
73. Walker, *Jesus and the Holy City*, 269, 271.

2.7. Conclusion

In conclusion, we find in the NT an assertion that Jesus is the ultimate holy place. He embodies in himself the presence of God. Theophany and encountering God are possible through him. In addition, Jesus takes upon himself in his ministry the role and function of the temple and its rituals. In short, holiness is no longer associated with a place, but with a person. Jesus is the holy space *par excellence*.

This assertion leads to very important questions: What about Jerusalem and the temple – and by implication the land? Do they cease to be "holy territory"? The answer the NT authors give to this question is "yes." The NT not only claims that Jesus replaced and embodied holy space, it also implies and concludes that this embodiment nullified the notion that Jerusalem or the land are special "holy places." The judgment on Jerusalem and temple in the NT, as we have seen, is conclusive and final. Unlike the prophetic tradition, there is no mention of a future restoration of the temple and Jerusalem.[74] To speak of a future physical temple would be to ignore that Christ at his first coming began to fulfill the hopes of the OT.[75]

---

74. For some, however, Jesus' words in Matt 23:39 (also Luke 13:35b) "For I tell you, you will not see me again, until you say, 'Blessed is he who comes in the name of the Lord'" – give the impression that Jesus is envisioning a time in the future in which Jerusalem will accept Jesus as Messiah. See for example C. Blomberg, *Matthew. The New American Commentary* (Nashville: Broadman & Holman Publishers, 1992), 351. It will be hard to build a whole theological argument about a future significance for Jerusalem from this verse, while completely ignoring the witness of the NT as a whole. Moreover, Matt 23:39 is not necessarily a prediction, but could be simply a general statement that when Jesus returns, "even those who had rejected him will of necessity affirm him as the coming one, the crucified, risen Messiah, whether in gladness or remorse." Hagner, *Matthew 14-28*, 681. Moreover, and as Allison has shown, "until you say" can be read as stating a condition upon Jerusalem. In other words, Jerusalem will not see Jesus again unless it repents and acknowledges him as the one coming from the Lord. D. C. Allison, "Matt 23:39 = Luke 13:35b As a Conditional Prophecy," *JSNT* 18 (1983): 75–84.

75. Some see in 2 Thess 2:4, which speaks about the man of lawlessness taking his seat at the temple of God, a prediction of a future significance for the temple of Jerusalem. See for example R. L. Saucy, "The Church as the Mystery of God," in *Dispensationalism, Israel and the Church: The Search for Definition*, ed. D. L. Bock, W. C. Kaiser and C. A. Blaising (Grand Rapids: Zondervan, 1992), 151. However, it is more probable from the context of 2 Thess 2 that the reference to the temple should be taken "symbolically." See F. F. Bruce, *1 & 2 Thessalonians. Word Biblical Commentary* (Dallas: Word Books, 1982), 169. Moreover, Wright suggests that Paul here reflects the early Christian tradition, going back to Jesus himself, according to which Jerusalem was to be destroyed, and according to which that destruction was to be interpreted as the wrath of God against his sinful people. Wright, "Jerusalem in the New Testament," 54.

Holiness is now defined in relation to Jesus. Divine Presence in biblical theology narrows from land, to Jerusalem, to temple, to Jesus – and will expand again, as we will see, from Jesus, to Jerusalem, to the ends of the earth. The NT redefines holy place – in reference to Jesus. Even so, however, this redefinition should not be viewed as a rejection of the OT tradition. No, the NT authors clearly held a high regard to the Scriptures. Rather, what we have is a redefinition of these traditions as an unavoidable consequence of the climactic Jesus-event. The NT is reading the holiness traditions through new eyes – as finding their *telos* in Christ.

3. The Church as Holy Space

An important implication of Jesus' embodiment of holiness is that the church, as the body of Christ,[76] derives its holiness from Jesus who dwells in her midst, and as a result she, too, is declared as the temple of God in the NT. Paul says to the Corinthians:

> Do you not know that *you are God's temple* and that God's Spirit dwells in you? If anyone destroys God's temple, God will destroy him. For God's temple is holy, *and you are that temple.* (1 Cor 3:16–17)[77]

> For *we are the temple of the living God*; as God said, "I will make my dwelling among them and walk among them, and I will be their God, and they shall be my people. Therefore go out from their midst, and be separate from them, says the Lord, and touch no unclean thing; then I will welcome you, and I will be a father to you, and you shall be sons and daughters to me, says the Lord Almighty." (2 Cor 6:16–18)[78]

---

76. Rom 12:5; 1 Cor 10:17, 12:27; Eph 4:12, 5:23; Col 1:24.
77. See also 1 Cor 6:19.
78. Compare with Lev 26:11–12; Isa 52:11; Jer 31:9.

These two passages explicitly declare that, in the theology of Paul, the church *is* the temple of God. The temple image is not simply used as a metaphor. Rather, and by citing OT passages that speak about the time of restoration, Paul "is saying that Christians are indeed the real beginning fulfillment of the actual prophecy of the end-time temple."[79] According to Paul, God now dwells *in* his people.[80] It is important to note that Paul "is not saying that each individual Christian is a temple within which God's Spirit dwells, but rather that the Spirit of God dwells in the Christian community *corporately as a community*."[81]

Furthermore, Paul's use of these OT promises that are related to the time of Israel's restoration not only indicates that in Paul's mind the time of restoration has arrived, but that this restoration will now include or incorporate Gentile believers. In a striking manner, Paul follows his citation of these Israelite promises (2 Cor 6:16–18) with the astonishing claim that today "we have these promises" (2 Cor 7:1) – clearly implying that Gentile Corinthians are co-recipients of these promises.

The same is evident in Ephesians 2:17–22, where Jews and Gentiles *together* in Christ constitute a new building that grows into a temple for God:

> In whom the whole structure, being joined together, grows into a holy temple in the Lord. In him you also are being built together into a dwelling place for God *by the Spirit*. (Eph 2:19–22)

The reference to Christ as the cornerstone is of extreme importance. Paul is citing Psalm 118:22 and/or Isaiah 28:16; in doing so, he links the Jerusalem temple in Zion with Christ as its cornerstone. This means that

---

79. Beale, *New Testament Biblical Theology*, 639. Beale remarks that some commentators, like Fee, speak of the temple Corinthians only as a metaphor; the church is merely "like" a temple. Beale argues against this interpretation in length. Ibid., 635–639; G. D. Fee, *The First Epistle to the Corinthians* (Grand Rapids: Eerdmans, 1987), 260.

80. Davies observes that Paul in 2 Cor 6:16 departs from the LXX when he uses the phrase ἐνοικήσω ἐν αὐτοῖς (which literary means "dwells in you"), in order "to emphasize that God no longer dwells *with* his people in a tent or temple, but actually dwells *in* them." Davies, *The Gospel and the Land*, 187 (emphasis in the original).

81. A. C. Thiselton, *The First Epistle to the Corinthians: A Commentary on the Greek Text* (Grand Rapids: Eerdmans, 2000), 316 (emphasis in the original).

the church, both Jews and Gentiles, can be "a holy temple in the Lord" because of Christ and through Christ, and also because of the dwelling of the Holy Spirit in her midst.[82] The same rationale is also found in 1 Peter 2:4–6, where a reference is also made to Isaiah's prophecy. But in 1 Peter, the church is not only a temple; she is also a "holy priesthood":

> As you come to him, a living stone rejected by men but in the sight of God chosen and precious, you yourselves like *living stones are being built up as a spiritual house*, to be a *holy priesthood*, to offer spiritual sacrifices acceptable to God through Jesus Christ. For it stands in Scripture: "Behold, I am laying in Zion a stone, a cornerstone chosen and precious, and whoever believes in him will not be put to shame."(1 Pet 2:4–6)

The reference to "holy priesthood" evokes memories from Israel's call in the wilderness (Exod 19:5). Yet, the holiness of the people of God, according to Peter, clearly derives from the cornerstone of the house – Jesus himself. God's people thus have a derivative holiness – one dependent on Jesus the prime focus of holy space. We can see this principle of derivative holiness in the words of Jesus to his disciples in John 17:17–19:

> *Sanctify* them in the truth; your word is truth. As you sent me into the world, so I have sent them into the world. And for their sake *I consecrate myself, that they also may be sanctified in truth*.

The verb ἁγιαζω is used for both "consecrate" and "sanctify," and is the same one used in John 10:36 about the Father "consecrating" Jesus. Jesus' holiness is the source of the holiness of the disciples. This is probably

---

82. Walker says that this is what is distinct about the Paul's teaching of the community as a temple, as compared with the Qumran community, which also viewed itself as an alternative temple. He says: "Paul's doctrine of the Church (and its members) as the true *locus* of God's Temple was therefore founded on distinctively Christian assumptions: the reality of the Holy Spirit, and also the person of Christ himself." Walker, *Jesus and the Holy City*, 121.

behind Paul's calling the believers "saints" or ἅγιοι[83] and more precisely "sanctified in Jesus Christ" or ἡγιασμένοις ἐν Χριστῷ Ἰησοῦ (1 Cor 1:2). Furthermore, in 1 Corinthians 6:11 Paul says that his addressees are "sanctified" in the name of Jesus and by the Spirit, and in 1 Corinthians 1:30 Jesus has become "sanctification" to them.

In conclusion, the NT teaching that Jesus himself is the new temple leads by implication to the church as a corporate entity being described as the holy temple of God. The holiness of the church in the NT is a *derivative* holiness. It derives from Jesus who is the cornerstone of the holy temple, and from the presence of the Holy Spirit in her midst. If earlier we concluded that holiness is no longer located in a *place*, but in *a person*, the conclusion now is that holiness has been located – by extension – in the community of Jesus.

4. Universal Holiness

These two realities – the fact that holiness is no longer confined to one space (the land, Jerusalem, or the temple), but is to be found in the person of Jesus, together with the fact that the church with Christ as her cornerstone and the Spirit in her midst is the temple of God – lead to the conclusion that holiness as a result of the coming of Jesus is no longer confined to one territory, but is now universalized. In other words, since the church today is spread all over the universe, holiness – which is the mark of the church as a temple – is located where the church is.

We can see this already beginning in the ministry of Jesus. Admittedly, most of Jesus' ministry was confined within the holy territory of Israel, and on one occasion when he sent the twelve disciples to preach the kingdom he told them: "go nowhere among the Gentiles and enter no town of the Samaritans, but go rather to the lost sheep of the house of Israel" (Matt 10:5–6). Yet Jesus' decision to focus most of his ministry in Galilee remains quite startling, given the significance that Jerusalem had for his contemporaries as the holy territory *par excellence*. Moreover, as the story with the

---

83. Rom 1:7; 2 Cor 1:1; Eph 1:1.

Canaanite women tells us (Matt 15:21–28), Jesus never hesitated to meet with Gentiles; thus, though being "sent only to the lost sheep of the house of Israel" (15:24), he healed the woman's daughter and even praised her (15:28). More importantly, on many occasions Jesus visited and ministered in the non-Jewish Decapolis.[84] Anticipating his own people's rejection to his message, Jesus predicted a time in which many would "come from east and west and recline at table with Abraham, Isaac, and Jacob in the kingdom of heaven."[85] So we can argue that the Gospels portray a gradual shift, moving beyond the sacred geography of Israel, which culminated in the commission to make disciples of "all nations" (Matt 28:19) and to "go into all the world and proclaim the gospel to the whole creation" (Mark 16:15).[86]

We can also observe some universal implications in some of Jesus' other teachings. For example, in Mark 2:27 Jesus reminds his audience "the Sabbath was made for man, not man for the Sabbath."[87] Jesus here takes a Jewish teaching about creation and the Sabbath and gives it a more general and universal application, by saying that the Sabbath was made for *humanity in general*.

Then again, the cleansing of the temple includes a hint of the movement towards the universalization of holiness. The synoptic Gospels mention Isaiah 56:7 as behind Jesus' rationale for his actions. Only Mark quotes the verse in full, but the message is implied by the other evangelists: "My house shall be a house of prayer *for all nations*" (Mark 11:17). The original verse in Isaiah speaks of foreigners coming to God's holy mountain and offering accepted burnt offerings and sacrifices. Jesus' citation then "picks up on one element of the sacred traditions concerning the restored or eschatological temple: it was to be the focus of the eschatological ingathering of the Gentiles."[88]

---

84. Cf. Matt 15:21; Mark 5:1; 7:24.
85. Matt 8:11–12. See also Luke 13:28–29.
86. Mark 16:9–20 is commonly known as the "long ending" of Mark, and is not found in the oldest manuscripts of the Gospel of Mark. Evans, among others, believe that it is a later secondary ending. Evans, *Mark 8:27-16:20*, 545–551. Our analysis, however, has shown that – at least thematically – this passage fits well with the overall structure of the Gospel of Mark and with the themes we find in the synoptic Gospels.
87. See Dunn, *The Partings of the Ways*, 152–153.
88. Bryan, *Jesus and Israel's Traditions*, 222.

Could this citation be a critique of the temple arrangement in the first century, which separated between Jews (holy) and the Gentiles (unholy) and which, through dedicating a court for the Gentiles, prevented them from entering the actual temple? Could Jesus be announcing that the time of restoration prophesied by Isaiah is arriving, and as a result the offerings of the Gentiles can be accepted now?[89]

The book of Acts takes this expansion of holiness to a new level. There is a movement from Jerusalem, to Judea and Samaria, and to the ends of the earth (1:8). At Pentecost Peter declares that the prophecy of Joel about the eschatological Zion has been fulfilled and so the Spirit now falls on "all flesh" (2:17). The incident with Peter and Cornelius in Joppa (Acts 10) breaks the boundaries of holiness with regard to food laws, to people, and to territory. God tells Peter: "What God makes clean, do not call common" (10:15) in reference to his encounter with Gentiles in their home – something that was clearly against the purity laws of the Jews in the first century (11:2–3). We need to keep in mind that many discussions among the Jews in those days centered not only on the question of "who is pure?" but also "where is pure?"[90] In this light, we can safely presume that Caesarea Maritima, the capital of the Romans in Palestine, was not considered pure. In other words, Peter extends the commandment "What God makes clean, do not call common" to apply to territory, and not just food and people. He concludes that "God shows no partiality but in *every nation* anyone who fears him and does what is right is acceptable to him"

---

89. Furthermore, Bryan suggests reading the cleansing incident in the light of Zech 14:21: "there shall no longer be a trader in the house of the LORD of hosts on that day." The Hebrew word translated "trader" here is כנעני, which could also be translated as "Canaanite." Bryan comments: "Zechariah anticipates an eschaton in which the distinction between sacred and common, pure and impure, disappears . . . Thus it is entirely plausible that against the backdrop of Zechariah 14's expectation of the eschatological Temple, Jesus' action as well as his citation of Isaiah 56.7 served as an indictment of the Temple for having failed to become the eschatological Temple." Bryan, *Jesus and Israel's Traditions*, 223–224. If Bryan is correct, then this would serve to enforce the conclusion that Jesus was critiquing the temple for failing to live up to the eschatological expectations of being an *inclusive* temple. See also Dunn, *The Partings of the Ways*, 48–49. We may recall here Gordon's comments on Zech 14:21 that what we have in this verse is the implication that "holiness would extend beyond its normal confines." Gordon, *Holy Land, Holy City*, 72.
90. Weinfeld, *The Promise of the Land*, 75.

(Acts 10:34–35). The incident in Cornelius' house in Caesarea culminates in the pouring of the Spirit over the new Gentile Christians (10:44), to the amazement of the Jews present.

In short, the story of the Spirit and of the church in Acts knows no geographical limits: the Ethiopian did not received the Spirit in Jerusalem (8:28), and Paul himself was given the Spirit, not in the land, but in Damascus. As Davies concludes, "the geographical question need not concern us: the territorial limits of Jewish expectation have been transcended."[91]

That holiness is no longer confined to the land is also evident in Ephesians 6:1–3. There, Paul applied the commandments related to the land to people and places *outside of the land*:

> Children, obey your parents in the Lord, for this is right. "Honor your father and mother . . . that it may go well with you and that you may live *long in the land* (γῇ)."

Paul is quoting the fourth commandment (Exod 20:12). Yet it is important to notice how Paul omits the final part in the verse in Exodus which says "in the land *that the LORD your God is giving you.*" By doing so, he is basically expanding the holy territory over which this commandment has affect. What applied to the land of promise applies now in Ephesus.

The above discussion shows that holiness is no longer confined to the land or the people of the land, but has been universalized as it pertains to both territory and peoplehood. All lands can be holy: holiness applies to the Ephesians where they are. All peoples can be holy: Gentiles can join the holy city. This confirms what the whole of the NT gives testimony to: *Holiness as a result of the Jesus-event is now a-territorial: it is not limited to one territory.* This shift has already been anticipated in the OT. The work of the Spirit opens the possibility of breaking down the barriers between preconceived notions of "holy" and "profane," resulting in new holy lands and new holy peoples.

---

91. Davies, *The Gospel and the Land*, 272.

5. The Demand for Ethical Holiness

We have seen in the OT that the land demanded holiness, and that the presence of God in the midst of his people also demanded holiness.[92] The demand for holiness is still as important in the NT. Paul gives at least two reasons why holiness still matters. First, since the church is a holy temple, Christians should do their best not to destroy the temple of God (1 Cor 3:17), which parallels the call in the OT not to defile the land. Second, the Spirit now dwells in believers (1 Cor 3:16); this again parallels the demands for holiness in the OT, which were based on the fact that God dwelled in the midst of his people.

At the same time, we must observe that holiness in the NT has been redefined. It is no longer tied to places, times, or diets. The focus in the NT is ethical and moral, not cultic or spatial. This redefined holiness, as we might expect to see, started in Jesus.

Jesus' radical statement about pure food ran against the traditions of his day regarding holiness: "It is not what goes into the mouth that defiles a person, but what comes out of the mouth; this defiles a person."[93] Upon hearing this, the Pharisees "were offended" (Matt 15:12), for purity laws were considered an essential part of living in the land.[94] In Jesus' days, purity in the society was not portable, but "located and related with a concern for the holiness of the land."[95] Jesus overturned this at a stroke!

Moreover, Jesus' parable about the Good Samaritan (Luke 10:25–37) provides, according to Bryan, another window into how Jesus challenged the purity laws of his days. The question the lawyer asked, "who is my neighbor" (10:29) "is bound up with the question 'who is pure'?" Bryan concludes:

---

92. See chapter 2 above, section 1.
93. Matt 15:11; see also Mark 7:15; Matt 12:1–8. Similarly, Jesus' very harsh woes against the religious leaders of his day in Matt 23 culminates in his criticism on the Pharisees for focusing on external purity and neglecting the heart (Matt 25:23, 25–26).
94. See Bryan, *Jesus and Israel's Traditions*, 157.
95. Wenell, *Jesus and Land*, 102.

Yet Jesus' parable strongly implies that the Samaritan who was deemed by Jews to be irremediably impure and a defiler of the Land but who keeps the divine will by showing neighbourly love is approved by God, and those who most rigorously defend the holiness of the Temple, the Land and the people but fail to love their neighbours are not.[96]

So Jesus in this parable is doing what he did with the dietary laws: he shifts the focus from external ritual, racial, and territorial purity into internal purity and now into social justice. Jesus clearly had challenged the notions of purity common in his times.[97] For him, the heart is the source of holiness and defilement. The purity that Jesus offered was radically different from the customs of his day, and it challenged the concept of "holy space":

> This is not the purity of the Pharisees. It does not emphasize new *halakhic* interpretations, or attempt to define who is pure and who is less pure, or *where* is pure and where is less pure. It is not the purity of the Sadducees. There is no focus on the temple and its holiness. It is not the purity of Qumran. Enemies are not condemned as defiled, but included in the commandment to love. It is not even the purity of John. There is no emphasis on the ritual practice of sacred space.[98]

This redefining of purity can be also seen in Paul's letters in his treatment of the dietary debates. In Romans 14:14–20, purity is measured in brotherly relationships and not in what one eats, because "the kingdom of God is not a matter of eating and drinking but of righteousness and peace

---

96. Ibid., 185.
97. Minear even argues that "Jesus was crucified because he seemed to be the enemy of holy places (like Jerusalem and the temple) and holy times (like the Sabbath and the festivals) and holy things (like "clean" foods and dishes)." P. S. Minear, "Holy People, Holy Land, Holy City. The Genesis and Genius of Christian Attitudes," *Interpretation. A Journal of Bible and Theology* 37, no. 1 (1983): 22.
98. Wenell, *Jesus and Land*, 102.

and joy in the Holy Spirit" (14:17).[99] In 1 Timothy 4:3–4 Paul goes so far to declare that "everything created by God is good, and nothing is to be rejected if it is received with thanksgiving, for it is made holy by the word of God and prayer." This is a radical statement, especially when one considers that it is coming from a first-century Jew, with their strict dietary laws. Something massive has taken place and has caused Paul to redefine what it means to be holy. Similarly, when Paul called the church a temple in his letters to the Corinthians, the discussion did not include any cultic notions, but centered on the ethical behavior of his readers. The holiness to which Christians have been called "evokes not spatial but moral undertones."[100]

The book of Hebrews, as already discussed, is against offering physical sacrifices and cultic or food rituals, and instead calls for a new way offering sacrifices (Heb 13:9, 12, 15–16). The same pattern can be seen in Peter's first letter, which focuses on the holy living of the Christians: "As he who called you is holy, you also be holy in all your conduct, since it is written, 'You shall be holy, for I am holy.'" (1 Pet 1:14–16). Peter argues here that the Christian community inherits not just the privileges but also the demanding responsibilities of being the holy people of God.

In conclusion, holiness in the NT is indeed demanded, but it has also been redefined. It is no longer a cultic purity that relates to food diets, circumcision, or Sabbath – as was the situation for example with the diaspora Jews. Instead, holiness is ethical and social, and should be evident in the daily lives of the Christian community. The articulation of these new standards of living distinguished the Christian community and *set them apart* from the other communities around them as *holy* people. In this, however, it no longer matters *where* the community is located. What matters is the presence of God in their midst – a presence that makes them a temple for God and that demands holy living. As such, any land could be a "holy" land where "holy" people lived "holy" lives.

---

99. See also 1 Cor 6:12–13; Col 2:16; Titus 1:15.
100. Davies, *The Gospel and the Land*, 187.

6. Conclusion –
The Arrival of the Eschatological Temple

We have explored how the Jesus-event affected and redefined the concept of sacred geography. "In his death and resurrection, Jesus' holiness or sanctification became the measure and standard of all holiness, whether of places, times, things, or persons."[101] Walker gives a good summary of the redefinition that took place in the NT and how it affects the concept of holy place:

> When the one came who would embody the incarnate presence of God, the true *shekinah* presence, then the Temple as the previous focused location of the divine name would need to be laid aside. When the Spirit came, Jerusalem's role as witnessing to the presence of God in the midst of his people would no longer be necessary. When the time came that the gospel could go out "to all nations," then the previous particularity associated with Jerusalem would need to give way. When Gentiles could at last enter "the people of God," then the necessary distinction between Jew and Gentiles emblazoned within the Temple would have to be "broken down."[102]

The fact that Jesus replaced in his person and ministry the notion of holy space led to important developments. First, the traditional understanding of holy space was challenged and nullified. "Holy territory" expanded to include every place and every community where Christ is present and where the Spirit dwells in the midst of the community. This redefinition then affected what it meant to be holy: it was an ethical and moral holiness – no longer tied to territory.

Holiness is now "a-territorial." By "a-territorial" we mean that it is no longer confined to one particular territory. However, holiness is still an earthly experience – related to the daily living of the Christian here and now in this world. As such, it is possible to argue that according to the

---

101. Minear, "Holy People, Holy Land," 23.
102. Walker, *Jesus and the Holy City*, 315.

NT, if a Christ-centered community in which the Spirit dwells, inhabits a locality, and if this community exhibits holy living, then a holy reality is created, and this renders that locality as "holy." Holiness is a-territorial, but it is still an earthly – indeed "earthy" – experience. A "holy land reality" is still possible.

The conclusion of all of this is that Jesus has inaugurated the eschatological temple spoken of by the OT prophets. He accomplished this in his person and ministry, and through the dwelling of the Spirit in the church. Jesus is the epitome of the presence of God on earth, the one in whom the glory of the Father was revealed. The coming of Jesus announced that the new history has arrived and so holiness is now universalized. The eschatological presence of God in the new era knows no limits to race, age, or geography. It is an all-inclusive presence.

CHAPTER 9

Jesus and the Covenanted Land

Introduction

In this chapter, we will look at how the NT treated the theme of the covenant as it pertains to the theology of the land. It will be argued that Jesus is portrayed as the ideal Israelite and the faithful seed of Abraham, the one who kept the covenant and inherited the land. We will also argue that the covenanted people are also defined as those who are in Jesus; thus they have been universalized, and in Jesus they inherit the land. The land continues to be a mandated land, and there are continuous demands on the people of God to produce fruits.

The fulfillment in Jesus of the OT covenant with Israel has important consequences for how we interpret this covenant today. Israel broke the covenant with God, and did not live as children of Abraham. Arguably, the church as the seed of Abraham, Jews and Gentiles, continues the story of Israel.

1. Background: Covenantal Nomism

The covenant was a major element in defining Israel's identity in the first century. Dunn, following Sanders,[1] argues that despite the variety of the

---
1. E. P. Sanders, *Paul and Palestinian Judaism: A Comparison of Patterns of Religion* (London: SCM, 1977), 422.

Jewish theology in the first century, we can speak of a common pattern of "covenantal nomism" as a characteristic of Judaism that was taken for granted by most Jews.[2] Covenantal nomism is the belief that "God had made a special covenant with Israel to be his own, and as integral to that covenant had given Israel the law to provide Israel with the means of living within that covenant."[3] The law, on this understanding, marks the people of God and distinguishes them from other nations. Israel's obedience to the law is seen as an act of gratitude for his covenantal promises and election. In particular, three aspects of the law functioned as markers for the distinctiveness of the Jews: circumcision, observing the Sabbath, and the dietary laws.[4]

This Jewish belief in their continuing covenantal relationship with God included, of course, the belief that the land was still part of the covenantal arrangement. Therefore, when we read statements in the NT about God's remembering his covenant with Abraham, we should presume that the land is part of this covenant. Matthew introduces Jesus in his story as the Son of David and the *son of Abraham* (Matt 1:1), in a clear reference that Jesus continues the story of Israel. Luke's introduction includes two important references to the covenant with Abraham, through the mouths of Mary and Zechariah (1:54–55, 73–75). By introducing the story of Jesus as such, Matthew and Luke underscore the fact that the Abrahamic covenant provides the backdrop of the story of Jesus, and that the land was still under promise.[5] The message is clear: God has *remembered his covenant* with Abraham and the promises of restoration and of a new eschatological covenant are about to be fulfilled.[6] In addition, if N. T. Wright is correct about the meaning of δικαιοσύνη θεοῦ (commonly translated as the

---

2. Dunn, *The Partings of the Ways*, 35.

3. Ibid., 35.

4. It is worth noting here that what Sanders and others characterize as "covenantal nomism" is not an invention of Second Temple Judaism. Its roots and basis are grounded in the OT. God's calling to Abraham was accompanied by a demand for obedience and circumcision. God's election of Israel and his redemptive acts towards her were accompanied with calls to obey the law. Second Temple Judaism simply inherited and adopted this concept and applied it to the context of the first century.

5. Brueggemann, *The Land*, 161.

6. See J. Hamilton, "The Seed of the Woman and The Blessings of Abraham," *Tyndale Bulletin* 58, no. 2 (2007): 271.

"righteousness of God"), then this would give us further insight into how the NT authors understood the significance of the Jesus-event. For, according to Wright, δικαιοσύνη θεοῦ is "God's own faithfulness to his promises, to the covenant."[7] So when Paul declares in Romans 1:16–17 that the gospel of Christ reveals the righteousness of God, what is in mind here is precisely his *covenantal faithfulness*. In other words, the NT teaches that in the Jesus-event God has remembered his covenant with Israel. This will have important consequences for our understanding of the theology of the land.

2. Israel and the Land Redefined

2.1. Jesus the Faithful Israelite in the Gospels

Many have observed how in the Gospel of Matthew, more than any other Gospel, Jesus is presented as encapsulating in his life the story of Israel – a new Israel.[8] Jesus' birth circumstances echo those of Moses: a ruthless king hunts both. Jesus goes in his infancy to Egypt, just as Israel did. This is what Matthew intended to communicate when he cited Hosea 11:1: "When Israel was a child, I loved him, and out of Egypt I called my son." Matthew claims that, "this was *to fulfill* what the Lord had spoken by the prophet" (Matt 2:15). Yet the original context in Hosea is not a prophecy about the Messiah or about the future. Hosea is narrating the story of Israel *in the past* – and this is precisely the point behind Matthew's citation. Jesus now is God's Son who is called out of Egypt. This is Israel's story retold in Jesus.[9]

Matthew introduces John the Baptist's ministry using Isaiah's words, "The voice of one crying in the wilderness: Prepare the way of the Lord" (Matt 3:3). Matthew's citation is a not just reference to one verse (Isa 40:3), but also to the whole episode in Isaiah 40–55, which speaks of God's servant Israel. Matthew here is using the words of John to communicate that

---

7. N. T. Wright, *What Saint Paul Really Said: Was Paul of Tarsus the Real Founder of Christianity?* (Grand Rapids: Eerdmans, 1997), 96.
8. Holwerda, for example, says: "In Matthew, "these two questions coincide: Who is Jesus? and who is Israel? Jesus is Israel, and Israel is Jesus." Holwerda, *Jesus and Israel*, 44.
9. See Burge, *Jesus and The Land*, 30–31; Holwerda, *Jesus and Israel*, 37–39.

the time of comfort has arrived and that John is preparing the way for the Lord *and his Servant*. When Jesus is baptized, he is introduced as "God's Son" (Matt 3:17), which echoes the sonship of Israel in the OT, and the calling of Israel as the Servant of YHWH (Isa 42:1). His baptism is in essence an act of identification with Israel, as Israel's representative.[10]

Jesus was baptized in the Jordan River at the beginning of his ministry, which echoes Israel's crossing of the same river to enter the Promised Land. The temptation narrative is another sign that Jesus is re-living the story of Israel. Jesus' forty days in the "wilderness" (Matt 4:2) echo Israel's forty years of testing in the wilderness. What is also interesting is that each of the three temptations faced by Jesus is one faced by Israel in the wilderness. This is why in all three incidents Jesus' response came not simply from Scripture, but from the book of Deuteronomy in particular[11] – a book that describes Israel's wilderness experience and focuses on the importance of obedience. The message is clear: whereas Israel failed to obey God and to keep the covenant in the wilderness, Jesus, the new and ideal Israelite, obeyed God and kept the covenant. In short, Jesus relives the story of Israel.

N. T. Wright argues at length that the whole of Jesus' ministry should be seen as a "retelling" of Israel's story, and in particular of her return from exile. Jesus "claimed in word and deed that the traditional expectation was now being fulfilled. The new exodus was under way: Israel was now at last returning from her long exile."[12] Further, he argues convincingly that *it was Jesus himself* who conveyed the notion that he was re-enacting the story of Israel, and not merely the evangelists:

> If scholars are ready to credit Matthew, say, or Luke with the ability to understand how the geographical symbolism of Israel's traditions could function – and if, equally, John the Baptist and many others were able to understand these same symbols and re-enact them – there is no reason whatsoever to deny Jesus the same skill . . . Jesus does seem to have had

---

10. D. A. Hagner, *Matthew 1-13. Word Biblical Commentary* (Dallas: Word Books, 1993), 57.
11. Deut 8:3; 6:16; 6:13.
12. Wright, *Jesus and the Victory of God*, 243.

a keen awareness of the symbolism of place. His movement took its origin, after all, from that of John the Baptist, who like several other Jewish prophets of the time was gathering people in the Jordan valley, re-enacting the exodus in which Israel had for the first time come in to possess the land.[13]

Moving from Matthew into John, we can see the same theme even intensified. In one important passage (John 15:1–6) Jesus redefines and personalizes what it means to be "Israel in the land."[14] Jesus claims that he is the "*true* vine" (15:1), indicating indirectly that there is another "false" vine. Jesus' use of the vine metaphor is not uncalculated. The vine in the OT is Israel planted in the land.[15] Jesus claims here that he has replaced Israel:

> The crux for John 15 is that Jesus is changing the place of rootedness for Israel. The commonplace prophetic metaphor (the land as vineyard, the people of Israel as vines) now undergoes a dramatic shift. God's vineyard, the land of Israel, now has only one vine: Jesus.[16]

In short, the history of Israel narrows down and focuses on one person: an Israelite and a descendant of Abraham by the name of Jesus. This new Israelite re-enacts the story of Israel and encapsulates what it means to be Israel. In addition, Jesus is also portrayed as the obedient and thus ideal Israelite – the one with whom God is well pleased (Matt 3:17). The implication of this redefinition of Israel is that the covenant blessings and motifs that concerned Israel must undergo a similar transformation in order to accommodate the new reality. The land is then one of those covenant motifs that we can expect to undergo some redefinition.

---

13. Ibid., 430. In addition, Wright observes how Jesus' actions and use of symbols fit exactly into the overall grid of Second Temple retellings of Israel's and how other retellings, too, involved substantial adjustments at the level of praxis, symbol and questions-and-answers (p. 200).
14. See Davies, *The Gospel and the Land*, 333.
15. Ps 80:8; Jer 2:21; Isa 5:2.
16. Burge, *Jesus and the Land*, 54.

2.2. Jesus the Seed of Abraham in Paul

The same theme of Jesus as the ideal Israelite is articulated in Paul, yet from a different angle. In Galatians 3 Paul uses the example of Abraham in his discussion with the Judaizers. He reminds them that the nations were supposed to be blessed through Abraham (3:8; see Gen 12:3), and then claims that this blessing came to the Gentiles *in Christ* (3:14). He then states explicitly that there is only one "offspring" to Abraham, and this "offspring" is the only recipient of the promises to Abraham:

> Now *the promises* were made to Abraham and to his offspring. It does not say, "And to offsprings," referring to many, but referring *to one*, "And to your offspring," *who is Christ*. (Gal 3:16)[17]

This is indeed a massive statement – one that Hays calls Paul's "essential theological presupposition for his hermeneutical strategies."[18] Paul affirms that Jesus is the *only legitimate recipient* of the Abrahamic promises, denying in essence any other claims by any person or people group to the benefits of this covenant. The story of Israel narrows down in Paul's thinking until it is summed up in one person: Jesus.

Jesus, according to Paul, *earned this right* to channel the blessing of Abraham to the nations and to be recognized as Abraham's only legitimate heir. The fact that Abraham's blessing to the Gentiles came *in Jesus* is based

---

17. See Gen 12:7: "To your offspring (לזרעך) I will give this land." See also Gen 13:15; 15:18; 17:8; 24:7, all are promises of the land to the זרע of Abraham. See also, "and in your offspring (בזרעך) shall all the nations of the earth be blessed." The Hebrew word זרע is a collective noun. It is singular in form but both singular and plural in meaning, just like the English word seed. In Greek, the word is σπέρμα, and has both a singular (σπέρματι) and a plural (σπέρματιν) form, and Paul uses both in the verse to make his point. The use of the Hebrew word in Genesis has clearly a plural meaning. According to Enns, "Paul here is employing a technique that was common in his day, namely, capitalizing on the interpretive flexibility of certain words or grammatical features." Enns, *Inspiration and Incarnation*, 136. In other words, Paul's play with words here, though cannot be justified by grammar, was nevertheless acceptable in his context. Paul's point is theological: The promise is fulfilled in Christ. Interestingly, in Gal 3:26, Paul tells the Galatians: "You are Abraham's offspring." He uses the singular form of σπέρμα with the second person plural form of the verb to be (εστε).

18. Hays, *Echoes of Scripture*, 121.

on Jesus' obedience in his death on the cross – as evident by the use of ἵνα εἰς (in order that) in the beginning of Galatians 3:14:

> Christ redeemed us from the curse of the law by becoming a curse for us – for it is written, "Cursed is everyone who is hanged on a tree" – so that (ἵνα εἰς) in Christ Jesus the blessing of Abraham might come to the Gentiles, so that we might receive the promised Spirit through faith. (Gal 3:13–14)

Jesus' death was his taking upon himself the curse of breaking the covenant. Paul is not saying here that Jesus broke the covenant and therefore deserved the curse. Rather, since Jesus has become Israel, part of becoming Israel is taking upon himself the curse of Israel. Whereas in the Gospels the focus is on Jesus' active obedience in his life and ministry, the focus in Paul is on his passive obedience, which was evident in his death.

2.3. Jesus Inherits the Land

The inevitable implication of this – both the Gospels' teaching that Jesus is the new Israel, and Paul's claim in Galatians 3:16 that Jesus is *the* seed of Abraham – is that Jesus now receives the promises and benefits of the Abrahamic covenant, *including the land*.

Paul uses the land promises in Genesis to indicate that Jesus received the land. Notice how Paul's phrase in Galatians 3:16 "to your offspring" is a quotation from the land promises "to the offspring" (Gen 12:7). If he had used "in your offspring," he would have referred to the promise that nations will be blessed "in the offspring" (Gen 12:3). The fact that Paul does not mention the land here does not mean that we can exclude the land from the equation, for "while the Abraham image undoubtedly is transformed, it is inconceivable that it should have been emptied of its reference to land. *The Abraham imagery apart from the land promise is an empty form."*[19] We can therefore conclude that Jesus inherited the land promised to Abraham. He is the only legitimate inheritor of the land. The land promises have been transferred from Israel to Jesus the faithful Israelite.

---

19. Brueggemann, *The Land*, 166 (emphasis added).

The land that Jesus inherits is the whole earth. Matthew claims that Jesus has been given all authority on heaven and *earth* (Matt 28:18). *Jesus here receives all the lands of the earth as his inheritance.* Similarly, Paul makes it clear in Philippians. 2:7–10 that every knee on earth should bow to Jesus – which underscores his universal sovereignty. The land has been universalized. We can see this theme of the universalization of the land even more clearly in Romans 4:13. Notice how Paul describes the geographical extent of the promises to Abraham:[20]

> For the promise to Abraham and his offspring that he would be *heir of the world* did not come through the law but through the righteousness of faith.

Abraham, according to Paul, received the world – and not Canaan – as his inheritance. The word Paul uses is κόσμος, which could be interpreted as the world or even the order of the universe.[21] *The Promised Land is in fact, according to Paul, the promised earth.* This is not an invention of Pauline theology, as if it did not have its basis in the Jesus-event and even in the Genesis narratives. Matthew claimed, as we just saw, that Jesus' sovereignty was universal (Matt 28:18). Conceivably, Paul could have known this Mathean tradition; certainly his own teaching has reached a parallel conclusion.

In addition, we have seen that inherent in the promise of the land to Abraham (defined from the "river to the river") is a promise of universal dominion, and how Psalm 2 promises the king of Israel the "ends of the earth" as his possession.[22] Furthermore, some strands of Second Temple Judaism have begun to universalize the land promises.[23] If so, we cannot exclude the

---

20. See K. E Bailey, "St. Paul's Understanding of the Territorial Promise," *The Near East School of Theology Theological Review* XV, no. 1 (1994): 59–69.
21. S. Zodhiates, *The Complete Word Study Dictionary: New Testament* (Chattanooga: AMG Publishers, 2000).
22. See above chapter 4, section 5.
23. See section on First-Century Jewish Theology of the Land (p.179 of this book) for more on the universalization of the land in Second Temple Judaism. Tendencies to universalize the promises of the land in Second Temple Judaism are well established in modern scholarship. Beale, for example, observes: "Both the OT and Judaism viewed

possibility that these strands could have influenced Paul. Moreover, Paul's own involvement in spreading the gospel to Gentiles no doubt also have influenced Paul to move forward with this universalization process.

However, we must emphasize that for Paul, just as is the case for the Second Temple theologians who universalized the land, the basis for such a move was scriptural. Indeed, for Paul, Romans 4:13 is "a unique return to Israel's highest calling for the world."[24] This is precisely why Paul used Abraham as his basis for this universal theology. Abraham is "the father of many nations." In him the nations of the world would be blessed. In other words, in the mind of Paul, he was bearing faithful witness to the teachings that were foreseen and "pre-preached" in Scripture (Gal 3:8). He viewed himself as still within the tradition.

This is important to realize since Paul was writing in a diverse theological Jewish context. Even if diaspora Judaism universalized the land, there were other Jewish voices, which maintained strong nationalistic and territorial theologies of the land.[25] Some of Paul's readers in Romans and Galatians might well have been influenced by such views on the land. Thus, if he was not to be discredited, Paul would have to argue for this position, not only from the perspective of the risen Christ, but also from OT Scriptures.

Paul was writing with the conviction that the Abrahamic blessing had now been realized in the Jesus-event. Yet this fulfillment of the Abrahamic covenant in Jesus would necessarily have important ramifications for both the people and the land. The people of God now must be universalized, so too the land. The land in Paul's theology is the whole earth. However, this is not a spiritualization of the land promises, nor is it a rejection of the promises. On the contrary, this is the realization of the original intent

---

Israel's land promises as containing within themselves a notion that the boundaries of the promised land would be expanded to encompass the entire earth." Beale, *New Testament Biblical Theology*, 756. See also Bailey, "St. Paul's Understanding," 60; Amaru, "Land Theology in Philo," 65–93 (in particular p. 85–86); Wright, *The New Testament*, 495–496. See also Jub. 32:19; Sirach 44:21; Enoch 40:9; 2Baruch 14:13; 51:13.

24. Burge, *Jesus and the Land*, 86.

25. Davies observes: "The exegesis of Jewish history – not surprisingly – had pressed upon the Abrahamic promise a "national," territorial stamp which often tended to obliterate its universal range." Davies, *The Gospel and the Land*, 177.

behind the promises. What Paul rejects is the limiting of these promises to one people and one territory. The land has been universalized.

2.4. Conclusion

The Gospels and Paul portray Jesus as the new and ideal Israel as well as the faithful seed of Abraham who kept the covenant; he is the one in whom the history of Israel finds its climax. The covenant between God and Israel, of which the land was an integral part, becomes the covenant between God and Jesus – or between the Father and the Son (Matt 3:17). The land, in this new arrangement, is the earth. This new development highlights the centrality of the Jesus-event as a pivotal point in biblical theology, which announced the arrival of a new era in history. As Dunn argues:

> [The] transfer of the decisive identifier of the people of God, of the church of God, from the ethnic seed of Abraham and the land promised to Abraham to the Christ as the one whom Israel's whole history and purpose aspired is one of the most revolutionary features of the earliest Christian movement . . . Christianity is defined by Christ and by reference to Christ – period![26]

The coming of Jesus thus has redefined what it means to be Israel. Israel is now understood in reference to him. It has also redefined the concept of the Promised Land, allowing the promise to break out of its particularistic phase and to refer now to the whole earth – fully in line with God's original intention. Next we will see how Jesus has redefined what it means to belong to the people of God.

---

26. Dunn, *New Testament Theology*, 117 (emphasis in the original).

3. The Covenanted People Redefined

3.1. Covenantal Membership through Christ

Jesus' selection of the twelve disciples was a symbolic act in which Jesus was redefining Israel around himself. The twelve disciples "recall the promises of the past and evoke a twelve-tribe constitution of Israel."[27] They represent a new Israel. The teachings and acts of Jesus will be the defining boundaries of this new community. Jesus also called his followers in general to form a new family around himself. He claimed that "whoever does the will of God, he is my brother and sister and mother" (Mark 3:35). Jesus envisioned loyalty to himself as creating an alternative community.[28]

We have already observed how John portrays Jesus as taking the place of Israel as the true vine (John 15:1–6). The disciples of Jesus must be *in him* in order to produce fruit. Indeed any branch that is not *in him* will be cast out (John 15:4–6). The equation is simple: *If Jesus is the new Israel, then being in Jesus means being part of Israel.*

We have also seen how Paul claims in Galatians 3:16 that Jesus is the heir of the Abrahamic promises. Paul then takes his argument to the next stage and makes it his basis for redefining what it means to be a descendant of Abraham today:

> For in Christ Jesus you are all sons of God, through faith. For as many of you as were baptized into Christ have put on Christ. There is neither Jew nor Greek, there is neither slave nor free, there is no male and female, for you are all one in Christ Jesus. *And if you are Christ's, then you are Abraham's offspring*, heirs according to promise. (Gal 3:26–29)

---

27. Wenell, *Jesus and Land*, 105. Wenell gives a thorough analysis of the number twelve and the symbolism behind it in both the Old and New Testaments. She also argues that the tradition behind the twelve disciples goes back to Jesus himself, and was not a later development (p. 104–135).
28. Wright, *Jesus and the Victory of God*, 401. See also Matt 10:34–39; 12:46–50; 19:29; Mark 10:29–30; Luke 8:19–21; 9:59–60; 11:27–28; 12:51–53; 14:25–27; 18:29.

There are many key issues to underline in these verses. First, it is important to emphasize that Paul builds his argument here on his already established arguments that Jesus is *the* "offspring" (3:16), and that inheritance is through faith and not through the law (3:18). Second, Paul is here talking about people who have believed in Christ (3:26), have been "baptized into Christ" and have "put him on" (3:27). The metaphor of baptism communicates incorporation: "To be 'baptized into Christ' is to be incorporated into him by baptism, and hence to be 'in Christ.'"[29] The conclusion of all of this is natural for Paul: if you belong to Christ, then by implication you belong to Abraham as well, because Jesus is the seed of Abraham.

In short:

> Jesus sums up true Israel in his one person; all those who identify with him and are represented by him are deemed to be, in a positional or legal sense, literally true Israel, though one cannot see this reality with physical eyes.[30]

This summing of Israel into the person of Christ has massive implications for the theology of the land. In the new covenant era, the blessing of Abraham is now open to all who are in Christ – Jews and Gentiles alike. This also means that the inheritance of the land – now redefined as the earth – is something of which both Jews and Gentile can be beneficiaries.

3.2. The Universalization of the People of God

The people of God in the new era thus include both Jews and Gentiles. We can already observe in the Gospels some hints of this expansion. A few examples will suffice. Jesus declared, "many will come from east and west and recline at table with Abraham, Isaac, and Jacob in the kingdom of heaven" (Matt 8:11–12; see also Luke 13:28–29). He also said, in a clear reference to Gentiles: "I have other sheep that are not of this fold. I must bring them also, and they will listen to my voice. So there will be one flock,

---

29. F. F. Bruce, *The Epistle to the Galatians: A Commentary on the Greek Text* (Grand Rapids: Eerdmans, 1982), 185. See also 1 Cor 10:2 which takes about being baptized into Moses to communicate being joined under his representation.

30. Beale, *New Testament Biblical Theology*, 772.

one shepherd" (John 10:16). The disciples are commissioned by Jesus before the ascension to go to "all nations" and to the "ends of the earth."[31] In addition, Peter says in Acts 2:39 that "the promise is for you and for your children and for *all who are far off,* everyone whom the Lord our God calls to himself." This could be seen as a hint towards the inclusion of those who are far off – the Gentiles, echoing Joel 2:32.[32]

The inclusion of Gentiles with the people of God in the NT was progressive. The Gentile Pentecost, Peter's encounter with Cornelius, the mission of Paul, and the Jerusalem council – these were all major events that led to the realization of this inclusion. Paul then gives the inclusion of Gentiles a strong theological basis.[33] He claims in his letters that there is no difference in the new economy of salvation between Jews and Gentiles.[34] The basis for Paul for this universalization is clear: membership in the covenant people today is through faith in Jesus.[35] He also goes back to Abraham to argue for the universalization of the people of God and the land,[36] showing that this had always been God's intention,[37] and underscoring that membership in the people of God has always been through faith, not through the law (which was what had marked the Jews as the people of God).[38]

---

31. Matt 28:19; Mark 16:15; Acts 1:8. See chapter 8 section 4 above for more examples about the universalization tendency in the Gospels.

32. Polhill, *Acts*, 117.

33. For Dunn, it was Paul who challenged the external boundaries of Judaism, and not Jesus. Jesus only challenged the internal boundaries of covenant membership, by sitting and having fellowship with "sinners." Dunn, *The Partings of the Ways*, 183. Sinners, for Dunn, are those within Judaism who were perceived as breaking the Torah and not within the covenant circle (p. 148–150). It is highly unlikely that such a radical shift in biblical history will have its basis only in Paul without any traces for it in Jesus. In addition, Dunn has to deal with many references in the Gospels, which hinted towards the universalization of the mission of Jesus and his disciples. Dunn thus had to conclude that these references reflect a late stage. Talking about Matt 28:19, he says (p. 156), "it is almost certain that the 'great commission' of Matt 28.19–20 reflects an understanding of mission which only came to such clear and full expression at a later stage – whatever may have been the historical root of the saying itself." It is more plausible, in my opinion, to argue that Paul did not start the universalization of the people of God, but that he was the one who pushed it forward and gave it its theological basis.

34. Rom 10:12; 1 Cor 12:13; Gal 3:28; 5:6; Eph 3:18.

35. Gal 3:16, 29.

36. Rom 4:12, 13, 16; Gal 3:8, 14.

37. Rom 3:29; Gal 3:8.

38. Rom 4:13; Gal 3:18.

Hays' detailed analysis of Paul's use of the OT is vital for our study. He argues that Paul's interpretive strategies look at Scripture in such a way that the church – composed of Jews and Gentiles together – comes into focus as the goal of God's redemptive action.[39] Paul operates with an "ecclesiocentric hermeneutic,"[40] which has christological foundations.[41] Commenting on Romans 3:21–4:25, he argues:

> Paul, speaking from *within* the Jewish tradition, contends that the Torah itself provides the warrant for a more inclusive theology that affirms that the one God is God of Gentiles as well as Jews and that Abraham is the forefather of more than those who happen to be his physical descendants.[42]

Hays' argument is important because it confirms, once again, that for Paul, the inclusion of Gentiles into the people of God is *the original intent* of the election and calling of Abraham, and not a surprising uncalculated new development as a result of the new Christian movement. What is new in Paul's theology is the conviction that this inclusion of Gentiles is a *present* reality as a result of the recent Jesus-event.

We must also observe that the inclusion of Gentiles in Pauline theology makes them *equal beneficiaries* of the people of God. Paul explicitly states: "There is neither Jew nor Greek" (Gal 3:28). The same is evident in Ephesians 2 in the passage on the joining and reconciliation of Jews and Gentiles in Christ. He starts the discussion by claiming that Gentiles *were* "separated from Christ, alienated from the commonwealth of Israel and strangers to the covenants of promise" (2:12). Notice how Paul equates separation from Christ with alienation from the commonwealth of Israel. This means two things. First, Jesus is now the true center of Israel. Second, Jews who are outside of Christ are now outside of Israel. Thus, the redefinition of what it means to be Israel has already taken place in Paul.

---

39. Hays, *Echoes of Scripture*, 84.
40. Ibid., 86.
41. Ibid., 120.
42. Ibid., 55 (emphasis in the original).

Further, the alienation is not simply an alienation from God. Paul is not taking here about sin and sinners from the perspective of an individualistic standing in front of God. The alienation is from *Israel and her covenantal promises*. It is important to remember that being part of Israel is what gave a right standing with God in the OT. Now one has to be *in Christ* to enjoy the same privileges. Paul's conclusion of this passage is important. As a result of the cross of Jesus, Gentiles "are no longer strangers and aliens," but "fellow citizens with the saints and members of the household of God" (2:19). Paul cannot be more conclusive: Gentiles have an equal share in the commonwealth of God. Ephesians 3:6 declares this unequivocally:

> The Gentiles are *fellow heirs*, members of the same body, and *partakers of the promise* in Christ Jesus through the gospel.

We can observe the same conclusion in Romans 11, where Paul uses the metaphor of the olive tree. The wild olive shoots that are grafted in among the others in the tree "*share in the nourishing root of the olive tree*" (11:17). The new branches do not only join the new tree. They join *and share* the nourishing root of the tree, and in effect become natural members of it.

The church today, consisting of Jews and Gentiles, thus *inherits the story of Israel*. It is not simply that Gentile Christians share some of Israel's blessings. They joined Israel. Hays uses the term "incorporation": Gentiles have been incorporated into Israel as a result of their faith in Christ.[43] He also observes how in 1 Corinthians 10:1, Paul calls the attention of the Corinthians to the experience of "our fathers,"[44] and in 1 Corinthians 12:2 Paul says to the Gentiles that they "*were* Gentiles": these phrases indicate that Paul "thinks of the Corinthian Christians as Gentiles no longer."[45] The reason for this is:

> Paul can treat Scripture as a word for and about Gentile Christians only because these Gentiles have become – in a

---

43. Ibid., 96.
44. Ibid., 95.
45. Hays, *Echoes of Scripture*, 96.

remarkable metonymic transfer – Abraham's seed, heirs of God's word to Israel, as a result of God's act in Jesus Christ.[46]

All of this is probably behind the coining of the phrase "the Israel of God" in Paul: "And as for all who walk by this rule, peace and mercy be upon them, and upon *the Israel of God*" (Gal 6:16). Some argue that the phrase "Israel of God" applies to Israel in the flesh – and not to the church.[47] Davies, for example, says that the term applies "to the Jewish people as a whole," and argues that Romans 9–11, where Paul deals extensively with Israel as a separate entity, gives support to this.[48] Yet this conclusion is doubtful, especially at the climax of an epistle that has argued so extensively and passionately that in Christ there is no Jew or Gentile. Furthermore, the epistle does not deal with the future of the Jewish people; so it is most unlikely that Paul would have brought up this new and complex issue in his final sentences. It seems far more logical, then, taking the whole epistle as the direct context (and not Rom 9–11), to argue that Paul uses the phrase to describe the true children of Abraham – those who are in Christ:

> In the context of the total argument of Galatians, where the issues focus on the question "Who really are the children of Abraham?" . . . to conclude with a declaration that Gentile converts are rightfully "the Israel of God" would be highly significant and telling.[49]

---

46. Ibid., 121.

47. Some have even re-punctuated the verse to read: "Peace on all those who follow this rule, and mercy on the Israel of God." Longenecker convincingly refutes this interpretation. R. N. Longenecker, *Galatians. Word Biblical Commentary* (Dallas: Word Books, 1990), 297–298.

48. W. D. Davies, "Paul and the People of Israel," *New Testament Studies* 24, no. 1 (1977): 10. See also Bruce, who identifies the phrase with "all Israel" in Rom 11:26, and applies it to a remnant within the Jewish people. As such, Paul here hopes that this remnant will increase in the future. Bruce, *1 & 2 Thessalonians*, 275.

49. Longenecker, *Galatians*, 298. See also G. W. Hansen, *Galatians* (Downers Grove: InterVarsity Press, 1994), 201. Moreover, Paul makes this statement immediately after declaring that "neither circumcision counts for anything, nor uncircumcision, but a new creation" (Gal 6:15). It seems then that the "new creation" of Gal 6:15 is the "Israel of God" of Gal 6:16. This "Israel of God" does not depend on circumcision" but on being in Christ.

It is then better to understand the phrase as applying to the "new community of Gentile and Jewish believers."[50] This is indeed a radical statement by Paul:

> Paul is willing to attach to that same community one of Judaism's most sacred titles for itself: Israel . . . This is perhaps the apostle's most stark example of universalizing the new identity of the people of God.[51]

In short, the NT's vision of the people of God, as a result of the Jesus-event, is one of inclusivity. The "people of God" has been universalized. Paul thus can champion a salvation that is pan-ethnic or "supra-national."[52] The inclusion of Gentile Christians made them equal citizens or members in the commonwealth of God. The natural implication of all this, is that both Jews and Gentiles who are in Christ inherit the promises to Abraham, including the land. To this we move next.

3.3. The Inheritance of the Land by the People of God

We have argued that for Paul, Jesus is the heir of the Abrahamic promises, including the land. Paul then takes this particular argument about the inheritance of the land onto the next level. In Galatians 3:29 he claims: "And if you are Christ's, then you are Abraham's offspring, *heirs according to promise.*"

Paul here is expanding the beneficiaries of this inheritance to include all those who are Christ's. He is not denying his earlier statement that Christ is the seed of Abraham (3:16). He is expanding it by making it the basis for the inheriting by all those who are in Christ. "Paul insists that Gentiles who believe in Jesus gain nothing less than the full inheritance that had belonged exclusively but temporarily to Israel before."[53] The direct and straightforward implication of all of this is simple: *the land belongs*

---

50. Hays, *Echoes of Scripture*, 96.
51. Burge, *Jesus and the Land*, 83.
52. Ibid., 79.
53. Wright, *Old Testament Ethics*, 193.

to all those who are Christ's. Brueggemann rightly stresses that we cannot exclude the land from the inheritance in Galatians 3:29 "unless we are to succumb to an otherworldly hermeneutic."[54] He then adds: "The heirs in Christ are not heirs to a new promise, but the one which abides, and that is centrally land."[55]

The use of the concept of "inheritance" is not limited to Galatians 3:29, but is a common theme in the Paul.[56] What is the nature of this inheritance? We have already seen how in Romans 4:13 Paul interprets the promises to Abraham to be about the inheritance of the *earth*. We can equally conclude that since Christ inherited the earth, in fulfillment to the promise of Abraham, then those who are in Christ inherit the earth as well (Matt 5:5). As Bailey puts it, "the promise *had to expand*, because the very 'people of God' had expanded."[57] In other words, the inheritance of the land has been expanded or "universalized": the focus is now not on the Promised Land but on the whole earth, inherited by Jews and Gentiles in Christ.

Paul therefore can challenge believers in Ephesians about a commandment that had previously related namely to life in the land (Eph 6:1–3). He tells the Ephesians to obey their parents "that you may live long in the land" (Eph 6:3). The privileges and demands of Israel in their land became those of Ephesian believers *in Ephesus*.

Many scholars speak of the concept of inheritance in the theology of the land in the NT. However, because of preconceived beliefs about the nature of the inheritance, they conclude that the inherited land is now either a futuristic concept or a spiritual one – and for the most part something only enjoyed by *individuals*. Beale, for example, speaks of the inheritance as related to the "hope of the believer's bodily resurrection," and as having "its

---

54. Brueggemann, *The Land*, 167.

55. Ibid. The application of this inheritance in Brueggemann's theology is a little bit vague. He says that it is about having "a place in a displacing world" (p. 167), and it seems that he is engaged in a more existential interpretation, although he denies this (p. 166).

56. On three occasions – Gal 5:21; 1 Cor 6:9; 15:50 – Paul mentions the kingdom as the inheritance, in a context of a warning against unethical behaviours. See also Rom 8:17 where "The children of God are heirs of God and fellow heirs with Christ." See also Gal 4:7; Eph 1:14.

57. Bailey, "St. Paul's Understanding," 68 (emphasis in the original).

end-time inaugurated fulfillment in those who believe in Christ."[58] Waltke says that Paul replaces "Abraham's physical seed's attachment to the land with Abraham's spiritual seed's attachment to a life in Christ," and that "Israel's inheritance of the land of Canaan is a foretaste of the Christian's inheritance in the regeneration of all things."[59]

There is no denying a futuristic element in Paul theology.[60] It seems, however, that Beale and Waltke undermine both the *present* and the *earthly* dimensions of the inheritance today. Instead, we must interpret the concept of inheritance according to its role in the biblical story. *The church inherits the story of Israel, which is a story that includes a promise of land*. For Paul, the universalization of the promise represents the promise's original intention, and is now realized in Christ. In addition, this universalization for Paul is more than the transfer of this promise into particular new places in the universe where Christ is present, and where believers have a spiritual experience in him. Rather, the whole inhabited world, indeed the universal order (the *kosmos*), is the Promised Land. *The land universalized is not the land spiritualized.*

Above all, what these scholars miss is that when Paul speaks of inheriting the promises, he is *not talking about individuals* inheriting the promises. He is talking about the believers, the seed of Abraham and the new people of God, as a corporate entity. They inherit the land as a community. We must remember that in Paul's mind the church continues the story of Israel. Therefore, we cannot interpret the statements about inheritance as referring to private individualistic spiritual experiences. Such a thought is alien to the biblical concept of inheritance and promise, and indeed to the concept of redemption in the OT.

Israel's inheritance of a *land* serves as a model for the inheritance of *lands* by many new communities in new geographical locations. Believers in Christ are called to start new covenantal communities that embody a Christ-centered version of the theology of the land of Israel in new geographies, and thus "universalize" the land, and this will serve as a foretaste

---

58. Beale, 2011, 761, 765.
59. Waltke, *Old Testament Theology*, 578, 581.
60. See chapter 11 below, sections 3–4.

for the ultimate fulfillment of the land in the future consummation. This is what it means to say that the land has been universalized.

3.4. Conclusion

The people of God in the NT are defined in reference to Christ. A new Israel is formed, and it continues the story of Israel, as found in the OT, bringing it to its climax. The people of God are no longer limited – either by ethnicity or by geography. Anyone who believes in Christ is Abraham's seed. The natural conclusion is that this redefined people now receive the earth as an inheritance, in fulfillment of the original intention behind Abraham's call. Those who are in Christ live out the theology of the land of Israel in new places, and thus universalize the land. At the same time, we must remember that the land is covenanted, and that the inheritance is better understood as a mandate. This will have important consequence on the calling and identity of the church. To this we move next.

4. The Inheritance as a Mandate

Inheriting the privileges of the Abrahamic covenant means at the same time inheriting the responsibilities of the covenant. The concept of inheriting the land does not mean that the land becomes a possession, as if the ownership transfers from God to the people.[61] God remains the ultimate owner of the earth. Rather, the land is received as mandate, and as such, it is still a gift under condition. The gift is still conditional. Those who receive the inheritance must keep the covenant stipulations in order to continue to be worthy of the inheritance. We will next see how the NT redefines what it means for the people of God to keep the covenant.

4.1. Jesus Redefines the Covenant

According to Matthew, Jesus claimed in the Sermon on the Mountain that he had not come to abolish the law and the prophets but to fulfill (πληρῶσαι) them (Matt 5:17). The verb πληρόω has the notion of making

---

61. See chapter 3 section 3 above on the land as a mandate.

full – presumably something that is yet incomplete. Jesus speaks here with a sense of authority (Matt 7:28–29), and claims that his mission is to fulfill or bring to completion the message of the OT. It is true that he is not contradicting the OT, "*but neither is he preserving it unchanged*"[62] – as evident in his frequent use of the phrase "but I say to you."[63]

Jesus brought a "new teaching" (Mark 1:27). He gave his own words authority equal to the sacred books: "Heaven and earth will pass away, but my words will not pass away" (Matt 24:35).[64] He also challenged certain aspects of the law. For example, he clearly challenged the dietary laws of his days, especially in his statement that "there is nothing outside a person that by going into him can defile him" (Mark 7:15). The same applies to the Sabbath. It is true that discussions about what is permitted on the Sabbath were common in that period.[65] Yet what is striking (and radically not in line with the Jewish context) is Jesus' massive claim that he is the "lord of the Sabbath" (Matt 12:8; Mark 2:28). These two brief examples give clear evidence that Jesus saw himself as bringing a new teaching.[66]

We can thus conclude that Jesus redefines what it means to keep the law. Further support for this comes from Matthew's portrayal of Jesus being seated on a mountain. As already noted, Matthew structures his Gospel on the idea that Jesus re-enacts the story of Israel. So when he portrays Jesus delivering the sermon from "a mountain" (Matt 5:1) – in contrast to Luke 6:17 which speaks of a level place – it is probable that he is paralleling Jesus with Moses, who gave the people the law. If so, then the statement that he came to "fulfill the law" takes on a new dimension. Jesus is absorbing the law and giving it a new whole meaning. As N. T. Wright observes:

---

62. Blomberg, *Matthew*, 103.
63. Matt 5:22, 28, 32, 34, 39, 44.
64. Compare with Matt 5:18: "Until heaven and earth pass away, not an iota, not a dot, will pass from the Law until all is accomplished."
65. Dunn, *The Partings of the Ways*, 131.
66. For Dunn, Jesus did not really challenge the authority of the law, but he was joining already existing debates among Second Temple Jews about the law and its interpretation. He concludes that overall "Jesus' teaching was within the range of the then acceptable debate regarding the interpretation and application of the law." Dunn, *The Partings of the Ways*, 134. Yet our brief discussion shows that Jesus is not really within the level of interpretation in all of these discussions, and that despite his respect to the law (Matt 23:2–3; Mark 1:44; 10:19; Luke 17:14), he did challenge and add to certain aspects of it.

For Jesus, the symbolic praxis that would mark out his followers, and which therefore can be classified as, in that sense, redefined Torah, is set out in such places as the Sermon on the Mount.[67]

In short, by claiming to "fulfill" the law, Jesus redefines the law and brings a new teaching. In the same manner in which Jesus redefines Israel around himself, he redefines the law around himself. We cannot ignore this new Jesus-dimension to what it means to keep the covenant in the new history inaugurated by Jesus – and it will have important implications for the theology of the land.

4.2. Paul and the Law

We have seen that "covenantal nomism" meant that for first-century Jews the law represented the distinctive marker of God's people. For Paul, however, faith in Jesus now becomes the mark of Israel in the new era (Rom 3:28). Covenant membership is through faith in Christ, and not through the law. The law therefore is seen to have a temporary function as a guardian (Gal 3:24–26). The guardian was a personal slave-attendant and had a temporary role in the life of a person. His role was mainly disciplinary, until a person was old enough to take responsibility.[68] Paul is saying that now that Jesus is here, the law is no longer needed. It has achieved its purpose.

At the same time, Paul speaks about the importance of works of love, and considers these works as the fulfillment of the law. The law is now summed up in one commandment: "love your neighbor as yourself," and therefore, *"love is the fulfilling of the law"* (Rom 13:8–10).[69] We cannot say with certainty whether Paul here was consciously echoing Jesus in his conversation with the lawyer (Matt 22:37–40). What we can say with certainty is that the law is no longer for Paul the distinctive mark of the covenant community – works of love are what count now. Similarly, he says in Galatians 5:6 that in Christ "neither circumcision nor uncircumcision

---

67. Wright, *Jesus and the Victory of God*, 431.
68. See Bruce, *1 & 2 Thessalonians*, 182.
69. See also Gal 5:14.

counts for anything, but only faith working through love." As Dunn observes, the love command for Paul "meant an opening out of Judaism itself, to lose its ethnic distinctiveness; and that meant that the rituals which set Jews apart from Gentiles become an unjustified restriction of the love command."[70] Acts of love took the place of the law.

Paul, like Jesus, redefines what it means to keep the covenant. He moves beyond the cultic notions of first-century Judaism and argues that the law in its original form is no longer binding. Moreover, it seems that what Paul relativized are the law aspects that separated Jews and Gentiles, but not those that were ethical and moral. Instead, the law as a result of the coming of Christ is summed up in the commandment of love.

4.3. The Jesus-Community and the Demand of "Fruits"

The NT, as we have just seen, redefines what it means to keep the covenant. This new definition is seen in the NT in the many demands for "good fruits" (John 15:1–4). It is important that we read these demands with the story of Israel as a background. When we do so, we can compare or parallel these demands with the conditions or the stipulations of the covenant, which were necessary to keep the land. We will observe that the emphasis in the NT is more on the social and ethical issues, and not on the cultic ones, which opens the door for Gentiles to keep the covenant. In addition, we will see that obedience to God is seen now in reference to Christ.

We start with the most obvious example in the NT about inheriting the land: "Blessed are the meek, for they shall inherit the earth" (Matt 5:5). We can of course read the Beatitudes as eschatological in nature: pointing towards the future. In other words: the meek shall *ultimately* – in the consummation – inherit the earth. We can, and should, at the same time read them as instructions from Jesus on how to live as a covenant community. Matthew 5:5 is a direct quote from Psalm 37:11. In the psalm, the qualities of those who inherit the land were: waiting for the Lord, meekness, being blessed by the Lord, righteousness, and keeping the way. In addition, justice, righteousness and care for the poor are emphasized as good qualities

---

70. J. D. G. Dunn, *Romans. 9–16. Word Biblical Commentary* (Dallas: Word Books, 1988), 781.

all over the psalm. We should also read Matthew 5:5 with all the Beatitudes as a background. The eight Beatitudes describe the qualities of the people of God in the new history. These are descriptions of the community as a whole, and not of different individuals with different qualities. This means that those who inherit the land are not just the meek, but also the poor in spirit, the mourners, those hungry for justice, the merciful, the pure in heart, the peacemakers, and the persecuted for the sake of justice and Jesus' name. The reward in each of these Beatitudes – whether it is the kingdom, the comfort, or the land – is from the Jewish tradition. Jesus reasserts here, in the spirit of Psalm 37, what it means to be the covenantal people of God – the light and salt of the world (Matt 5:13–16). "The sermon is a challenge to Israel to *be* Israel."[71]

Obviously, we should notice the universalization that is already taking place in the mind of Jesus, through his use of the word γῆ,[72] which commonly means in the NT "the earth."[73] In the Sermon, Jesus emphasizes that right behavior is a matter of the heart. The qualities described in Matthew 5–7 are not primarily qualities of individuals, but are the collective qualities of the followers of Jesus – qualities that distinguishes them as his followers. Those who obey Jesus' law will stand like a house on the rock, and those who do not will fall (Matt 7:24–27). Such a warning, spoken with such an authority (7:29), brings to mind the prophetic warnings about the consequences of breaking the covenant. In this terminology, the fall of the house built on sand echoes the fall of Jerusalem and the exile. Jesus' words are the new law – or the covenant stipulations – in the new era in history.

The parable of the vineyard speaks of the vineyard as an "inheritance" (Matt 21:38).[74] It concludes with Israel losing the inheritance, and with another nation receiving it – a nation that is marked by producing fruit: "Therefore I tell you, the kingdom of God will be taken away from you and given to a people *producing its fruits*" (Matt 21: 43). God is *the owner* of the

---

71. Wright, *Jesus and the Victory of God*, 288.
72. For more on the use of γῆ in the NT, see Burge, *Jesus and the Land*, 34.
73. For more on this verse as it relates to the theology of the land, and the interpretation of γῆ as earth, see Burge, *Jesus and the Land*, 43; Beale, *New Testament Biblical Theology*, 756; Walker, "The Land and Jesus Himself," 101; Robertson, *The Israel of God*, 26.
74. Matt 25:33–44; see also Mark 12:1–12; Luke 20:9–19.

vineyard, and his tenants are *accountable* to him. This again parallels what we discovered about God as the owner of the land in the OT, and about the land as a mandate. This also parallels the prophetic tradition of warnings of an impending exile. In addition, the image of the vineyard and the fence around it is an allusion to Isaiah's parable (Isa 5:1–7) about Israel in the land. In the original context, the emphasis was on justice and righteousness (Isa 5:7). The message of Jesus is clear: producing fruits, particularly justice and truth, remains a demand, even a condition, for the people of God.

In Jesus' law, loving God and loving neighbor are given the same value (Matt 22:36–40). This shows the emphasis on love in Jesus' teachings (John 13:34–35). In fact, when Jesus stated explicitly that he is bringing a new teaching, it had to do with love: "*A new commandment* I give to you, that you love one another: just as I have loved you, you also are to love one another" (John 13:34). The new covenant community that will center on Jesus is to be marked by love. "By this all people will know that you are my disciples, if you have love for one another" (John 13:35). The force of this statement can be seen when we read it in contrast to the markers of Jewish communities in the first century: circumcision, dietary food, and keeping the Sabbath. Jesus is again redefining the covenant boundaries and what it means to be a member of the covenant community.

This also shows the social concern in Jesus. He repeated the prophetic message: "I desire mercy, and not sacrifice" (Matt 9:13; 12:7) to show that social purity is more important than cultic purity (see also Matt 23). In particular, Jesus showed a strong concern for the poor and the marginalized.[75] In Matthew 25:31–46, a passage about the final judgment, he made a remarkable claim that *inheriting* the kingdom (25:34) is for those who care for the hungry, the homeless, the poor, and the sick – and equates himself with these categories. What Jesus says here is in line with the Pentateuch with its emphasis on the sojourners and the powerless in the land (including non-Israelites), and with the prophetic tradition in its emphasis on social justice. The pattern of Israel's experience in the land is echoed. Instead of the land, Jesus talks about inheriting the kingdom (25:34) and eternal

---

75. Mark 10:21–22; 12:41–44; Luke 6:21; 14:12–14; 16:19–25.

life (25:46); and instead of exile, he talks about eternal damnation (25:46). In both cases, the marginalized in the land are prioritized.

The same emphasis on fruits, especially in a Jesus-centered and social context, is evident in Paul and the Epistles. In Romans 11, the grafted branches could be cut off if they do not abide in faith (in Jesus) (11:20–24). Membership in the olive tree is conditional. Paul also speaks of the fruits of the Spirit (Gal 5:22) as qualities that would cause one to *inherit* the kingdom of God (5:21).

The emphasis on serving the poor is also evident in Pauline epistles.[76] He also talks about the concept of economic equality and gives warning against greed. Paul's social and economical argument is theological in nature:

> For I do not mean that others should be eased and you burdened, but that as a matter of fairness your abundance at the present time should supply their need, so that their abundance may supply your need, that there may be fairness. As it is written, "Whoever gathered much had nothing left over, and whoever gathered little had no lack." (2 Cor 8:15)

Paul quotes Exodus 16:18, which speaks about Israel's experience in the wilderness on their way to the land, and how God provided for them on a daily basis. The Corinthians' Christian community is thus built after the example of Israel – one which emphasized equality and social justice.

In a similar vein, the writer of Hebrews follows his statement that his readers are now receiving a kingdom that cannot be shaken (12:28) with a commandment about hospitality to strangers (13:2). The two are anchored together. The Christian community to which he writes is founded on the principles in the OT, which emphasized hospitality.

James speaks of social equality and respect to the poor (2:1–13), and bases his argument on the call to love the neighbor (2:8). Meeting the needs of the poor, according to James, is the evidence of faith (2:15–16). His famous statement that faith without works is dead is directed to those who do not care for the poor (2:17). In fact:

---

76. Rom 15:26; 2 Cor 9:11–12; Gal 2:10.

> Religion that is pure and undefiled before God, the Father, is this: to visit orphans and widows in their affliction, and to keep oneself unstained from the world (Jas 1:27).

In summary, the examples mentioned above are not random acts of kindness that Christians should do. Rather, these acts reveal their nature and calling as the people of God. In addition, these are all not simply good morals or good ethics for individual believers. These are markers of the new communities of faith as a whole – communities that inherited not just the privileges of being the new Israel, but also the demands and responsibilities of that privilege. The church inherits both the privileges and responsibilities of Israel (1 Pet 2:9). The responsibilities of the believers are reminiscent of those required of the people who inherited the land in the OT – except that now they are applicable for all peoples in all lands.[77]

4.4. Conclusion

There is no cheap grace in the Bible. The people of God are always accountable to the giver of all good things. It is true that Jesus and Paul redefined what it means to keep the covenant, yet the demand for fruit still holds. In addition to faith in Christ, the new covenant community is to show a strong social awareness and care for one another and for their neighbors, and in particular the poor. The people of God must exhibit fruit that reveals their calling and identity as God's people of earth. The biblical commandments for godliness are not simply about individual piety, but they are first and foremost communal identifications of the people of God. When Christians live in such a manner, they are revealed as a new Israel and embody a Christ-centered Israelite theology of the land – in lands far away from the original Promised Land.

---

77. Wright, *Old Testament Ethics*, 192.

5. The Nullification of the Old Covenant

The above discussion raises questions about "Israel according to the flesh" (Rom 9:3). The question is this: what happens to the "particular" after the "universal" has been achieved? What happens to Israel and her land? What about the old covenant with Israel? According to the NT, do ethnic Jews still have a claim to the Promised Land based on the old covenant?

Some argue that a repentant Israel could still claim the benefits of her covenant with God, including that of the land.[78] Paul refers to the historic privileges of ethnic Israel in Romans 9:4–5 in these words: "To them belong the adoption, the glory, the covenants, the giving of the law, the worship, and the promises. To them belong the patriarchs." Kaiser argues, "For Paul, no one of the previous promises has changed – not even the promise of the land."[79] In other words, the covenant with Israel, in its old terms, is still valid, and will be reinstituted one day with ethnic Israel. Ware argues that the church is not given "territorial and political aspects of the new covenant," since that is reserved for "Israel." The church and Israel are "distinguishable covenant participants." They are "one by faith in Christ and common partaking of the Spirit, and *yet* distinct insofar as God will yet restore Israel as a nation to its land."[80]

Such views, however, must respond to the challenge raised by the NT about Jesus as the new and ideal Israelite. It also must deal with the redefinition by Jesus of the covenant, the covenant boundaries, and the covenant

---

78. See for example D. Juster, "A Messianic Jew Looks at the Land Promises," in *The Land Cries Out: Theology of the Land in the Israeli-Palestinian Context*, ed. S. Munayer and L. Loden (Eugene: CASCADE Books, 2012), 63–68; Kaiser, "The Promised Land," 302–312. Such views could be loosely labelled today as "Christian Zionism," and they vary in their form and beliefs about a future for the Jewish people. It is beyond this study to analyze and respond in detail to each of these views. For more see Sizer, *Zion's Christian Soldiers?*; G. M. Burge, *Whose Land? Whose Promise?: What Christians are not Being Told about Israel and the Palestinians*, illustrated ed. (Cleveland: Pilgrim Press, 2003); Chapman, *Whose Promised Land?*; N. Ateek, C. Duaybis and M. Tobin, *Challenging Christian Zionism: Theology, Politics and the Israel-Palestine Conflict* (London: Melisende, 2000).
79. Kaiser, "The Promised Land," 311.
80. B. A. Ware, "The New Covenant and the People(s) of God," in *Dispensationalism, Israel and the Church: The Search for Definition*, D. L. Bock, W. C. Kaiser and C. A. Blaising (Grand Rapids: Zondervan, 1992), 96–97 (emphasis in the original).

community. In addition, if Paul claims that those who are in Christ are Abraham's offspring and heirs according to the promise, can there be two "offsprings" of Abraham, with each receiving a different promise? And if Paul reads the promise of the land as a promise of the earth for those who are in Christ, can we still read the promise as one of a particular land for a particular people? Katanacho rightly argues that "any theological claims that replace Christ's ownership with Israel's must deal with the difficulties of defining Israel and with the New Testament claims that Christ receives the Abrahamic inheritance of [the land]."[81] In addition, the following arguments can be made for the nullification of the old covenant.

5.1. Who is Abraham's Seed?

The question of who is the real or authentic seed of Abraham is an important and old one; indeed it was common among Second Temple Jews. This is evident in John the Baptist's conversation with the Pharisees and Sadducees, who claimed that Abraham was their father (Matt 3:8–9). For John, being a physical descendant of Abraham does not make one a child of Abraham, but repentance does. God can also raise up children of Abraham who are not physical descendants of Abraham. Jesus himself in the gospel of John echoes the same rationale. During a dialogue with some Jews who told him that Abraham was their father, he answered: "If you were Abraham's children, you would be doing the works Abraham did" (John 8:39).

Paul joins the discussion as well and expands it to what it means to be a Jew and an Israelite. Circumcision for Paul, which was the sign of the Abrahamic covenant, and being a Jew, is not an outward thing:

> For no one is a Jew who is merely one outwardly, nor is circumcision outward and physical. But a Jew is one inwardly, and circumcision is a matter of the heart, by the Spirit, not by the letter. His praise is not from man but from God. (Rom 2:28–29)

---

81. Y. Katanacho, "Christ is the Owner of Haaretz," *Christian Scholars Review* 34, no. 4 (2005): 440.

This is a striking statement. Not every Jew is a real Jew, and not every circumcised person is authentically a member of the covenant. Similarly, "not all who are descended from Israel belong to Israel, and not all are children of Abraham because they are his offspring" (Rom 9:7). This is because "it is not the children of the flesh who are the children of God, but the children of the promise are counted as offspring" (Rom 9:8). Paul is talking here about Israel of the OT, and to prove his point he goes again to the OT and gives the examples of Isaac and Jacob. For Paul, this is not a new teaching. *This is how things have always been.* Racial ethnicity alone does not guarantee the benefits of the Abrahamic Covenant.

5.2. Israel Broke the Covenant

Over and over in both Testaments, it is clear that one can lose the benefits of the covenant, including the land, by breaking the covenant.[82] John the Baptist could not have been more explicit: "Even now the axe is laid to the root of the trees. Every tree therefore that does not bear good fruit is cut down and thrown into the fire" (Matt 3:10). We have already looked at the parable of the Tenants, and many other parables convey the same message: The kingdom of God – the inheritance – "will be taken away from you and given to a people producing its fruits."[83] "Those invited were not worthy" of the wedding invitation.[84] The fig tree, which did not produce fruit, and used up the ground, would be "cut off" (Luke 13:6–9), and Jesus said to that tree: "May *no one ever* eat fruit from you again" (Mark 11:14). Any branch in the vineyard that does not produce fruits will be cut off (John 15:1). Paul also said that some of the branches of the olive tree had been cut off (Rom 11:17). All of these examples simply show that breaking the covenant (or not yielding fruits) will lead to being cut off from the covenant family. Covenant membership is not something that can be taken for granted – not even by race. In addition, it is not the case here that God has rejected Israel, but it is that Israel has rejected God by breaking the covenant he made with her. *A broken covenant is not a binding covenant.*

---

82. See chapter 3 above, sections 3 and 4.
83. Matt 21:43; see also Mark 12:9; Luke 20:16.
84. Matt 22:8; see also Luke 14:24.

5.3. Gentiles and Jews United

Jesus spoke of "other sheep" that will be included in the flock of Israel: "There will be *one flock, one shepherd*" (John 10:16). We have also seen how for Paul, Gentiles are "fellow citizens with the saints and members of the household of God" (Eph 2:17), and they "share in the nourishing root of the olive tree" (Rom 11:19). This shows that those who joined the covenant community, along with those who stayed in it (the first believers were all Jews), constitute *one community*. Moreover, this new community *continues the story of Israel*, and does not start a new one.

Admittedly, there have been some modifications as a result of the Jesus-event, and the covenant has been redefined or renewed; *yet renewal of the covenant is itself part of the story of Israel*, and something that has been already anticipated – most notably in the writings of Jeremiah. This means that what we have in the NT is not a rejection of Israel or of the OT, but the continuation of Israel's story. As Hays stresses:

> The church discovers its true identity only in relation to the sacred story of Israel, and the sacred story of Israel discovers its full significance – so Paul passionately believed – only in relation to God's unfolding design for salvation of the Gentiles in the church . . . *The experience of the Christian community stands in continuity with the story of Israel, not in contradiction with it.*[85]

Gentile believers do *not* replace Israel in the covenant. This is not replacement theology, but incorporation theology. Gentile believers are incorporated into Israel, and as such become full members. The church does not replace Israel. The church is the continuation of Israel, because those who are in Christ are the seed of Abraham.[86]

To insist on maintaining a distinct exclusive "inheritance" for the Jewish people (the Promised Land) is to deny the rights of those who have been

---

85. Hays, *Echoes of Scripture*, 100, 102 (emphasis added).
86. The term "replacement theology" is controversial and polarizing, and it has a negative connotation today, due to the long history of anti-Semitism that was associated with it. It is advisable that we seek new terminologies and avoid the word "replacement."

incorporated in the covenant community and who have inherited the story of Israel. It would also be to deny the right of these Gentile believers to call Abraham and the patriarchs as their "forefathers," and to sing the songs of Israel and call God their shepherd (Ps 23), and to claim the story of Israel – even that of the ideal Israelite Jesus Christ – as their own story.

5.4. The Jewish People Are Part of the New Covenant: Romans 10–11

Jews are not rejected in the new covenant, and in fact can be members of the new community. This is an obvious statement, yet it has major implications for the theology of the land. Any hope for the redemption of the Jewish people falls within the story of the people of God in the new era – or the Christian faith – and not within another special one (that includes a particular land and particular covenant). The time of salvation for the Jews is *now*, and it is through faith in Christ.

In Romans 10–11, Paul also makes it clear that his desire for the Jewish people is that they repent and join the Jesus-community: "My heart's desire and prayer to God for them is that they may be saved" (10:1). He stresses that "everyone who believes in [Jesus] will not be put to shame. For there is no distinction between Jew and Greek; for the same Lord is Lord of all" (10:11–12). Yet despite the rejection of Israel to Jesus (10:16–21), God has not rejected his people (11:1a). However, Paul immediately explains what it means that God did not reject his people. He gives himself as an example of someone who is not rejected: "For I myself am an Israelite, a descendant of Abraham, a member of the tribe of Benjamin. God has not rejected his people whom he foreknew" (11:1b–2). In other words, Paul, an Israelite, is evidence that God did not reject his people. God not rejecting his people means for Paul that they can still join the Jesus-community through faith in Jesus (and not through the law). Those who join the Jesus-community continue to be part of Israel and are part of the remnant of grace. This remnant has always been part of the story of Israel, and "so too *at the present time* (ἐν τῷ νῦν καιρῷ) there is a remnant, chosen by grace" (11:5).

The time for the Jewish remnant is the present time (and not the future). We should interpret the phrase "ἐν τῷ νῦν καιρῷ" theologically. This is not a simple temporal phrase, but points to an "opportune time."[87] More importantly, as confirmed by the use of the same phrase in Romans 3:26, the phrase seems to have an eschatological tone in Paul's mind.[88] Paul is speaking about the new era – the one defined by the Christ-event. Just as in Elijah's days he thought he was the only one remaining, only to discover that there are "seven thousand men who have not bowed the knee to Baal" (11:4), so it is in the present age: there *is* a remnant of grace.

The door is still open "in the present time" for more Jews to *re*-join the covenant community: "And even they, if they do not continue in their unbelief, will be grafted in, for God has the power to graft them in again" (11:23). Again, Paul is still talking about the present time. This is key to our understanding Paul's words that all Israel will be saved:

> Lest you be wise in your own sight, I do not want you to be unaware of this mystery, brothers: a partial hardening has come upon Israel, until (ἄχρι) the fullness of the Gentiles has come in. And in this way *all Israel will be saved*, as it is written, "The Deliverer will come from Zion, he will banish ungodliness from Jacob"; "and this will be my covenant with them when I take away their sins." As regards the gospel, they are enemies for your sake. But as regards election, they are beloved for the sake of their forefathers. For the gifts and the calling of God are irrevocable. (Rom 11:25–29)

This is one of the most debated passages in all of Paul's writing. For some, this passage says that God has a future distinct role for the Jewish people, and this includes a restoration to the land. For example, Kaiser argues:

> This is not a matter of individual salvation nor a matter of converting to a Gentile brand of Christendom, but it is a matter of God's activity in history when the nation shall once again, as in the days of blessing in the past, experience the

---

87. See Zodhiates, *Complete Word Study Dictionary*.
88. Dunn, *Romans. 9-16*, 638.

blessing and joy of God spiritually, materially, geographically, and politically.[89]

The following points can be made in response. First, Paul is talking about "the present time," and not about a distinctive future era or age. It is true that the preposition ἄχρι, used in 11:25, suggests a temporal sequence, but as Dunn explains:

> It does not follow, however, that Paul had a clear perception of the final events as happening in strict sequence . . . His conviction is simply of a mounting climax with the incoming of the Gentiles as a trigger for the final end in which Israel's conversion, Christ's *Parousia*, and the final resurrection (v. 15) would all be involved.[90]

The quote from Isaiah 59:20 is important. This is an eschatological passage pointing to things which were future to Israel. There is no reason why we should conclude that in Paul's mind this verse is still talking about the future (i.e. Paul's future). Paul quotes the verse in the original form, where it is in the future tense – "the deliverer *will* come." However, for Paul in general, the eschatological time has already arrived in Christ, and therefore we can and should interpret the reference to the deliverer as speaking about *what has already happened*. The deliverer (Jesus) has *already come* and brought forgiveness of sins, just as Isaiah said he would come. As Walker explains:

> Paul's reason for quoting this verse is to indicate that when the Deliverer finally comes (and he now has), the sure result of that coming will be his turning 'godlessness away from Jacob.' In other words, the promise which Paul looks forward to being fulfilled does not lie in the first half of the quotation, but in the second: because he believes that Jesus was

---

89. Kaiser, "The Promised Land," 310.
90. Dunn, *Romans. 9-16*, 680.

truly the Deliverer sent by God (v. 26b) he has faith that the divinely intended consequences will follow: 'he *will* banish ungodliness from Jacob' (v. 26c). In this way . . . 'all Israel will be saved' (v. 26a). Paul is not predicting a 'large-scale,' last-minute salvation of Jews' but speaking of an ongoing process which has now begun through the gospel.[91]

Second, we must not undermine the change in the quotation made by Paul. The original verse in Isaiah says: "and a Redeemer will come *to* Zion" – not "*from* Zion," as Paul has it. In saying "*from*," Paul intentionally changes the Hebrew text and its Greek paraphrase, thereby removing any implication that Jerusalem will play a future role in God's salvation history.[92]

Third, the hope for the Jewish people throughout Romans 9–11 is their "salvation" – defined as faith in Christ. Their restoration (regardless whether it is a future or present phenomenon) means their re-grafting in the olive tree – the same one in which the new branches, the Gentiles, have been grafted. The restoration is not, therefore, about a distinct plan, or a distinct branch in the tree. As such, Jews and Gentiles in the olive tree "share in the nourishing root of the olive tree" (11:17). If the Jews inherit a land, then so will the Gentiles, and *vice versa*. And as we have seen, the land that both Jews and Gentiles inherit in Christ is the whole earth. There is thus no place in Paul's theology for a particular distinct inheritance reserved for those of just one ethnicity.

In short, it seems that any attempt to load Romans 11:26 with nationalistic implications for ethnic Israel must include a form of *eisegesis* that imports foreign preconceptions to the text and that ignores the overall ecclesiology of Paul, which was shaped by the Jesus-event. The crux of Paul's theology in Romans 9–11, and indeed in the entire letter, is that Jews

---

91. Walker, *Jesus and the Holy City*, 141 (emphasis in the original).
92. Waltke, *An Old Testament Theology*, 575. Similarly, Dunn comments on the change from "to" into "from": "The implication once again is of Paul's readiness to reaffirm the eschatological significance of Jerusalem without reinforcing the old Jewish assumption that Zion would literally be the focus of the eschatological climax (cf. again Gal 4.25–26)." Dunn, *The Partings of the Ways*, 114.

and Gentiles are branches in the same tree, and not that they are distinct in their membership.

5.5. The New Nullifies the Old

The NT clearly claims that the Jesus-event initiated a new covenant. Jesus explicitly declares this in the Last Supper: This is my blood of the [new] covenant, which is poured out for many for the forgiveness of sins (Matt 26:28).[93] The reference to the "(new) covenant" and the forgiveness of sins brings to mind Jeremiah's famous prophecy about the new covenant (Jer 31:31–34). Such words cannot have any other meaning in the first century – especially among Jewish listeners. As Blomberg says:

> Here is the inauguration of Jeremiah's new covenant (Jer 31:31–34)...The covenant language implies the creation of a community, now to be constituted of those who in their eating and drinking identify with the benefits of Jesus' sacrificial death. This "true Israel" stands over against the natural Israel of the old covenant.[94]

The book of Hebrews also claims that Jesus is the minister of a "new covenant."[95] Again, these words had only one meaning for the recipients of the letter – as confirmed when Hebrews quoted in full the central passage in Jeremiah's prophecy (Heb 8:8–12; Jer 31:31–34). There can be no doubt that in the mind of the writer of Hebrews the new covenant that Jeremiah spoke about has been fulfilled in Jesus. In addition: The new covenant is not only or mainly a question of definition, or an exegetical conclusion based on a proof-text in Jeremiah; the new covenant is a *new act of God*, to which Scripture bears witness.[96]

---

93. Some manuscripts have the words "new" before covenant, possibly influenced by Luke 22:20 and 1 Cor 11:25. See France, *The Gospel of Matthew*, 987.
94. Blomberg, *Matthew*, 391.
95. Heb 7:22; 8:6; 9:15; 12:24.
96. Ellingworth, *Epistle to the Hebrews*, 418 (emphasis added). Furthermore, and as Ellingworth points out, Hebrews claims that God has acted and spoken in Jesus "these last days" (Heb 1:2). The phrase "ἐπ' ἐσχάτου τῶν ἡμερῶν τούτων," used in the Septuagint in eschatological contexts (Num 24:14; Dan 10:14), sets the context of the whole Epistle (p.

The natural consequence of the teaching in the NT – that Jesus' coming is the fulfillment of the hopes of the OT – is that the covenant with Israel in its old form is no longer binding; and this is what the book of Hebrews explicitly claims. Because "the law made nothing perfect" (Heb 7:19), God sent Jesus as the "guarantor of a better covenant" (Heb 7:22). In fact,

> Christ has obtained a ministry that is as much more excellent than the old as the covenant he mediates is better, since it is enacted on better promises. For if that first covenant had been faultless, there would have been no occasion to look for a second. (Heb 8:6–7)

Then, after quoting Jeremiah 31:31–34, the writer of Hebrews claims:

> In speaking of a new covenant, he makes the first one obsolete. *And what is becoming obsolete and growing old is ready to vanish away.* (Heb 8:13)

The point is clear and simple. "The mere use of the word 'new' implies the superannuation of the old."[97] According to Ellingworth, the writer of Hebrews is simply presupposing the rabbinic principle that a new act of God supersedes the old.[98] Moreover, it was Jeremiah who used the term "new," not the writer of Hebrews; so this "newness" has been anticipated. It is not a surprising or *completely new* development in the story.

Hebrews 8:13 clearly indicates that the newness that came as a result of the Jesus-event makes the old "obsolete." Admittedly, within the context of Hebrews 7–8, the old that is now "obsolete" is primarily the Mosaic covenant (Jer 31:32; Heb 8:9); yet the comparison does not require us to apply it only to the Mosaic covenant. Jeremiah is speaking after the exile about Israel's history as a whole, and the renewal he talks about is a renewal to all the people of Israel. Furthermore, the book of Hebrews, taken as a whole,

---

93). In other words, the writer is talking about the new eschatological era, in which God has spoken through Jesus. We must read the reference to the new covenant in this context.

97. Gordon, *Hebrews*, 94.

98. Ellingworth, *Epistle to the Hebrews*, 418.

talks about the revelation in Jesus which fulfills the story of Israel in its entirety. The newness that started with Jesus is a comprehensive newness, and as new, it makes the old obsolete.

5.6. Conclusion

It is vital to read the old covenant through the lens of the new. Israel's story has reached its climax in the Jesus-event. To insist that the old covenant continues today *with its terms unchanged* is to deny in essence that Jesus continued Israel's story, and that he is the ideal and faithful Israel, *the* seed of Abraham, and the inheritor of the land. It also fails to acknowledge that the universalization of the inheritance was something foreseen and anticipated in the OT, and it denies the fact that this inheritance is only possible in the present age in Christ for those who are in union with him. Finally, it fails to see the land as a mandate, insisting instead on treating the gift of land as a "possession." We must remember the question: "*Why* a land?" or "What was its intended purpose?" and then wonder: "Did the promise of the land achieve this intended purpose and destiny?" The answer the NT gives to the later question is "yes": Jesus inaugurated a new era in history in which the land became a source of blessing to the entire world, which was precisely the divinely intended purpose of the land. According to Paul, Jesus made the blessing of Abraham a possibility to all the families of the earth. As such, any future restoration for ethnic Israel to the Promised Land would not be in harmony with the biblical narrative.

6. Conclusion – The Church as the Eschatological Covenant Community

The natural conclusion of this chapter is that the "new covenant" that was anticipated in the OT has now arrived in the Jesus-event. The implication of the arrival of the new covenant is that those who are in Christ *are the eschatological covenant community* and, as such, it is they who receive the inheritance. We have seen how Jesus gathered twelve disciples as a symbol that he was reconstituting Israel around himself. In addition, many have argued for an eschatological significance to this act.[99] Jesus' ministry arguably aimed at establishing new eschatological communities, marked by certain distinguishing elements.[100]

In the book of Acts, the apostles did not set out simply to convert people into a new belief. They were establishing new communities (Acts 2:42–47). This communal dimension to Christianity was not limited to the church in Jerusalem, but extended to wherever the new faith arrived. These communities continued the story of Israel in new locations, and as such they were modeled after the example of Israel in the land. We can look at these communities as new Israel(s) in new land(s). Their vocation as God's people on earth was to be a testimony to God and a blessing to their surrounding culture, in fulfillment to the mandate given to Abraham and Israel. As such, these new Christian communities were fulfilling the goal or intent behind the calling of Israel to be a "light to the nations," a "chosen nation" from among the nations. This is probably what Jesus meant when he called his followers to be like a "city on a hill" (Matt 5:14). As von Rad comments:

> It is more probable that the reference here to the "city set on a hill" is concerned with something more than a simple analogy drawn from everyday experience. The saying about the city which is visible to all is closely bound up with that concerning the light of the world: the eschatological congregation of the faithful is the city set on a hill, and their light will be visible to the whole world.[101]

We may elaborate on this quote and add that we are talking now about multiple *eschatological congregations* in multiple new lands. These congregations

---

99. See for example Bryan, *Jesus and Israel's Traditions*, 105–106.
100. Wright, *Jesus and the Victory of God*, 276. Wright observes that John the Baptist's followers were recognizable as small collective entities within local communities. He then recalls that in the first century world 'private life' was virtually non-existent. He then says, "the clear implication, which we would be quite wrong to locate only in the post-Easter period, is that those who gave their allegiance to Jesus, just like those who gave their allegiance to John, formed a distinct group with a distinct praxis – and that Jesus himself saw them in these terms."
101. G. Von Rad, "City on a Hill," in *The Problem of the Hexateuch and Other Essays*, ed. G. Von Rad (New York: McGraw-Hill, 1966), 242.

should view themselves and self-identify as a light and a source of blessing to the peoples around them. At the same time, these congregations in new lands are a foretaste and a signpost to the ideal realities that will define things in the consummation.

CHAPTER 10

Jesus and the Kingdom of God on *Earth*

Introduction

This chapter looks at the theme of the kingdom of God in the NT as it pertains to the land. The kingdom is a central theme in the Jesus-event. We will see that Jesus inaugurated the reign of God on earth and took upon himself the role of God's vicegerent on earth. It will be further argued that the domain of Jesus' reign is the whole earth. In other words, the land associated with Jesus' kingdom is the whole earth.

We will also argue that Paul shares the theology of the Gospels that the kingdom is indeed a present reality, though with a future dimension. Paul sees the declaration of Jesus as king as a central theme, and he sees the resurrection as the pivotal moment in which Jesus was declared as king. Finally, we will see how the mission of the church expands the kingdom of God, and the means by which the kingdom's territories expand from one land to the whole earth. The church declares and manifests the reality of the reign of God in new lands.

1. Background: Expectations of Restoration in Jesus' Time

There were strong Jewish expectations of restoration in the time of Jesus, which were inherently tied with the concept of the kingdom of God. Even though the term "kingdom of God" does not appear in the OT, what is implied by the term is a central theme in the biblical narrative. Beasley-Murray, quoting Psalm 99, says that God's kingdom is affirmed in the OT in the assertions of the sovereignty of God.[1] However, the kingdom of God in the OT has to do with more than general statements about God's sovereignty. As we have already seen, the reign of the God of Israel was a hoped-for eschatological *event*, in which God would restore the fortunes of Israel (e.g. Isa 52:7–10). Ladd observes that in the time of Jesus the "age to come" (*olam haba*) and the "kingdom of God" were interchangeable terms.[2] In other words, the kingdom of God in the OT is an eschatological event in which God would *become* king.

According to Chilton:

> When people used the phrase "kingdom of God" in early Judaism, they were striving to understand how God relates to his world. Use of the phrase both reflected and encouraged a vivid attempt to conceive God's vindication of his people. What would he do? When would he act? To the benefit of precisely which people? How would we know how to cooperate with God's rule?[3]

These hopes of restoration were translated in Jesus' day into a nationalistic vision, so that in many Second Temple Judaism texts, "the reign of God is considered nationalistically, as God's exaltation of Israel over the nations."[4] There were groups that called for re-establishing a Jewish kingdom and cleansing the land, and some like the Zealots even called for the use of force to achieve this. Naturally, the land was viewed as a central element in these hopes. N. T. Wright says:

---

1. G. R. Beasley-Murray, "The Kingdom of God in the Teaching of God," *JETS* 35, no. 1 (1992): 19.
2. G. E. Ladd, *A Theology of the New Testament* (Grand Rapids: Eerdmans, 1993), 44.
3. B. Chilton, *Pure Kingdom: Jesus' Vision of God* (London: SPCK, 1996), 56.
4. McCartney, "Ecce Homo," 8. See also G. R. Beasley-Murray, *Jesus and the Kingdom of God* (Grand Rapids: Eerdmans, 1986), 39–70.

Although "kingdom of God" referred more to the fact of Israel's God becoming king than to a localized place, the sense of Holy Land was invoked by the phrase as well, since YHWH had promised this country to his people.[5]

It is in this environment that Jesus came and announced his message of the arrival of the kingdom of God, and in which the first Christians declared the gospel and the Lordship of Jesus. As Davies reminds us, Christianity arose in the land at a time when, in varying degrees of emotional intensity and geographic distribution, the expectations of restoration were "the constant concern, if not the preoccupation, of many Jews, inside the land especially, and also outside of it."[6] It is vitally important, then, to read Jesus' message in dialogue with his contemporaries. When we do so, we will discover that this has important implications for the theology of the land and how it relates to the kingdom of God.[7]

In addition, we must also remember the political state of affairs in the wider world in Jesus' day. The Christian gospel expanded in an era when the world was controlled by the Roman Empire. Caesar as Emperor was revered and worshipped.[8] In a time when the Jewish people were expecting the good news (gospel) of the coming of God as king, and when Christians were declaring (as we shall see below) that Jesus was the embodiment of the reign of God, in the Greek world, the word εὐαγγέλιον was "a regular technical term, referring to the announcement of a great victory, or to the birth, or accession, of an emperor."[9] In other words, to announce that YHWH

---

5. Wright, *Jesus and the Victory of God*, 206.
6. Davies, *The Gospel and the Land*, 161.
7. Luke seems to allude to these aspirations of restoration when he talks in his Gospel about the Davidic Messianic figure who would rescue Israel from her enemies (Luke 1:69–71), and when he has the disciples talking about "redeeming Israel" (Luke 24:21) and "restoring the kingdom to Israel" (Acts 1:6). These terms in Jesus' time referred to the "restoration of the nation, the cleansing of the land, and a divinely endorsed inheritance of the Holy Land." Burge, *Jesus and The Land*, 26.
8. For a brief yet comprehensive look on the Roman Empire in the first century, see D. N. Schowalter, "Churches in Context. The Jesus Movement in the Roman World," in *The Oxford History of the Biblical World*, ed. M. D. Coogan (Oxford: Oxford University Press, 1998), 388–419. See also R. A. Horsley, *Jesus and Empire: The Kingdom of God and the New World Disorder* (Minneapolis: Fortress Press, 2003).
9. Wright, *What Saint Paul Really Said*, 43.

is king is to announce that Caesar is not, and to announce that Jesus is Lord is to announce that Caesar is not. So the Christian gospel of the kingdom of God must have been perceived as a counter-message to Rome's "gospel" of the kingdom of Caesar.[10]

2. The Jesus-Event and the Reign of God on Earth

The kingdom of God in Jesus' life and ministry is one of the most discussed topics in the NT studies.[11] The aim of this section is to answer the following question: How does the theology of the kingdom of God in the Gospels affect our understanding of the theology of the land?

Despite the different views, "modern scholarship is quite unanimous in the opinion that the kingdom of God was the central message of Jesus."[12] In addition, we must interpret Jesus' actions (and not just his message) as kingdom-actions. The Jesus-event can be, therefore, described as a kingdom-event. Our question can be thus framed as follows: How does this kingdom-event affect our understanding of the theology of the land?

To answer this question, certain episodes and themes from the Jesus-event will be briefly examined. Selectivity is unavoidable due to the wealth of material about the kingdom of God in the Gospels.[13] The following is not a comprehensive study of episodes and themes, but will hopefully be sufficient as a window into Jesus' kingdom ministry and teachings.

---

10. Ibid., 43–44.

11. It is beyond this study to cover all the different interpretations to the theology of the kingdom. For a concise summary of the different interpretations of the theology of the kingdom of God in the last 200 years, see Ladd, *Theology of the New Testament*, 55–58. It is also very difficult to cover the theme of the kingdom from all the necessarily angles, although there are many good studies that attempt to do so. See for example Chilton, *Pure Kingdom*; Ladd, *Theology of the New Testament*; Beasley-Murray, *Jesus and the Kingdom of God*; Wright, *Jesus and the Victory of God*; H. N. Ridderbos, *The Coming of the Kingdom* (New Jersey: Presbyterian and Reformed, 1962); J. D. G. Dunn, *Jesus Remembered* (Grand Rapids: Eerdmans, 2003).

12. Ladd, *Theology of the New Testament*, 54.

13. Beasley-Murray's book *Jesus and the Kingdom of God* (1986) is a comprehensive study of the theme of the kingdom in the Gospels.

2.1. The Kingdom Now, and the Vicegerency of Jesus

This section looks at multiple passages in the Gospels that speak about the kingdom of God, and argues that the Jesus-event inaugurated the reign of God on earth. The Gospels claim, as we will see, that the time of the kingdom is *now*. We will also see that the Gospels speak of Jesus as God's agent – his vicegerent – who inaugurated God's reign on earth. They did so through their descriptions of his ministry as the one who fulfilled the hopes of the OT, and through the titles that they gave to him.

2.1.1. *The Launching of Jesus' Public Ministry of Jesus: Mark 1*

Mark summarizes the message of Jesus as follows:

> Jesus came into Galilee, proclaiming the *gospel of God*, and saying, "The time is fulfilled, and the *kingdom of God is at hand*; repent and believe in the gospel." (Mark 1:14–15)

Mark has just set Isaiah 40–55 as the context of Jesus' ministry, by introducing John as the "voice crying out in the wilderness" (Mark 1:3). Therefore, the term "gospel of God" should be understood with this background in mind, and in particular Isaiah 52:7:

> How beautiful upon the mountains are the feet of him who brings good news, who publishes peace, who brings *good news of happiness*, who publishes salvation, who says to Zion, *"Your God reigns."*

Mark here "depicts Jesus' coming in terms of Isaiah as the one who heralds the good news from God."[14] The gospel is the good news that the moment in history has arrived in which God will become king, in accordance with the prophecy of Isaiah. The gospel and the kingdom are interchangeable here: the gospel is the announcement of the kingdom, and the kingdom is the good news that God is becoming king.

---

14. R. Guelich, *Mark 1-8:26. Word Biblical Commentary* (Dallas: Word Books, 1989), 43.

This pivotal moment in history is "at hand" (ἐγγίζω). This verb is better understood by considering the immediate context: "the time is fulfilled." This phrase is better translated as "the appointed time has come to pass."[15] Mark has Jesus speaking here about the inauguration of a new era – an eschatological one – which would necessitate the conclusion of an old one. Using the Jewish terminology of those times, Jesus was announcing that the *olam hazeh* is concluded and that the *olam haba* is about to launch. Further, the word καιρός (translated as "time") has the notion of an "appointed time." Jesus is thus announcing the arrival of a decisive and divinely appointed moment in history. Clearly, then, the kingdom is an eschatological event.

Going back to the verb ἐγγίζω, Guelich observes that whereas the context denotes "arrival," the Greek generally denotes "nearness."[16] However, we should not polarize the notions of "nearness" and "arrival." In other words, the kingdom is about to arrive. The term speaks of an "eschatology which is not yet realized, but about to be realized."[17]

We must not also miss the main point Mark is making at this stage in his Gospel: the public ministry of Jesus itself, the content of Mark's Gospel, is the inauguration of the kingdom which would shortly be established.[18] The kingdom is at hand because Jesus is about to start his ministry. In the spirit of Isaiah, Jesus is, therefore, the anointed servant of God and the agent of the kingdom. His baptism explicitly shows this. The descending of the Spirit upon him and the voice from heaven are direct references to the anointing of the Servant of YHWH in Isaiah 40–55:

---

15. Ibid.

16. Ibid., 44. See also p. 44–45 for a discussion of the different views on translating this verb in this verse.

17. R. T. France, *The Gospel of Mark: A Commentary on the Greek Text* (Grand Rapids: Eerdmans, 2002), 92. Similarly, Dunn observes that the use of the perfect tense of the verb (ἤγγικεν) "indicates an action already performed and resulting in a state or effect which continues into the present." He then comments on the verse: "It is not a timeless nearness which is in mind; something had happened to bring the kingdom near." Dunn, *Jesus Remembered*, 407.

18. See Wright, *Jesus and the Victory of God*, 472.

Behold *my servant*, whom I uphold, my chosen, in whom my soul delights; I have put my *Spirit upon him*; he will bring forth justice to the nations. (Isa 42:1)	And when he came up out of the water, immediately he saw the heavens being torn open and the *Spirit descending* on him like a dove. And a voice came from heaven, "You are my *beloved Son*; with you I am well pleased." (Mark 1:10–11)

With the echoes of Isaiah 40–55 in Mark chapter 1, we can safely conclude that Mark declares here that the "Servant of YHWH" is the "beloved Son." The whole episode of the beginning of the ministry of Jesus, therefore, is meant to communicate that Jesus is the Servant of YHWH who will be instrumental in the breakthrough of the long-awaited rule of YHWH. The kingdom of God is breaking through in history.

Moreover, we have observed that Isaiah describes the ministry of the servant as having universal implications (42:1; 49:6). If this identification between the servant as the agent of the kingdom in Isaiah 40–55 and Jesus as the Son of God in Mark 1 is maintained, then we can argue that Mark is setting the stage here for his conclusion – where Jesus tells his disciples that the gospel must be proclaimed "to all nations" (Mark 13:10), "in the whole world" (Mark 14:9), and to "the whole creation" (Mark 16:15).[19]

2.1.2. Exorcism: Luke 10:1–24, 12:20

In Luke 10 Jesus sends seventy-two of his disciples in pairs to the villages to declare that "the kingdom of God has come near to you" (10:9b, 11b); this again uses the verb ἐγγίζω, as in Mark 1:15. They return reporting to him that "even the demons are subject to us in your name," to which Jesus responds, "I saw Satan fall like lightning from heaven" (10:17–18). There is a strong connection here between the declaration of the kingdom of God and the falling of Satan. Jesus sets out his kingdom as opposed to that of Satan, and he frequently cast out demons throughout his ministry.[20] In addition, he told his disciples "in the same hour" that many prophets and kings desired to see what they see, and did not see it, and to hear what

---

19. See no. 642 above.
20. Matt 8:16; Mark 1:34; 3:11; Luke 4:40–41.

they hear, and did not hear it (10:24); this is a clear indication that the long-awaited eschatological hopes of the OT are a present reality.

In Luke 11, following the casting out of a demon, Jesus declares: "But if it is by the finger of God that I cast out demons, then the kingdom of God *has come upon you*" (Luke 11:20).[21] The use of the verb φθάνω, which means "to come upon," "necessitates the conclusion that the kingdom of God has in some sense actually become present."[22] Jesus is unambiguously claiming that the kingdom of God is a present reality in and through his ministry of casting out demons. Jesus is fighting here Israel's enemies – not the Romans but the demons.

Moreover, the casting out of demons by Jesus, as a sign of the coming of the kingdom, shows that Jesus himself is portrayed here as God's kingdom-agent or his vicegerent. Jesus is leading the fight on behalf of his Father. He declares in this context that the Father has handed to him "all things" (Luke 10:22). McCartney also argues that there is an added significance to the acts of exorcism, in that they restore the vicegerency of human beings, which was lost with Adam:

> When Jesus as man, empowered by the Spirit, exercises authority over the demons, the proper vicegerency of man under God is restored. Jesus did what Adam should have done; he cast the serpent out of the garden.[23]

The casting out of demons is thus a sign of the presence of the kingdom of God through God's vicegerent – Jesus. By declaring Satan as the real enemy (and not the Romans) Jesus is engaged in a cosmic battle with Satan that goes beyond the borders of Israel and extends to "all the kingdoms of the world" – a term Luke ascribes to Satan in the temptation narrative

---

21. See also Matt 12:29 where it is the "spirit of God" instead of "finger of God." The meaning is the same in both cases. See Hagner, *Matthew 1-13*, 639–640.
22. Ibid., 343. Hagner also says that using φθάνω is a clearer statement about the presence of the kingdom – stronger than ἐγγίζω (is near), which is used in Mark 1:15 and Luke 10:9 discussed above.
23. McCartney, "Ecce Homo," 9.

(Luke 4:5). Jesus is thus restoring not simply the fortunes of Israel, but those of the whole world.

2.1.3. *The Deeds of the Christ: Matthew 11:1–15; Luke 4:16–21*

In Matthew 11, John the Baptist sends his disciples to Jesus to inquire whether he was "the one who is to come" (11:3) – clearly a "title referring to the Messiah."[24] John was motivated to ask this question by the "deeds of the Christ" (11:2). Jesus' response, which used images from Isaiah, was a confirmation that these deeds were indeed *messianic* deeds:

> Go and tell John what you hear and see: the blind receive their sight and the lame walk, lepers are cleansed and the deaf hear, and the dead are raised up, and the poor have good news preached to them. (Matt 11:4–5)[25]

Jesus then comments on the person of John the Baptist, and confirms John's identity as the "messenger of YHWH" of Malachi 3:1 and the "Elijah" of Malachi 4:5 (11:10, 14). He declares him the greatest "among those born of women," but then paradoxically declares that "the one who is least in the kingdom of heaven is greater than he" (11:11).[26] Jesus is here contrasting not individuals, but eras. The reason that kingdom members are greater than John is because the new kingdom era is greater than the old one. This is evident in two ways: first, by identifying John with the messenger in Malachi, Jesus quotes from the last book in the *Nevi'im*, to show that John

---

24. Hagner, *Matthew 1-13*, 300. See Matt 3:11; Ps 118:26; Dan 7:13.
25. Hagner observes that the deeds described here are both a description of Jesus' miracles in Matt 8–9 and phraseologies from Isaiah that refer to the promised Messianic age. The blind receive sight: Isa 29:18; 42:18; 35:5 and Matt 9:27–31. The lame walk: Isa 35:6 and Matt 9:1–8. Lepers are cleansed: Isa 53:4 and Matt 8:1–4. The deaf hear: Isa 29:18; 35:5; 42:18 and Matt 9:32–34. The dead are raised: Isa 26:19 and Matt 9:18–26. The poor has good news preached to them: Isa 61:1 and Matt 9:35. Hagner, *Matthew 1-13*, 301.
26. The phrase "the kingdom of the heavens" occurs only in Matthew, where it is used thirty-two times. According to Ladd, it is "a Semitic idiom, where heavens is a substitute for the divine name." In addition, Ladd argues that "it is possible that 'the kingdom of the heavens' is native to the Jewish-Christian milieu, which preserved the gospel tradition in Matthew rather than reflecting the actual usage of Jesus." Ladd, *Theology of the New Testament*, 61.

concludes the prophetic era. Second, by implication, Jesus now inaugurates the new era – the kingdom one:

> From the days of John the Baptist until now the kingdom of heaven has suffered violence, and the violent take it by force. For all the Prophets and the Law prophesied until John. (Matt 11:12–13)

This is one of the most difficult verses in Matthew, and it is beyond this study to summarize the different opinions.[27] Regardless of what is or who is implied by the violence and the suffering, we can safely say that Jesus here is declaring that the kingdom of heaven is now "powerfully operative among men in the labors of Jesus."[28] John is a "transitional figure between two separate orders."[29] In other words, the kingdom era has begun.

Luke 4:16–21 offers a similar correlation between the messianic deeds and the arrival of the kingdom. In the synagogue in Nazareth, Jesus reads from Isaiah 61:1–2, which in its context is a prophecy about the eschatological era. The prophecy lists different deeds that the anointed one will perform. Jesus' comment after he finished reading is monumental: "*Today this Scripture has been fulfilled in your hearing*" (Luke 4:21). This is one of the strongest declarations in the entire NT that the new age has been launched in Jesus' ministry.

The original context of this prophecy in Isaiah 61 is that of Israel's restoration and the end of exile. The same applies to the different references to Isaiah in Matthew 11:4–5. By identifying his deeds with those of the one who is to come – the Messiah – Jesus is declaring that the restoration of Israel and the end of exile are happening through his ministry. The kingdom of God is breaking through, because the agent of that kingdom, the one with authority over sickness and death, is present.

Moreover, the correlation between the healing acts and the kingdom is not arbitrary, nor is it simply a matter of fulfillment of prophecy. Rather,

---

27. See Hagner, *Matthew 1-13*, 306–307; Beasley-Murray, *Jesus and the Kingdom of God*, 91–96.
28. Beasley-Murray, *Jesus and the Kingdom of God*, 95.
29. Hagner, *Matthew 1-13*, 305.

the reign of God is the restoration into order and wholeness, as the references to Isaiah confirm. Israel's restoration has always meant a restoration of the world into a state of wholeness. That is why declaring the kingdom of God and the healing of every sickness and weakness often go hand in hand in the Gospels (e.g. Matt 4:23; 9:35); nor is it any coincidence that Gentiles benefited from these healing acts (e.g. the Canaanite women in Matt 15:21–28). The healings symbolize that God is restoring the creational order, and point towards a future place that will be characterized by wholeness.

2.1.4. The Kingdom Is in Your Midst: Luke 17:20–21

In Luke 17:29, the Pharisees asked Jesus "when the kingdom of God would come?" The question, naturally, presupposes that the kingdom, in the mind of the Pharisees, is yet to come. Jesus' answer to this question is very important:

> "The kingdom of God is not coming in ways that can be observed, nor will they say, 'Look, here it is!' or 'There!' for behold, *the kingdom of God is in the midst of you*." (Luke 17:20–21)

The phrase ἐντὸς ὑμῶν ἐστιν, translated here "in the midst of you," does not mean that the kingdom is "within you" as a matter of a private, inner spiritualized reality. Rather, "the most common modern view" is that the phrase should be understood as meaning "among/in the midst of," thus seeing the kingdom of God as "present in the person and ministry of Jesus."[30]

Green argues that Jesus here revisits the question of the kingdom's "temporality and geography." Jesus pronounces the kingdom as "already active, present, even where it is unacknowledged – not least among the Pharisees."[31]

---

30. J. Nolland, *Luke 9:21–18: 34. Word Biblical Commentary* (Nashville: Thomas Nelson, 1993), 853. Nolland rejects the interpretation of this phrase as matter of a private inner spiritualized reality on two bases: first, it requires that "you" be taken impersonally, which is a little unnatural. Second, it represents a view of the kingdom of God not found elsewhere in the Gospel tradition (p. 853).

31. J. B. Green, *The Gospel of Luke* (Grand Rapids: Eerdmans, 1997), 630 (emphasis added).

The message of Luke 17:21, considered along the wider ministry of Jesus, is simple: the kingdom of God is a present reality, and is located in the ministry and person of Jesus. Israel no longer has to wait: the time of the kingdom is *now* – without denying its future dimension.[32]

2.1.5. Entering Jerusalem

The entry of Jesus to Jerusalem on a donkey is one of the very few stories that is reported in all four Gospels.[33] In all of them "Jesus' symbolic act in approaching Jerusalem on a donkey is interpreted in terms of royalty."[34] According to Matthew, the crowd welcoming Jesus shouted "Hosanna to the *Son of David*! Blessed is he who comes in the name of the Lord!" (21:9; see Ps 118:24–25). According to Mark (11:10), they shouted, "Blessed is the *coming kingdom* of our father David!" In Luke (19:38), it is "Blessed *is the King* who comes in the name of the Lord!" and in John (12:13) "Blessed is he who comes in the name of the Lord, even *the King of Israel*!" In other words, the Gospels portray the entrance of Jesus as that of royal arrival: the king is coming! It is a kingdom-event.

Both Matthew (21:5) and John (12:15) claim that the incident is a fulfillment of Zechariah 9:9:

> Rejoice greatly, O daughter of Zion! Shout aloud, O daughter of Jerusalem! Behold, your king is coming to you; righteous and having salvation is he, humble and mounted on a donkey, on a colt, the foal of a donkey.

Jesus' calculated and planned action is, therefore, a direct claim that he is the "king of Zion" prophesied by Zechariah, and as such, he is claiming that he is bringing the misery of Israel into an end. Israel's restoration is about to happen, and what better venue than Jerusalem to host this event? In addition, because the return of God himself to Zion was an integral part

---

32. Wright warns in this context that Luke 17:21 does not support a "simplistic present kingdom viewpoint," but the more nuanced blend of present and future, which characterizes Jesus' proclamation throughout. Wright, *Jesus and the Victory of God*, 469.
33. Matt 21:1–11; Mark 11:1–10; Luke 19:28–40; John 12:12–16
34. Wright, *Jesus and the Victory of God*, 279.

of the restoration package,[35] N. T. Wright argues that "Jesus intended not only to announce, but also to symbolize and embody, YHWH's return to Zion."[36] It is an astounding claim – Jesus identifies himself as the true king of Zion, in effect embodying YHWH!

Yet the prophecy of Zechariah is about more than just restoring the fortunes of Israel. The prophecy continues as follows:

> I will cut off the chariot from Ephraim and the war horse from Jerusalem; and the battle bow shall be cut off, and he shall speak peace to the nations; *his rule shall be from sea to sea, and from the River to the ends of the earth.* (Zech 9:10)

Jesus, through his action, is claiming cosmic dominion – in the tradition of Zechariah 9:10 as well as Psalm 2:8. Jerusalem might be the battlefield, but the goal of the battle goes beyond Jerusalem. The king of Israel is God's vicegerent who will restore the whole creation to God; Jesus is claiming to be that king.

The entrance to Jerusalem is thus a pivotal kingdom-event. Its place in the narrative clearly intends to introduce the final week in Jesus' life, and in particular his death and resurrection, as the climax of the story of Israel and as the moment in history when God will become king through his vicegerent – the Messiah. Jesus is entering Jerusalem to establish the rule of God on earth. It had to be Jerusalem.

2.1.6. The Passion and the Resurrection

We can look at Jesus' death and resurrection, among many other ways, as a kingdom-event. After all, Jesus was crucified as "king of the Jews."[37] This will become clearer when we note the link in Isaiah of the Servant of YHWH being the one who is a royal figure and who introduces God's kingdom.[38] Jesus himself identified his death as the death of the servant:

---

35. See Isa 40:2–3, 9; 52:7–9; Ezek 43:2–7; Zech 2:10; 8:3.
36. Wright, *Jesus and the Victory of God*, 642.
37. Matt 27:37; Mark 15:24; Luke 23:38; John 19:19.
38. See chapter 5 above, section 4.2.

"For even the Son of Man came not to be served but *to serve*, and to give his life as a ransom for many" (Mark 10:45; also Matt 20:28). According to Evans, "there are good reasons to understand the ransom saying in terms of themes and images drawn from Second Isaiah, particularly the Suffering Servant Song."[39]

The connection between Jesus and the Servant of YHWH in Isaiah is strengthened when we consider other places in the Gospels and in the sayings of Jesus that make this connection.[40] Matthew claims that Jesus' healing actions were "to fulfill what was spoken by the prophet Isaiah: 'He took our illnesses and bore our diseases'" (8:17; see Isa 53:4). In Luke 22:37 Jesus explains his death using the servant song of Isaiah: "For I tell you that this Scripture must be fulfilled in me: 'And he was numbered with the transgressors'" (see Isa 53:12). Jesus' silence in his trial (Matt 26:63; 27:12–24) could be seen as a resemblance to Isaiah 53:7. And finally, the fact that he was buried in a rich man's tomb (Matt 27:57–60) could be seen as a resemblance to Isaiah 53:9.[41] There is thus a strong case that the gospel traditions have Isaiah 53 in mind as an explanation for the death of Jesus.

However, Dunn is hesitant in associating the Servant of YHWH tradition with Jesus himself.[42] He argues that Mark 10:45 and Luke 22:37 cannot be Jesus' words, but an elaboration on an early tradition that

---

39. Evans, *Mark 8:27-16:20*, 120. Evans discusses the themes of servanthood, ransom, giving life, and the phrase "for many" in both passages, and concludes that "Jesus' life would constitute the ransom that would free Israel from divine penalty." Similarly, Jeremias argues that the "representative surrender of life for the countless multitudes is in fulfillment of the saying about the Servant in Isa 53:10f., understood as a prophecy." J. Jeremias, *New Testament Theology*, trans. J. Bowden (London: SCM Press, 1971), 293. See also Ladd, *Theology of the New Testament*, 155.

40. Admittingly, the LXX never uses the διακον- root for the Servant of YHWH in Isa 42–53, but rather παῖς or δοῦλος. France observes that "διακονέω here is not, then, a verbal echo of the LXX of those passages, especially as the 'service' there rendered is to Yahweh, not, as here, to other people. In view of the echo of the language of Is. 53 in the following clause, however, Mark's readers may well have found, and been intended to find, a portrait of Jesus 'the Servant' also in the paradoxical notion of the Son of Man as a διάκονος." France, *The Gospel of Mark*, 419–420.

41. We can also make a reference to Acts 8:26–35 and the Ethiopian official encounter with Philip, which shows that the death of Christ was associated with the suffering Servant account. Wright also mentions Mark 9:12 (the Son of Man should suffer many things and be treated with contempt) as possibly alluding to Isaiah 53:12. Wright, *Jesus and the Victory of God*, 602.

42. Dunn, *Jesus Remembered*, 816.

understood Jesus' death as an offering sacrifice.[43] In other words, Dunn recognizes the echoes of Isaiah 53 in the text, but he does not believe that these echoes are original to Jesus.

N. T. Wright, on the other hand, gives a compelling argument for seeing not only Isaiah 53, but the whole of Isaiah 40–55, as being the background for Jesus' own understanding of his own death.[44] He first shows how in Second Temple Judaism some Jews believed that the great deliverance would come through a period of intense suffering.[45] He argues that the prophecy of Isaiah – particularly chapters 40–55, and particularly, within that, the figure of the servant – is the source for this belief.[46] In the understanding of Second Temple Judaism, however, the suffering would be of the nation, and in some cases her righteous representatives, but not of a single individual. This suffering is explained on the basis of Israel's own sin, being understood to hasten the moment when Israel's tribulation would be complete and her exile would come to an end.[47] Wright then argues that since Jesus' whole ministry program was the announcement and inauguration of the rule of God, as in Isaiah 40–55, then it follows that:

> Jesus regarded Isaiah 53, in its whole literary and historical context, as determinative . . . Jesus therefore intended not only to share Israel's sufferings, but to do so as the key action in the divinely appointed plan of redemption for Israel and the world.[48]

It is important to see Jesus as the servant, not just of Isaiah 53, but also of Isaiah 40–55 as a whole. The mission of the Servant in Isaiah is

---

43. Ibid., 813.
44. Wright, *Jesus and the Victory of God*, 577–604. See also N. T. Wright, "The Servant and Jesus: The Relevance of the Colloquy for the Current Quest for Jesus," in *Jesus and the Suffering Servant: Isaiah 53 and Christian Origins,* ed. W. R. Farmer and W. H. Bellinger (Harrisburg: Trinity Press International, 1998), 281–297.
45. Wright, *Jesus and the Victory of God*, 577.
46. Ibid., 588. He also alludes to the possibility that Daniel, Zechariah, and Ezekiel 4 provided additional basis for this belief.
47. Ibid., 591.
48. Ibid., 603.

universal; he is the "light for the nations" that "salvation may reach to the end of the earth" (49:6). His suffering will result in Jerusalem "expanding its tent," "spreading abroad" and "possessing the nations" (54:2–3), because the God of Israel is "the God of the whole earth" (54:5). Jesus, the righteous Israelite, as the Servant of YHWH, restored the fortunes not only of Israel, but also of the world through his death. He suffered and died as Israel, for Israel, and for the world. The kingdom of God goes out to the world through him, and in particular through his suffering – something that was indeed hard to grasp or expect (52:13, 15; 53:1).

The identification of Jesus as the Servant of YHWH is important for the theology of the land. It is an indication that the universal expansion of God's kingdom on earth has begun. The cross was a defining moment in the history of the kingdom. *The suffering of Jesus paved the way for the expansion of the kingdom.*

After his resurrection, Jesus declares his sovereign and universal rule as God's vicegerent: "All authority in heaven and *on earth* has been given to me" (Matt 28:18). It was not possible for Jesus to make such an assertion before his resurrection. His resurrection is his Father's vindication, following his obedience unto death. Moreover, we can look at the resurrection as the moment in history in which the kingdom of God was officially inaugurated on earth, and in which Jesus was declared as God's vicegerent. This is precisely the point of Peter' sermon in the Pentecost (Acts 2:22–39). He claims that the promises of Psalm 16 are fulfilled in Jesus, and arguing that Jesus is the prophesied Messiah that will come from the seed of David. The resurrection, according to Peter, is not simply the proof that Jesus is the Messiah, but the moment in history, in accordance to Psalm 110, when he was declared to be the Messiah:

> For David did not ascend into the heavens, but he himself says, "The Lord said to my Lord, 'Sit at my right hand, until I make your enemies your footstool.'" Let all the house of Israel therefore know for certain that God *has made him both Lord and Christ,* this Jesus whom you crucified." (Acts 2:34–36)

The resurrection thus marks the transition from the old age into the new one – the kingdom age.[49] If Jesus was indeed appointed as Lord and Messiah in his resurrection, then this means that the kingdom has been inaugurated and that the restoration of Israel has taken place.[50] When Peter claims that God has made Jesus the Messiah, he is claiming in essence "that Israel's destiny has reached its fulfillment in him."[51] Israel's exile is coming to an end and her fortunes are being restored.

2.1.7. *The Vicegerency of Jesus*

The above discussion sheds light on the vocation of Jesus as God's vicegerent – the agent who brought the kingdom of God to earth.[52] According to McCartney, an examination of Jesus' teaching and preaching shows that the "restored rule of humankind through the representative man does lie behind the arrival of 'the kingdom of God' which Jesus announces."[53] Jesus as vicegerent represents humanity in front of God, and embodies the rule of God on his behalf on earth. His role and actions as the herald of the kingdom, the one who exercises dominion over demons, the healer and restorer, the cosmic ruler of Jerusalem, and the Suffering Servant – all point to his vicegerency as ruling on God's behalf on the one hand, and the one through whom the vicegerency of humanity (lost in Eden) is restored on the other. In other words, Jesus achieved two things: (1) he brought the reign of God to earth, and (2) restored the human vicegerency. The two concepts are intertwined:

> But if it is *human* vicegerency that is restored, why is it called God's kingdom or reign? It is called God's reign because the proper created order of his sovereign rule on earth is *with man as vicegerent*. The kingdom of God is given to Jesus (Luke

---

49. See Ladd, *Theology of the New Testament*, 44.
50. See Walker, "The Land and Jesus Himself," 108.
51. Wright, *The New Testament*, 408.
52. Many of the concepts in this section come from McCartney's article, "Ecce Homo"
53. Ibid., 8.

22:29–30) and thus becomes his kingdom, the kingdom of the Son of Man. (Matt 13:41)[54]

The vicegerency of Jesus is also seen in the titles given to Jesus in the NT, and in particular the following four titles: Son of Man, Son of God, Shepherd, and the Christ. Each of these titles has royal and eschatological tones in it, and speaks of a role or a position that was given to Jesus in the NT to describe his ministry of earth.

First, Jesus' own self-designation as the "Son of Man" is understood to carry within it a notion of authority on earth:[55]

> *The Son of Man has authority on earth* to forgive sins . . . the Son of Man is lord even of the Sabbath. (Mark 2:10, 28)

The Son of Man's authority on earth clearly brings to mind Daniel 7:13–14, where the one who is like the Son of Man was given dominion and kingdom.[56] Evans argues that Jesus understood his own identity and vocation as that of the Son of Man of Daniel 7:13–14. He stresses the importance of the link between Jesus and the figure of Daniel 7, arguing that "fundamental elements of Jesus' proclamation of the kingdom of God, especially with regard to the perceived struggle with the kingdom of Satan, cannot be properly understood apart from appreciation of the contribution of Daniel 7."[57]

Jesus referred to Daniel 7:13–14 in his trial, when he was asked whether he was the Christ – the Son of God:

---

54. Ibid., 14 (emphasis in the original).
55. See I. H. Marshall, "Son of Man," in *Dictionary of Jesus and the Gospels*, ed. J. B. Green, S. McKnight and I. H. Marshall (Downers Grove: InterVarsity Press, 1992), 775–781. For the term Son of Man in the NT, see also D. Guthrie, *New Testament Theology* (Downers Grove: InterVarsity Press, 1981), 270–291; Dunn, *Jesus Remembered*, 705–764; C. Colpe, "ὁ υἱὸς τοῦ ἀνθρώπου," in *Theological Dictionary of the New Testament. Volume VIII*, ed. G. Bromiley and G. Friedrich (Grand Rapids: Eerdmans, 1972), 400–477.
56. See M. B. Shepherd, "Daniel 7:13 and the New Testament Son of Man," *WTJ* 86 (2006): 99–111.
57. C. A. Evans, "Defeating Satan and Liberating Israel: Jesus and Daniel's Visions," *JSHJ* 1, no. 2 (2003): 161.

You have said so. But I tell you, from now on you will see the Son of Man seated at the right hand of Power and coming on the clouds of heaven. (Matt 26:63–64)

Jesus gave this answer as a response to the question about his identity as Messiah. His answer combines both Daniel's vision and that of Psalm 110:1: "The Lord says to my Lord: 'Sit at my right hand, until I make your enemies your footstool.'" Daniel and the psalm speak of God's vindication of his vicegerent – the Son of Man in Daniel and the Son of God in the Psalm.[58] As such, the allusion to Daniel 7:13 is made, as Bauckham confirms, because "it is appropriate to the thought of eschatological vindication."[59] In addition, Jesus' response not only confirms his messianic identity – which would eventually result in his execution – but it also confirmed his role as God's vicegerent, who is about to suffer and be vindicated. "He is the true representative of YHWH's people, and will be vindicated as such."[60]

The identification of Jesus with the Son of Man of Daniel 7:13–14 is very important. The Son of Man in Daniel appears in a context of successive worldly kingdoms, all of which had fallen – only for God to establish his own kingdom, by giving dominion and kingdom to the Son of Man. This dominion is universal and multi-national. If Jesus is indeed the Son of Man of Daniel, then this is a claim to his universal sovereignty as God's vicegerent.

Second, Jesus was also declared as the "Son of God" – notably in his baptism and in the transfiguration. The Son of God in the OT, as we have seen above, was God's royal representative of God on earth: thus, for example, the king of Israel was celebrated as the son of God (Pss 2; 110). The declaration of Jesus as the Son of God in the Gospels is, therefore, a declaration of his royalty – as God's representative on earth. So we can interpret

---

58. Wright rightly insists that Dan 7:13 has nothing to do with the Son of Man figure coming from heaven to earth, but rather it is about him being elevated and vindicated. Wright, 1996, p. 524.
59. R. J. Bauckham, "The Son of Man: 'A Man in My Position' or 'Someone'," *JSNT* 23 (1985), 31.
60. Wright, *Jesus and the Victory of God*, 524.

the voice from heaven in the transfiguration in a kingdom-context.[61] In this context, this is a functional or vocational statement, more than an ontological one. Unlike the baptism, the voice this time speaks of Jesus in the third person – an indication that the voice was addressing those around Jesus. This is a public declaration, saying effectively: "This is my royal representative on earth; my Son; my vicegerent; and he deserves obedience as such." Jesus' transfiguration is his enthronement.[62]

Third, Jesus also saw himself as the shepherd.[63] Whereas the image of the shepherd and the sheep could be simply viewed as a daily-life image from the context of Palestine in the first century, many have argued for a theological and eschatological connotation behind the use of this image – linking it to the image of David-like figure as the shepherd in Ezekiel. The shepherd is one who restores Israel's fortunes and ends her exile.[64] In other words, by claiming to be the Shepherd, *Jesus is claiming to be the royal figure of Ezekiel who restores the fortunes of Israel.*

Matthew also unambiguously refers to Jesus as the royal shepherd of Micah 5:

> And you, O Bethlehem, in the land of Judah, are by no means least among the rulers of Judah; for from you shall come a ruler who will *shepherd my people Israel*. (Matt 2:6)

This is Matthew's summary of Micah 5:2–5, a passage which declares that the messianic figure "shall be great to the ends of the earth" (Mic 5:4). This description of Jesus as a universal ruler fits well with the theology of Matthew, who speaks of *Gentile* Magi worshipping the new-born baby

---

61. See also Luke 9:35 and Matt 17:5. Matthew adds the phrase "with whom I am well pleased" to the statement, possibly to make it similar to the statement in Jesus' baptism (3:17).

62. In Donaldson's study on the Mountain motif in the Gospel of Matthew, he argues that "the possibility presents itself that the mountain setting of the Transfiguration Narrative functions as a mountain of enthronement." Donaldson also argues for an influence of Ps 2:7 on the declaration voice. T. L. Donaldson, *Jesus on the Mountain: A Study in Matthean Theology* (Sheffield: JSOT Press, 1985): 147–148.

63. See Matt 2:6; 9:36; 10:6; 15:24; 26:31; Mark 6:34; 14:27; John 10:11.

64. Ezek 34:23–31; 37:22–28. See above chapter 5, section 4.1. See also Brueggemann, *The Land*, 164; Wright, *Jesus and the Victory of God*, 533; McCartney, "Ecce Homo," 10.

(and of a pagan king trembling when that baby was born), and who concludes his narrative with the gospel going to the ends of the earth after Jesus received authority over all the earth.

Finally, it now becomes apparent why Jesus was called "the Christ" in the Gospels and the NT. When Peter confessed him as "the Christ" (Matt 16:17), he was declaring his royalty, as the awaited king of Israel, the Son of David.[65] This title in a first-century Jewish context is loaded with meaning and realities that have to do with the awaited Messiah, the Son of David, who will establish God's throne in Zion, and all of this is related to the land. To declare Jesus as Messiah is to declare that both the restoration of Israel and the rebuilding of God's kingdom in Zion have begun.

These four titles, alongside Jesus' kingdom ministry, speak of Jesus in his humanity as the agent of God who brings God's reign on earth. They also describe him as the one representing humanity before God. In other words, the NT uses these titles to designate a role upon Jesus – namely that of a vicegerent. Such a designation is very important for our study of the land. Since, as we have argued, the restoration of man's vicegerency and that of the land go hand in hand, this designation indicates that Jesus as God's appointed vicegerent will reverse the fortunes of the land.

2.1.8. Conclusion: *The Kingdom Is Now*

We can conclude from the above discussion that the Gospels portray Jesus as the appointed vicegerent of God who inaugurated the reign of God on earth. Jesus' life, ministry, teachings, and death and resurrection are the embodiment of the kingdom of God. The Jesus-event, thus, inaugurates the reign of God on earth. The time of the kingdom is *now*. This basic NT teaching will no doubt have a profound impact of how we interpret the prophecies in the OT about the Messiah and the restoration of Israel – and will, naturally, alter our understanding of the theology of the land.

---

65. Matt 12:42; Mark 12:35; Luke 20:41.

2.2. The Kingdom Not Yet

We have already established the fact that in the teachings and ministry of Jesus, "eschatological salvation was now."[66] At the same time, and as Ladd explains, the majority of scholars have approached a consensus that the kingdom is "in some real sense both present and future."[67] In other words, Jesus' ministry achieved the beginning, but not the end of the kingdom of God. The kingdom of God was inaugurated, but not consummated. Dunn explains it as follows:

> A consistent aspect of the NT teaching on salvation is that it is a three-phase process, with a beginning, or decisive initiating event, an ongoing experience, and an end, the outcome to be attained.[68]

The fact that the Lord's Prayer says "your kingdom come" (Matt 6:10) reveals the futuristic element in Jesus' teaching. "One does not pray for something to come if it is already present."[69] The parable of the weeds in Matthew 13 explains this dynamic. Jesus gives this parable and many other parables in Matthew 13 to explain the kingdom. He speaks of an initial event in which seeds were sown, referring to his own ministry: "The one who sows the good seed is the Son of Man" (13:37). He then adds, "the field is the world, and the good seed is the sons of *the kingdom*. The weeds are the sons of the evil one" (13:38). Clearly, then, the sons of kingdom *are a present reality on earth*, alongside those of the evil one. He then speaks of a future event – the end of the age – in which "the Son of Man will send his angels, and they will gather out of *his kingdom* all causes of sin and all law breakers" (13:41). After that, "the righteous will shine like the sun in *the kingdom of their Father*" (13:43). This is clearly a reference to the kingdom in the future. The kingdom of God, therefore, began in the sowing

---

66. Dunn, *New Testament Theology*, 83.
67. Ladd, *Theology of the New Testament*, 56.
68. Dunn, *New Testament Theology*, 92.
69. Dunn, *Jesus Remembered*, 409.

ministry of the Son of Man, is present in the sons of the kingdom, and will be consummated in the future kingdom of the Father.

Jesus also explains his second coming as a kingdom-event:

> When the *Son of Man* comes in his glory, and all the angels with him, then he will sit on his glorious throne. Before him will be gathered all the nations, and he will separate people one from another as a shepherd separates the sheep from the goats. And he will place the sheep on his right, but the goats on the left. Then *the King* will say to those on his right, "Come, you who are blessed by my Father, *inherit the kingdom* prepared for you from the foundation of the world." (Matt 25:31–34)

This passage shows Jesus as king and judge. The Son of Man, God's vicegerent, will exercise the role of the judge in the consummation. Here is Israel's king finally judging the nations on behalf of YHWH, and exercising universal dominion (e.g. Ps 110:1; Isa 2:4; Dan 7:13–14). Jesus' language about the consummation is rooted in the biblical tradition of Israel, just as his language about the inauguration of the kingdom is.

We will come back in more detail to the question of the consummation in chapter 11. Meanwhile, it is important to underscore that the current period is a tension period, one in which the new age and the old age overlap. It is a "tension between realized eschatology and future eschatology."[70] The kingdom of God was established on earth alongside other kingdoms, and we live in a world that is the arena of a conflict between the kingdom of God and the kingdoms of this world – a tension that will finally be resolved when Christ returns. This tension will no doubt impact the mission and experience of the kingdom-communities here and now, as citizens of the kingdom of God and embodying this kingdom, while at the same living in the midst of the kingdoms of this world.

---

70. Hagner, *Matthew 1-13*, 148.

2.3. The Land of the Kingdom

We have so far seen that the kingdom is a present reality awaiting its future consummation. The kingdom is now – and in the future. It is already – but not yet. This section will argue that the kingdom is not only now; it is also *here*. The kingdom of God in this present age is an earthly phenomenon. It is the rule of God *on earth*. The earth is the sphere of the dominion of God. In other words, the *land* of the kingdom is the *earth*.

2.3.1. The Lord's Prayer: Matthew 6:10

Jesus taught his disciples to pray: "Your kingdom come, your will be done, *on earth* as it is in heaven" (Matt 9:10). This is a prayer for the Father to bring his "eschatological kingdom."[71] It is important to notice that this prayer shows where the rule of God must come – on earth (γῆ). As Wright explains, "the Jewish roots of this prayer leave no room for any idea of a purely abstract kingdom, a semi-Gnostic escape to another world."[72] The kingdom of God will come when the will of God is honored on earth just as it is in heaven. The kingdom, as the whole of the Sermon on the Mountain shows, is to live by heavenly rules and principles on earth. It is an earthly phenomenon.

2.3.2. Inheriting the Earth: Matthew 5:5

Jesus declares in the Beatitudes, "the meek shall inherit the earth" (Matt 5:5). We have already looked at this through the window of the covenant and Psalm 37.[73] In the context of the kingdom, however, Jesus is saying that the domain of the rule of God is the whole earth. One way to read the Beatitudes is to read them together as a unit. As such, Beale argues that "earth" in verse 5 is parallel with "kingdom of heaven" in verses 3 and 10, so that the "earth" here is "wider than the Promised Land's old borders and is coextensive with the kingdom of heaven."[74] Jesus is not talking about spiritual abstract realities that are not anchored in the world in which we

---

71. Ibid., 148.
72. Wright, *The New Testament*, 460.
73. See chapter 9 above, section 4.3.
74. Beale, *New Testament Biblical Theology*, 757.

live. He is applying the concept of the land and the people of God in the OT to his own followers (the meek, poor in Spirit, those hungry for righteousness, etc.).

2.3.3. Kingdom Parables

Jesus speaks about the kingdom in Matthew using many parables (e.g. Matt 13; Mark 4). The parables themselves indicate that the kingdom is a present reality in accordance with Isaiah's prophecy (Matt 13:13–15). Among the many things described in these parables is the concept of the gradual and somehow unspectacular growth of the kingdom. The parables in Matthew 13 are a good example. The parable of the sower concludes with the seeds that fell on good soil producing grain, "some a hundredfold, some sixty, some thirty" (13:8). This is a sign of expansion and growth. The same is evident in the mustard seed. Hagner observes that, even though the parable in itself is mainly about contrast rather than growth, "it is impossible to rule out an allusion to growth."[75] The parable shows that:

> The kingdom has begun inconspicuously, yet *it has begun*, and in the end the greatness of the kingdom in size will provide as amazing a contrast as that between mustard seed and the tree.[76]

This growth suggests not just personal or spiritual growth, but instead the geographical and territorial expansion of the kingdom as it spreads around the world. In addition, many have observed that Jesus might possibly be alluding to Ezekiel 17:23 and Daniel 4:12 when he talked about a tree which "the birds of the air come and make nests in its branches" (Matt 13:32).[77] The allusion to Daniel, if maintained, is quite interesting. In Daniel 4, the tree symbolizes Nebuchadnezzar's empire whose dominion stretched to the "ends of the earth" (Dan 4:22). France thus suggests that,

---

75. Hagner, *Matthew 1-13*, 387.
76. Ibid. (Emphasis in the original).
77. See for example Hagner, *Matthew 1-13*, 386; France, *The Gospel of Matthew*, 527; Blomberg, *Matthew*, 220.

This parable invites a comparison between the great but short-lived earthly empire of Babylon and the far greater and more permanent kingdom of heaven. The inclusion of all nations in that kingdom might be a bonus point for the sharp-eyed reader who knew the Daniel text and understood the birds as symbolic of the nations, but it is not emphasized.[78]

Whether we agree with this correlation between the parable of the mustard seed and Daniel 4 or not, the parables in Matthew 13 clearly speak of the kingdom of God in terms of growth and expansion. This expansion necessitates that the kingdom goes beyond the land, and into the earth. The mustard seed might have fallen first in one land, but the end-result is a tree that covers the whole earth, and all the nations can benefit from its fruit.

2.3.4. *The Great Declaration: Matthew 28:18–20*

The declaration of Jesus at the conclusion of Matthew's Gospel is perhaps one of the most important statements in the NT on the theology of the land:

> All authority in *heaven and on earth* has been given to me. Go therefore and make disciples *of all nations*, baptizing them in the name of the Father and of the Son and of the Holy Spirit, teaching them to observe *all that I have commanded you*. And behold, I am with you always, to the end of the age.

Jesus here declares his authority over all the earth ($γῆ$), and indeed the entire creation. This is a kingdom declaration. The vicegerent of God now rules the entire earth. There are no boundaries to his domain of authority. His royal land is the earth. This authority of Jesus, which he acquired at his resurrection, is the basis for the commission that he gave his disciples. "The universal authority of Jesus is the basis of the universal mission of the church."[79]

---

78. France, *The Gospel of Matthew*, 527.
79. Hagner, *Matthew 14-28*, 887.

According to Chris Wright, what is not often noticed is how thoroughly covenantal and *Deuteronomic* is the form and content of this passage.[80] He notices in particular a resemblance with Deuteronomy 4:39–40:

> Know therefore today, and lay it to your heart, that the Lord is God in *heaven above and on the earth beneath*; there is no other. Therefore you *shall keep his statutes and his commandments*, which I command you today, that it may go well with you and with your children after you, and that you may prolong your days *in the land that the Lord your God is giving you for all time.*

According to Wright, in Matthew 28:18 Jesus paraphrases the affirmation of Deuteronomy about YHWH . . . and calmly applies them to himself. *The risen Jesus thus claims the same relationship and sovereignty over all creation as the Old Testament affirms for YHWH.* The whole earth, then, belongs to Jesus.[81]

Notice how in Deuteronomy the commandments *of God* relate to Israel' presence *in the land*. In Matthew, the commandments of *Jesus* – God's vicegerent – relate to the mission of the disciples *on earth*. Jesus was thus expanding the territory from land to earth in accordance with the original plan. For the creator God is the God of heavens and earth.

Walker also argues that Matthew here is possibly contrasting Jesus with Moses. Matthew has Jesus saying this declaration on a mountain (28:16), which may be an echo of Moses on Mount Nebo, before the Israelites entered the land (Deut 34). According to Walker, if this comparison is maintained,

> This would endorse the argument that the particularistic Jewish emphasis on the "land" was now being eclipsed by an emphasis on the whole world: the "land to be possessed"

---

80. Wright, *The Mission of God*, 354.
81. Ibid., 403 (emphasis in the original).

was not the "land of Israel" . . . but rather the peoples of "all nations."[82]

Donaldson, on the other hand, argues that Mt Zion is in Matthew's mind here (as a theological background), and not Mt Sinai.[83] He argues that in Second Temple Judaism literature, the mountain frequently functioned as a site for eschatological events and that Mt Zion in particular was at the center of hopes of Israel's eschatological restoration. Matthew's closing scene on the mountain in Galilee, according to Donaldson, is "a highly eschatological pericope, for it inaugurates an age in which Jesus exercises universal authority and in which the long anticipated, but formally prohibited, mission to the Gentiles is to take place."[84]

Whether it was the Sinai tradition or the Zion one that influenced Matthew's theology, the implications are the same. This is an eschatological event in which Jesus declares his universal dominion. The "Promised Land" has been eclipsed by the breakthrough of what we may call the "promised earth." The borders of the land, after the resurrection, are "definitively transcended."[85]

The kingdom of Israel is now a universal kingdom. It is not limited to one land or one people, because the king in this kingdom has authority over heaven and earth. This is indeed a fulfillment of the original vision regarding the kingdom of God in the OT. Psalm 2:8 is now a reality: "You are my Son; today I have begotten you. Ask of me, and I will make the nations your heritage, *and the ends of the earth your possession.*" The risen Christ can now claim this psalm and make it his: He was appointed as the "Son of God"; the nations are his "heritage"; the "ends of the earth" are his "possession." This massive declaration is the basis of the great commission. Yet, for our purposes, it is clear evidence of a major shift in the biblical narrative – the land has now been replaced by the earth.

---

82. Walker, *Jesus and the Holy City*, 40.
83. Donaldson, *Jesus on the Mountain*, 174–192.
84. Ibid., 180.
85. Marchadour and Neuhaus, *Land, the Bible, and History*, 65.

2.3.5. Conclusion: Jesus, the Kingdom, and the Land

The Jesus-event inaugurated the reign of God *on earth*. The kingdom of God is both *now* and *here*.[86] The theology of the land serves to remind us that the kingdom of God is not a spiritual reality. The kingdom is God's rule on earth, just as in the OT God ruled on earth through his elected representatives – from Adam, to Israel, to the monarch. However, God's representatives in the OT – his vicegerents – failed to actualize and expand his rule on the entire earth. But Jesus, the Christ, finally achieved this reign and inaugurated the kingdom on earth, and as such he was declared the Son of God.

The land of Christ that he inherited as God's Son – his vicegerent – is the earth. The expansion of the land in the OT had been anticipated in several places: in the commandment in Eden to multiply and subdue the earth; in the promise to Abraham that in him all the families of the earth will be blessed; in the exaltation of the king of Israel as having a cosmic rule; and in the prophetic visions of a universal Zion. The land of Canaan, consequently, has served its purpose. It has been expanded and now covers the entire earth. In the theology of the kingdom, the land has been "universalized."

3. The Kingdom and the Vicegerency of Jesus in the Epistles

After we have looked at the theme of the kingdom of God in the Gospels, we move next to look at the theme as it appears in the rest of the NT, in

---

86. The statement of Jesus in John 18:36 may appear to contradict this conclusion. There, Jesus says: "My kingdom is not of this world. If my kingdom were of this world, my servants would have been fighting, that I might not be delivered over to the Jews. But my kingdom is not from the world." Yet as Beasley-Murray says, "it is essential that Jesus' statement [John 18:36] should not be misconstrued as meaning this his kingdom is not *active* in this world, or *has nothing to do with* this world." G. R. Beasley-Murray, *John. World Biblical Commentary* (Waco: Word Books, 1987), 331 (emphasis in the original). See also McCartney, "Ecce Homo," 14. What Jesus is saying is simply that his kingdom does not have its source or origin from this world. As we have seen, the kingdom of heaven came into this world through Jesus' ministry. It is a heavenly kingdom that broke through the earth (Matt 6:10). John 18:36 is not denying that the kingdom of God is active in the world.

particular in Pauline letters and Hebrews. The phrase "kingdom" appears in Pauline letters only fourteen times,[87] but this does not mean that the concept or the theme is missing in Paul. A quick look at the verses where the term "kingdom" appears in Pauline epistles shows that the kingdom is often the object of "inheritance."[88] In addition, Paul seems to speak about it as both a *present* reality (Rom 14:27) and a *future* one (1 Cor 15:50), which is consistent with his eschatology as a whole. Paul was convinced that he was "living in the final age towards which the eternal purpose of God has been aiming from the beginning of time";[89] and the arrival of the rule of God – his kingdom – was a central part in this theological moment. We can trace Paul's theology of the kingdom of God, mainly but not exclusively, in two places: the Epistle to Romans, and 1 Corinthians 15. We will then examine Hebrews 1–2, which deal with the vicegerency of Jesus.

3.1. The Kingdom of God in Romans

The introduction to Romans includes one of the most important statements in Paul regarding this theme of the kingdom:

> Paul . . . set apart for the *gospel of God*, which he promised beforehand through his prophets in the holy Scriptures, concerning *his Son*, who was descended from David according to the flesh and *was declared to be the Son of God* in power according to the Spirit of holiness *by his resurrection from the dead*, Jesus Christ our Lord, through whom we have received grace and apostleship to bring about the obedience of faith for the sake of his name among all the nations. (Rom 1:1–5)

Paul declares in this passage that the gospel of Christ, the one he is preaching, is the climax of the OT. The gospel is the proclamation that Jesus, the Son of God and Israel's Messiah, has been appointed Son of God through his resurrection. The first "Son" in this passage (1:3) refers to Jesus'

---

87. Rom 14:17; 1 Cor 4:20; 6:9–10; 15:24; 15:50; Gal 5:21; Eph 5:5; Col 1:13; 4:11; 1 Thess 2:12; 2 Thess 1:5; 2 Tim 4:1; 4:18.
88. 1 Cor 6:9–10; 15:50; Gal 5:21; Eph 5:5.
89. Hays, *Echoes of Scripture*, 100.

"uniquely intimate relationship to God."[90] The second "Son" (1:4) refers to a unique role exercised in a way not previously recognized – in the sense that he was not the "Son of God" before he was "declared to be Son of God."[91] Paul is talking about a distinctive critical moment in salvation history – the resurrection – in which Jesus was *appointed* as the Son of God:

> What Paul is claiming, then, is that the preexisting Son, who entered into human experience as the promised Messiah, was appointed on the basis of (or, perhaps, at the time of) the resurrection to a new and more powerful position in relation to the world.[92]

The gospel, according to Paul, is "the narrative proclamation of King Jesus."[93] It is about Jesus as the Davidic Messiah, who was appointed "Son of God." We have already observed that this term has royal connotations. Kings in the OT and the ANE – and even closer to home, the Caesar of Rome – were all celebrated as the "Son of God." The gospel to Paul is the declaration of the kingship of Jesus. "Paul's theology in Romans is, at its heart, royal."[94]

The fact that Jesus is Israel's Messiah leads to the proclamation of his gospel among all the nations. In fact, it is precisely because Jesus is *Israel's* Messiah that Paul is able to declare the gospel among *the nations*. As Dunn observes, "the full extent of God's purpose could only be realized through Jesus as Messiah (of Israel) risen from the dead to become the Son of God in power (for all)."[95] Paul starts in Israel, but ends with the nations. He starts in Jerusalem, but ends in Rome. This is not simply how he understood his own mission as an apostle to the Gentiles, or how he understood

---

90. D. J. Moo, *The Epistle to the Romans* (Grand Rapids: Eerdmans, 1996), 44.
91. The verb ὁρίζω is better translated as "appointed" or "designated" and not "declared." See J. D. G. Dunn, *Romans. 1-8. Word Biblical Commentary* (Dallas: Word Books, 1988), 13; Moo, *The Epistle to the Romans*, 47.
92. Moo, *The Epistle to the Romans*, 48.
93. Wright, *What Saint Paul Really Said*, 45.
94. Ibid., 54.
95. Dunn, *The Theology of Paul the Apostle* (Grand Rapids: Eerdmans, 1998), 14.

the Christian mission. For Paul, this is what the OT had always declared: Abraham is a "father of us all" (Rom 4:16); God is the God of both Jews and Gentiles (Rom 3:29); and God has promised "the world" to Abraham (Rom 4:13). Paul's theology of the gospel of the kingdom is universal, even if it appears historically to the Jew first and then to the Gentile (Rom 1:14–16). For Hays,[96] the phrase "to the Jew first and also to the Greek" in Romans 1:16 has echoes of Psalm 98:2–3:

> The Lord has made known his *salvation*; he has revealed his *righteousness* in the sight of the nations. He has remembered his steadfast love and faithfulness to the house of Israel. *All the ends of the earth have seen the salvation of our God.*

Hays then comments:

> The hope of the psalmist is that God's eschatological vindication of Israel will serve as a demonstration to the whole world of the power and faithfulness of Israel's God, a demonstration that will bring even Gentiles to acknowledge him. Paul shares the psalmist's eschatological vision; that is why he insists in Rom 1:16 that the gospel is a word of salvation to the Jew first and then subsequently also the Greek.[97]

In other words, salvation can be extended to the Gentiles only after Israel is vindicated. This eschatological vindication has taken place, according to Paul, when Jesus was appointed "Son of God" in power. As such, the gospel can now extend to the ends of the earth.

The gospel, therefore, is the declaration of the reign of God through his Messiah *even in Rome*. This gospel can save "everyone who believes," and we can add *"everywhere* he/she believes." The "obedience of faith" (Rom 1:5) that Paul is seeking from his audience is the obedience to Jesus as Israel's Messiah and the king of all the nations. In the theology of Paul in Romans,

---

96. Hays, *Echoes of Scripture*, 36–41.
97. Ibid., 37.

the eschatological kingdom of God is a realized reality. He believed he was witnessing the inauguration of the eschatological age that the OT pointed to – a time when Israel's Davidic Messiah ruled the nations and established the reign of God on earth. Paul's kingdom theology in Romans is thus universal. The world is the sphere of God's rule, and the nations are the object of his reign. The territory of the kingdom, in Paul's theology, is the world.

3.2. Paul and The Vicegerency of Jesus: 1 Corinthians 15:20–28

Paul argues in 1 Corinthians 15 for the centrality of the resurrection of Christ. The resurrection is the basis of the Christian faith (15:14). In the midst of this long chapter comes one of the most important passages in Paul about the reign of God through the vicegerency of Jesus, and the relationship of the resurrection to this concept:

> But in fact Christ has been raised from the dead, the firstfruits of those who have fallen asleep. For as by a man came death, by a man has come also the resurrection of the dead. *For as in Adam all die, so also in Christ shall all be made alive.* But each in his own order: Christ the firstfruits, then at his coming those who belong to Christ. Then comes the end, when he delivers the kingdom to God the Father after destroying every rule and every authority and power. For he must reign until he has put all his enemies under his feet. The last enemy to be destroyed is death. For "God has put all things in subjection under his feet." But when it says, "all things are put in subjection," it is plain that he is excepted who put *all things* in subjection under him. When all things are subjected to him, then the Son himself will also be subjected to him who put *all things* in subjection under him, that God may be all in all. (1 Cor 15:20–28)

Paul first parallels Jesus with Adam (15:22). This parallelism is based on the capacity of both to function as vicegerents. As vicegerents, both Adam and Jesus represent God on earth, and represent humanity in front of God.

What Paul seems to stress in this particular comparison is precisely the notion of *ruling on God's behalf,* which is evident in the allusions to Daniel 7, Psalm 8, and Psalm 110. The point Paul is making is that the resurrection marks "the beginning of the representative humanity of the last Adam."[98] The risen Christ is God's vicegerent *par excellence.* He accomplished what Adam failed to do: subduing the world on God's behalf. The climax of Christ's rule over all things, in this passage, is his own submission to God – "the very antithesis of Adam's sin."[99] In other words, the *role* of Jesus in this passage is that of a vicegerent. He rules on behalf of his Father, and one day when "all things are subjected to him," he will also "be subjected to him who put all things in subjection under him" (15:28). Jesus fulfills the role of Adam as the human vicegerent.[100]

N. T. Wright argues that Paul's Adam-christology is in fact an Israel-christology.[101] He explains how in Second Temple Judaism Israel was viewed as God's "true humanity," and then argues that Paul's theology of Adam is a Jewish one in which "the role traditionally assigned to Israel has devolved on to Jesus Christ." Paul now regards Jesus, not Israel, as God's "true humanity."[102] Wright then comments on 1 Corinthians 15:20–28 as follows:

> The resurrection of Jesus is thus interpreted by Paul through the widening categories of Messiahship, Israel and humanity . . . God's plan, to rule his world through obedient humanity, has come true in the Messiah, Jesus. That which was purposed in Genesis 1 and 2, the wise rule of creation by the obedient human beings, was lost in Genesis 3 . . . The Messiah, however, has now been installed as the one through whom God is doing what he intended to do, first through humanity and

---

98. Dunn, *Christology in the Making: A New Testament Inquiry into the Origins of the Doctrine of the Incarnation* (London: SCM Press, 1989), 108.
99. Ibid., 109.
100. McCartney, "Ecce Homo," 16.
101. N. T. Wright, *The Climax of the Covenant: Christ and the Law in Pauline Theology* (Minneapolis: Fortress Press, 1992), 21–26.
102. Ibid., 26.

then through Israel. Paul's Adam-christology is basically an Israel-christology, and is predicated on the identification of Jesus as Messiah, in virtue of his resurrection.[103]

We can thus conclude that the parallelism with Adam shows that the kingdom of God in Paul's theology is a universal kingdom. At the same time, the parallelism with Israel is also an indication that the kingdom is universal – since Israel perceived her ministry and the ministry of the Messiah as universal. The kingdom of God is about the reign of God through Christ over "all things." The creational language of Adam and Psalm 8 confirms this conclusion. The ministry of Jesus as God's vicegerent is a restoration of the creational order, and a defeat of the ultimate enemies – "every rule and every authority and power" even unto "death" (15:24–26). By setting death as the ultimate enemy, Paul reveals that he has a more cosmic view of the ministry of Jesus. He has moved beyond the narrow Jewish theology of his day, because he believed that he was witnessing the inauguration of the eschatological and universal rule of God – evident by his statement that "God has put all things in subjection under his feet" (15:27). Yet he also speaks of a future eschatological moment when Christ himself hands "all things" back to his Father (15:28). In both stages, kingdom "now" and kingdom "then," Paul's theology of the kingdom of God is universal. The land over which Christ rules is the world.

Finally, Paul's identification of Jesus with Adam is very important for our study of the land through the lens of Eden. The vocation of vicegerency is redeemed in Jesus, and this means that the curse of Eden on the ground can now be reversed. Eden as a land of blessing, peace, and order can now be restored.

3.3. Hebrews 1:8–9, 13; 2:6–9

The book of Hebrews opens by saying that "in these last days" God has spoken to us by his Son "whom he appointed *the heir of all things*, through whom also he created the world" (Heb 1:2). This is not a general statement about the identity of Jesus as the Son of God from eternity. Hebrews is

---

103. Ibid., 29.

speaking about a gradual historical and salvific process, which culminated in this appointment of the Son of God as the heir of all things; and, as Beale comments, "the likely time of this appointment to inherit the earth as God's Son was at Christ's resurrection."[104]

The book of Hebrews contains important statements about the royalty of Jesus. These statements appear in the context of comparison between Jesus and the angels, and are aided by the use of the Psalms. In Hebrews 1:8–9, the author quotes Psalm 45:6–7 and applies it to Jesus:

> But of the Son he says, "Your throne, O God, is forever and ever, the scepter of uprightness is the scepter of your kingdom. You have loved righteousness and hated wickedness; therefore God, your God, has anointed you with the oil of gladness beyond your companions." (Heb 1:8–9)

Psalm 45 in its original context gives the king of Israel divine attributes (45:6) and celebrates him as just and righteous (45:4, 7–8). It also speaks of his universal dominion (45:16–17). The author of Hebrews reads the psalm eschatologically. The hopes of an ideal king – an ideal "Son of God" – are now transferred to Jesus. The royalty of Jesus means that he is now addressed with divine attributes. Yet Lane is correct in asserting that the writer's primary interest in the quotation is "not the predication of deity but of the eternal nature of the dominion exercised by the Son."[105] This is further advanced by quoting Psalm 110, which is another "royal" psalm, and which Hebrews again claims is now fulfilled in Jesus.

Hebrews 2:6–9 continues the comparison between Jesus and angels, and this time quotes Psalm 8:4–6:

> It has been testified somewhere, "What is man, that you are mindful of him, or the son of man, that you care for him? You made him for a little while lower than the angels; you

---

104. Beale, *New Testament Biblical Theology*, 760.
105. W. L. Lane, *Hebrews 1-8. Word Biblical Commentary* (Dallas: Word Books, 1991), 29.

> have crowned him with glory and honor, putting everything in subjection under his feet." Now in putting everything in subjection to him, he left nothing outside his control. At present, we do not yet see everything in subjection to him. But we see him who for a little while was made lower than the angels, namely Jesus, crowned with glory and honor because of the suffering of death, so that by the grace of God he might taste death for everyone. (Heb 2:6–9)

The psalm in its original context celebrates God as creator. The references to "man" and "son of man," and the subjection of "everything" under his feet are clearly references to Genesis 1:26–28. The psalm interprets the creation of man in terms of royalty. The author of Hebrews, however, seems to "mock" this royalty: "At present, we do not yet see everything in subjection to him" (2:8b).[106] He then makes his point: it is Jesus who fulfills the vocation of humankind (2:9). He is the one crowned with glory and honor. Further, it is precisely in his suffering that he achieved this royal status. His path to glory is through his resurrection.

These two statements in Hebrews celebrate the royalty of Jesus by claiming that he fulfills the role of *both Israel's Messiah and Adam*. Hebrews thus celebrates Jesus as the ultimate vicegerent who rules on behalf of humanity. The reign of Jesus is not limited in Hebrews, for God has made him "heir of all things" (Heb 1:2). The fact that Jesus fulfills the vocation of the Messiah of Israel confirms the universality of his reign – a point underlined by the use of Psalms 45 and 110.

Finally, it is important to observe that the celebration in Hebrews of Jesus as God's vicegerent is based on his "suffering of death" (Heb 2:9). The cross of Jesus is his path to glorification, and it is his cross that opens the door for the restoration of order on earth.

---

106. Ibid., 47.

3.4. Conclusion

The three examples discussed above are not exhaustive, but they reveal that the NT shared many of the theological themes of the Gospels.[107] Jesus, whether proclaimed as crucified (as in Hebrews) or as raised from the dead (as in Paul), is the cornerstone of the theology of the kingdom. The death and resurrection of Christ, viewed as one event, is the climactic moment in salvation history in which Jesus was declared the Son of God and king of the world. It announced the arrival of the eschatological era and the restoration of Israel. This opened the door for the expansion of the gospel into the ends of the earth.

In Paul and Hebrews, Jesus' position is understood as God's vicegerent, who exercises dominion on God's behalf and restores the world to him. He restores the role of Adam and brings life to the world. As such he also takes the place of Israel as God's representative humanity. He reigns now on earth from heaven, and one day he will consummate the reign of God on earth.

4. The Mission of the Church and Universal Dominion

4.1. Jesus Bestows Vicegerency on His Disciples

Jesus often sent his disciples and followers on "kingdom missions."[108] When he sent his disciples, he "gave them power and authority over all demons and to cure diseases, and he sent them out to proclaim the kingdom of God and to heal" (Luke 9:1–2). We can describe this as a bestowal of authority upon the disciples. Jesus empowers them to become kingdom-agents, just

---

107. In addition to Rom and 1 Cor 15, we can talk about the theme of the Servant of YHWH in Paul's theology, and in particular in 2 Cor 5:14–21. See Gignilliat's important study on this theme. He argues that in 2 Cor 5:14–21, "Paul's understanding of the action of God through the agency of Christ on behalf of mankind is in some sense mediated by God's redemptive portrayal in Isaiah 40–55." M. S. Gignilliat, *Paul and Isaiah's Servants: Paul's Theological Reading of Isaiah 40-66 in 2 Corinthians 5:14-6:10* (London: T&T Clark, 2007), 107.

108. Matt 10:1–4; Mark 3:13–15; 6:7–13; Luke 9:1–6; 10:1–12.

as he is.[109] The acts they are commissioned to do are "kingdom-acts" – they are signs of the presence of the reign of God. In fact, Jesus also declares that his followers will do "greater works" than his, because he is "going to the Father" (John 14:12–13).

The vicegerency of the disciples is also seen in the statement that Jesus will give them "the keys of the kingdom," so that whatever they "bind on earth shall be bound in heaven," and whatever they "loose on earth shall be loosed in heaven" (Matt 16:19). This is a declaration of the disciples' authority as the representatives of God on earth. Moreover, Jesus bestowed upon his disciples the role of judging. They, too, will "sit on twelve thrones, judging the twelve tribes of Israel" (Matt 19:28). The disciples will share in the vicegerency of Jesus in the consummation of the kingdom, just as they will serve as kingdom-agents on earth after his ascension.

That is why the mission of the early church (or evangelism) can be defined as the disciples acting as kingdom-agents in their declaring the reign of God through his risen "Christ." We have already seen that the great commission in Matthew 28:19 is based on the great declaration of the kingship of Jesus in 28:18. Moreover, in the Markan account of the commission, Jesus sends his disciples to "proclaim the gospel to the whole creation," and then promises that "signs" will accompany those who believe in him (16:17–18). These signs included exorcism and healing, which had been signs in Jesus' ministry that the kingdom was breaking through. The disciples are the ones now acting as kingdom-agents and as God's vicegerents, whereas Jesus now sits down "at the right hand of God" (16:19) – a sign of his own vicegerency.[110]

In the book of Acts the disciples and followers of Jesus begin acting as kingdom-agents on behalf of Jesus. Luke summarizes the preaching of the disciples as preaching the "kingdom of God."[111] Empowered by the Spirit, they perform miracles and cast out demons (e.g. 2:43; 3:6–7) and declare the risen Christ "with great power" (4:33).

---

109. Wright, *Jesus and the Victory of God*, 203.
110. See no. 642 above.
111. Acts 8:12; 19:8; 20:25; 28:23, 31.

Moreover, the vicegerency of the twelve disciples is a restoration of the vicegerency of Israel. Israel as a priestly kingdom was supposed to embody the reign of God on earth. Israel's king was also supposed to bring the world into submission to God. Now this task has been mandated to the twelve Jewish disciples of Israel's Messiah; and in due course this mandate will be extended to all those who believe in this Messiah. This is a new Israel. The community of believers in Christ embodies the reign of God on earth, by declaring Jesus as the risen Christ, and by making disciples of this risen Christ.

4.2. Conquering the Land: The Book of Acts

We have argued that for both Jesus and Paul the sphere of the kingdom is the *earth*. The boundaries of the land of the kingdom have expanded to achieve the original vision of universal dominion. The book of Acts is a testimony to the beginning of the realization of this vision. In Acts, the gospel of the kingdom expands, and the reign of God is declared in new lands – not just the Promised Land.

Jesus' answer to the disciples' question in the opening of the book of Acts about the time of restoring the kingdom of Israel (1:6) is a declaration of the territory which will come under Jesus' reign in the course of the book:

> It is not for you to know times or seasons that the Father has fixed by his own authority. But you will receive power when the Holy Spirit has come upon you, and you will be my witnesses *in Jerusalem and in all Judea and Samaria, and to the end of the earth.* (Acts 1:7–8)

Some have taken Jesus' answer to mean that there will be a future restoration of an Israelite kingdom (naturally in the land). Yet the whole of Jesus' ministry, and no less his answer here in Acts 1:8, seems to indicate that (a) the kingdom is being restored through Jesus the Christ, and (b) the land of this kingdom has expanded now in accordance with the original plan. Jesus' answer, which is the blueprint of the geographical development of events in the book of Acts, indicates that the land of the kingdom now includes Jerusalem, Judea, Samaria (and, by implication, anywhere else the disciples bear witness to his reign) – even to the "ends of the earth." Jesus is speaking here about a process of progression and territorial growth to the kingdom of God. He is in essence denying the aspirations of many contemporary Jewish movements (and possibly some of his disciples' hopes) that sought to establish a national Jewish kingdom in the land.[112] In short, "the newly inaugurated kingdom claims as its sacred turf, not a single piece of territory, but the entire globe."[113]

Moreover, this theme of the kingdom of God in Acts constitutes the "book-ends" of the book – appearing in both the introduction and conclusion (1:3; 28:31). The book concludes with Paul "proclaiming the kingdom of God" in Rome. This indicates that for Luke *the restoration of Israel has begun* – but not in a nationalistic manner, as most first century Jews expected.[114] N. T. Wright makes a connection between the introduction and the conclusion of Acts, arguing that Paul as a kingdom-agent is proclaiming nothing less than the kingdom of Israel:

> Here at last is a Jew living in Rome itself . . . and declaring that, in and through Jesus, Israel's God is the sole king of the world. This is Luke's full answer to the question the disciples asked of Jesus in Acts 1:6. Israel's God has restored his kingdom for his people.[115]

It is appropriate in the context of Acts to speak of the disciples' mission as an act of conquering the earth – echoing the conquering of the land of Canaan by the Israelites in the days of Joshua. Several scholars have noticed

---

112. This is why many argue that Jesus is in fact *correcting* his disciples through his answer. See for example Burge, *Jesus and the Land*, 61; Walker, "The Land and Jesus Himself," 108; Waltke, *An Old Testament Theology*, 570; Davies, *The Gospel and the Land*, 265. For more on this verse and on the disciples' question, see section 5 of this chapter below.

113. Wright, *Jesus and the Victory of God*, 218.

114. Walker says that another evidence that for Luke the restoration had already been inaugurated through Jesus "comes in Paul's repeated declaration that the resurrection was to be seen in terms of the 'hope of Israel'." Walker, *Jesus and the Holy City*, 98. See Acts 23:6; 24:15; 26:6–7; 28:20.

115. Wright, *Jesus and the Victory of God*, 375.

the similarities between the structure of Acts and Joshua.[116] Most notable among them is Crawford, who argues that:

> Luke not only depended heavily on the Joshua story but in fact reworked some of its major emphases in ways which would allow the new narrative to serve as a foundational story for the emerging Christian movement.[117]

Crawford observes many similarities in the development of the narratives in Joshua and Acts.[118] He argues that the conquest of the land is the thrust of the book of Joshua, but in contrast, the commission to the disciples to be witnesses first in Jerusalem and then in ever-widening circles provides the thrust of the book of Acts.[119] Among many things, the comparison for Crawford shows that "unlike Joshua, Acts is not about building a kingdom for Israel in the land of promise; it is about building the kingdom of God in the world."[120]

We can conclude that the kingdom of God in Luke-Acts "is a twofold entity – inaugurated through Jesus' death and resurrection, but implemented through the disciples' mission."[121] Luke's *kerygma* in his Gospel is that the kingdom of God has been inaugurated in Jesus. Luke's *kerygma* in Acts is that the reign of God is being implemented in the universal mission of the church.

The territory associated with this kingdom thus necessarily will expand outwards – no longer confined to the Promised Land. It will become any

---

116. See for example Burge, *Jesus and the Land*, 59; P. W. L. Walker, "The Land in the Apostles' Writings," in *The Land of Promise*, ed. P. Johnston and P. Walker (Downers Grove: InterVarsity Press, 2000), 96.

117. T. G. Crawford, "Taking the Promised Land, Leaving the Promised Land: Luke's Use of Joshua for a Christian Foundation Story," *Review and Expositor* 95 (1998): 251.

118. He talks, for example, about the striving for holiness in both communities (p. 252). He also observes that the missionary journeys of Acts echo the various military campaigns of Joshua (p. 253). There is of course, the analogy between Achan on the one hand, and Ananias and Sapphira on the other (p. 256). He also suggests an analogy between the conversions of Rahab and Cornelius, since both were considered "unclean" (p. 257).

119. Crawford, "Taking the Promised Land," 252.

120. Ibid., 253.

121. Ibid., 96.

land where the risen Jesus is declared and followed as *the Christ*: Israel's Messiah and king of the world. In this new era, inaugurated by Jesus, the original "land of promise" has been left behind, and a new, larger "land of promise," has been laid enticingly before the eyes of Jesus's disciples – the whole inhabited world.

4.3. Subduing the Nations and the Inclusivity of the Kingdom: Acts 15:6–21

The council of Jerusalem in Acts 15 is also important for our study. It helps us to see Luke's understanding of the restoration of Israel, the inclusivity of this kingdom, and the theology of the land in general.

The issue of dispute – whether Gentile believers in Christ and the God of Israel should be circumcised and keep the law of Moses (Acts 15:1, 5) – does not concern us directly. Rather, we will focus on James' contribution to this dispute:

> Brothers, listen to me. Simeon has related how God first visited the Gentiles, to take from them a people for his name. And with this the words of the prophets agree, just as it is written, "After this I will return, and I will rebuild the tent of David that has fallen; I will rebuild its ruins, and I will restore it, that the remnant of mankind may seek the Lord, and all the Gentiles who are called by my name, says the Lord, who makes these things known from of old." Therefore my judgment is that we should not trouble those of the Gentiles who turn to God. (Acts 15:13–19).

James' quotation of the prophecy of Amos 9 in this context is remarkable. This is one of the passages in the prophetic tradition that speaks about the restoration of Israel using Edenic language (9:13–14). It also speaks about the end of exile and the restoration of Israel *in her land* (9:15), and about Israel possessing other nations (9:12). James astonishingly quotes this passage as his rationale for incorporating Gentile believers into Israel without needing to circumcise or keep the law. Why does he do so? Bock argues that James' quotation of Amos is not merely "an affirmation of analogous fulfillment," but rather "a declaration that this is now taking place. God had promised Gentile inclusion; now he is performing it."[122] In other words, James is not simply making an analogy between what is happening in his day and the prophecy of Amos. He is declaring that Amos 9 is being fulfilled.

For James, the fact that Gentiles are coming to faith *confirms* the restoration of Israel, the end of exile, and also the possession of other nations by Israel. Israel's restoration is now a "present reality."[123] Amos' prophecy is being fulfilled in the mission of the church. In this way, the "tent of David" is being rebuilt, and the blessing to the nations "is part and parcel of Israel's own restoration."[124]

The Gentile mission, seen from this angle, is the coming of nations under the "tent of David," and a means whereby "David" subdues of the nations for God. This is a remarkable interpretation of the nature of the kingdom – especially when one considers the context of first-century Jerusalem, and the aspirations of many for a political and national kingdom. The Jesus-event forced James and the disciples to interpret the OT prophecies about the restoration of Israel *in her land* as already being fulfilled in Christ, and which in turn led to a radical transformation to the disciples' understanding of the kingdom and the restoration of Israel.

4.4. Conclusion: The Kingdom of God and the Mission of the Church

The church in the NT is delegated and empowered by God to expand his reign until it reaches the ends of the earth. As such, believers participate in the expansion of the kingdom as vicegerents. The OT themes of Israel's inheriting the earth, Israel's possessing other nations, the Messiah's defeating his enemies, and the subduing of the nations under the God of Israel – all these are seen in new light. They are fulfilled today not through worldly

---

122. D. L. Bock, *Acts* (Grand Rapids: Baker Academic, 2007), 503.
123. Walker, *Jesus and the Holy City*, 97. Walker also argues that the fact that James' ruling was accepted indicates that "the apostles finally laid aside any earlier belief that Israel's restoration consisted either in political independence or in its people coming *en masse* to faith in Jesus. They now realized that the inclusion of the Gentiles, being seen as the 'ingathering of the nations', signified that Israel had already been restored." Ibid., 294.
124. Dunn, *New Testament Theology*, 115.

power or violence, but through the mission of the church and the coming of the nations to faith in Israel's God and Messiah. The theology of the land, as a result, has gone under radical transformation.

5. A Future Israelite Kingdom?

The argument that in Jesus the kingdom of God has been inaugurated, yet not consummated, raises the question about the possibility of a future Israelite kingdom in the land in the future consummation. Even if in the present era of the church's mission the NT speaks only of a universal kingdom, does that necessarily close the door on a more narrowly focused kingdom at the eschatological end of the biblical story? In light of the Jesus-event, does the NT leave a room for such a kingdom in Jerusalem?

Bock, among others,[125] argues that this consummation of the kingdom of God will indeed include a "political" restoration of Israel.[126] He does not deny that the kingdom of Christ has been inaugurated. The current stage is one in which Christ rules "invisibly" among his followers.[127] The church is a "new institution," and is the "showcase of God's present reign" through Jesus.[128] But he also argues that in the era of consummation Israel will be restored nationally and politically:

---

125. See for example: D. L. Bock, W. C. Kaiser, and C. A. Blaising, eds., *Dispensationalism, Israel and the Church: The Search for Definition* (Grand Rapids: Zondervan, 1992); R. K. Soulen, *The God of Israel and Christian Theology* (Minneapolis: Fortress Press, 1996); Juster, "A Messianic Jew," 63–81.

126. D. L. Bock, "The Reign of the Lord Christ," in *Dispensationalism, Israel and the Church: The Search for Definition,* ed. D. L. Bock, W. C. Kaiser and C. A. Blaising (Grand Rapids: Zondervan, 1992), 37–67. See also Kaiser who argues for a dual fulfillment of the OT, first in Jesus and the church, and then in Israel. Commenting on Acts 15 and James' interpretation of the prophecy, he argues that while James believed that the prophecy is being fulfilled and that Gentiles are now being blessed through David – that does not negate "the political and national aspects of that same promise." W. C. Kaiser, "The Davidic Promise and the Inclusion of the Gentiles (Amos 9:9–15 and Acts 15:13–18): A Test Passage for Theological Systems," *JETS* 20 (1977): 100.

127. Bock, "Reign of the Lord Christ," 67.

128. Ibid., 65.

> When Jesus returns, he will do all that the prophets of the Old Testament promised. The language chosen specifically [in Acts 3:17–26] ties itself to the concept of Israel's restoration, which is an element that is totally absent in the current activity of Jesus. Certain political, earthly expectations tied to Israel, such as those expressed in Luke 1 and Acts 1 are in view here. There is no indication that earthly and Israelitic elements in Old Testament promises have been lost in the activity of the two stages. In the "not yet" visible, consummative kingdom, Jesus will rule on earth. He will rule before and over all. He will rule with justice. He will restore Israel's role, as that is a characteristic of the period.[129]

Bock's main NT support for this argument is Acts 3:17–26, and in particular the phrase "*the time for restoring all the things* about which God spoke by the mouth of his holy prophets" (3:21). He stresses the importance of the term ἀποκαταστάσεως (restoring), and links it with the disciples' question in Acts 1:6 about restoring (ἀποκαθιστάνεις) Israel. This verb root, he observes, is commonly used in LXX for God's "political restoration of Israel."[130]

Bock, however, fails to comment on the fact that Peter here is speaking about "restoring *all things*," and not "restoring *Israel*." If the two were synonyms, then Luke would have used the same phraseology as that found in 1:6 – "restoring Israel." Rather, what we have here is precisely a development in the understanding of the concept of restoration in the mind of the disciples – something that Luke brilliantly captures in using these two different phrases. Whereas before Pentecost the disciples were thinking of God's restoring *Israel*, they are now speaking of God's restoring *all things*. Bruce rightly asserts, "the sense here cannot be restricted to the restoration

---

129. Ibid., 67.
130. Ibid., 56.

of the kingdom of Israel . . . but in the sense of all creation."[131] In other words, the hope in Acts 3:21 is a universal and not a nationalistic one.[132]

Bock also implies in his interpretation that there are two phases of the restoration: one for the church (present, invisible) and another for Israel (future, visible). This is difficult to defend exegetically. In fact, the parable of the seed in Matthew 13 shows that the future kingdom is the inauguration and continuation of the same present kingdom. *The consummation continues or consummates what has already been inaugurated* – it does not inaugurate a new national kingdom. Those who insist on a future "political" and "earthly" Israelite kingdom are forced to conclude that the NT authors in fact spiritualized the OT promises, and did not see the Jesus-event as the true fulfillment of these promises. They are also forced to conclude that the current manifestation of the kingdom in the church's mission, which Bock described as "invisible," is a spiritual one – apolitical and non-earthly. This dichotomy between "earthly" and "spiritual," however, is a form of eisegesis to the NT, and is foreign to the theology of the NT as a whole.

In addition, the NT never speaks of a particular political "Israelite" kingdom in Jerusalem that is distinct from the current inaugurated kingdom. Moreover, the expected Israelite kingdom in the OT was itself always universal in scope.[133] The apocalyptic and poetic nature of the language used in expressing these hopes of an Israelite kingdom was the very foundation which encouraged the NT authors to claim these expectations as fulfilled universally in Christ. Thus, they did not feel the need to defend this interpretation as though it were radically or unrecognizably new; nor did it leave them with any hankering after a more narrow and particularistic Israelite kingdom in the future– in addition to the one already inaugurated in Christ.

Bock's argument ultimately means that Israel has not been restored. Yet our above discussion shows that Jesus' ministry, death and resurrection are

---

131. F. F. Bruce, *The Acts of the Apostles: the Greek Text with Introduction and Commentary* (Grand Rapids: Eerdmans, 1990), 144.
132. Walker also says: "Hope of a more widespread or 'universal' restoration has now . . . been deferred to the period of Jesus' return; and at that time God's purpose will be to restore 'everything', not just the 'kingdom of Israel'." Walker, *Jesus and the Holy City*, 96.
133. See above chapter 4, section 5, and chapter 5, sections 2.2, 3.2, and 4.2.

portrayed in the NT as *the* beginning of the restoration of Israel. Jesus himself evoked this language of restoration through his actions and words. It would be strange indeed if Luke included the expectations of the restoration of Israel in the introduction of his Gospel (which Bock mentions in the quote above) only to conclude that Israel's hopes were not met in Jesus, but postponed for several thousand years until Jesus comes again. Quite the opposite: Luke, like Mark and Matthew, started his Gospel with these expectations to confirm that what he was about to narrate – the Jesus-event – was *the* fulfillment of these expectations.[134]

As for the introduction of Acts, and the disciples' question about the kingdom of Israel (1:6), Bock argues that Jesus' reply "does not deny that this will happen; it just affirms that the timing will not be revealed and that they have another calling to pursue in the meantime."[135] Yet, as we have already observed, many scholars believe that Jesus was in fact *correcting* the disciples, by pointing their attention to the universal mission of the church.[136] His reply to go from Jerusalem to the ends of the earth indicates that Jesus has a different understanding to that of the disciples about the nature and sphere of the kingdom of Israel. Jesus *challenged* the narrow and political Jewish expectations of his days – not *postponed* them. Furthermore, the conclusion of Acts shows Paul "proclaiming the kingdom of God" in Rome (28:31) – which gives a clear indication of the meaning of the term "kingdom" in Acts. It is hard to imagine that when Paul was proclaiming the kingdom of God in Rome, he was talking about a future political and national Israelite kingdom in the land.[137]

Finally, concerning "national" Israel, the NT clearly teaches that Israel lost her right of vicegerency when they rejected Jesus.[138] "The kingdom

---

134. The fact that the expectations in the beginning of Luke were fulfilled in a manner that was against the expectations of Jewish leaders and theologians in Jesus' time does not mean that these expectations were not met. Walker's statement that "the great hopes for Israel and Jerusalem adumbrated at the beginning of Luke's Gospel do not materialize" is not strictly accurate. The hopes *were* materialized, but not in the manner expected by the Jewish leaders. Walker, *Jesus and the Holy City*, 79

135. Bock, *Acts*, 60.

136. See no. 871 above.

137. As we have seen, Wright argues that Acts 28:31 is Luke's answer to the disciples' question about the kingdom in Acts 1:6. Wright, *Jesus and the Victory of God*, 375.

138. McCartney, "Ecce Homo," 18.

of God will be taken away from you and given to a people producing its fruits" (Matt 21:43). This does not mean that every Jew is rejected and prevented from taking part in the new kingdom. It is important to re-emphasize that the first believers were all Jews. However, what "national" Israel lost – viewed collectively – is her vicegerency. The presence of the church today as God's vicegerent eliminates the necessity and the possibility of a future Israelite kingdom. The role of Israel has been absorbed first in Christ, and through him in the church.

6. Conclusion: The Land and the Kingdom

There are many correlations between the theology of the land and that of the kingdom. For example, salvation is expressed in the OT in terms of inheriting the land,[139] while the NT speaks of inheriting the kingdom. As we saw in the Beatitudes, "for theirs in the kingdom of heaven" could be seen as equal to "inheriting the land" (Matt 5:3, 5). In addition, Jesus in Matthew speaks about inheriting "the earth" (5:5), "eternal life" (19:29), and "the kingdom" (25:34): arguably these are different ways of referring to the same reality.

Paul commonly used the verb "inherit" with "the kingdom" as its object[140] – so much so that Holwerda argues that in Paul "the promise that the land will be inherited has become the promise that the kingdom of God, which embraces all nations, the entire creation, and even the cosmos itself, will be inherited."[141] In a sense, one could argue that the theology of the land is absorbed in the theology of the kingdom.

Since the kingdom is an earthly experience, this means that we cannot spiritualize the land in the NT – as if territory and geography no longer matter. It is important to stress this fact, as it safeguards us from "spiritualizing" the nature of the kingdom. The kingdom is the reign of God *on earth*. Therefore, as Marchadour and Neuhaus say:

---

139. See for example Amos 9:14; Ezek 36:24; Jer 32:41.
140. Gal 5:21; 1 Cor 6:9; 15:50.
141. Holwerda, *Jesus and Israel*, 104.

> It would be wrong to attribute only a spiritual meaning to the concept. The kingdom is to become a reality in this world by taking flesh in the social, economic, political, religious and spiritual values taught first in the Torah and then by Jesus himself.[142]

The values that Marchadour and Neuhaus refer to are what we can term as "kingdom-realities" in "new lands." These kingdom-realities can be seen in the teachings and actions of Jesus. Jesus announced an alternative way of living, which touches on all areas of life. These kingdom-realities, together with the declaration of Jesus as Lord and king, unavoidably challenged other kingdoms in the world, and caused the church to suffer from hostility and resistance. Yet these realities were also attractive and distinctive hallmarks of the early church and the basis of the kingdom's growth and expansion into new lands. At the same time, these kingdom-realities pointed forward to the time of consummation when the kingdom of God will be the only reality that defines this world. The present time, thus, is a time of tension. The church embodies the kingdom, but waits for its consummation. It models the kingdom, but waits for the king.

Land matters, and Jesus' kingdom ministry, seen as the climax of Israel's story, confirms this. Wenell's conclusion of her study on Jesus and land is worth quoting in length:

> Jesus did recall the land promise and tapped into hopes that God would soon fulfill his promises to the nation. Yet he did this in a very different way from other contemporary groups: the Sadducees, Pharisees, or even the Qumran covenanters. He did so as a prophetic figure, offering a symbolic alternative to the present structures of his society. His vision . . . tapped into deeply held hopes for a new and better world, and new spatial arrangement with God as king. Jesus' message established a new sacred space, and a new relationship between God, people and kingdom. It is not necessary to decide

---

142. Marchadour and Neuhaus, *Land, the Bible, and History*, 64.

whether the mathematical statement 'kingdom equals land' is true or false; *but it is important [to] establish that the message of the kingdom evokes the promises to Abraham and defines a new sacred space with its own symbolic associations and practical implications.*[143]

The implication of the above arguments is that the Jesus-event is the inauguration of the long-awaited reign of God on earth. The "age to come" is now a *present reality*, and the resurrection of Christ is a declaration that a new era has begun – an eschatological one. The story of Israel, therefore, has reached its climax. However, it was not what the Jewish people themselves in the time of Christ had envisioned.

According to the gospel witness, Israel's restoration is already taking place in Jesus through the expansion of the kingdom. The awaited kingdom has been launched. Such a reality necessarily demands that we re-examine our understanding of concepts such as "restoration" and "end of exile," and conform them to the biblical understanding of these terms – as revealed partially in the OT, but now fully in Christ.

Seen in this light, the land in this era of biblical history has been eclipsed by the whole earth. Israel's Messiah, the Son of David, returned to the land, and achieved victory over Israel's enemies, and in him the restoration of Israel has begun. The kingdom of God became a reality in that land – and in particular at Golgotha and the empty tomb. Importantly, this climactic event that launched this kingdom – Jesus' death and resurrection – did indeed take place in Jerusalem (Matt 16:21), but from there the kingdom of God will now expand to include the whole earth (Acts 1:8). As a result, new nations and new lands will be subdued under the authority of the one to whom all authority in heaven and on earth has been given (Matt 28:18–20).

---

143. Wenell, *Jesus and Land*, 139 (emphasis added). The practical implications of this will be unpacked in chapter 12.

CHAPTER 11

The Land as Eden Restored

Introduction

We have started this study by arguing that the garden of Eden should be the starting point of the biblical theology of the land. From Eden came the three main themes of this study: divine presence, the covenant, and the reign of God. It is only logical, then, after examining these three main themes in the NT, that we go back to our starting point – Eden – and ask: Can we see echoes of Eden in the NT? And how does this aid our understanding of the theology of the land? The first part of this chapter, thus, looks at the Jesus-event through the Eden motif. We will also examine certain passages in the NT that explicitly mention the garden.

Eden appears in the final part of the Revelation, which speaks of the era of consummation. This leads us to consider Eden as it relates to the ultimate purposes of God as revealed in the NT. The second part of this chapter, thus, considers how the NT authors looks at the land theme in the future consummation. It will become apparent that the land continues to be a major theme in biblical theology and that it plays an important role in defining the realities of the consummation. The chapter argues that the NT biblical theology of the land moves from land to earth: the biblical hope is the renewal of the earth.

1. Echoes of Eden in the Jesus-Event

In the previous three chapters, we have looked at the Jesus-event through the lenses of divine presence, covenant, and kingdom. We can summarize the main findings of these chapters about these three themes using the language of Eden. When we do so, it will become apparent that there continues to be a strong correlation between Jesus and Adam, and by implication, between Eden and the land.

First, and when it comes to divine presence, the NT presents a Jesus who is the "the epitome of God's presence on earth."[1] Theophany is possible only through him. As such, the development of the biblical narrative from the Eden sanctuary, to God's presence with Israel in the wilderness, to the temple and the "Zion tradition," has reached a climactic point. God's original purposes of expanding the Edenic sanctuary through Adam are now being fulfilled through Jesus.

Second, when it comes to the covenant theme, we can trace echoes of Eden in the temptation narrative.[2] We cannot overlook the fact that it was *Satan* who tempted Jesus in the wilderness, and this takes us back to Eden. Jesus succeeds where Adam failed. He kept the covenant and overcame the temptation of Satan. It is no coincidence, then, that Luke takes the genealogy of Jesus all the way to Adam (Luke 3:38), and that Paul calls Jesus the last Adam.[3]

Finally, and when it comes to the kingdom motif, we can look at the inauguration of the reign of God on earth as a restoration of the royal garden of Eden and the vicegerency of humanity. Jesus' kingdom ministry shifted the focus onto Israel's real enemy: Satan (and not the Romans). Satan's re-emergence in the Gospels is significant. Jesus revives Israel's role as God's vicegerent on earth, and fights a cosmic fight against Satan and overcomes him. Therefore, we can say that the kingdom of God, inaugurated by Jesus, is the beginning of the restoration of Eden.

---

1. Beale, *New Testament Biblical Theology*, 632.
2. Matt 4:1–11; Luke 4:1–13.
3. 1 Cor 15:22, 45; see also Rom 5:12–14. These passages will be considered in more detail below.

The mission of the church is to establish new "Edenic realities" in new lands. These realities are ideal realities that remind us of Eden – as a place of divine presence and "rest." The church, thus, should be defined as the community in a certain land that seeks to embody the presence of God and to proclaim the reign of God in that land through his Christ, and that at the same time seeks to model and proclaim the Edenic ideals of justice, equality, and wholeness in these lands. The church does this with a sense of hope as it keeps an eye towards the future, when the Edenic realities will be the only ones defining our existence, as we shall momentarily see.

Restoration of what was broken and lost in Eden has begun in Christ. Reading the Jesus-event through the lens of Eden gives the Jesus-event a universal backdrop. The universal dimension to Eden is being fulfilled. The NT portrays Jesus' ministry in a cosmic setting. As we have seen, this is something familiar in Israel's theology. The land in the OT is portrayed as Eden restored. Adam as proto-Israel had a universal mission, and so did Israel. As such, Jesus as the last Adam fulfills the role of both Israel and Adam, and in both cases, this has universal ramifications.

2. Eden in the NT

Having summarized the Jesus-event through the lens of Eden, we move next to consider the passages in the NT which mention Eden and Adam explicitly. The garden of Eden is mentioned only a few times in the NT. The main two references to the Eden narrative are found in Paul's argument that Jesus is the last Adam, and in the final chapter of Revelation. Interestingly, the Christian canon ends where the Jewish canon started: in a garden. The following is a very brief discussion of the instances in which the garden theme is mentioned in the NT, with a focus on Revelation 22:1–5.

2.1. Luke 23:42–43

> And he said, "Jesus, remember me when you come into your kingdom." And he said to him, "Truly, I say to you, today you will be with me in Paradise." (Luke 23:42–43)

Luke records this statement by Jesus while on the cross as a response to the request from one of the thieves to remember him when he comes into his kingdom. Jesus evokes here the image of the garden of Eden. The word used here is παράδεισος, which is the same one used in the LXX in Genesis 2–3 to describe the garden. In Jesus' day, there was an understanding of paradise as the pleasant resting place of some of the privileged dead, prior to the great day of resurrection.[4] Marshall could be right in saying that in the present passage "paradise" represents the state of bliss which Jesus promises to the criminal directly after death.[5]

The significance of this verse for our purpose is in the claim that Jesus is re-opening the door to Eden through his death. Access to Eden was denied, to prevent Adam and Even from eating from the tree of life. The irony here is that Jesus, through his death, gives access to life again. The cross makes Eden a possibility again.

Moreover, restoration to Eden *begins* at the cross. Jesus claims that the moment of this renewed entrance to Eden is *today* (σήμερον) – or "the same day as the day of a discourse."[6] We do not need to take this verse literally (asserting that Jesus did in fact go to paradise immediately after his death) to appreciate the force of this claim. The use of σήμερον here refers to the day of crucifixion "as the day of entry into paradise."[7]

The cross of Christ is thus both the *means* by which mankind gains access into Eden again, and the redemptive-historical *moment* in which this access became possible. The main thrust of this study of the theology of the land so far has been the argument that the original promise of the land represents the first step in the restoration of the loss of the original special land – Eden. Now, in the next era of salvation, inaugurated by Jesus, Eden is restored in and through the cross of Christ.

---

4. Nolland, *Luke 9:21-18:34*, 1153.
5. I. H. Marshall, *The Gospel of Luke: A Commentary on the Greek Text. New International Greek Testament Commentary* (Exeter: Paternoster Press, 1978), 873.
6. J. P. Louw and E. A. Nida, *Greek-English Lexicon of the New Testament: Based on Semantic Domains (Vol. 1)* (New York: United Bible Societies, 1996), 653.
7. Marshall, *The Gospel of Luke*, 873.

2.2. 2 Corinthians 12:2–4

> I know a man in Christ who fourteen years ago was caught up *to the third heaven* – whether in the body or out of the body I do not know, God knows. And I know that this man was caught up *into paradise* – whether in the body or out of the body I do not know, God knows. (2 Cor 12:2–3)

Paul speaks here about a vision that he once had in which God revealed some things to him. It is difficult fully to comprehend what Paul was referring to in his vision – especially when it comes to being "out of body" and in the "third heaven." Harris argues convincingly that Paul's cosmology here reflects a Jewish interpretation of "heaven" and "the heaven of heavens" in 1 Kings 8:27; according to this there were three heavens, so that the third heaven was the highest heaven. Therefore, when Paul says "to the third heaven," he means "into the immediate presence of God."[8]

Interestingly, then, Paul seems to equate the "third heaven" with "paradise."[9] The garden is now a reality that belongs to the heavenly realms, and, if Harris is correct in his interpretation of the "third heaven," then paradise represents the immediate presence of God. This can explain why Paul boasts about this experience and that he heard things that cannot be told and that one may not utter (2 Cor 12:4). We can make a reference here to the heavenly homeland and the heavenly city in Hebrews 11, and even to the Jerusalem of Revelation 21. Heaven is described in all of these

---

8. M. J. Harris, *The Second Epistle to the Corinthians: A Commentary on the Greek Text*. New International Greek Testament Commentary (Grand Rapids/Carlisle: Eerdmans/Paternoster Press, 2005), 840. Even though there was a more popular view in Second Temple Judaism that spoke of seven heavens, Harris argues that it is unlikely that Paul was operating with this cosmological scheme, for if he could claim to have ascended only to the third of seven heavens, his opponents could easily depreciate the significance of his ascent, especially if they were able to claim ascent to a higher heaven.

9. There are typically three options to the relationship between "the third heaven" and "paradise." The first is to argue that they describe two distinct experiences and thus places. This option is dismissed in modern scholarship. The second is to equate the two places and to argue that paradise is the third heaven. See R. Martin, *2 Corinthians. World Biblical Commentary* (Waco: Word Books, 1986), 404. The third option is to view paradise as a place within the third heaven. See Harris, *Second Epistle to the Corinthians*, 845.

passages as a "place": a homeland, a city and now paradise. For Paul, these are not mere imaginations. This is something real – and he has been there.

2.3. Jesus as the Last Adam: Romans 5:17–19; 1 Corinthians 15:22, 45

> For if, because of one man's trespass, death reigned through that one man, much more will those who receive the abundance of grace and the free gift of righteousness reign in life through the one man Jesus Christ. Therefore, as one trespass led to condemnation for all men, so one act of righteousness leads to justification and life for all men. For as by the one man's disobedience the many were made sinners, so by the one man's obedience the many will be made righteous. (Rom 5:17–19)

> For as in Adam all die, so also in Christ shall all be made alive. . . . Thus it is written, "The first man Adam became a living being"; the last Adam became a life-giving spirit. (1 Cor 15: 22, 45)

The comparison between Jesus and Adam is possible because of their roles as representative figures. In both Romans and Corinthians, Paul is clearly talking about the Adam of Eden (Gen 2–3), the one that we have come to understand as proto-Israel. Moreover, in both places Paul argues that Jesus *reverses* the consequences of Adam's sin. In particular, the reversal takes humans *from death to life*. In the context of Genesis 2–3, death is exile from Eden. Jesus now brings life, and becomes "a life-giving spirit" (1 Cor 15:45). So we can make the argument that as the last Adam he makes the return to the garden possible again, for life is to be found in the garden. Furthermore, death in Genesis 2–3 is also the loss of man's vicegerency. The reversal here as a result of the ministry of Jesus is the restoration of this lost vicegerency. "The purpose for which God made 'man,' a purpose which failed in Adam, has been achieved in Christ."[10]

Dunn observes that when Paul uses the language of Adam to talk about Christ, he is referring primarily to the risen Christ.[11] We have also argued that Luke 23:43 claims that the cross is the moment when access to paradise was made possible again. Thus, the death and resurrection of Jesus, viewed as one event, marks this transitional moment from death to life. Therefore, when Paul says in 1 Corinthians 15:45 that the last Adam *became* a life-giving spirit, he is referring to a particular moment in redemptive history: the death and resurrection.

These passages in Paul indicate that the vicegerency of humankind – lost in Eden – has now been restored in Christ. The loss of vicegerency in Genesis resulted in the loss of life, which in that context meant expulsion from Eden. That loss also caused the ground to be cursed. We can thus conclude that the death and resurrection of Christ launch a new era in salvation history: it is the moment in which the death that occurred in Eden is overturned and the redemption of the "land" is begun.

2.4. Revelation 2:7

> To the one who conquers I will grant to eat of the tree of life, which is in the paradise of God. (Rev 2:7)

This is probably one of the most direct references to the Eden narrative in the NT. It presents the garden of God as a *reward* for the one who conquers. In particular, the reward is permission to eat from the "tree of life" – an exact reversal of the punishment in Eden.[12] The "cherubim" and the "flaming sword" are no longer an obstacle. Eden is now granted to the one who conquers.

---

10. Dunn, *The Partings of the Ways*, 253.
11. Dunn, *Christology in the Making*, 107.
12. Interestingly, the same end-time hope is referred to with virtually identical language in several early Jewish texts. See G. K. Beale, *The Book of Revelation: A Commentary on the Greek Text. New International Greek Testament Commentary* (Grand Rapids/Carlisle: Eerdmans/Paternoster Press, 1999), 234–235; D. E. Aune, *Revelation. 17-22. Word Biblical Commentary* (Nashville: Thomas Nelson, 1998), 151–154.

Furthermore, since Jesus is the one addressing the seven churches (1:13–18), it is clearly the risen Jesus who now grants this permission to eat from the "tree of life." He speaks as the one who died but is now alive and has the "keys of Death and Hades" (1:18). Jesus speaks here with a sense of earned sovereignty. He is the one who can grant access to Eden.

The location of the "paradise of God" is not specified here. Some Jewish traditions spoke of paradise as a "heavenly region," and of eschatological access to the tree of life in the "heavenly paradise";[13] so one can be tempted to associate the paradise of God with "heaven" (see discussion above on 2 Cor 12:2–3). Yet Revelation 22:1–5 indicates that it will be located in the new Jerusalem which will descend from heaven *on earth*.

2.5. Revelation 22:1–5

> Then the angel showed me the river of the water of life, bright as crystal, flowing from the throne of God and of the Lamb through the middle of the street of the city; also, on either side of the river, the tree of life with its twelve kinds of fruit, yielding its fruit each month. The leaves of the tree were for the healing of the nations. No longer will there be anything accursed, but the throne of God and of the Lamb will be in it, and his servants will worship him. They will see his face, and his name will be on their foreheads. And night will be no more. They will need no light of lamp or sun, for the Lord God will be their light, and they will reign forever and ever. (Rev 22:1–5)

When we look at the passage carefully, we will see that it represents both an overturning of what went wrong in the original garden of Eden as well as a *step-beyond* it. It also builds on the prophetic visions of Ezekiel and Zechariah, who both described eschatological Jerusalem with Edenic language. Just as in Genesis 2–3, the language of Revelation 22:1–5 is loaded with symbolism. We will consider next some of the symbols.

---

13. Aune, *Revelation 17-22*, 153, 155.

2.5.1. The Water of Life

The water of the river in Revelation is the water of *life*. This is not mentioned about the river of Eden, but is nevertheless mentioned about the rivers that appear in some OT eschatological visions.[14] The river, like in Ezekiel's vision, comes out of the temple, (God and the Lamb are the temple, 21:22). Jewish literature has similar images of a future Eden with a river of living water.[15] The uniqueness of Revelation, when compared to Ezekiel and Jewish literature, is in the christological element. The Lamb is described here as a source of this water that gives life.

2.5.2. The Tree of Life

Whereas Ezekiel speaks of many trees, John speaks collectively of one tree of life.[16] Both Revelation and Ezekiel have in mind the tree of life of Eden. John elaborates on the imagery of Genesis and Ezekiel by declaring that the tree produces a *different* kind of fruit each month, which could be a symbol of continuous renewal. He also elaborates on Ezekiel by declaring that the leaves of the tree were for the healing *of the nations*. If the universality of healing was merely implied in Ezekiel, it is now explicitly declared. The tree of life heals all the nations.

2.5.3. No Longer Will There Be Anything Accursed

The statement that "no longer will there be anything accursed" is most probably a reference to Zechariah 14:11: "And it shall be inhabited, for there shall never again be a decree of utter destruction. Jerusalem shall dwell in security." In both places, the word used is κατάθεμα, which is the LXX Greek of the Hebrew term חרם (devoted to destruction). If John is indeed reflecting Zechariah 14:11, then what he has in mind is the state of peace and security that will govern Jerusalem when "the curse of war will no longer exist."[17]

---

14. Ezek 47:9; Zech 14:8. See also Ps 46:4 and Joel 3:18.

15. Aune shows many Jewish texts from the Second Temple period that show strong resemblance with Rev 22:1–5. Aune, *Revelation 17-22*, 1175–1176.

16. Aune, *Revelation 17-22*, 1177.

17. Ibid., 1178. Beale further suggests a possible allusion to Isa 34:1–2, where it says that God has devoted the nations to destruction (חרם). This is an attractive suggestion

Moreover, a case for a possible allusion to the curse in Genesis 3:17 could be made here. In Genesis 3:17, it says that the ground was "cursed," using the verb ארר, and in the LXX it is ἐπικατάρατος, which is different from what we find in Revelation 22:3. The reference is not linguistic, but thematic. The new Eden includes a promise, similar to the one made to Noah, that there would be no more curse, destruction, or ban on anything. In a sense, this is an overturning of what went wrong in Eden.

2.5.4. The Presence of God

In the new garden, God and Lamb are *constantly present* with his people. The garden is the dwelling place of God (21:3). The servants of God will not have to hide from his presence (Gen 3:8). Rather, they will see his face and he will be the light of this new place (22:4–5). Seeing the face of God is a metaphor in Judaism and early Christianity for a full awareness of the presence and power of God, for worshipping God in the temple, or for seeing him in the context of a prophetic vision.[18] In the OT, the presence of God was limited to the sanctuary (tabernacle and the temple). Access to his presence was only allowed to the priests, and only with limitations. In the new garden, "the whole community of the redeemed is considered priests serving in the temple and privileged to see God's face in the new holy of holies, which now encompasses the entire temple-city."[19]

2.5.5. Vicegerency Restored

The servants of God will worship him and will reign forever and ever. The notion of participating in the eschatological reign of God has been anticipated throughout the biblical tradition.[20] Humanity is now restored to its ultimate position as God's vicegerent on earth. The people of God are portrayed as servants, worshippers, and kings. The word used for worship

---

– especially as it links well with the previous statement about the healing of the nations. "If this allusion is in mind, then Rev 22:3 pictures the time when the converted from among the nations, who have become citizens of the new Jerusalem, will experience complete removal of the curse that was pronounced on them in the OT." Beale, *The Book of Revelation*, 1112.

18. Aune, *Revelation 17–22*, 1179.
19. Beale, *The Book of Revelation*, 1114.
20. Isa 60:3, 12–14; Dan 7:18, 22, 27; Matt 19:28; 1 Cor 6:2; 2 Tim 2:12; Rev 5:10.

is λατρεύω, which "refers particularly to the performing of the Levitical service."[21] In other words, humanity is restored to its role as "kingdom of priests." Adam and Israel's vicegerency is fulfilled now in the redeemed community in the new garden. This redeemed community declares to God that "by your blood you ransomed people for God from every tribe and language and people and nation, and you have made them a kingdom and priests to our God, and they shall reign on the earth" (Rev 5:9–10).

2.5.6. No Tree of Knowledge of Good and Evil

Finally, we should pay attention to what this new garden does *not* include in comparison with the original garden of Eden, namely: the tree of knowledge of good and evil, together with the commandment not to eat from it. The absence of this tree is indicative of the fact that this vision represents the final and completed picture. This is not a project anymore. The mission does not depend on the obedience of the people of God. Victory has been accomplished by the Lamb. The possibility of failure is excluded.

2.5.7. The Garden as the Ultimate Place

In conclusion, Revelation 22:1–5 speaks of a new and better garden that goes beyond Eden, Canaan, and Zion. In this final and completed picture, Eden has reached its potential as the ultimate sanctuary, a place where God is fully and constantly present with his people. It has reached its potential as a royal garden, a place where God and the Lamb reign supreme over all the creation. Humanity has also reached its potential in this garden as kings and priests – God's partners on earth. Revelation 22:1–5 is a picture of perfection and wholeness. It is a land – *the* land *par excellence*.

2.6. Conclusion

The references to the garden motif in the NT show several important developments. *Eden is now a possibility again.* Christ as the last Adam has opened the doors to Eden through his death and resurrection. The curse of Eden is overturned at the cross. *The cross is both the means and the moment in which entry to Eden is made possible again.*

---

21. Zodhiates, *Complete Word Study Dictionary*.

Yet though the cross is the moment when Eden was made a possibility again, it is not until the consummation that the believer actually "returns to Eden." The current period, as we have repeatedly argued, is one that is characterized by tension, in which the believer awaits the arrival of the new Jerusalem – and the new Eden – described in the book of Revelation. Revelation, as already seen, describes the final and ultimate place as a new garden of Eden. The garden is a place of life, and is open to people from all nations. In this garden, human beings are restored to their original role as God's vicegerents on earth. They maintain order and rule with God. The possibility of another failure and curse is excluded – symbolized by the absence of the tree of knowledge of good and evil.

The land in biblical theology can now be seen to have been part of the restoration process towards Eden. The ideal realities – which Eden, Canaan, and Zion successively aspired to have – are now found in this one temple-city, and in particular in the garden in its midst. The universal mission of Eden is now fulfilled, and Eden is a true source of blessing to the rest of the universe.

3. The NT and the Restoration of Creation

The discussion of Eden in the vision of Revelation leads us to consider the theme of the consummation in the NT, especially as it pertains to the land. We will see next that the NT's vision of the future consummation focuses solely on the redemption of the whole creation – not the land. The NT speaks of universal and cosmic restoration. It assumes that since the restoration has already begun and the mission of the church has already expanded and reached to the ends of the earth, then it is only appropriate to speak of the renewal of the earth. There is no point or need to go backwards in salvation history and speak only of the restoration of Israel's land.

We have already looked at two important passages in the NT that speak of this holistic restoration. In Acts 3:21 Peter speaks of "the time for restoring *all the things* about which God spoke by the mouth of his holy prophets long ago." We also looked at 1 Corinthians 15:25–28, where Paul claims that God has put *all things* in subjection under Jesus' feet. This is not, of course, the only place in which Paul speaks of holistic restoration. In Ephesians 1:10 he speaks of a time in which God will unite *all things* in Jesus, things in heaven and things on earth. In Colossians 1:20 he speaks of how God will to reconcile to himself *all things* through Jesus, whether on earth or in heaven. The references to "heavens" and "earth" in these two verses are clearly an allusion not only to the creation of the world (Gen 1:1), but also to Isaiah's vision of a "new heavens and new earth" (Isa 65:17).

We will consider next in more details other key passages in the NT that talk about the renewal of the whole earth.

3.1. Romans 8:18–23

Perhaps no other place reflects Paul's vision of a holistic restoration more than Romans 8:18–23. Before we look at this passage, we need to consider the transitional phrase γὰρ in 8:18, which links this passage with what Paul has already declared in 8:17 – namely that the children of God are fellow *heirs with Christ*, provided they "suffer with him in order that they may also be glorified with him." The topic of "glorification" in 8:18 is thus mentioned in reference to suffering as "heirs of Christ" (8:17). The language of "inheritance" in the context of Romans refers to the inheritance of Abraham to the world (4:13). Paul's words about the renewal of creation in this passage are therefore spoken in a context in which the world – not just the land – is the real inheritance of the believers. This world in its current state, declares Paul, is under bondage and is awaiting its freedom:

> For *the creation* waits with eager longing for the revealing of the sons of God. For the creation was subjected to futility, not willingly, but because of him who subjected it, in hope that *the creation itself will be set free* from its bondage to corruption and obtain the freedom of the glory of the children of God. For we know that *the whole creation* has been groaning together in the pains of childbirth until now. And not only the creation, but we ourselves, who have the *firstfruits of the Spirit*, groan inwardly as we wait eagerly for adoption as sons, the redemption of *our bodies*. (Rom 8:19–23)

The language of "sons of God," formerly applied in the OT to Israel, applies now to believers in Christ. The goal of redemption here includes the whole creation. Paul's statement that creation is now subjected to futility must be the result of his understanding of Genesis 3; yet N. T. Wright observes that the language used here also evokes images of Israel's bondage. Creation's subjection to corruption and decay is the equivalent of Israel's slavery in Egypt.[22] Notice also that Paul, by saying "not deliberately," makes it clear that creation itself was not the rebel against God. Rather, it was humankind that rebelled, thus caused God to subject the creation to futility. This highlights again the vicegerency of Adam in the creation narrative, as the one to whom God subjected all things, and whose rebellion can have such consequences.[23]

This subjection to futility is not the end of God's dealing, but a stage in his purpose.[24] Paul has a strong sense of hope. According to N. T. Wright, the basis of Paul's hope must be a combination of two things. First, it comes from the biblical promise of new heavens and new earth.[25] Paul's belief in the renewal of creation is entirely Jewish. It stems from the goodness of creation, and from the prophetic visions of renewal of the land, of nature, and of the entire creation.

Second, Paul's hope comes from the creation story in which human beings, made in God's image, are appointed as God's stewards over creation.[26] We have seen how the role of God's steward or vicegerent on earth was given to Israel, and then to Christ. Through Christ, believers become "fellow heirs." It is then logical that this passage combines the restoration of creation with that of the "sons of God" (8:19, 23). Just as creation will be restored, believers will be restored when they receive the redemption of their bodies (not souls).

Paul thus speaks of the restoration of both believers and creation as part of the same eschatological event. This restoration is rooted in the OT belief

---

22. N. T. Wright, *The Letter to the Romans: Introduction, Commentary, and Reflections* (Nashville: Abingdon Press, 2002), 596.
23. See Dunn, *Romans. 1-8*, 471.
24. Ibid, 471.
25. Wright, *The Letter to the Romans*, 597.
26. Ibid.

of holistic restoration. The resurrection of Christ, his glorification, and the indwelling of the Spirit as the firstfruits – all these allow Paul to speak with a new confidence and certainty about this hope of restoration.

3.2. 2 Peter 3:10–13

The NT's hope of a new creation can be also seen in 2 Peter 3. This chapter speaks about the delay of the second coming (3:4, 9).

> But the day of the Lord will come like a thief, and then the heavens will pass away with a roar, and the heavenly bodies will be burned up and dissolved, and the earth and the works that are done on it will be exposed. Since all these things are thus to be dissolved, what sort of people ought you to be in lives of holiness and godliness, waiting for and hastening the coming of the day of God, because of which the heavens will be set on fire and dissolved, and the heavenly bodies will melt as they burn! But according to his promise we are waiting for *new heavens and a new earth* in which righteousness dwells. (2 Pet 3:10–13)[27]

These verses contain many difficult elements for interpretation. Although on the surface it seems that the passage teaches that heavens and earth will be *annihilated*,[28] a more careful reading shows otherwise. Bauckham argues that this passage uses Jewish apocalyptic language and adopts a Jewish eschatology – evident not only in the reference to Isaiah 65:17 and 66:22, but also to many Second Temple references.[29] He then argues that the cosmic dissolution described in 2 Peter 3:10, 12, was "a return to the primeval chaos, as in the flood (3:6), so that a new creation may emerge." In other words, the verses describe a "renewal, not an abolition, of creation."[30]

---

27. For the variation in the text of 2 Peter 3:10, see R. J. Bauckham, *Jude, 2 Peter. Word Biblical Commentary* (Waco: Word Books, 1983), 316–321.
28. See for example R. L. Overstreet, "A Study of 2 Peter 3:10–13," *Bibliotheca Sacra* 137(548), (1980): 354–371.
29. See for example e.g. Jub. 1:19; 1 Enoch 45:4–5; 72:1; 91:16; 4 Ezra 7:75.
30. Bauckham, *Jude, 2 Peter*, 326.

This passage reveals that the early church continued to hold on to the OT belief of the renewal of creation and the arrival of new heavens and new earth. It also shows that the church now associates the consummation with the second coming of Jesus (2 Pet 3:4). The "day of the Lord" is still a day of judgment upon the world. At the same time, this passage makes no reference to Israel or the land. The movement in NT theology from the land to a more universal fulfillment is, as it were, taken for granted. The focus is entirely on the restoration of *creation* now and the coming of new heavens and a new earth.

3.3. Hebrews 11

Hebrews 11 contains an intriguing interpretation of the Abrahamic narrative and the promise of the land. It claims first that the patriarchs never actually received the land but lived as strangers and exiles in the land (11:9, 13, 39); this is an apparent reference to either Genesis 17:8 (which calls the land "the land of your sojourning"), and/or to Genesis 24:3 (where Abraham calls himself a stranger and a sojourner among the Hittites). According to Hebrews, this shows that *the land was not Abraham's ultimate hope*. Abraham and the patriarchs were waiting for a different homeland, not Canaan or his original homeland in Ur:

> For he was looking forward to *the city that has foundations, whose designer and builder is God* . . . These all died in faith, not having received the things promised, but having seen them and greeted them from afar, and having acknowledged that they *were strangers and exiles on the earth [γῆ, or land]*. For people who speak thus make it clear that they are seeking a homeland. If they had been thinking of that land from which they had gone out, they would have had opportunity to return. But as it is, they *desire a better country*, that is, *a heavenly one*. Therefore God is not ashamed to be called their God, for he *has prepared for them a city*. (11:10, 13–16)

This is a stunning claim. Hebrews rereads the patriarchal narrative based on the fact that we live now in "these last days" in which God has spoken through the Son. This new reading of the tradition sees the land as not the actual or intended goal of the promise. Abraham and the patriarchs were waiting for a completely different homeland. The land is viewed now as a foreign land, and it is "merely a shadow of the genuine promise God wants to give . . . a foretaste, a metaphor perhaps, of a more profound location with God."[31] In other words, the promise of the land according to Hebrews, "whilst real and valid in its own terms, pointed typologically to something greater."[32]

The reference to the city that has foundations almost certainly alludes to Psalm 87; if so, this is extremely significant. This psalm envisions Zion – the city of God – as an inclusive multi-ethnic and glorified city. This is truly a "heavenly homeland." This, says Hebrews, was the real goal of the promise, and not Canaan.

There is a temptation in the Christian tradition to defer all future hopes to "heaven." As Holwerda observes, in contrast to the Jewish faith, "the faith of many Christians has been more heaven-oriented than land-oriented. The biblical themes of land and city have been spiritualized and focused elsewhere than on this earth."[33] It is important in this context to stress, then, that the "heavenly" in Hebrews 11:16 should not be viewed as an antithesis to the "earthly" – as if Hebrews is anticipating an escape from this earth (Gnosticism). Rather,

> The perspective of the writer is thoroughly Jewish and eschatological. Thus the "heavenly" is that which God intends to bring to birth on earth, and which therefore already exists in his intention; the "city" which he has prepared for them is therefore not simply a "mansion in the sky," but a human community of the redeemed in the coming Kingdom, when there will be new heavens and a new earth.[34]

---

31. Burge, *Jesus and The Land*, 100.
32. Walker, *Jesus and the Holy City*, 212.
33. Holwerda, *Jesus and Israel*, 87.
34. Wright, "Jerusalem in the New Testament," 71.

Hebrews 11 brings a very important perspective with regards to the theology of the land in the NT – namely that *we are not fully restored until the time of the consummation*. Hebrews thus reflects the tension between the already and the not yet. On the one hand, it declares that we are already there: "You *have come* to Mount Zion and to the city of the living God, the heavenly Jerusalem" (12:22). On the other hand, it also reminds us, especially in times of tribulation, that we are not fully there yet, and that we are still on the way to the Promised Land: "Therefore, since we are surrounded by so great a cloud of witnesses, let us also lay aside every weight, and sin which clings so closely, and *let us run with endurance* the race that is set before us" (12:1).

The theology of the land in Hebrews has a new function. It is in a sense an image of motivation to perseverance and holy living. It provides the language needed to describe the relationship between the present reality and the future consummation. It also points to a glorious and ideal picture in the future – described in terms of a "heavenly homeland" and "a city that is to come" (11:16; 13:14).

3.4. Revelation 21: A Completed Picture

We have already analyzed in the previous section the passage in Revelation 22:1–5 which speaks about the consummation using the language and metaphor of Eden. The creational dimension of this passage should not be overlooked. Revelation clearly envisions a time of a new creation.

Revelation 21 is a climactic point in the whole book. The description here evidently concerns the *final* stage. This is it. "It is done" (21:6). John talks about the new heavens and the new earth (21:1). He describes the heavenly city Jerusalem that came down from heaven to earth. Heaven and earth meet and embrace in this final scene. God now dwells on earth (21:3). Pain and death are no longer a possibility (21:4). This is the new creation in its final stage: "Behold, I am making *all things* new" (21:5).

The image of "new heavens and a new earth" in Revelation 21 confirms the trend in the NT of an expected cosmic restoration – as anticipated by the OT. Revelation's contribution is that it unites the image of the "new heavens and new earth" with that of the "new Jerusalem":

> Then I saw *a new heaven and a new earth*, for the first heaven and the first earth had passed away, and the sea was no more. And I saw the holy city, *new Jerusalem*, coming down out of heaven from God, prepared as a bride adorned for her husband. And I heard a loud voice from the throne saying, "Behold, *the dwelling place of God is with man*." (Rev 21:1–3)

In this vision, heaven and earth embrace each other as the heavenly Jerusalem descends into earth. Once again the goodness of God's creation is confirmed. Thus, the final picture is not one in which people escape to heaven. Rather, heaven comes down to earth. In addition, Revelation gives an image of God dwelling with his people on earth. Later in this final vision, John declares: "And I saw no temple in the city, *for its temple is the Lord God the Almighty and the Lamb*" (21:22). This is a striking statement. The temple, which embodied the presence of God on earth, is no longer needed, because there will be no limit to God's presence on earth.

Revelation is also entirely universal when it comes to the scope of salvation. The Abrahamic blessing that was supposed to extend to all the families of the earth is now a celebrated reality, and the people of God in this vision are multi-ethnic – being drawn from "every tribe and language and people and nation" (Rev 5:9; see also 7:9). Moreover, the language in the final image of new heavens and a new earth is also covenantal:

> He will dwell with them, and *they will be his people* (λαοί), and God himself will be with them as *their God* . . . The one who conquers will have *this heritage*, and I will be his God and he will be my son. (Rev 21:3, 7)

The covenantal language in 21:3 reflects the formula used in the OT to describe God's relationship with Israel (Lev 26:11–12). In Ezekiel 37:27 the same language is used to describe Israel's fortunes in the age to come. So John's use of it here is significant, because he now applies this covenantal formula to *all* people universally, not just to a specific group – as evident by his use of the word λαοὶ.[35]

The language of inheritance in 21:7 is also important (κληρονομήσει ταῦτα literally translates "will inherit these things"). The pronoun ταῦτα could be a reference to the blessings of "eschatological salvation" listed in verse 4 (no tears, no death, no mourning)[36] or indeed the multiple promises of the whole section so far (21:1–6).[37] In other words, those who conquer will inherit the new heavens and earth. Moreover, it is important to underscore the inclusivity of the promise. Anyone who conquers, regardless of his/her ethnicity or background will inherit "these things." The inheritance is now open to all.

Before we conclude our brief discussion on Revelation, there is the important question as to whether the use of the language of Jerusalem in Revelation is an indication that the earthly Jerusalem will play a significant role in God's plans for the future. In other words, does Revelation have a place for a revived literal earthly Jerusalem?

As we have seen, the Jerusalem of Revelation 21 is a heavenly Jerusalem – one that comes down from heaven to earth. The description of the city is entirely symbolic. So at first glance, it looks clear that John is not describing here the literal city of Jerusalem. Furthermore, it is a "new" city, and as such, we assume it takes the place of the old Jerusalem. This is confirmed when we note that the old Jerusalem in Revelation has ceased to function as the city of God. Rather, it has been "trampled" (11:2) and is viewed negatively as the place where "the Lord was crucified" (11:8). If, as is probable, John was writing after Jerusalem's destruction in AD 70, then that event may well have influenced his view of the city. As Bauckham says, "in its rejection of Jesus, Jerusalem forfeited the role of holy city (11:2), which John therefore transfers to the new Jerusalem."[38]

This understanding of the physical Jerusalem should then guide our interpretation of Jerusalem in Revelation. For example, Revelation 14:1,

---

35. Aune, *Revelation 17-22*, 1123.
36. Ibid., 1129.
37. Beale, *The Book of Revelation*, 1058.
38. R. J. Bauckham, *The Climax of Prophecy: Studies on the Book of Revelation* (Edinburgh: T&T Clark, 1993), 172.

which speaks of the Lamb standing on Mount Zion, is clearly not a reference to the earthly Jerusalem, but to the heavenly one (and the scene is in heaven anyway, Rev 14:1–5). Similarly, the reference in Revelation 20:9 to the "beloved city" is most probably a reference to the "the church."[39] In short,

> To argue that John was teaching about the future of the physical Jerusalem is to run entirely in the opposite direction. For John was not drawing attention *to* Jerusalem, but drawing material *from* Jerusalem that would be of lasting importance for the congregation for whom he was writing.[40]

Like the OT prophets, who used the familiar images and vocabulary of Israel (land, temple, end of exile) to describe the future restoration of Israel, John is using familiar concepts, but he is clearly giving them a new meaning. The focus in Revelation is on the *new* and *heavenly Jerusalem* that will come down to earth – not on the physical Jerusalem. The picture in mind is cosmic and universal – that of Eden restored. Revelation looks to the future, not to the past.

In conclusion, the focus throughout the book of Revelation is cosmic. Therefore, the presence, blessing, and reign of God in the book are all *universal* realities. The biblical story in Revelation finds its culmination in one complete and comprehensive picture of a *restored place* in the midst of the *restored creation*.

4. Conclusion: A Better *Place*

The NT claims that in Jesus the vicegerency of humankind has been restored and therefore Eden is a possibility again. The moment of the inversion of

---

39. Beale, *The Book of Revelation*, 1027. Beale reminds us here that Rev 3:12 has said that all believers, Jewish and Gentile, who "overcome" will be identified with "the name of the city of God . . . the new Jerusalem, which descends from heaven from God."
40. Walker, *Jesus and the Holy City*, 262 (emphasis in the original).

what went wrong in Eden is the death and resurrection of Christ. Eden's potential of blessings and expansion can now realized.

The universalization of the land in the NT continues in the era of consummation. The NT shares the hope of the OT of a new heaven and a new earth. It is a hope of universal restoration. This means that the ultimate hope of the people of God is not to go to "heaven." Rather, chapters 21–22 of Revelation clearly show that the ultimate hope is an actual place *on earth*. The city comes down from heaven to earth. The new garden is a heavenly one that is located on this earth. The transformation of this earth is only possible when the heavenly realities touch and embrace it. In other words, the earth will be surely renewed, but it will still be "earthly."

The hope for the restoration of the earth underscores and emphasizes the goodness of God's creation. The heavens and the earth were "very good" (Gen 1:31). As such, it would not make any sense for God to create something good, placing human beings in it, only to take them away from it in the consummation. Yes, this earth needed redemption: the ground has been cursed (Gen 3:17); and the Promised Land has been defiled by Israel; and other nations defiled their own lands. Yet redemption means renewal, not annihilation. The place of the land in the theology of the OT serves to remind us that God's intention is and has always been to redeem this earth. This is the renewal that the prophets spoke about over and over again. The prophetic hope was not of a place in heaven, but of a renewed land in a renewed earth. Seen in this light, the "Promised Land" of the consummation *inevitably has to be* on this earth – after it has been renewed.

The theology of the land also reminds us that what we ultimately hope for is a redeemed *place* – not merely redeemed *souls*. A redeemed place means the redemption of everything that this place holds and represents: societies, relationships, and nature. In addition, both the status and mission of humankind needs restoration. In other words, redemption is not only about going back to Eden, but it is also about taking on the responsibility of being God's co-workers in creation – or his vicegerents.

Finally, it is important to remember that eschatology and ethics go hand in hand. We must take seriously what God is doing (and is about to do) in this world. The tension between the "already" and the "not yet" demands that we hold fast to both sides of the tension, by trying as much as possible to reconcile the realities of the "not yet" homeland in our "already" homelands. This means that in the experience and life of the church we should be an embodiment to a certain degree of God's presence and reign on earth – as well as an elevated sense of responsibility towards the neighbor. Christian communities should aspire to create ideal Edenic spaces on earth, while continuing to look forward to the time when the new Jerusalem – with the new Eden in its midst – comes down to this earth.

CHAPTER 12

Conclusions: Towards a Missional Theology of the Land

Introduction

This chapter brings together and summarizes the discussions of the previous chapters and gives a proposal for the place and role of the land in biblical theology. It also argues for the importance of the land as a theological concept in Christian theology, over against any attempts to spiritualize the land or make it irrelevant. It finally proposes a model in which the theology of land aids the mission of the church.

1. The Land and Biblical Theology: A Paradigm

We have approached the theology of the land through a diachronic-thematic approach. There were three major themes through which we looked at the narrative: the land as a sanctuary, the land as covenanted, and the land as the sphere of the reign of God. These three themes came about through analyzing the garden of Eden narrative. They then became the framework of this study, and were used as a lens through which we analyzed both the Old and New Testament materials. The structure of this study is illustrated in the following diagram:

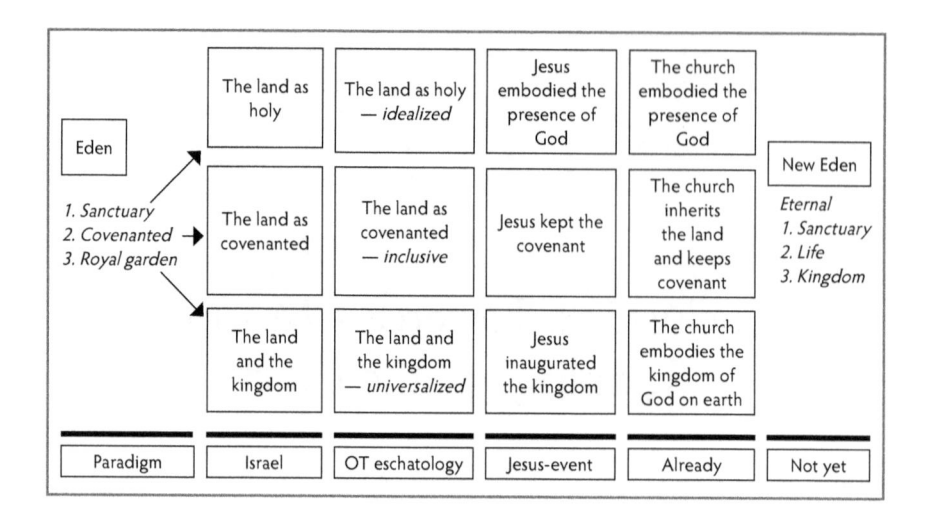

Paradigm	Israel	OT eschatology	Jesus-event	Already	Not yet
Eden 1. Sanctuary 2. Covenanted 3. Royal garden	The land as holy	The land as holy — *idealized*	Jesus embodied the presence of God	The church embodied the presence of God	New Eden Eternal 1. Sanctuary 2. Life 3. Kingdom
	The land as covenanted	The land as covenanted — *inclusive*	Jesus kept the covenant	The church inherits the land and keeps covenant	
	The land and the kingdom	The land and the kingdom — *universalized*	Jesus inaugurated the kingdom	The church embodies the kingdom of God on earth	

The Eden narrative, we have argued, was written in such a way so as to mirror the story of Israel. Adam in Eden reflects Israel in the land. Adam could be viewed as proto-Israel, and since Israel descends in the flesh from Adam, we could even argue that Adam is the first Israelite. Therefore, the story of Israel and her theology of the land could be seen as the restoration of humankind into Eden.

The NT authors assumed that Jesus is the continuation and climax of the story of Israel. He came in the flesh from Israel, re-enacted the story of Israel, and brought the story of Israel into a new era with expanded, new horizons. Jesus is the ideal Israelite as well as being, simultaneously, the last Adam.

When we bring the two sides of this story together – Israel as Adam and Jesus as Israel – a paradigm in biblical theology develops. *Israel in the land echoes Adam in Eden, and Jesus in the land echoes Israel in the land. Therefore Jesus echoes Adam.* We can then construct a biblical paradigm that explains the biblical theology of the land in the following three diagrams, which are to be understood as overlapping with one another and can thus be superimposed upon one another:

We can see by looking at these diagrams how there is a common pattern in all of them. Israel is repeating the story of Adam. For example, Israel was brought into the land, just as Adam was brought into Eden. Israel broke the covenant and was exiled outside of Canaan, just as Adam broke

Conclusions: Towards a Missional Theology of the Land 349

Adam ---→ brought into **Eden** ---→ chosen and given a mission

Proto-Israel — *was formed outside of Eden then brought into it* — *Priest and vicegerent*

Eden as a sanctuary / covenanted / royal garden ---→ **Eden** to expand

Proto-Promised Land — *Be fruitful, multiply and fill the Earth (Gen 1:28)*

Adam broke the commandment ---→ exiled outside of Eden

Proto-exile

failure to fulfil the universal mission ---→ a promise of redemption

The seed of the woman (Gen 3:15)

Israel ---→ brought into **Canaan** ---→ chosen and given a mission

Second Adam — *Called outside of Cannan then brought into it* — *Kingdom of priests*

Cannan as holy, covenanted, and sphere of the monarchy ---→ **Canaan** to expand

Promised Land — *Universal Dominion*

Israel broke the covenant ---→ exiled outside of the land

Exile

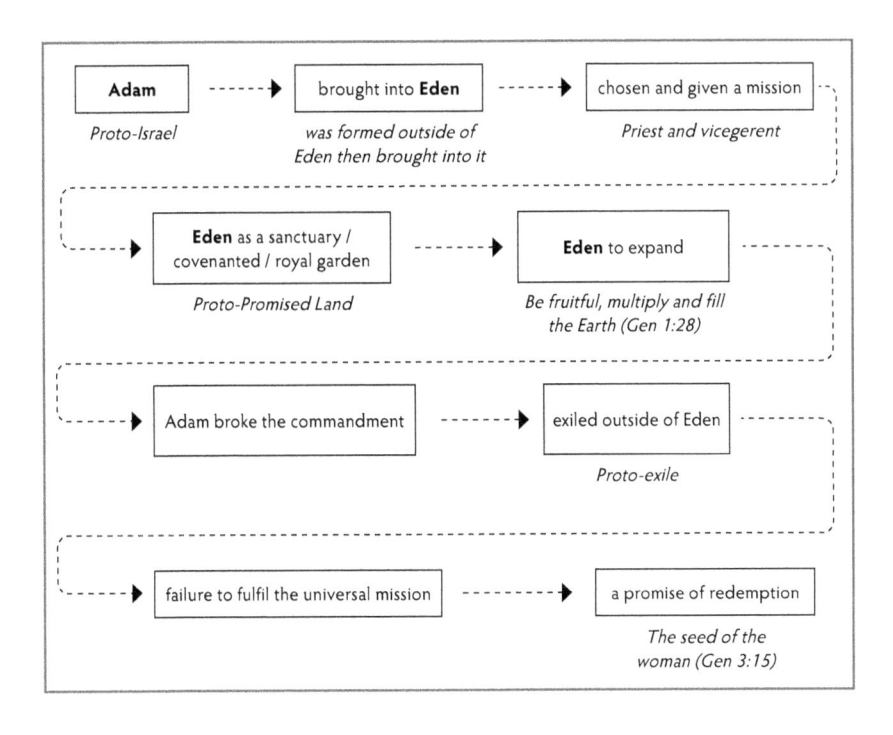

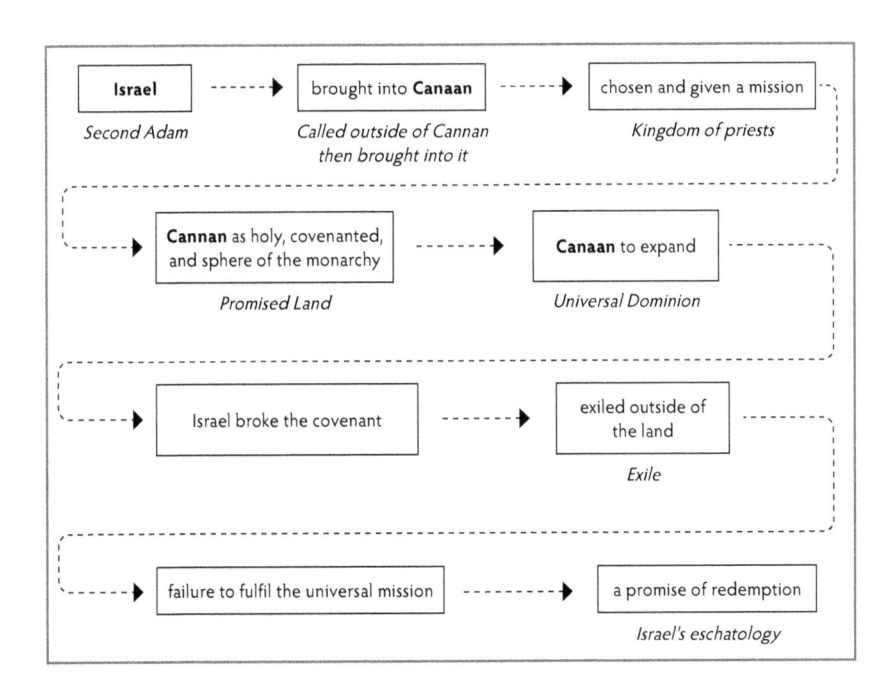

failure to fulfil the universal mission ---→ a promise of redemption

Israel's eschatology

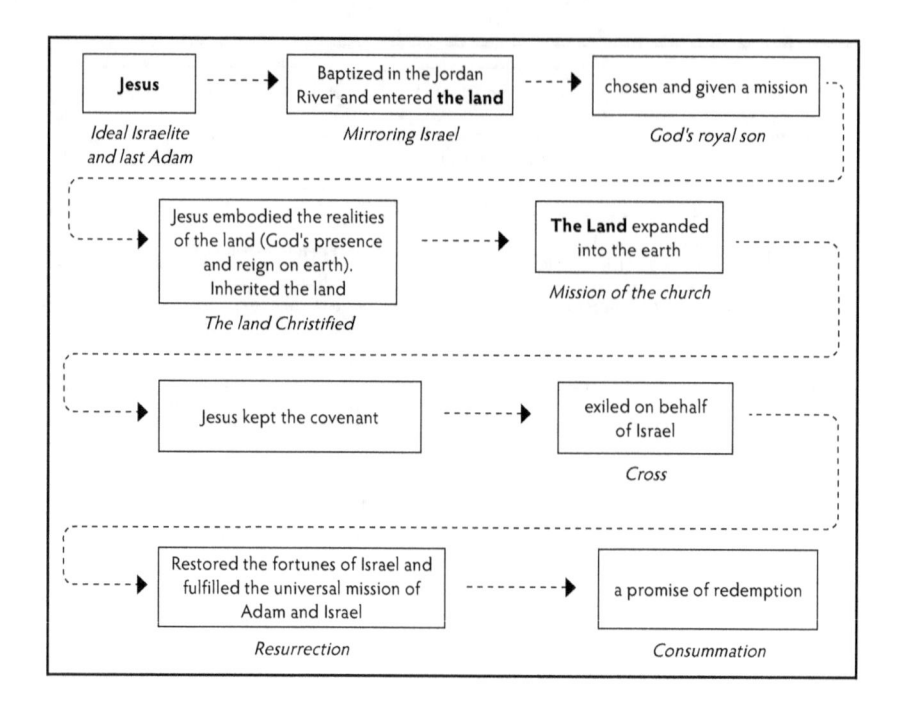

```
┌─────────────────────────────────────────────────────────────────────┐
│  ┌─────────┐       ┌──────────────────┐       ┌──────────────────┐  │
│  │  Jesus  │──────▶│ Baptized in the Jordan │──▶│ chosen and given │──┐
│  └─────────┘       │ River and entered the land │ │   a mission    │  │
│                    └──────────────────┘       └──────────────────┘  │
│  Ideal Israelite      Mirroring Israel          God's royal son     │
│  and last Adam                                                      │
│  ┌────────────────────────────────────────────────────────────────┘ │
│  │  ┌──────────────────────┐       ┌──────────────────┐             │
│  └─▶│ Jesus embodied the   │──────▶│  The Land expanded │──────────┐│
│     │ realities of the land│       │  into the earth    │          ││
│     │ (God's presence and  │       └──────────────────┘          ││
│     │ reign on earth).     │         Mission of the church        ││
│     │ Inherited the land   │                                      ││
│     └──────────────────────┘                                      ││
│       The land Christified                                         ││
│  ┌────────────────────────────────────────────────────────────────┘│
│  │  ┌──────────────────────┐       ┌──────────────────┐            │
│  └─▶│ Jesus kept the covenant │────▶│  exiled on behalf │──────────┐│
│     └──────────────────────┘       │    of Israel     │          ││
│                                    └──────────────────┘          ││
│                                          Cross                    ││
│  ┌────────────────────────────────────────────────────────────────┘│
│  │  ┌──────────────────────┐       ┌──────────────────┐            │
│  └─▶│ Restored the fortunes│──────▶│   a promise of   │            │
│     │ of Israel and fulfilled │    │    redemption    │            │
│     │ the universal mission│       └──────────────────┘            │
│     │ of Adam and Israel   │         Consummation                   │
│     └──────────────────────┘                                        │
│         Resurrection                                                 │
└─────────────────────────────────────────────────────────────────────┘
```

the covenant and was exiled outside of Eden. Then Jesus comes and, to a certain degree, he overlays the same pattern, but this time he goes through the common sequence or stages *perfectly*.

These diagrams reveal some very important considerations for biblical theology in general and for the theology of the land in particular. The land evidently has a vital role to play in the biblical narrative. It is an integral part of the story, as it provides the necessary platform for a holistic and comprehensive mission that is intended eventually to bring about the whole created order into the right relationship with the creator. We can now consider the following considerations for biblical theology:

1.1. The Universal Dimension of Redemption

The land from the origin has a universal potential. Eden and Canaan are not the ultimate goal. They point beyond themselves towards a bigger and more inclusive goal. Israel's mission demands by definition a potential for expansion. Israel views herself as God's first created humanity because she believes that she is God's ideal and representative humanity on this earth.

She clearly believes that her domain of influence has to expand beyond its land.

1.2. Jesus and Adam, Eden and the Land

The vicegerency of Adam and Israel is restored in Jesus, and so the land can now reach its potential as an ideal expanding geography. Jesus universalizes the land, not as a surprising development in the narrative, but as the long-awaited expansion of the mission of Adam/Israel. As a result of the Jesus-event, people from every nation *and every land* join the people of God. *Eden begins to reach its potential.* New communities in new lands begin to embody the presence of God, keeping his covenant, and submitting to his authority.

1.3. Subduing the Earth

The driving force in biblical theology is God's first recorded commandment: "Be fruitful and multiply and *fill the earth* and *subdue it*" (Gen 1:28). Man's mission in Eden fulfills this commandment. This is also the appropriate background for Abraham's first calling (Gen 12:1–3). In other words, Abraham's call is supposed to set right what Adam failed to do. This is Israel's own self-understanding. It is how Israel understands the reign of her king (Ps 2:8) and how the prophets portray the ministry of Israel's future Savior and Messiah. This is also Jesus' own self-understanding. The "great commission" (Matt 28:18) therefore echoes these previous important themes in biblical history: the call in Genesis 1:28 to "fill the earth"; the promise of Psalm 2:8 that the king will have the "ends of the earth" as his "possession"; and the prophetic tradition of a Messiah whose influence extends to the "ends of the earth" (e.g. Mic 5:4). Acts 1:8 is the beginning of the actualization of this expansion. This expansion will be fully realized in the consummation only – in the new heavens and new earth.

1.4. Redemption as Restoration of Commissioning

This paradigm also reveals a very important theme in biblical theology: redemption as the restoration of commissioning. Redemption in the Bible is not a goal in itself. It is the means through which mankind is restored to its potential as created in the image of God to be anointed for his service.

Redemption is *missional* in purpose. It brings humanity back into his role as God's vicegerent. Redemption transforms the Promised Land into a *promising* Land.

Humanity's return to Eden in the consummation is not simply a reward in which the people of God eternally enjoy ideal realities. Rather, they return to fulfill the human task: implementing the reign of God on earth (only this time they reign *with* God and not only *for* God). The Eden of Genesis 2 and that of Revelation 22 are both places in which human beings are active.

This should help us avoid some misconceptions. The big picture in biblical theology has often been portrayed in many Christian circles as follows:

Creation ---➔ Fall ---➔ Redemption[1]

The paradigm has at least two strengths. First, it affirms the goodness of creation. Second, it affirms that "the redemption achieved by Jesus Christ is *cosmic* in the sense that it restores the whole creation."[2] However, this paradigm seems to make redemption as the ultimate goal of God's dealing in history. This has the potential of producing people whose main concern is to be redeemed, but not commissioned. This paradigm, we suggest, needs a very important adjustment, to become:

Creation ---➔ Commissioning ---➔ Fall ---➔
Redemption ---➔ Re-commissioning

This is a crucially important adjustment, because it emphasizes that "salvation" or the "rescuing" of humankind is not the ultimate goal of redemption. Rather, the ultimate goal is the restoration of humanity *into its potential – to be God's co-worker on earth*. The people of God are redeemed

---

[1]. An excellent exposition of this worldview is found in A. M. Wolters, *Creation Regained: Biblical Basics for a Reformational Worldview* (Grand Rapids: Eerdmans, 2005).

[2]. Ibid., 69 (emphasis in the original). Wolters further adds: "redemption means *restoration* – that is, the return to the goodness of an originally unscathed creation and not merely the addition of something supracreational . . . Restoration affects the *whole* of creational life and not merely some limited area within it" (emphasis in the original).

and then re-commissioned to become his agents on earth – both now and in the consummation. Thus, when Paul declares that "by grace you have been saved" (Eph 2:8), he immediately explains why this gracious saving act took place: "For we are his workmanship, *created in Christ Jesus for good works*, which God prepared beforehand, that we should walk in them" (Eph 2:10).

To be redeemed is thus to be brought back into a right relationship, not only with God, but also with neighbor, self, and creation. The land sets the stage for such a redemption. This explains the phenomenon of Israel. When God chose Abraham, he brought him into a land and promised him a family (society) and gave his descendants (Israel) instructions on how to live as a society in that particular land; by this they could become a visible sign to the nations around them of what it would mean to be redeemed. That is also why the first church was described as an active community: people who lived together, took care of one another, and shared all their possessions. In a sense, therefore, redemption is the re-creation of a re-commissioned community on earth.

2. A Christ-Centered Theology of the Land

2.1. The Land Christified

We cannot speak about a Christian theology of the land if we bypass Jesus and the NT witness to the Jesus-event. All Christian theology must be done in reference to Christ and to Christ alone. Christ lived in the land, died in the land, ascended from the land, and promised to return to the land. He claimed in word and deed that his ministry was the climax of the story of Israel – which was all along a story about the land. The NT is then written from the perspective that Israel has already been restored in Jesus. The post-resurrection Christians understood themselves to be living in the beginning of the inauguration of the kingdom of God on earth – the fullness of time.

The land in the NT has, therefore, in a sense, been "Christified."[3] All that pertained to the land in the OT found its full meaning and realization in Christ. The potentials of the land became a reality in Jesus. Jesus embodied the *presence of God* on earth; divine manifestation in its fullness was in Jesus. He *kept the covenant* and inherited the land and also managed to begin the expansion of his inheritance. He also inaugurated the *reign of God* on earth; he is the Messiah of Israel and the universal ruler of the world; God reigns on the land through Jesus.

Jesus also redefined what it means to be Israel. Israel now includes peoples from all the nations, and the basis of inclusion in the people of God is the faithfulness of Jesus. Membership in the people of God is dependent upon faith in Jesus – and not upon obedience to the law. Naturally, if Jesus is identified with Israel, then the land of Israel is now the land of Jesus. Since the people of God expanded, the land also must expand to make possible the incorporation of peoples from all the nations. In Christ, the land finds its potential, and is universalized.

The ideal realities that were to be found in the land in the OT period now find a fuller meaning *in Christ*, and by extension in the community defined around him – the new Israel. Realities of belonging, life, inclusion, restoration, wholeness, community, equality, truth, justice, contentment, being provided for, and accountability – all these realities that previously were characteristics of living in the land begin now to find their true meaning in Christ and in the life of Christ-centered communities. *To be in the land becomes to be in Christ*.

2.2. Land Matters

By no means, however, does this Christo-centric interpretation of the land negate the importance of the land in Christian theology. Land is still important. Commitments to the goodness of creation, to the bodily resurrection of believers, and to incarnational theology demand a commitment to *place* as having significance.

---

3. This term, the land Christified," has been first coined by Davies. Davies, *The Gospel and the Land*.

Conclusions: Towards a Missional Theology of the Land

Some Christian traditions seem to de-emphasize the importance of the land as a category in the Christian faith. The apparent lack of attention given to the land in the NT, and the way Jesus and the NT writers diverted attention away from the Jewish nationalistic hopes in the first century have caused many to conclude that land is no longer important.

Davies' important study of the theology of the land seems to go in this direction. He emphasizes throughout the study that the Christian faith "cut loose from the land," and that the Gospels demanded a breaking out of its "territorial chrysalis." For him, this is another way of saying that Christianity "increasingly abandoned the geographical involvement of Judaism which was deeply cherished by many Jews."[4]

Davies' understanding of the theology of the land in NT as a "spiritual" reality affects how he understands concepts like kingdom and inheritance, evident in his interpretation of Matthew 5:5:

> Kingdom transcends all geographic dimensions and is spiritualized. Despite the use of the term "earth," we need not be removed from such spiritualization in Matt. 5:5, because we have previously recognized that in Judaism itself, as elsewhere in the New Testament, the notion of "entering the land" had been spiritualized.[5]

Yet what does it really mean that the land has been "spiritualized"? Davies fails to clarify exactly what he means by "spiritualized"; as such leaves the possibilities open for how we perceive this notion. Does it mean non-physical? Non-earthly? Does this imply that the kingdom is only concerned with "spiritual" realities, as opposed to social and political ones? Does that mean that the land as a theological theme is no longer important?[6]

---

4. Ibid., 336
5. Ibid., 362.
6. Davies talks about personalization of the land: "To do justice to the personalism of the New Testament, that is, to its Christo-centricity, is to find the clue to the various starta of tradition that we have traced and to the attitudes they reveal: to their freedom from space and their attachment to spaces." Davies, *The Gospel and the Land*, 367.

Davies is right in contrasting the NT with the Jewish hopes of the times of Jesus (and, of course, these hopes arose from their understanding of the OT). The NT did not support the national and political Jewish hopes for the land, but that does not necessarily mean that it cut loose from the land. The land is still important – but now it has been expanded or universalized, and "it has been universalized precisely with reference to land."[7]

Moreover, the hope for eternity in heaven is very common in popular Christianity. Many Christians are heaven-oriented and not land-oriented, and many theological traditions provide an environment for such ideas to flourish. Dispensationalism, for example, which directly and indirectly influenced many Christian circles (especially among Evangelical Protestants), emphasized the dichotomy between the OT and the NT.[8] Whereas the OT is about an earthly kingdom and earthly blessings, the NT is about a spiritual kingdom and spiritual blessings. Jesus did not fulfill all the promises of the OT, especially when it comes to promises about national Israel

---

7. Holwerda, *Jesus and Israel*, 102.

8. Dispensationalism is a popular system among many Protestant Christians to interpret the Bible, especially as it pertains to the progression of the biblical narrative and the relationship between the two testaments. There are many forms of Dispensationalism, and each form divides the human history into different "dispensations" in which God deals with humanity in a different way. Probably the main two essential beliefs of Dispensationalism are (1) its insistence of what advocates of Dispensationalism call "literal" or "plain" interpretation of the Bible, and (2) the distinction between Israel and the church in the Bible. The church age, in which we are today, will one day come to an end when the church is raptured to heaven, and God will once again deal with Israel and send Jesus again to rule over Israel in the land. For an articulation of the main beliefs of Dispensationalism, see C. C. Ryrie, *Dispensationalism* (Chicago: Moody Publishers, 2007); Bock, Kaiser, and Blaising, *Dispensationalism*. For a critique of Dispensationalism, see A. W. Donaldson, *The Last Days of Dispensationalism: A Scholarly Critique of Popular Misconceptions* (Eugene: Wipf & Stock, 2011); V. S. Poythress, *Understanding Dispensationalists* (Phillipsburg: P&R, 1994); Sizer, *Zion's Christian Soldiers?*. It is commonly believed that Dispensationalism contributed to the birth of Christian Zionism in the 20th century. Christian Zionism believes that the creation of the State of Israel in 1948 is the fulfillment of Old Testament prophecies regarding Israel, and as such advocates Christian support to modern Israel, often ignoring the plight of Palestinians who live in the land. For the historical and theological roots of Christian Zionism, see S. Sizer, *Christian Zionism: Road Map to Armageddon?* (Downers Grove: IVP Academic, 2004). For a critique of Christian Zionism, see P. Church, "Dispensational Christian Zionism: A Strange but Acceptable Aberration or a Deviant Heresy?" *WTJ* 71 (2009): 375–398; I. Abraham and B. Roland, "'God Doesn't Care': The Contradictions of Christian Zionism," *Religion & Theology* 16, no. 1–2 (2009): 90–110; Chapman, *Whose Promised Land?*; Ateek, Duaybis, and Tobin, *Challenging Christian Zionism*.

and her land. This dual hermeneutics deferred all Christian hopes into both the *future* and *heaven*. The Christian mission is thus defined as primarily about *then* and *there*, not the *here* and *now*. The Christian hope is one of *escape* from this earth into heaven, not the *restoration* of this earth.[9] At the same time, there is an emphasis for a future hope of restoration for the Jewish people, which will include their return to the land on earth. In other words, the land continues to play a part in this theology, but only as it pertains to the Promised Land and the future of the Jewish people.

Moreover, many Christians who challenge the belief of a future restoration of the Jewish people to their land (specially within the "covenantal" stream of theology),[10] and who emphasize that Jesus did in fact fulfill the promises of Israel and continued the story of Israel, fall into a similar trap, by emphasizing that he did so in a somehow *spiritual* manner. The land in this perspective is also spiritualized. A good characterization of this trend can be seen in Waltke's summary:

> The NT redefines Land in three ways: first, *spiritually*, as reference to Christ's person; second, *transcendentally*, as a reference to heavenly Jerusalem; and third, *eschatologically*, as a reference to the new Jerusalem after Christ's second coming.[11]

Yet we must again question this "transcendentalization" of the land, especially as it gives the impression that the land is no longer important in the present era. Such a perspective – not unlike Dispensationalism, with which it disagrees – ends up paradoxically deferring all Christian hopes

---

9. For a good critique of this position, see R. J. Middleton, "A New Heaven and a New Earth: The Case for a Holistic Reading of the Biblical Story of Redemption," *Journal for Christian Theological Research* 11 (2006): 73–79. Middleton argues (p. 96): "But 'heaven' simply does not describe the Christian eschatological hope. Not only is the term 'heaven' never used in Scripture for the eternal destiny of the redeemed, but continued use of 'heaven' to name the Christian hope may well divert our attention from the legitimate biblical expectation for the present transformation of our earthly life to conform to God's purposes. Indeed, to focus our expectation on an other worldly salvation has the potential to dissipate our resistance to societal evil and the dedication needed to work for the redemptive transformation of this world."
10. See for example Robertson, *The Israel of God*.
11. Waltke, *An Old Testament Theology*, 14.

into "heaven." In other words, the land *spiritualized* has the potential of becoming the land *heavenized*. Moreover, this line of thought seems to flounder on the same dichotomy between the spiritual and the earthly, by characterizing the difference between the inauguration and the consummation as that between earthly and spiritual. This can be seen in Beale's interpretation of the land:

> Land promises will be fulfilled in a physical form, but . . . the inauguration of this fulfillment is mainly spiritual until the final consummation in a fully physical new heaven and earth . . . Invisible, spiritual, new-creational realities will be completed in the physical and visible land of the entire earth.[12]

We must question again what is the intended meaning of terms like "spiritual" and "invisible." These terms might be perceived as portraying the mission of the church as "spiritual" – meaning not related to this world. It is true that the kingdom of God comes in two stages (inaugurated, then consummated), but there is a continuation between what was inaugurated and what will be consummated. *The consummation consummates what has already been inaugurated.* This is different from speaking about two seemingly distinct phases, one spiritual and another physical.

Finally, we must proceed with caution when it comes to the assertion that "in Christ" replaced "in the land." This belief, though indeed advocated in this study, might give the impression that what is in view is the experience of the *individual* being in Christ: as such it becomes an existential and experiential reality. However, to be "in Christ" is to be with him *here* and *now*, and is at the same time a *community experience*. To be "in Christ" is to be in him with the community of the believers – and this is directly related to the land of that community. The theology of the land emphasizes the role of the community:

> To be *in Christ,* just as to be *in the land*, denotes first, a status and relationship that have been *given* by God; second, a

---

12. Beale, *New Testament Biblical Theology,* 751, 768.

position of inclusion and security in God's family; and third, a commitment to live worthily by fulfilling the practical responsibilities towards those who share the same relationship with you.[13]

It is very important that this status of being "in Christ" demands responsibilities by and to those within the community. The social dimension of the theology of the land helps reclaim this community element in redemption. Chris Wright further proposes that ancient Israel's mission in the land can become a model for the experience of being "in Christ" today. He calls this a "typological understanding of the significance of Israel's land":[14]

> The typological interpretation of the land, which relates it to the person and work of Jesus the Messiah, does not come to a "dead end" with Jesus himself. Rather, it carries the social and economic thrust of Old Testament ethics onwards into the ethics of practical relationships within New Testament Israel, the messianic community. Citizenship of the kingdom of God most certainly has a social and economic dimension.[15]

Wright's contribution to the theology of the land is immensely important. He avoids any spiritualization or heavenization tendencies by anchoring the thesis "In Christ = In the Land" in the experience of the community of believers on earth; also by linking this to a Christian version of Israel's theology of the land. As such, the theology of the land continues to be an important category of faith in Christian theology – with an important role to play in defining the mission of the church.

Thus we can say: *Land matters.* The biblical narrative is a story about land. Covenant, as Brueggemann stresses, never concerned only people and God, "*but the land is always present to the interaction and is very much a*

---

13. Wright, *Old Testament Ethics*, 192 (emphasis in the original).
14. Ibid., 193.
15. Ibid., 196.

decisive factor."[16] In many Christian circles, the transition from the OT to NT resulted in two dissimilar versions of redemption: the covenant in the OT between God, people, and land became in the NT a covenant between God and *individuals – with no reference to land or community*. However, a serious biblical theological approach to the Bible as a whole must, however, challenge such an approach – especially in the light of the fact that the NT authors so clearly present the Jesus-event as the continuation and climax of the story of Israel.

Furthermore, such a reductionistic understanding of God's dealings with humanity – as only with individuals (regardless of place) – minimizes the effects of the fall. The fall not only affected our relationship with God, but it affected our relationship with self, neighbor, and land. The fall affected every sphere of life: social, economical, and ecological. Defining redemption must deal with all of these issues. This can only be done through a serious biblical theological approach that keeps land (together with all that pertains to it) as part of the covenant between God and humanity. *The fall was comprehensive, and as such it demands the redemption of peoples and that of lands.*

2.3. The Universalization of the Land

The main thesis of this study is that the land as a result of the Jesus-event has been universalized in the present era of the new covenant. However, this universalization of the land is by no means a negation of the role and importance of the land in Christian theology, but instead serves only to emphasize its importance. Nor is this universalization a spiritualization of the theme. This universalization is what the OT anticipated from the very beginning. We will next see that the universalization of the land takes shape in three ways: through expansion, through reproduction, and finally in the consummation.

2.3.1. Universalization by Expansion

The coming of Jesus caused the borders of the land to expand. This is particularly evident in Acts 1:8: "You will be my witnesses in Jerusalem and in

---

16. Brueggemann, *The Land*, 200 (emphasis added).

all Judea and Samaria, and to the end of the earth." The image envisioned here is that of progression or expansion. As the gospel of the kingdom moved from Jerusalem, into Judea, into Samaria, and into the ends of the earth, the borders of the land also shifted outwards to include these new places. In this image, the Promised Land grows until it reaches the ends of the earth. In other words, the "land" grows into the "earth." This notion is aided by the fact that in both Hebrew and Greek, the word for "land" and "earth" is the same: ארץ, and γῆ.

This aspect of the universalization reminds us of the historical nature of Christianity. That is why the Jesus-event had to take place in the land of promise, and that is why the first church had to be a Jerusalemite church. The land plays an integral role in the NT biblical theology. The reign and presence of God began expanding to the rest of the world *from the land*.[17]

2.3.2. Universalization by Reproduction

Second, the land is universalized in that the mission of the church establishes new "holy places" in new lands. We can refer to this as establishing new "land realities" in new lands. As new communities of believers in new lands embody the presence and reign of God, taking responsibility for their territory, they recreate the story of Israel in new lands. In this process, Jerusalem no longer has to play a central place in relation to the other new locations, because Jesus is now the cornerstone – the center of the new Christian movement. The NT thus has a decentralized ecclesiology – but it is still territorial. Any place has the potential to become a "holy place." Any land has the potential to become a holy land. Any city has the potential to become a holy city or a city on a hill – as evident by the role of Antioch in the early stages of Christianity (Acts 11:25–30). As Burge explains:

---

17. So Davies says, "The emergence of the Gospels – kerygmatic as they may be – witnesses to a historical and, therefore, geographic, concern in the tradition, which retains for the *realia* their full physical significance. The need to remember the Jesus of History entailed the need to remember the Jesus of a particular land. Jesus belongs not only to time, but to space; and the space which he occupied took on significance, so that the *realia* of Judaism continued as a *realia* in Christianity. History in the tradition demanded geography." Davies, *The Gospel and the Land*, 366.

> The New Testament . . . brings an ecclesial alternative to the problem of Holy Land. Christians in other lands, lands deeply valued by God, bring with them the possibility of bearing the reality of Christ to these places. Which explains the fundamental basis of Christian mission. This is a divinely appointed task to bring that which the Temple and the land once held – the presence of God – into the nations of the world.[18]

The church, however, brings more than just the "presence of God" to new lands. It speaks prophetically for God in new lands. It cares for the neighbors and sojourners in new lands. It promotes and embodies the kingdom ideals of justice and equality in new lands. As such, it creates new land realities in new lands. *The land is universalized when Israel's model is Christified and replicated in new lands.* In addition, the new "land realities" function as a signpost and point forward to the time of consummation, when all the earth will be fully redeemed.

2.3.3. Universalization in the Consummation

Third, the universalization of the land is intended to point towards a time in which the whole created order is renewed in the form of a "new heavens and a new earth." This holistic and universal redemption serves to remind us of the goodness of creation. The land is part of God's good creation. The restoration of the land is an integral part of the restoration of the earth – a moment towards which history is moving. Until this happens, however, the lands continue to groan.

These three aspects of the universalization of the land together make a complete picture. The land is universalized as it expands beyond Jerusalem into new lands. This expansion includes an element of decentralization, which no longer necessitates that Jerusalem continues to play a central role in redemptive history. Rather, new land realities are created in new lands, as Israel's model is replicated in new places. This process culminates in a "new heavens and a new earth" when God intervenes in time and space – by bringing complete redemption to the universe.

---

18. Burge, *Jesus and The Land*, 131.

2.4. Two Testaments. One Story

Theology and hermeneutics are inevitably related. This topic of the land is one area in theology where this is very evident. In particular, the relationship between the Old and New Testaments is central to one's theology of the land. The theology of the land, as argued for here, is based on certain assumptions and presuppositions regarding the nature of the Jesus-event – in particular that it continues the story of Israel. Jesus did not invent a new tradition. He did not start a new story. He came as Israel's Messiah and, as Israel's Messiah, he brought God's reign and salvation to the ends of the earth. *The Old and New Testaments talk about one story.*

As such, when it comes to understanding the relationship between both Testaments, we can say that the Old finds its climax in the New, and the New is only understood in light of the Old. No doubt, there are new developments in the narrative. Jesus and Paul redefined certain elements in the OT, for example, regarding purity and rituals. The NT brings something new to the table, and by implication it causes some things to become old. *Yet this is all part of the plot. The renewal has been anticipated.*

When it comes to the land, this newness is manifested in the ways argued for above: Christ embodies the realities of the land, and as a result the land is universalized. This interpretation is not the spiritualization, allegorization, or the negation of the promises of the land in the OT. Rather, this interpretation simply recognizes that Christ is the fulfillment of the hopes of the OT. It also follows the lead of what the NT itself does. *Interpreting land promises with reference to Christ is precisely what the NT did.*

Furthermore, it must be emphasized that the theology of the land proposed here is entirely an "Israelite" theology. Jesus was a Jew. He lived and ministered in the land of promise. He restored his people. In other words, the story of Israel narrowed down until it became the story of one ideal Israelite who represented all of Israel. Through this ideal Israelite, the story expanded again – this time to incorporate new nations into the people of God and to declare new lands as belonging to this Jewish Messiah. Through Jesus, the ideal Israelite, Israel lived out its potential and calling as a light to the world. From the land of Israel came out a message of salvation to all lands. The OT is thus not negated. It is emphasized, realized, and fulfilled.

Moreover, Jews are not "replaced" by Gentiles. The first church, after all, consisted of mainly Jewish believers. Rather, Gentiles joined Israel or were incorporated into Israel *as anticipated in the OT*.[19] The incorporation is part of the plot and is in fact a main goal towards which the plot has been moving all along. In other words, using Paul's metaphor, there is and has always been one olive tree. "God has not uprooted the olive tree of Israel and replaced it with another. On the contrary, uncultivated branches of wild olives (Gentiles) have been grafted into the olive tree of Israel – the same original planting."[20] The addition of the new branches necessitates the growth of this tree, and consequently the land has been expanded. There has been a parallel growth and expansion with the land.

In short, a Christ-centered universalized theology of the land is not an abnormal development in the story, and is not a spiritualization of the OT. It is precisely what the OT anticipated all along and what the NT claimed to be witnessing. To argue otherwise is a misrepresentation of both the vision of the OT and the claims of the NT.

3. From Land to Lands: A Missional Theology of the Land

3.1. Israel as a Paradigm

The theology of the land is in its essence *missional*. Israel in the land could and should function as a paradigm for the mission of churches in new lands. A missional theology of the land attempts to apply a Christian version of Israel's theology of her land in new lands. It is eventually a movement, as it were, from land (singular) to lands (plural).

The theology of the land acknowledges:
- The land mediates the presence of God and demands holiness;
- The land is covenanted. It is always a mandate and not a possession, and as such it requires accountability;

---

19. Hays, *Echoes of Scripture*, 96.
20. Dunn, *New Testament Theology*, 120.

- The land is where the reign of God takes place and it calls for God's agenda to be applied through his vicegerents.

As such, a missional theology of the land seeks to take these beliefs, to "Christify" them, and to make them a reality in new lands. This is the natural implication of the universalization of the land. A missional theology of the land, in other words, *replicates a Christian version of Israel in new lands.*

Such an approach emphasizes the continuity between the OT vision of redemption and that of the NT. It also goes beyond treating the land in the OT as merely an earthly type or a shadow that simply points towards another seemingly quite different heavenly reality. Instead, the fact that the Jesus-event fulfills the OT enhances the possibility of applying the paradigm of Israel in new locations. As Chris Wright argues:

> Christ and the kingdom he proclaimed and inaugurated "fulfill" the Old Testament, taking up its socio-economic pattern and transforming it into something that can be the experience not just of a single nation in a small slice of territory but of anyone, anywhere, in Christ.[21]

A missional theology of the land, therefore, engages with the social, political, and economical spheres. It will not do for the church to focus only on the salvation of souls or on the sins of the individuals. The biblical vision of redemption involves the redemption of lands and societies. The kingdom that Jesus inaugurated is not a spiritual or irrelevant one. The kingdom shapes social actions, such as how to treat the poor, marginalized, neighbor, enemy, money, and possessions.[22]

Needless to say, this does not mean that perfection will define the experience of the church here on earth. The church seeks to replicate the theology of the land of Israel while fully acknowledging that as long as she lives in this fallen world, she will fall short from coming close to fully achieving the biblical ideals.

---

21. Wright, *Old Testament Ethics*, 196.
22. See Wenell, *Jesus and Land*, 142.

Finally, a missional theology of the land demands that we re-evaluate our definition and understanding of terms like "evangelism" and "gospel." This will help us avoid the dichotomy that exists among many Christians today between defining the gospel as "the salvation of souls" on the one hand and "social action" on the other.[23] *The gospel includes both, and the two cannot be separated.* This is not simply a matter of "both . . . and . . . .." Rather, the two are one. To accept the salvation of Christ is to submit and participate in his kingdom agenda. To be saved is to join the community of faith that is committed to applying and promoting God's kingdom agenda on earth. To be engaged in social action is to call people to believe in Jesus. When Jesus sent his disciples to the world he commanded them to "teach them to keep my commandments" – and Jesus certainly commanded acts of love, compassion, generosity and justice. *God's mission, as seen in his instruction to ancient Israel and the great commission, is holistic, and therefore the mission of the church must be holistic as well.*

3.2. The Individual and the Community

In a missional theology of the land, the role of the community is emphasized alongside that of the individual – perhaps even above it. The biblical context of redemption is the community. In many Christian circles, salvation has become a private matter that is not related to land and community. The focus is on God's encounters with individuals and God is relevant only as he is involved in personal and private matters. But as we have seen, covenant has always been between *God, communities, and land*. As Brueggemann powerfully argues:

> It will not do to make the individual person the unit of decision-making because in both Testaments the land possessed or promised concerns the whole people. Radical decisions in obedience are of course the stuff of biblical faith, but now it cannot be radical obedience in a private world without brothers and sisters, without past and futures, without turf to be

---

23. See e.g. Wright, *What Saint Paul Really Said*, 154. See also V. Samuel and C. Sudgen, eds., *Mission as Transformation: A Theology of the Whole Gospel* (Oxford: Regnum, 1999).

managed and cherished as a partner in the decisions. The unit of decision-making is the community and that always with reference to the land.[24]

God is the God of nations and lands, and not just the God of individuals. The focal point in biblical theology is the community and not the individual. This is not a denial of the need for individuals to make faith decisions. God is the one who meets individuals where they are. However, once an individual believes in the gospel of the reign of God through Christ, he or she becomes a member of a community – a family. The individual is accountable to the community just as they are to him. *Meaning, mission, and identity can only be defined in the context of the community.*

This is where the NT concept of fellowship comes into play. Fellowship is not merely a symbolic spiritual articulation of Christian unity in Christ. Rather, "the experience of *fellowship* – in its full, rich, concrete NT sense – fulfills analogous theological and ethical functions for the Christian as the possession of *land* did for Old Testament Israelites."[25] Christian fellowship, therefore, manifests itself in the socio-economic sphere and is interpreted in socio-economic actions, such as sharing possessions, meeting the needs of the community, and maintaining a system of equality among the members of the fellowship. The experience of the community is central to what it means to be a Christian.

3.3. Territorial Ecclesiology

A missional theology of the land requires that churches define their mission in relation to territory. Churches do not exist in a vacuum or an ethereal reality. Location and context do matter. The mission of the church should be a response to the context and as such is defined by this context. Tarazi, arguing from an Eastern Orthodox perspective, says:

> This is why Orthodoxy has consistently taken the New Testament expression "the church of God in such and such

---

24. Brueggemann, *The Land*, 199.
25. Wright, *Old Testament Ethics*, 195 (emphasis in the original).

a place" to be a basic truth at the core of sound ecclesiology. There is no such thing as an ethereal church of God at large, but the same church of God taking different shades and colors according to its various dwelling places on this earth.[26]

This understanding of ecclesiology is extremely important. It emphasizes the rootedness of the church in the land. *A church in a particular land exists for the sake of that land and takes her mission agenda from it.* The church, in other words, derives much of its purpose from its locale. This is not simply a matter of contextualizing the Christian gospel and making it more "relevant." This has to do with the self-definition of the church. This requires that each church identifies its territory and claims this territory as the realm of her vicegerency. The mission of the church in the world is, after all, a declaration of the sovereignty of the Son of God over all the lands of the world. The local church needs to apply this global reign of Christ in its own distinctive locality.

Churches today are defined more in terms of doctrine and beliefs than territory. Mission is defined in reference to individuals and people groups – not territory. Yet the biblical vision of holistic redemption and the paradigm of Israel together suggest a different way of doing church and mission. *The church in a particular land exists with the view that this land will one day become a new restored creation.* Therefore, the church of a particular land must embody, advocate, and implement God's agenda for that land. God's agenda for a particular land must then unify the churches that exist in a particular land towards fulfilling this agenda. *A missional theology of the land thinks territorially.*

3.4. Embodying the Presence and Reign of God on Earth

The church must also take seriously the theology of being made in God's image and of being entrusted with vicegerency. The community of believers collectively represent God on earth. The local church represents God in a particular village, or city, or land. The believers should take this

---

26. P. N. Tarazi, "Covenant, Land and City: Finding God's Will in Palestine," *The Reformed Journal* 29 (1979): 14.

responsibility seriously. God and the land demand holiness, and the covenant that God made with his people always demands fruits.

The church in all its community-based activities, creates, as it were, a sacred arena where God can be encountered. The church community is thus the natural medium of theophany today. The community, liturgy, and sacraments embody and manifest the presence of God within a particular land. The presence of God is a sanctifying presence: it transforms individuals, communities, societies, and lands.

The church should also take its priestly task seriously. The church not only represents God within a certain land, but also represents a certain land and the people of that before the face of God. As such, it must continuously engage in prayers of intercession on behalf of the nation and the land (1 Tim 2:1–2).

A church must also recognize its identity as the "light" and "salt" of the land. A corrupt salt or a fading light is a recipe for the corruption and darkness of society and land. The church in a particular land must have a sense of accountability towards that land and the people and society of that land. With election comes responsibility.

3.5. The Cross as the Paradigm

We have seen how the cross and the resurrection of Jesus signify the moment in salvation history in which the new kingdom era begins. The cross, in a sense, is the moment and the means when Eden began to be restored. We can add to this that the cross is also the paradigm of restoration. *The cross exemplifies true vicegerency and sets the pattern for how the land is to be restored.* The path to exaltation always goes through suffering (Isa 52:13–53:12; Phil 2:5–11). This has important implications for how churches carry the role of vicegerency today.

It is crucial to underscore that declaring a territory as belonging to God and announcing Jesus as Lord over new lands is not done through military or political means. The church cannot rely on power or the secular authorities to implement the reign of God in new lands. The church in the past has erred in trying to enforce the kingdom of God over people and territory – evident for example on occasions in the Byzantine Empire, the

Crusades, Calvin's Geneva, and the Puritans. The role of the church cannot be confused with that of political rulers or civil authorities.

The church conquers the world not by weapons or force. The kingdom of God expands through preaching and evangelism in both words and deeds. *The non-violent and sacrificial approach of the Messiah determines the nature of his reign and the method and approach of his followers.* The kingdom, though violently resisted (Acts 14:22), is to expand non-violently – through sacrificial service and the power of the Spirit (1 Cor 2:3–5).

3.6. Practical Implications

This paradigm of a missional theology of the land will take a different shape in each new land, depending on the cultural, social, political and economical context. This is not a straight-jacket or a "one size fits all." The mission and shape of the church in a wealthy land or where Christians are the majority, is naturally different from the mission and shape of the church in a land where there is poverty and where Christians are a minority. Christianity by its nature is an adaptable faith that takes into consideration the context of the land. Yet we can briefly propose some common practical missional strategies that arise from our thesis that the theology of the land provides a paradigm for the mission of the church. Each of these four strategies properly deserves a chapter of its own.

Tenancy and Equality: God owns the land – every land. No one can claim possession or ownership of any land. Human beings are only tenants in the land, and as such must share the blessings of the land with their neighbors. A Christian theology of the land also emphasizes that the land is something to share, not to possess. It is given as a gift for the good of the society, and is shared equally between the members of the community. The principle of shared and inclusive land means that an ideal land is a place where people of all ethnicities and social backgrounds are treated equally. This can be seen in issues like racism, having equal access to education, health care, and job opportunities. Equality also means that people should have freedom of thought, faith, and conscience.

Social Justice: The theology of the land also reminds us that the land is a place where the vulnerable in the society, such as the widows, orphans, and the sojourner (and their equivalent in today's world) are cared for. This goes beyond acts of charity. Political and economical systems in which a certain privileged minority control the majority of the land or the majority of the economy should be challenged and opposed.

The Bible includes many principles that could aid the Christian voice and mission as it pertains to socio-economic justice. In today's world, where material possessions are valued more than anything else, Christians should promote adaptable versions of principles such as releasing the land and forgiving debts (the Jubilee).[27]

Reconciliation: The gift of land is viewed in the Bible as a step towards the restoration to Eden – a place where Adam exercised his vicegerency for the good of creation. An ideal land, following the pattern of Eden, is thus a place where order reigns. This means that we must make every effort to make the land a place of peace, fellowship, and reconciliation. The principle of redemption reminds us that we must make the land a place where enemies meet and are reconciled. The principle of re-commissioning reminds us that the church should be a community of peacemakers. It must be engaged in active and sacrificial peacemaking in the land.[28]

Care for Creation: Finally, the theology of the land (also following the pattern of Eden) realizes the goodness of God's creation. God's intention is to *redeem* this world, not to annihilate it. God's vision and agenda for his world should be the vision and agenda of his church. The theology of the land realizes that we as humans have been entrusted with this earth and we should do our best to use its resources in a responsible way. The church as God's redeemed vicegerent must thus be actively engaged in care for creation, and participate in discussions about issues like climate change and

---

27. For more on equity and socio-economic justice, see Hartropp, *What Is Economic Justice?*; Herron, "Land, the Law, and the Poor," 76–84; Goldingay, "Jubilee Tithe," *Transformation* 19, no. 3 (2002): 198–205; J. D. Mason, "Biblical Teaching on Assisting the Poor," in *The Bible and Christian Ethics,* ed. D. E. Singh and B. C. (Oxford: Regnum Books, 2012), 23–50; R. J. Sider and S. Mott, "A Biblical Paradigm for Economic Justice," in *The Bible and Christian Ethics,* ed. D. E. Singh and B. C. (Oxford: Regnum Books, 2012), 84–116. C. E. Armeding, "Borrowing and Lending: Is There Anything Christian About Either?" in *The Bible and Christian Ethics,* ed. D. E. Singh and B. C. Farr (Oxford: Regnum Books, 2012), 128–142.

28. For more on this issue, see M. Volf, *Exclusion and Embrace: A Theological Exploration of Identity, Otherness, and Reconciliation* (Nashville: Abingdon Press, 1996); Munayer, "From Land of Strife," 234–265; G. H. Stassen, *Just Peacemaking: Transforming Initiatives for Justice and Peace* (Louisville: Westminster John Knox Press, 1992).

recycling.[29] *The theology of the land means that ecological concerns can never be merely a "side-issue" for the church.*

We have only scratched the surface with this very brief discussion. These issues are mentioned here only as points that need to be seriously studied and developed in Christian theology and practice, for they are at the heart of what the church should be. For in the end, the theology of the land reminds us that, in the words of the psalmist, "The earth/land is the Lord's and the fullness thereof, the world and those who dwell therein" (Ps 24:1).

---

29. For more on this issue, see Wright, "Biblical Reflections on Land," 153–167; W. E. March, *God's Land On Loan: Israel, Palestine, and the World* (Louisville: Westminster John Knox Press, 2007); I. W. Provan, *Tenants in God's Land: Earth-Keeping and People-Keeping in the Old Testament* (Cambridge: Grove Books, 2008); C. B. DeWitt, ed., *The Environment and the Christian: What Can We Learn from the New Testament* (Grand Rapids: Baker Book House, 1991); Simkins, *Creator & Creation*; F. F. Bruce, "The Bible and the environment," in *Living and Active Word of God. Essays in Honor of Samuel J. Schultz*, ed. M. Inch and R. Youngblood (Winona Lake: Eisenbrauns, 1983), 15–29.

Epilogue

1. The Promised Land Today

The argument of this book – that the land has been universalized in and through Christ – begs the question: what about the original "Promised Land" itself? What about Palestine and Israel today? Is there a special place for the original land in Christian thought and theology? In addition, what is a proper Christian response to the conflict taking place these days in that very same land? What does a missional theology of the land look like in Palestine and Israel today?[1]

First, and as we have argued extensively, the original Promised Land has lost its strictly *theological* significance. It is no longer a distinct "holy land" that is set apart for God. Christians who continue to advocate that the land today belongs to the Jewish people based on God's eternal covenant with Abraham have to respond to the many challenges raised in this book. For example: What were the original borders of this land? Who is Israel? Were the promises conditional or unconditional? And most importantly, what was the original purpose behind the promise of the land? And were these purposes achieved? In addition, we have also argued from the perspective of the NT, that Jesus, the true Israelite, is the legitimate heir of the Abrahamic promises, including that of the land, and that those who are in him are therefore heirs of the Abrahamic promises today. The NT claims that Jesus is the ultimate fulfillment of the OT story, and that after his

---

1. By Palestine and Israel I mean the land that was known as Palestine under the British Mandate (1920–1948) and which was later divided between the Jews of the State of Israel that was established in 1948 and the Arabs.

death and resurrection, the land has been universalized. In this sense, the land has lost its theological significance.[2]

However, once this critical point has been granted, we can readily acknowledge that the land continues to act as a witness to God's work in history. It will always be the historical backdrop or scenery in which the biblical drama took place in actual time and space: the call of Abraham, the birth, death and resurrection of Christ, the place where the church first began. So, in this sense, the Land still has a special role that it can play within Christian faith – *as a witness*. This is why many have called the land "the fifth Gospel." The land tells a story! It tells the story of a God who has chosen a people and land, and dwelt in their midst – eventually bringing from that people and that land a powerful redemption which can reach to all the families and the lands of the earth. It tells the story of a God who blesses but also demands holiness and justice. It also tells the story of a God who in meekness died in that land in order to restore every land, so that we can inherit the land again.

In this sense, the land can be considered sacred, as Inge argues, "sacred places will be those which have been associated with sacred stories, places linked with divine disclosure."[3] The land gives a testimony to thousands of years of salvation history. It can, as such, become a place where God is encountered in a special way – especially by people who find themselves in places which they are familiar with from their reading of Scripture. The land functions as a stimulus for spiritual reflection, prayer, and fresh encounters with God. That is why over the centuries Christian pilgrims have visited this land, seeking a deeper encounter with God.[4]

---

2. Some have suggested that the land could possibly be the theatre of the final drama in salvation history, namely the place where Christ will return. See R. L. Wilken, *The Land Called Holy: Palestine in Christian History and Thought* (New Haven: Yale University Press, 1992), 47. However, as we have seen, the focus in the final vision of the NT is on the new heavens and the new earth, and the New Jerusalem, not on the land.

3. J. Inge, "Towards a Theology of Place," *Modern Believing* 40, no. 1 (1999), 47. Inge argues extensively for what he called an "Incarnational" theology of the land where a place in which God is experienced in a special way can become sacred. It is important to observe that any place or land for Inge, like the cathedral, could become sacred, and not just the original land of promise. See also his book: J. Inge, *A Christian Theology of Place* (Burlington: Ashgate, 2003).

4. See the book by Wilken, *The Land Called Holy*. See also P. W. L. Walker, *Holy City, Holy Places?: Christian Attitudes to Jerusalem and the Holy Land in the Fourth Century* (Oxford:

However, we must warn against idolizing the land – something to which this very same land itself testifies. *Our connection is with the God of the land, the God whose story the land tells, and not with the land itself.* The Crusades and the Crimean War are just examples of how far Christians are willing to go when the land is absolutized over the God of the land. In addition, and as we have seen, there is no guarantee that a holy place will continue to be holy forever – as Jerusalem itself testifies.

Furthermore, Christians must remember that the people of the land are as important as the land itself when it comes to narrating the biblical story and the story of the land over the centuries. Christians who visit the land must have a connection not just with old stones of old churches, but more importantly, with the "living stones" of the land – the community of faith where God in reality dwells. The presence of God by his Holy Spirit in the midst of the community of faith in the land is what makes this land, as indeed any other land, to be holy. The people of the land are an integral part of the witness of the land. The testimony of the land apart from the people of the land is an empty testimony. If the land is the fifth Gospel, then the people of the land are the sixth Gospel.[5]

2. Religion, Christian Theology, and the Palestinian Israeli Conflict

With regards to the conflict in the land today, it is evident that the land today is a place of hostility, strife, and division. It is far removed from the ideals of the biblical vision of Eden, which, as we saw, was supposed to be a land of peace, wholeness, and reconciliation.

The Palestinian Israeli conflict is one of most complex conflicts in modern history. At its core, it is a conflict about territory and control. It is a conflict about land, and not merely any land, but the biblical land. Over

---

Oxford University Press, 1990).
5. See the important article by Palestinian theologian M. Raheb, "Towards a New Hermeneutics of Liberation: A Palestinian Christian Perspective," in *The Biblical Text in the Context of Occupation: Towards a New Hermeneutics of Liberation*, ed. M. Raheb (Bethlehehm: Diyar, 2012), 11–28.

the years, religion has been used in this conflict by many parties to justify acts of violence and land confiscation. Both sides make claims that the land belongs to them, based not only on historical and political claims, but also on religious ones. These claims are more often than not *exclusive* in nature.[6] Israeli leaders, supported by Jewish religious leaders, insist today that Israel is defined as a *Jewish* State. At the same time, the state of Israel continues its expanding policy by building settlements on Palestinian land, and these settlements are often occupied by religious Jews who believe that *all the land* belongs to them because of the promises to Abraham.

In places like Bethlehem today, Jewish settlers seize control of Palestinian land by force, protected by the Israeli army, and motivated by their religious tradition. All historical Palestine, they argue, is "land of Israel" given to their ancestors, and by extension to them, as an eternal possession. Any attempt by Palestinians to prove ownership of the land by legal documents is deemed irrelevant by these fanatic Jewish groups.[7]

On the other hand, some Palestinian Islamic fundamentalist groups also claim the whole land as "*waqf*," a holy territory devoted to *Allah*, and therefore necessitating their action of *jihad* to cleanse the land from the control of the "infidels."[8]

To add up to an already complex situation where religion is used to justify a political claim, many Christian groups and churches around the world have taken sides in this conflict in the name of the Bible and the God of Bible. These are often called Christian Zionists. Christian Zionism comes in different backgrounds and theological shapes. The theological roots of Christian Zionism have been thoroughly examined by different scholars.[9] After the holocaust Christians rightly reevaluated their relationship and even theology regarding the Jewish people. "Post-holocaust theology" developed as a response to centuries of persecution of the Jewish people

---

6. See Munayer, "From Land of Strife," 263–265.
7. See M. Bravermann, *Fatal Embrace* (Texas: Synergy Books, 2010), 3–5.
8. See Munayer, "From Land of Strife," 263–265.
9. For the historical and theological roots of Christian Zionism, see Sizer, *Christian Zionism*; R. O. Smith, *More Desired than Our Own Salvation: The Roots of Christian Zionism* (Oxford: Oxford University Press, 2013). For the way in which Christian Zionism influences the Palestinian Israeli conflict, see Ateek, Duaybis, and Tobin, *Challenging Christian Zionism*.

in the West, a persecution that tragically culminated in the holocaust. It is a theology that looks very positively towards the biblical covenants with Israel and argues for their continuation with the Jewish people today, even after the Christ-event. In other words, the covenant with biblical Israel has *not* been *superseded*. The church has *not replaced* biblical Israel.[10]

In addition, many Christians around the world today believe that God will at the end times restore the Jewish people and bring them to the Promised Land, and that all of this will lead to the second coming of Christ. These views became very popular when the modern state of Israel declared its independence in 1948, and even more so when Israel illegally seized control of East Jerusalem in 1967.[11] Dispensationalism theology, which holds a distinctive place for the Jewish people in its theological framework, was the common "by default" theology of most evangelical churches and seminaries, in particular in USA.

Before moving forward we must ask: Does this book promote "replacement theology" or "supersessionism"? The answer depends on how one defines "replacement theology" to begin with. Simply speaking, "supersessionism" is "the view that the NT church is the new and/or true Israel that has forever superseded the nation Israel as the people of God."[12] Sadly, there are some forms of replacement theology that teach not only that God had rejected and replaced the Jews with Gentiles or the church, but also that the Jews today are rejected and under judgment for killing Jesus and for continuing to reject Jesus. This is sometimes called punitive replacement theology. Needless to say, this position must be strongly rejected. The history of the church in relation to the Jewish people is tragic and shameful. Anti-Semitism can be partially traced to the church's attitude towards the Jewish people.

The approach preferred in this book is that of *incorporation into* and *continuity with* biblical Israel, rather than *superseding* or *replacing* Israel. Gentile believers were incorporated into biblical Israel, forming a new

---

10. For a good representation of this theology, see Soulen, *The God of Israel*.
11. UN resolution 298 states that all legislative and administrative actions taken by Israel to change the status of Jerusalem are totally invalid and cannot change that status.
12. Michael J. Vlach, "Various Forms of Replacement Theology," *TMSJ* 20, no. 1 (Spring 2009): 57. The article explains the different kinds of replacement theology.

entity – the church – which stands in continuation with biblical Israel. The link between the two, the cornerstone, is Jesus Christ the Jewish Messiah. Such an approach looks positively to the OT and biblical Israel, and presupposes that biblical Israel and the OT do not stand in contradiction with the Christian faith.

Moreover, one of the main arguments of this book has been that in Christ, Jews and Gentiles were *united*. The new entity – the church – is by definition multi-racial. In fact, one could argue that it is this organic unity between Jews and Gentiles that gives the church its identity, and it could not have been any other way. One important implication of this is that Christianity must challenge racism *in all its forms*. It must also challenge any superior and prejudice attitudes towards any race or people group. A superior attitude towards any person or people – Christian, Jew or Muslim – cannot be the characteristics of a child of God who understands the true meaning of being justified by faith.

3. A Palestinian Christian Response: Towards a Shared Land Theology

The political solutions that are being discussed nowadays do not speak about sharing the land, but only about *dividing* it. They revolve around the question of "what is ours?" and "what is theirs?" The narratives that dominate the political space are also exclusive in nature.[13]

The reality in the land is one of injustice. There are oppressors and there are the oppressed. Not all the people of the land are equal. Most Palestinians continue to live under the harsh reality of the Israeli occupation. There are laws that differentiate between ethnicities and religion – against the biblical

---

13. Most of the political discussions today center around the idea of a "two states solution," in which Palestinians and Israeli divide the land. The practicality of this solution is now debated since it is becoming more and more impossible to define the borders of each side's territory as a result of the Israeli settlements. This is why many academics and activists today are calling for a "one state" solution, in which there is one country and one law, but two governments. I believe that the church must not get involved in suggesting political solutions. Rather, the message should be that regardless of which political solution is adopted and implemented – the vision and ideals of God of justice and equality in the land – indeed any land – must be respected.

vision of equality. The resources of the land are not shared equally. What is a Christian response to all of this?

In 2009 Palestinian Christian lay leaders, theologians, pastors, and activists from all church backgrounds issued an important document called "Kairos Palestine."[14] The document is bold and prophetic. It rightly calls the Israeli occupation to Palestinian land a "sin against God and humanity."[15] It rejects any use of the Bible or theology to support political options that are based upon injustice. It further emphasizes that:

> We believe that our land has a universal mission. In this universality, the meaning of the promises, of the land, of the election, of the people of God open up to include all of humanity, starting from all the peoples of this land. In light of the teachings of the Holy Bible, the promise of the land has never been a political program, but rather the prelude to complete universal salvation. It was the initiation of the fulfillment of the Kingdom of God on earth.[16]

A missional theology of the land must ask today: what does the "kingdom of God" look like in the land today? The church in the land must continue to bear witness to the holy God of the covenant who demands holiness and justice. It must take an active role in proclaiming the ideals of God for his earth. This is the "original" land that became the blueprint for all other lands. The failure of humanity to live in peace and harmony here is thus ironic and deeply sad.

The challenge raised in front of the church today is to preach a theology of a *shared land* – and I hope that this book pushes this forward. A theology of a *shared land* means that any exclusive claim to land of the Bible in the name of God must be rejected. Such a theology emphasizes that all the dwellers of the land must share the land and its resources *equally* and have the same rights – regardless of their ethnicity or religion. There are

---
14. To read the entire document and the names of the authors visit www.kairospalestine.com.
15. *The Kairos Palestine Document*, 2009, section 2.5.
16. Ibid., section 2.3.

no "second-class" citizens in this land. No one is marginalized in God's vision of the land. *A shared land is not simply an option; it is the only way forward.* This is the biblical vision and so it must be the prophetic vision of the church in Palestine and Israel. The reality on the ground is that of "walls," yet what is needed is a vision of "bridges." *Palestinians and Israelis must think collectively in terms of a common future in which they cooperate – not a divided future in which they separate.* As Palestinians and Israelis, we are indeed "able to love and live together." We can "organize our political life, with all its complexity," but only after "ending the occupation and establishing justice."[17]

I speak from personal experience – my ancestors have been living in this land for hundreds of years. For me and my family, the Promised Land is "home." We feel that we belong to the land, and that we are co-narrators of the story it tells. The reality I grew up in is one of tragedy and strife. I have lost land, and I have seen loved ones leave the land, and others forced to leave. I have seen people immigrate to this land freely from all over the world and call this land home, and at the same time there are many others, including some of my relatives, who wish to return to this land – the place where they were born – but are not allowed. The land I live in today is torn apart by walls and checkpoints. Will this land I call "home" become a place where God is experienced? Can it become a place where the justice of God reigns? Can it become a place where Jews, Muslims and Christians – while retaining their distinctive beliefs – can embrace each other as fellow human beings, and indeed as people of faith, and be reconciled in practice?

Regardless of the political reality, we must continue to hope! We must at the same time cling to our calling to be peacemakers, and promote and model meekness; for, as Jesus taught, it is the meek who will inherit the land – not the strong or the wealthy. It is only fitting to conclude this book with words from the *Kairos Document*:

> Our land is God's land, as is the case with all countries in the world. It is holy inasmuch as God is present in it, for God alone is holy and sanctifier. It is the duty of those of us who

---

17. Ibid., section 5.4.2.

live here, to respect the will of God for this land. It is our duty to liberate it from the evil of injustice and war. It is God's land and therefore it must be a land of reconciliation, peace and love. *This is indeed possible.* God has put us here as two peoples, and God gives us the capacity, *if we have the will,* to live together and establish in it justice and peace, making it in reality God's land.[18]

---

18. Ibid., section 2.3.1. (*Emphasis added*).

Bibliography

The Holy Bible: English Standard Version. Wheaton: Standard Bible Society, 2001.

Abraham, I. and B. Roland. "'God Doesn't Care': The Contradictions of Christian Zionism." *Religion & Theology* 16, no. 1-2 (2009): 90–110.

Aharoni, Y. *The Land of the Bible: A Historical Geography.* Louisville: Westminster John Knox Press, 1979.

Albright, W. F. "The Location of the Garden of Eden." *The American Journal of Semitic Languages and Literatures* 39, no. 1 (1922): 15–31.

Alexander, T. D. *From Paradise to the Promised Land: An Introduction to the Pentateuch.* Carlisle: Paternoster Press, 2002.

———. *The Servant King: The Bible's Portrait of the Messiah.* Vancouver: Regent College, 2003.

———. *From Eden to The New Jerusalem: Exploring God's plan for Life on Earth.* Nottingham: Inter-Varsity Press, 2008.

Allison, D. C. "Matt. 23:39 = Luke 13:35b As a Conditional Prophecy." *JSNT* 18 (1983): 75–84.

Alonso-Schökel, L. "Sapiential and Covenant Themes in Genesis 2–3." In *Studies in Ancient Israelite Wisdom,* edited by J. L. Crenshaw, 472–479. New York: KTAV, 1976.

Amaru, B. H. "Land Theology in Josephus' Jewish Antiquities." *The Jewish Quarterly Review* (1981): 201–229.

———. "Land Theology in Philo and Josephus." In *The Land of Israel: Jewish Perspectives,* edited by L. A. Hoffman, 65–93. Notre Dame: University of Notre Dame Press, 1986.

———. *Rewriting the Bible: Land and Covenant in Post-Biblical Jewish Literature,* Valley Forge: Trinity Press International, 1994.

Amit, Y. "Biblical Utopianism: A Mapmakers Guide to Eden." *Union Seminary Quarterly Review* 44 (1990): 11–17.

Anderson, A. A. *2 Samuel. Word Biblical Commentary.* Dallas: Word Books, 1989.

Anderson, B. W. *The Living World of the Old Testament.* Harlow: Longman, 1988.
Anderson, G. "Eden, Garden of." In *The New Interpreter's Dictionary of the Bible,* edited by Sakenfeld, 186–187. Nashville: Abingdon Press, 2006.
———. "Does The Promise Still Hold? Israel and The Land." *Christian Century* 126, no. 1 (2009): 22–25.
Armeding, C. E. "Borrowing and Lending: Is There Anything Christian About Either?" In *The Bible and Christian Ethics,* edited by D. E. Singh and B. C. Farr, 128–142. Oxford: Regnum Books, 2012.
Arnold, B. T. *Genesis. New Cambridge Bible Commentary.* Cambridge: Cambridge University Press, 2009.
Asselin, D. T. "The Notion of Dominion in Genesis 1–3." *The Catholic Biblical Quarterly* 16 (1954): 277–294.
Assis, E. "'How Long Are You Slack to Go to Possess the Land' (Jos. XVIII 3): Ideal and Reality in the Distribution Descriptions in Joshua XIII–XIX." *Vetus Testamentum,* (2003): 1–25.
Ateek, N. S. *Justice, and only Justice: A Palestinian Theology of Liberation.* Maryknoll: Orbis Books, 1989.
———. *A Palestinian Christian Cry for Reconciliation.* Maryknoll: Orbis Books, 2008.
Ateek, N., C. Duaybis and M. Tobin, eds. *Challenging Christian Zionism: Theology, Politics and the Israel-Palestine Conflict.* London: Melisende, 2005.
Attridge, H. W. "'Let Us Strive to Enter That Rest': the Logic of Hebrews 4:1–11." *The Harvard Theological Review* (1980): 279–288.
Aune, D. E. *Revelation. 17-22. Word Biblical Commentary.* Nashville: Thomas Nelson, 1998.
Baden, J. S. "The Morpho-Syntax of Genesis 12:1–3: Translation and Interpretation." *The Catholic Biblical quarterly* 72, no. 2 (2010): 223–237.
Bailey, K. E. "St. Paul's Understanding of the Territorial Promise." *The Near East School of Theology Theological Review* XV, no. 1 (1994): 59–69.
Baker, D. L. "The Jubilee and the Millennium. Holy Years in the Bible and Their Relevance Today." *Themelios* 24, no. 1 (1998): 44–69.
Barclift, P. "Zionism, Justice, And the 'Promised Land.'" *Lexington Theological Quarterly* 39, no. 4 (2004): 195–224.
Bartholomew, C. G. "Biblical Theology." In *Dictionary for Theological Interpretation of the Bible,* edited by K. J. Vanhoozer, C. G. Bartholomew and D. J. Treier, 84–90, Grand Rapids: Baker Academic, 2005.
Bauckham, R. J. *Jude, 2 Peter. Word Biblical Commentary.* Waco: Word Books, 1983.

———. "The Son of Man: 'A Man in My Position' or 'Someone.'" *JSNT* 23 (1985): 23–33.

———. "Jesus' Demonstration in the Temple." In *Law and Religion: Essays on the Place of the Law in Israel and Early Christianity*, edited by B. Lindars, 72–89. Cambridge: James Clarke & Co, 1989.

———. *The Climax of Prophecy: Studies on the Book of Revelation*. Edinburgh: T&T Clark, 1993.

Beale, G. K. *The Book of Revelation: A Commentary on the Greek Text*. New International Greek Testament Commentary. Grand Rapids/Carlisle: Eerdmans/Paternoster Press, 1999.

———. *The Temple and the Church's Mission*. Downers Grove: InterVarsity Press, 2004.

———. "Eden, The Temple, and The Church's Mission in the New Creation." *JETS* 48, no. 1 (2005): 5–31.

———. *A New Testament Biblical Theology: The Unfolding of the Old Testament in the New*. Grand Rapids: Baker Academic, 2011.

Beasley-Murray, G. R. *Jesus and the Kingdom of God*. Grand Rapids: Eerdmans, 1986.

———. *John*. World Biblical Commentary, Waco: Word Books, 1987.

———. "The Kingdom of God in the Teaching of God." *JETS* 35, no. 1 (1992): 19–30.

Berg, W. "Israel's Land, der Garten Gottes. Der Garten als Bild des Heiles im Alten Testament." *Biblische Zeitschrift* 32 (1988): 35–51.

Berkowitz, A. "The Law and the Land: Why Biblical Israel has Artificial Territorial Boundaries." *Tradition* 28, no. 2 (1994): 34–43.

Birch, B. C., W. Brueggemann, T. E. Fretheim, D. L. Petersen, eds. *A Theological Introduction to the Old Testament*. Nashville: Abingdon Press, 2005.

Blomberg, C. *Matthew. The New American Commentary*. Nashville: Broadman & Holman Publishers, 1992.

Bock, D. L. "The Reign of the Lord Christ." In *Dispensationalism, Israel and the Church: The Search for Definition,* edited by D. L. Bock, W. C. Kaiser and C. A. Blaising, 37–67. Grand Rapids: Zondervan, 1992.

———. *Luke 1:1-9:50,* Grand Rapids: Baker Books, 1994.

———. *Luke 9:51-24:53,* Grand Rapids: Baker Books, 1996.

———. *Acts*. Grand Rapids: Baker Academic, 2007.

Bock, D. L., W. C. Kaiser and C. A. Blaising, eds. *Dispensationalism, Israel and the Church: The Search for Definition*. Grand Rapids: Zondervan, 1992.

Boorer, S. "The Importance of a Diachronic Approach: The Case of Genesis-Kings." *The Catholic Biblical quarterly* 51, no. 2 (1989): 195–208.

Brand, J. "Sabbath-rest, Worship, and the Epistle to the Hebrews: Welebrating the Rule of Yahweh." *Didaskalia* 1, no. 2 (1990): 3–13.

Bravermann, M. *Fatal Embrace.* Texas: Synergy Books, 2010.

Bremmer, J. N. "Paradise: From Persia, via Greece, into the Septuagint." In *Paradise Interpreted: Representations of Biblical Paradise in Judaism and Christianity,* edited by G. Luttikhuizen, 1–20., Leiden: Brill, 1999.

Brown, F. "A Recent Theory of the Garden of Eden." *The Old Testament Student* (1884): 1–12.

Brown, F., S. Driver and C. Briggs. *The Brown-Driver-Briggs Hebrew and English Lexicon.* Peabody: Hendrickson Publishers, 1996.

Bruce, F. F. "The Bible and the environment." In *Living and Active Word of God Essays in Honor of Samuel J. Schultz,* edited by M. Inch and R. Youngblood, 15–29. Winona Lake: Eisenbrauns, 1983.

———. *This is That. The New Testament Development of Some Old Testament Themes.* London: Paternoster,1968.

———. *1 & 2 Thessalonians. Word Biblical Commentary.* Waco: Word Books, 1982.

———. *The Epistle to the Galatians: A Commentary on the Greek Text.* Grand Rapids: Eerdmans, 1982.

———. *The Acts of the Apostles: The Greek Text With Introduction and Commentary.* Grand Rapids: Eerdmans, 1990.

Brueggemann, W. "David and his Theologian." *Catholic Biblical Quarterly* 30 (1968): 156–181.

———. "From Dust to Kingship." *Zeitschrift für die Alttestamentliche Wissenschaft* 84, no. 1 (1972): 1–18.

———. "'Vine and Fig Tree': A Case Study in Imagination and Criticism." *Catholic Biblical Quarterly Washington, D. C.,* 43, no. 2 (1981): 188–204.

———. *Genesis: Interpretation: A Bible Commentary for Teaching and Preaching.* Atlanta: John Knox Press, 1982.

———. "The Earth is the Lord's: A Theology of Earth and Land." *Sojourners Magazine* 15, no. 9 (1986): 28–32.

———. "Genesis 17: 1–22." *Interpretation* 45, no. 1 (1991): 55–59.

———. *Theology of the Old Testament: Testimony, Dispute, Advocacy.* Minneapolis: Fortress Press, 1997.

———. "The Hope of Heaven . . . on Earth." *Biblical Theology Bulletin: A Journal of Bible and Theology* 29, no. 3 (1999): 99.

———. "The City in Biblical Perspective: Failed and Possible." *Word And World* 19 (1999): 236–250.

———. *The Land: Place as Gift, Promise, and Challenge in Biblical Faith,* Minneapolis: Fortress Press, 2002.

———. *An Introduction to the Old Testament: The Canon and Christian Imagination.* Louisville: Westminster John Knox Press, 2003.

———. "To Whom Does The Land Belong?" *Journal for Preachers* 30, no. 3 (2007): 28–35.

———. *Old Testament Theology: An Introduction,* Nashville: Abingdon Press, 2008.

Bruno, C. R. "'Jesus is Our Jubilee' . . . But How? The OT Background and Lukan Fulfilment of the Ethics of the Jubilee," *JETS* 53, no. 1 (2010): 81–101.

Bryan, S. M. *Jesus and Israel's Traditions of Judgement and Restoration.* Cambridge: Cambridge University Press, 2002.

Burge, G. M. *Whose Land? Whose Promise?: What Christians are not Being Told about Israel and the Palestinians,* illustrated ed. Cleveland: Pilgrim Press, 2003.

———. "Land." In *The New Interpreter's Dictionary of the Bible. I-Ma (Vol. 3),* edited by K. D. Sakenfeld, 570–575. Nashville: Abingdon Press, 2006.

———. *The Bible and the Land.* Grand Rapids: Zondervan, 2009.

———. *Jesus and The Land: The New Testament Challenge to 'Holy Land' Theology.* Grand Rapids: Baker Academic, 2010.

Burns, D. E. "Dream Form in Genesis 2.4 b-3.24: Asleep in the Garden." *Journal for the Study of the Old Testament* 12, no. 37 (1987): 3.

Callender, D. E. *Adam in Myth and History: Ancient Israelite Perspectives on the Primal Human.* Winona Lake: Eisenbrauns, 2000.

Cardin, N. B. "The Place of Place in Jewish Tradition." *CrossCurrents* 59, no. 2 (2009): 210–216.

Carson, D. A. and D. J. Moo. *An Introduction to the New Testament.* Grand Rapids: Zondervan, 2005.

Cassuto, U. *A Commentary on the Book of Genesis I.* Jerusalem: Magnes Press, Hebrew University, 1961.

Chanikuzhy, J. *Jesus, the Eschatological Temple: An Exegetical Study of Jn 2:13-22 in the Light of the pre-70 C.E. Eschatological Temple Hopes and the Synoptic Temple Action.* Leuven: Peeters, 2012.

Chapman, C. *Whose Promised Land? The Continuing Crisis Over Israel and Palestine.* Grand Rapids: Baker Books, 2002..

———. *Whose Holy City?: Jerusalem and the Israeli-Palestinian Conflict.* Lion: Oxford, 2004.

Charlesworth, J. H. "Paradise." In *The Anchor Bible Dictionary*, edited by D. N. Freedman, 154–155. New York: Doubleday, 1992.

Childs, B. S. *Exodus.* London: SCM Press, 1974.

———. *Biblical Theology of the Old and New Testaments: Theological Reflection on the Christian Bible.* Minneapolis: Fortress Press, 1993.

Chilton, B. *Pure Kingdom: Jesus' Vision of God.* London: SPCK, 1996.

Church, P. "Dispensational Christian Zionism: A Strange but Acceptable Aberration or a Deviant Heresy?" *WTJ* 71 (2009): 375–398.

Clements, R. E. *God and Temple.* Oxford: Basil Blackwell, 1965.

Clifford, R. J. *The Cosmic Mountain in Canaan and the Old Testament.* Cambridge: Harvard University Press, 1972.

Clines, D. J. A. "The Tree of Knowledge and the Law of Yahweh." *VT* 24 (1974): 8–14.

———. *The Theme of the Pentateuch.* Sheffield: JSOT Press, 1997.

Cohn, R. "From Homeland to the Holy Land: The Territoriality of Torah." *Continuum*, 1, no. 1 (1990): 4–14.

Colins, R. "Temple, Jerusalem." In *The Anchor Bible Dictionary*, edited by D. N. Freedman, 350–383, New York: Doubleday, 1992.

Collins, J. J. "The Exodus and Biblical Theology." *Biblical Theology Bulletin* 25, no. 4 (1995), 152.

Colpe, C. "ὁ υἱὸς τοῦ ἀνθρώπου." In *Theological Dictionary of the New Testament. Volume VIII*, edited by G. Bromiley and G. Friedrich, 400–477. Grand Rapids: Eerdmans, 1972.

Cooper, L. E. *Vol. 17: Ezekiel.* The New American Commentary. Nashville: Broadman & Holman Publishers, 1994.

Crawford, T. G. "Taking the Promised Land, Leaving the Promised Land: Luke's Use of Joshua for a Christian Foundation Story." *Review and Expositor* 95 (1998): 251–262.

Cundall, A. E. "Sanctuary." In *Baker Encyclopaedia of the Bible*, edited by W. A. Elwell and B. J. Beitzel, 1902. Grand Rapids: Baker Book House.

Curtis, A. *Oxford Bible Atlas.* Oxford: Oxford University Press, 2007.

Darr, K. P. "The Wall around Paradise: Ezekielian Ideas about the Future." *Vetus Testamentum* (1987): 271–279.

Dauphinais, M. and M. Levering. *Holy People, Holy Land: A Theological Introduction to the Bible.* Grand Rapids: Brazos Press, 2005.

Davies, W. D. "Paul and the People of Israel." *New Testament Studies* 24, no. 1 (1977): 4–39.

———. *The Territorial Dimension of Judaism.* Minneapolis: Fortress Press, 1991.

———. *The Gospel and the Land: Early Christianity and Jewish Territorial Doctrine.* Sheffield: JSOT Press, 1994.

DeWitt, C. B., ed. *The Environment and the Christian: What Can We Learn from the New Testament.* Grand Rapids: Baker Book House, 1991.

Derrett, J. D. M. "Whatever Happened to the Land Flowing with Milk and Honey?" *Vigiliae Christianae* (1984): 178–184.

Dillard, R. B. "Zion." In *Baker Encyclopaedia of the Bible*, edited by W. A. Elwell and B. J. Beitzel, 2199–2203, Grand Rapids: Baker Book House, 1988.

Dillard, R. B. and T. Longman. *An Introduction to the Old Testament.* Grand Rapids: Zondervan, 1994.

Donaldson, A.W. *The Last Days of Dispensationalism: A Scholarly Critique of Popular Misconceptions.* Eugene: Wipf & Stock, 2011.

Donaldson, T. L. *Jesus on the Mountain: A Study in Matthean Theology.* Sheffield: JSOT Press, 1985.

Dumbrell, W. J. *Covenant and Creation: An Old Testament Covenantal Theology.* Carlisle: Paternoster, 1984.

———. "The Prospect of Unconditionality in the Sinaitic Covenant." In *Israel's Apostasy and Restoration. Essays in Honor of Roland K. Harrison,* edited by A. Gileadi, 141–155. Grand Rapids: Baker, 1988.

———. *The Search for Order: Biblical Eschatology in Focus.* Grand Rapids: Baker Book House, 1994.

———. "Genesis 2:1-3: Biblical Theology of Creation Covenant." *Evangelical Review of Theology* 25, no. 3 (2001): 219–230.

Dunn, J. D. G. *Romans. 1-8. Word Biblical Commentary.* Dallas: Word Books, 1988.

———. *Romans. 9-16. Word Biblical Commentary.* Dallas: Word Books, 1988.

———. *Christology in the Making: A New Testament Inquiry into the Origins of the Doctrine of the Incarnation,* second ed. London: SCM Press, 1989.

———. *Jesus and the Spirit: A Study of the Religious and Charismatic Experience of Jesus and the First Christians as Reflected in the New Testament.* Grand Rapids: Eerdmans, 1997.

———. *The Theology of Paul the Apostle.* Grand Rapids: Eerdmans, 1998.

———. *Jesus Remembered.* Grand Rapids: Eerdmans, 2003.

———. *The Partings of the Ways: Between Christianity and Judaism and their Significance for the Character of Christianity.* London: SCM Press, 2006.

———. *New Testament Theology: An Introduction.* Nashville: Abingdon Press, 2009.

———. *The Epistle to the Galatians.* Grand Rapids: Baker Publishing Group, 2011.

Durham, J. *Exodus. Word Biblical Commentary.* Waco: Word Books, 1987.

Ellingworth, P. *The Epistle to the Hebrews: A Commentary on the Greek Text. New International Greek Testament Commentary.* Grand Rapids/Carlisle: Eerdmans/Paternoster Press, 1993.

Elwell, W. A. and B. J. Beitzel, eds. *Baker Encyclopedia of the Bible.* Grand Rapids: Baker Book House, 1988.

Enns, P. *Inspiration and Incarnation: Evangelicals and the Problem of the Old Testament.* Grand Rapids: Baker Academic, 2005.

———. *The Evolution of Adam: What the Bible Does and Doesn't Say About Human Origins.* Grand Rapids: Brazos Press, 2012.

Essex, K. H. "The Abrahamic Covenant." *Master's Seminary Journal* 10, no. 2 (1999): 191–212.

Estes, D. J. "Looking for Abraham's City." *Bibliotheca Sacra* 147(588), (1990): 399–413.

Evans, C. A. "Jesus' Action in the Temple: Cleansing or Portent Destruction?" *The Catholic Biblical Quarterly* 51 (1989): 237–270.

———. *Mark 8:27-16:20. Word Biblical Commentary.* Nashville: Thomas Nelson, 2001.

———. "Defeating Satan and Liberating Israel: Jesus and Daniel's Visions." *JSHJ* 1, no. 2 (2003): 161–170.

Farr, B. C. and D. E. Singh, eds. *The Bible and Christian Ethics.* Oxford: Regnum Books, 2012.

Fee, G. D. *The First Epistle to the Corinthians.* Grand Rapids: Eerdmans, 1987.

France, R. T. *The Gospel of Mark: A Commentary on the Greek Text.* Grand Rapids: Eerdmans, 2002.

———. *The Gospel of Matthew.* Grand Rapids: Eerdmans, 2007.

Frankel, D. *The Land of Canaan and the Destiny of Israel: Theologies of Territory in the Hebrew Bible.* Winona Lake: Eisenbrauns, 2011.

Freedman, D. N. 1975, "Son of Man, Can These Bones Live?" *Interpretation* 29, no. 2 (1975): 171–186.

Gignilliat, M. S. *Paul and Isaiah's Servants: Paul's Theological Reading of Isaiah 40-66 in 2 Corinthians 5:14-6:10.* London: T&T Clark, 2007.

Gillingham, S. *Psalms Through The Centuries.* Oxford: Blackwell Pub, 2008.

Gleason, R. C. "The Old Testament Background of Rest in Hebrews 3: 7-4: 11." *Bibliotheca Sacra* 157 (2000): 281–303.

Gnuse, R. K. "An Overlooked Message: The Critique of Kings and Affirmation of Equality in the Primeval History." *Biblical Theology Bulletin: A Journal of Bible and Theology* 36, no. 4 (2006): 146.

Goldingay, J. "Jubilee Tithe." *Transformation* 19, no. 3 (2002): 198.

———. *Old Testament Theology: Israel's Gospel (Vol. 1)*. Downers Grove: InterVarsity Press, 2003.

———. "Covenant." In *The New Interpreter's Dictionary of the Bible,* 767–778. Nashville: Abingdon Press, 2006.

Gordon, R. P. *Holy Land, Holy City: Sacred Geography and the Interpretation of the Bible*. Carlisle: Paternoster Press, 2004.

———. *Hebrews*. Second ed. Sheffield: Sheffield Academic Press, 2008.

Gowan, D. E. "Wealth and Poverty in the Old Testament. The Case of the Widow, the Orphan, and the Sojourner." *Interpretation* 41, no. 4 (1987): 341–353.

———. *Eschatology in the Old Testament*. Edinburgh: T&T Clark Publishers, 2000.

Green, J. B. *The Gospel of Luke*. Grand Rapids: Eerdmans, 1997.

Gregory, B. C. "The Postexilic Exile in Third Isaiah: Isaiah 61:1–3 in Light of Second Temple Hermeneutics." *JBL* 126, no. 3 (2007): 475–496.

Grundke, C. L. K. "A Tempest in a Teapot? Genesis III 8 Again." *Vetus Testamentum* 51, no. 4 (2001): 548–551.

Guelich, R. *Mark 1-8:26. Word Biblical Commentary*. Dallas: Word Books, 1989.

Guthrie, D. *New Testament Theology*. Downers Grove: InterVarsity Press, 1981.

Haag, E. *Der Mensch am Anfang. Die Alttestamentliche Paradiesvorstellung Nach Gn 2-3. (Trierer Theologische Studien vol. 24)*. Trier: Paulinus, 1970.

Habel, N. C. *The Land is Mine: Six Biblical Land Ideologies*. Minneapolis: Fortress Press, 1995.

Hagner, D. A. *Matthew 1-13. Word Biblical Commentary*. Dallas: Word Books, 1993.

———. *Matthew 14-28. Word Biblical Commentary*. Dallas: Word Books, 1995.

Hahn, S. "Covenant in the Old and New Testaments: Some Current Research (1994-2004)." *Currents in Biblical Research* 3, no. 2 (2005): 263–292.

Hall, S. L. *Conquering Character: The Characterization of Joshua in Joshua 1-11*. New York: T&T Clark, 2010.

Hamilton, J. "The Seed of the Woman and The Blessings of Abraham." *Tyndale Bulletin* 58, no. 2 (2007): 253–273.

Hamilton, V. P. *The book of Genesis. Chapters 1-17*. Grand Rapids: Eerdmans, 1990.

Hammock, C. E. "Isaiah 56: 1-8 and the Redefining of the Restoration Judean Community." *Biblical Theology Bulletin* 30, no. 2 (2000): 46.

Hansen, G. W. *Galatians*. Downers Grove: InterVarsity Press, 1994.

Harris, M. J. *The Second Epistle to the Corinthians: A Commentary on the Greek Text. New International Greek Testament Commentary*. Grand Rapids/Carlisle: Eerdmans/Paternoster Press, 2005.

Hartropp, A. *What Is Economic Justice?: Biblical And Secular Perspectives Contrasted*. Milton Keynes: Paternoster, 2007.

Havrelock, R. "The Two Maps of Israel's Land." *Journal of Biblical Literature* 126, no. 4 (2007): 649–667.

Hays, R. B. *Echoes of Scripture in the Letters of Paul*. New Haven: Yale University Press, 1989.

———. "Reading Scripture in Light of the Resurrection." In *The Art of Reading Scripture*, edited by R. B. Hays and E. F. Davis, 216–238. Grand Rapids: Eerdmans, 2003.

Herion, G. A. and G. E. Mendenhall. "Covenant." In *The Anchor Bible Dictionary (Vol. 1)*, edited by D. N. Freedman, 1179–1202. New York: Doubleday, 1992.

Herron, R. B. "The Land, the Law, and the Poor." *Word & World* 6, no. 1 (1986): 76–84.

Hill, A. "The Ebal Ceremony as Hebrew Land Grant?" *JETS* 31 (1988): 399–406.

Holwerda, D. E. *Jesus and Israel: One Covenant or Two?* Grand Rapids: Eerdmans, 1995.

Hoppe, L. J. *The Holy City: Jerusalem in the Theology of the Old Testament*. Collegeville: Liturgical Press, 2000.

Horbury, W. "Land, Sanctuary and Worship." In *Early Christian Thought in its Jewish Context*, edited by J. M. G. Barclay and M. D. Hooker, 207–224. Cambridge University Press, Cambridge; New York, 1996.

Horsley, R. A. *Jesus and Empire: The Kingdom of God and the New World Disorder*. Minneapolis: Fortress Press, 2003.

House, P. R. "Creation in Old Testament theology." *Southern Baptist Journal of Theology* 5, no. 3 (2001): 4–17.

Howard-Brook, W. *"Come Out My people!": God's Call Out of Empire in the Bible and Beyond*. Maryknoll: Orbis Books, 2010.

Hugenberger, G. P. "The Servant of the Lord in the 'Servant Songs' of Isaiah: A Second Moses." In *The Lord's Anointed. Interpretation of Old Testament Messianic Texts,* edited by P. E. Satterthwaite, R. S. Hess and G. J. Wenham, 105–140. Grand Rapids: Baker, 1995.

Hughes, P. E. *A Commentary on the Epistle to the Hebrews.* Grand Rapids: Eerdmans, 1977.

Hultgren, S. "The Origin of Paul's Doctrine of the Two Adams in 1 Corinthians 15.45-49." *Journal for the Study of the New Testament* 25, no. 3 (2003): 343.

Inge, J. *A Christian Theology of Place.* Burlington: Ashgate, 2003.

———. "Towards a Theology of Place." *Modern Believing* 40, no. 1 (1999): 42–50.

Janowski, B. "The One God of the Two Testaments: Basic Questions of a Biblical Theology." *Theology Today* 57, no. 3 (2000): 297–324.

Janzen, W. "Land." In *The Anchor Bible Dictionary,* edited by D. N. Freedman, 143–154. New York: Doubleday, 1992.

Japhet, S. "Conquest and Settlement in Chronicles." *Journal of Biblical Literature*, (1979): 205–218.

Jeremias, J. *New Testament Theology.* Translated by J. Bowden. London: SCM Press, 1971.

Jeschke, M. *Rethinking Holy Land: A Study in Salvation Geography.* Scottdale: Herald Press, 2005.

Johnston, P. S. and P. W. L. Walker, eds. *The Land of Promise: Biblical, Theological and Contemporary Perspectives.* Downers Grove: Intervarsity Press, 2000.

Joosten, J. *People and Land in the Holiness Code: An Exegetical Study of the Ideational Framework of the Law in Leviticus 17-26.* Leiden: Brill, 1996.

Juster, D. "A Messianic Jew Looks at the Land Promises." In *The Land Cries Out: Theology of the Land in the Israeli-Palestinian Context,* edited by S. Munayer and L. Loden, 63–81. Eugene: CASCADE Books, 2012.

Kaiser, W. C. "The Promise Theme and the Theology of Rest." *Bibliotheca Sacra* 130(518), (1973): 135–50.

———. "The Davidic Promise and the Inclusion of the Gentiles (Amos 9:9-15 and Acts 15:13-18): A Test Passage for Theological Systems." *JETS* 20 (1977): 97–111.

———. "The Promised Land: A Biblical-Historical View." *Bibliotheca Sacra,* 138(552), (1981): 302–12.

Kallai, Z. "The Southern Border of the Land of Israel: Pattern and Application." *Vetus Testamentum,* (1987): 438–445.

Kallai, Z. "The Patriarchal Boundaries, Canaan and the Land of Israel: Patterns and Application in Biblical Historiography." *Israel Exploration Journal* 47, no. 1-2 (1997): 69–82.

Katanacho, Y. "Christ is the Owner of Haaretz." *Christian Scholars Review* 34, no. 4 (2005): 425.

———. "Jerusalem is the City of God: A Palestinian Reading of Psalm 87." In *The Land Cries Out. Theology of the Land in the Israeli-Palestinian Context*, edited by S. Munayer and L. Loden, 181–199. Eugene: Wipf and Stock, 2012a.

———. *The Land of Christ*. Bethlehem: Bethlehem Bible College, 2012b.

———. "Reading the Gospel of John Through Palestinian Eyes." Paper presented at Institute of Biblical Research, Chicago, November 16, 2012.

Kawashima, R. S. "The Jubilee Year and the Return of Cosmic Purity." *The Catholic Biblical Quarterly* 65, no. 3 (2003): 370–389.

Kedar-Kopfstein, B. "עדִי." in *Theological dictionary of the Old Testament. 10, naqam - 'azab*, edited by G. J. Botterweck, H. Ringgren and H. Fabry, 481–491. Grand Rapids: Eerdmans, 2001.

Kennedy, J. M. "Peasants in Revolt: Political Allegory in Genesis 2-3." *Journal for the Study of the Old Testament* 15, no. 47 (1990): 3.

Keulen, E. J. "Reversal of a Motif: The Land Is Given into the Hand of the Wicked. The Gift of Land in Some Wisdom Texts." In *The land of Israel in Bible, History, and Theology: Studies in Honour of Ed Noort*, edited by J. Van Ruiten and J. C. De Vos, 197–209. Leiden: Brill, 2009.

Kline, M. G. "The Two Tables of the Covenant." *Westminster Theological Journal* 22 (1960): 133–146.

———. *Kingdom Prologue: Genesis Foundations for a Covenantal Worldview*, Overland Park: Two Age Press, 2000.

———. *Treaty of the Great Kings: The Covenant Structure of Deuteronomy*. Eugene: Wipf & Stock Publishers, 2012.

Korn, E. B. *The Jewish Connection to Israel, The Promised Land: A Brief Introduction for Christians*. Woodstock: Jewish Lights Pub, 2008.

———. "Jewish Reflections on Richard Lux's 'The Land of Israel (Eretz Yisrael) in Jewish and Christian Understanding.'" *Studies in Christian-Jewish Relations'* 3, no. 1 (2009): 1–5.

Kvalbein, H. "The Kingdom of God in the Ethics of Jesus." *Studia Theologica* 55, no. 1 (1997): 60–84.

Kwakkel, G. "The Land in the Book of Hosea," in *The Land of Israel in Bible, History, and Theology: Studies in Honour of Ed Noort*, edited by J. Van Ruiten & J. C. De Vos, 167–182. Leiden: Brill, 2009.

L'Hour, J. "Yahweh Elohim." *RB* 81 (1974): 524–556.

Laansma, J. "'I Will Give You Rest': The Background and Significance of the Rest Motif in the New Testament." *Tyndale Bulletin* 46 (1995): 385–388.

Ladd, G. E. *A Theology of the New Testament*. Grand Rapids: Eerdmans, 1993.

Landau, Y., "The Land of Israel in Jewish-Christian-Muslim Relations." *Studies in Christian-Jewish Relations* 3, no. 1 (2008): 17.

Lane, W. L. *Hebrews 1-8. Word Biblical Commentary*. Dallas Word Books, 1991.

Leder, A. C. "Paradise Lost: Reading the Former Prophets by the Rivers of Babylon." *Calvin Theological Journal* 37, no. 1 (2002): 9–27.

Léon-Dufour, Xavier. *Dictionary of Biblical Theology*. London: Geoffrey Chapman, 1973.

Lessing, R. R. "Isaiah's Servant in Chapters 40–55. Clearing up the Confusion." *Concordia Journal* (Spring 2011): 130–134.

Levenson, J. D. *Sinai & Zion: An Entry Into the Jewish Bible*. New York: HarperSanFrancisco, 1987.

———. "The Davidic Covenant and its Modern Interpreters." *The Catholic Biblical Quarterly* 41 (1979): 205–219.

Levine, E. "The Land of Milk and Honey." *Journal for the Study of the Old Testament* 25, no. 87 (2000): 43–57.

Lewis, A. H. "The Localization of the Garden of Eden." *Bulletin of the Evangelical Theological Society* 11, no. 4 (1968): 169–175.

Lewy, J. "The Two Strata of the Eden Story." *HUCA* 27 (1956): 93–99.

Lilburne, G. R. *A Sense of Place: A Christian Theology of the Land*. Nashville: Abingdon Press, 1989.

Lincoln, A. T. *Ephesus. Word Biblical Commentary*. Waco: Word Books, 1990.

Lindblad, U. "A Note on the Nameless Servant in Isaiah XLII 1-4." *Vetus Testamentum* 34, no. 1 (1993): 115–119.

Lipinski, M. "נחל." in *Theological Dictionary of the Old Testament (Vol. 9)*, edited by H. Ringgren and G. H. Botterweck, 319–335. Grand Rapids: Eerdmans, 1998.

Lohfink, N. *Das Siegeslied am Schilfmeer: Christliche Auseinandersetzungen mit dem Alten Testament*. Frankfurt am Main: Josef Knecht Verlag, 1965.

Longenecker, R. N. *Galatians. Word Biblical Commentary*. Dallas: Word Books, 1990.

Louw, J. P. and E. A. Nida. *Greek-English Lexicon of the New Testament: Based on Semantic Domains (Vol. 1)*. New York: United Bible Societies, 1996.

Luttikhuizen, G. P., ed. *Paradise Interpreted: Representations of Biblical Paradise in Judaism and Christianity*. Leiden: Brill, 1999.

Lux, R. C. "The Land of Israel (Eretz Yisra'el) in Jewish and Christian Understanding." *Studies in Christian-Jewish Relations* 3, no. 1 (2008): 4.

March, W. E. *God's Land On Loan: Israel, Palestine, and the World*. Louisville: Westminster John Knox Press, 2007.

Marchadour, A. and D. Neuhaus. *The Land, the Bible, and History: Toward the Land That I Will Show You*. New York: Fordham University, 2007.

Marshall, I. H. *The Gospel of Luke: A Commentary on the Greek Text*. New International Greek Testament Commentary. Carlisle: Paternoster Press, 1978.

———. *The Acts of the Apostles: An Introduction and Commentary*. Grand Rapids Eerdmans, 1980.

———. "Son of Man." In *Dictionary of Jesus and the Gospels*, edited by J. B. Green, S. McKnight and I. H. Marshall, 775–781, Downers Grove: InterVarsity Press, 1992.

Martin, R. *2 Corinthians*. World Biblical Commentary. Waco: Word Books, 1986.

Mason, J. D. "Biblical Teaching on Assisting the Poor." In *The Bible and Christian Ethics*, edited by D. E. Singh and B. C. Farr, 23–50. Oxford: Regnum Books, 2012.

McCartney, D. G. "Ecce Homo: The Coming of the Kingdom as the Restoration of Human Vicegerency." *The Westminster Theological Journal* 56, no. 1 (1994): 1–21.

McComiskey, T. E. *The Covenants of Promise: A Theology of the Old Testament Covenants*. Nottingham: Inter-Varsity Press, 1985.

———. *The Minor Prophets: An Exegetical and Expository Commentary*. Grand Rapids: Baker Book House, 1992.

McConville, J. G. "Jerusalem in the Old Testament." In *Jerusalem Past and Present in the Purposes of God*, edited by P. W. L. Walker, 21–51. Carlisle: Paternoster Press, 1992.

———. "Biblical Theology: Canon and Plain Sense (Finlayson Memorial Lecture 2001)." *Scottish Bulletin of Evangelical Theology* 19 (2001): 129–133.

———. *Deuteronomy*. Downers Grove: InterVarsity Press, 2002.

McIver, R. K. "The Parable of the Weeds among the Wheat (Matt 13:24-30, 36-43) and the Relationship between the Kingdom and the Church as Portrayed in the Gospel of Matthew." *Journal of Biblical Literature* 114, no. 4 (1995): 643–659.

Meadowcroft. "Method and Old Testament Theology. Barr, Brueggemann and Goldingay Considered." *Tyndale Bulletin* 57, no. 1 (2006).

Mendenhall, G. E. "Covenant Forms in Israelite Tradition." *The Biblical Archaeologist* 17, no. 3 (1954): 49–76.

Mettinger, T. N. D. *A Farewell to the Servant Songs: A Critical Examination of an Exegetical Axiom*. Lund: CWK Gleerup, 1983.

———. *The Eden Narrative: A Literary and Religio-Historical Study of Genesis 2-3*. Winona Lake: Eisenbrauns, 2007.

Middleton, J. R. "The Liberating Image? Interpreting the Imago Dei in Context." *Christian Scholars Review* 24, no. 1 (1994): 8–25.

———. *The Liberating Image: The Imago Dei in Genesis 1*. Grand Rapids: Brazos Press, 2005.

———. "A New Heaven and a New Earth: The Case for a Holistic Reading of the Biblical Story of Redemption." *Journal for Christian Theological Research* 11 (2006): 73–97.

Millar, J. G. "Land." In *New Dictionary of Biblical Theology*, edited by T. D. Alexander and B. S. Rosner, 623–627, Downers Grove: InterVarsity Press, 2000.

Millard, A. R. "The Etymology of Eden." *Vetus Testamentum* 34, no. 1 (1984): 103–106.

Miller, P. D. "The Gift of God: the Deuteronomic Theology of the Land." *Interpretation* 23 (1969): 451–465.

———. "Syntax and Theology in Genesis XII 3a." *Vetus Testamentum* (1984): 472–476.

———. "The Land in the Psalms." In *The land of Israel in Bible, History, and Theology: Studies in Honour of Ed Noort*, edited by J. Van Ruiten and J. C. De Vos, 183–196. Leiden: Brill, 2009.

Minear, P. S. "Holy People, Holy Land, Holy City. The Genesis and Genius of Christian Attitudes." *Interpretation. A Journal of Bible and Theology* 37, no. 1 (1983): 18–31.

Miscall. "Jacques Deridda: In the Garden of Eden." *Union Seminars Quarterly Review* 44 (1990): 1–9.

Mitchel, T. C. "Eden, Garden of." In *New Bible Dictionary*, edited by H. Marchal, A. R. Millard, J. I. Packer and D. J. Wiseman, 289–290, Nottingham: IVP Academic, 1996.

Moo, D. J. *The Epistle to the Romans*. Grand Rapids: Eerdmans, 1996.

Morray-Jones, C. R. A. "Paradise Revisited (2 Cor 12:1-12): The Jewish Mystical Background of Paul's Apostolato. Part 1: The Jewish Sources." *The Harvard Theological Review* 86, no. 2 (1993): 177–217.

———. "Paradise Revisited (2 Cor 12: 1-12): The Jewish Mystical Background of Paul's Apostolate. Part 2: Paul's Heavenly Ascent and Its Significance." *The Harvard Theological Review* 86, no. 3 (1993): 265–292.

Morris, P. "Exiled from Eden: Jewish Interpretations of Genesis." In *A Walk in the Garden. Biblical, Iconographical and Literary Images of Eden*, edited by P. Morris and D. Sawyer, 117–166. Sheffield: JSOT Press, 1992.

Motyer, S. "The Temple in Hebrews: Is it There?" In *Heaven on Earth*, edited by S. Gathercole and T. D. Alexander, 177–190. Carlisle: Paternoster Press, 2004.

Muilenburg, J. "Abraham and the Nations: Blessing and World History." *Interpretation* 19 (1965): 387–398.

Munayer, S. and L. Loden. *The Land Cries Out: Theology of the Land in the Israeli-Palestinian Context*. Eugene: CASCADE Books, 2012.

Munayer, S. "From Land of Strife to Land of Reconciliation." In *The Land Cries Out*, edited by S. Munayer and L. Loden, 234–265. Eugene: Wipf & Stock, 2010.

Munday, J. C. "Eden's Geography Erodes Flood Geology." *The Westminster Theological Journal*, 58, no. 1 (1996): 123–154.

Neher, A. "The Land as Locus of the Sacred." In *Voices from Jerusalem. Jews and Christians Reflect on the Holy Land*, edited by D. Burrell and Y. Landau, 18–29. New York : Paulist Press, 1992.

Neiman, D. "Eden, the Garden of God." *Acta Antiqua Academiae Scientiarum Hungaricae* 17 (1969): 109–124.

Neumann-Gosolke, U. "'And the Land Was Subdued Before Them ...'? Some Remarks On The Meaning of כבש in Joshua 18:1 and Related Texts." In *The Land of Israel in Bible, History, and Theology: Studies in Honour of Ed Noort*, edited by J. Van Ruiten and J. C. De Vos, 73–86. Leiden: Brill, 2009.

Niditch, S. "Ezekiel 40–48 in a Visionary Context." *Catholic Biblical Quarterly* Washington, D. C. 48, no. 2 (1986): 208–224.

Niehaus, J. "In the Wind of the Storm: Another Look At Genesis III 8." *Vetus Testamentum* 44, no. 2 (1994): 263–7.

Nolland, J. *Luke 1-9:20. Word Biblical Commentary*. Waco: Word Books, 1982.

———. *Luke 9:21-18:34. Word biblical Commentary*. Nashville: Thomas Nelson, 1993.

Noort, E. "Gan-Eden in the Context of the Mythology of the Hebrew Bible." In *Paradise Interpreted: Representations of Biblical Paradise in Judaism and Christianity,* edited by G. P. Luttikhuizen, 21–36. Leiden: Brill, 1999.

Odell, M. S. *Ezekiel.* Macon: Smyth & Helwys Pub, 2005.

Olson, D. T. "Biblical Perspectives on the Land." *Word & World* 6, no. 1 (1986): 18–27.

Orlinsky, H. M. "The So-Called 'Servant of the Lord' and 'Suffering Servant' in Second Isaiah." *Vestus Testamentum Supplements* 14 (1967): 1–134.

Orlinsky, H. M. "The Biblical Concept of the Land of Israel: Cornerstone of the Covenant between God and Israel." In *The Land of Israel: Jewish Perspectives,* edited by L. A. Hoffman, 27–64. Notre Dame: University of Notre Dame Press, 1986.

Otto, E. "Die Paradieserzahlung Genesis 2-3: Eine nachpriesterschriftliche Lehrerzahlung in ihrem religionshistorischen Kontex." *BZAW* 241 (1996): 167–192.

Ottosson, M. "ארץ." In *Theological Dictionary of the Old Testament,* edited by G. J. Botterweck and H. Ringgern, 388–405. Grand Rapids: Eerdmans, 1997.

Ottosson, M. "Eden and the Land of Promise." In *Congress Volume, Jerusalem 1986,* edited by J. A. Emerton, 177–188. Leiden: Brill, 1986.

Overstreet, R. L. "A Study of 2 Peter 3:10-13." *Bibliotheca Sacra* 137(548), (1980): 354–371.

Pawlikowski, J. "Land as an Issue in the Christian-Jewish Dialogue." *Cross Currents,* 59, no. 2 (2009): 197–209.

Pennington, J. T. and S. M. McDonough, eds. *Cosmology and New Testament Theology.* London: T & T Clark, 2008.

Pierce, R. W. "Covenant Conditionally and a Future for Israel." *JETS* 37 (1994): 27–38.

Polhill, J. B. *Acts. The New American Commentary (Vol. 26).* Nashville: Broadman & Holman Publishers, 1995.

Postell, S. D. *Adam as Israel: Genesis 1-3 as the Introduction to the Torah and Tanakh.* Eugene: Pickwick Publications, 2011.

Potter, H. D. "The New Covenant in Jeremiah XXXI 31-34." *Vetus Testamentum* (1983): 347–357.

Poythress, V. S. *Understanding Dispensationalists.* Phillipsburg: P&R, 1994.

Preuss, H. D. *Old Testament Theology. Volume I.* Louisville: Westminster John Knox Press, 1995.

———. *Old Testament Theology. Volume II.* Louisville: Westminster John Knox Press, 1996.

Primus, C. "The Borders of Judaism: The Land of Israel in Early Rabbinic Judaism." In *The Land of Israel: Jewish Perspectives*, edited by L. Hoffman, 97–108. Notre Dame: University of Notre Dame Press, 1986.

Provan, I. W. *Tenants in God's Land: Earth-Keeping and People-Keeping in the Old Testament.* Cambridge: Grove Books, 2008.

Raheb, M. "Towards a New Hermeneutics of Liberation: A Palestinian Christian Perspective. " In *The Biblical Text in the Context of Occupation: Towards a New Hermeneutics of Liberation,* edited by M. Raheb, 11–28. Bethlehehm: Diyar, 2012.

Ramsey, G. W. "Is Name-Giving an Act of Domination in Genesis 2:23 and Elsewhere?" *The Catholic Biblical Quarterly* 50, no. 1 (1988): 24–35.

Redford, D. B. "The 'Land of the Hebrews' in Gen. XL 15." *Vetus Testamentum* (1965): 529–532.

Rendtroff, R. "Canonical Interpretation: A New Approach to Biblical Texts." *Pro Ecclesia* 3, no. 2 (1994): 141–151.

———. *The Canonical Hebrew Bible: A Theology of the Old Testament.* Leiden: Deo, 2005.

Ridderbos, H. N. *The Coming of the Kingdom.* New Jersey: Presbyterian and Reformed, 1962.

Ridling, Z. *The Bible Atlas.* The Access Foundation, 2000.

Robertson, E. "Where Was Eden?" *The American Journal of Semitic Languages and Literatures* (1912): 254–273.

Robertson, O. P. *The Christ of the Covenants.* Grand Rapids: Baker Book House, 1980.

———. *The Israel of God: Yesterday, Today, and Tomorrow.* Phillipsburg P&R: 2000a.

———. "A New Covenant Perspective on the Land." In *The Land of Promise: Biblical, Theological and Contemporary Perspectives,* edited by P. W. L. Walker and P. S. Johnston, 121–141. Downers Grove: InterVarsity Press, 2000b.

Rowley, H. H. *The Servant of the Lord and other Essays on the Old Testament.* Oxford: B. Blackwell, 1952.

Ryken, L., J. Wilhoit, T. Longman, C. Duriez, D. Penney and D. G. Reid. *Dictionary of Biblical Imagery.* Downers Grove: InterVarsity Press, 1998.

Ryrie, C. C. *Dispensationalism.* Chicago: Moody Publishers, 2007.

Samuel, V. and C. Sudgen, eds. *Mission as Transformation: A Theology of the Whole Gospel.* Oxford: Regnum, 1999.

Sanders, E. P. *Paul and Palestinian Judaism: A Comparison of Patterns of Religion.* London: SCM, 1977.

---. *Jesus and Judaism*. Philadelphia: Fortress Press, 1985.
Sasse, H. "γῆ." In *Theological Dictionary of the New Testament,* edited by G. Kittel, 677–681. Grand Rapids: Eerdmans, 1969.
Saucy, R. L. "The Church as the Mystery of God." In *Dispensationalism, Israel and the Church: The Search for Definition,* edited by D. L. Bock, W. C. Kaiser and C. A. Blaising, 127–155. Grand Rapids: Zondervan Pub. House, 1992.
Schmitt, J. J. "Israel as Son of God in Torah." *Biblical Theology Bulletin: A Journal of Bible and Theology* 34, no. 2 (2004): 69.
Schowalter, D. N. "Churches in Context. The Jesus Movement in the Roman World." In *The Oxford History of the Biblical World,* edited by M. D. Coogan, 388–419. Oxford: Oxford University Press, 1998.
Schwartz, D. R. "The End of the ΓΗ (Acts 1:8): Beginning or End of the Christian Vision?" *Journal of Biblical Literature,* (1986): 669–676.
Seebass, H. "'Holy' Land in the Old Testament: Numbers and Joshua." *Vetus Testamentum* 56, no. 1 (2006): 92–104.
Selman, M. "The Kingdom of God in the Old Testament." *Tyndale Bulletin* 40, no. 2 (1989): 161–183.
Shepherd, M. B. "Daniel 7:13 and the New Testament Son of Man." *WTJ* 86 (2006): 99–111.
Sider, R. J. and S. Mott. "A Biblical Paradigm for Economic Justice." In *The Bible and Christian Ethics,* edited by D. E. Singh and B. C. Farr, 84–116. Oxford: Regnum Books, 2012.
Simkins, R. *Creator & Creation: Nature in the Worldview of Ancient Israel.* Peabody: Hendrickson Publishers, 1994.
Sizer, S. *Christian Zionism: Road Map to Armageddon?* Downers Grove: IVP Academic, 2004.
---. *Zion's Christian Soldiers? The Bible, Israel and The Church*. Nottingham: Inter-Varsity Press, 2007.
Sloan, I. B. "Ezekiel and the Covenant of Friendship." *Biblical Theology Bulletin: A Journal of Bible and Theology* 22, no. 4 (1992): 149.
Smith, A. "The Fifth Gospel." In *Eyes to See, Ears to Hear. Essays in Memory of J. Alan Groves,* edited by P. Enns, D. Green and M. Kelly, 77–91. Phillipsburg: P&R, 2010.
Smith, R. O. *More Desired than Our Own Salvation: The Roots of Christian Zionism.* Oxford: Oxford University Press, 2013.
Snaith, N. H. "Isaiah 40-66: A Study of the Teaching of the Second Isaiah and its Consequences." *Vetus Testamentum Supplements* 14 (1967): 135–264.

Soulen, R. K. *The God of Israel and Christian Theology.* Minneapolis: Fortress Press, 1996.

Speiser, E. A. "The Rivers of Paradise." In *Oriental and Biblical Studies,* edited by J. J. Finkelstein and M. Greenberg, 23–34. Philadelphia: University of Pennsylvania, 1967.

Spero, S. "Who Authorized Israelite Settlement East of the Jordan?" *Jewish Bible Quarterly* 35, no. 1 (2007): 11–15.

———. "Paradise Lost or Outgrown?" *Tradition* 41, no. 2 (2008): 256–274.

Stassen, G. H. *Just Peacemaking: Transforming Initiatives for Justice and Peace.* Louisville: Westminster John Knox Press, 1992.

Stern, P. D. "The Origin and Significance of 'The Land Flowing with Milk and Honey.'" *Vetus Testamentum* 42, no. 4 (1992): 554–557.

Stordalen, T. "Man, Soil, Garden: Basic Plot in Genesis 2-3 Reconsidered." *Journal for the Study of the Old Testament* 17, no. 53 (1992): 3–26.

———. *Echoes of Eden: Genesis 2-3 and Symbolism of the Eden Garden in Biblical Hebrew Literature.* Leuven: Peeters, 2000.

Stuhlmueller, C. "Yahweh-King and Deutero-Isaiah." *Chicago Society of Biblical Research* 15 (1970): 32–45.

Szubin, H. Z. and B. Porten. "Royal Grants in Egypt: A New Interpretation of Driver 2." *Journal of Near Eastern Studies* 46, no. 1 (1987): 39–48.

Tal, U. "Union Seminars Quarterly Review." *Jewish Self-Understanding and the Land and the State of Israel* (1970): 353–354.

Tarazi, P. N. "Covenant, Land and City: Finding God's Will in Palestine." *The Reformed Journal* 29 (1979): 10–16.

———. *Land and Covenant.* St. Paul: Ocabs Press, 2009.

Tate, M. E. "King and Messiah in Isaiah of Jerusalem." *Review and Expositor* 65 (1968): 409–421.

Taylor, V. "The Origin of the Markan Passion Sayings." *New Testament Studies* 1, no. 3 (1955): 159–167.

The Kairos Palestine Document, 2009, available at http://www.kairospalestine.ps/content/kairos-document

Thiselton, A. *The First Epistle to the Corinthians: A Commentary of the Greek Text.* Grand Rapids: Eerdmans, 2000.

Thomas, R. L. "The Mission of Israel and of the Messiah in the Plan of God." *The Master's Seminary Journal* 8 (1997): 191–210.

Thompson, M. E. W. "Israel's Ideal King." *JSOT* 24 (1982): 79–88.

Torrance, T. F. *Space, Time, and Incarnation.* Edinburgh: T&T Clark, 1997.

Toussaint, S. D. and J. A. Quine. "No, Not Yet: The Contingency of God's Promised Kingdom." *Bibliotheca Sacra* 164(654), (2007): 131–47.

Townsend, J. L. "Fulfilment of the Land Promise in the Old Testament." *Bibliotheca Sacra* 142(568), (1985): 320–337.

Tsumura, T. D. "The Doctrine of Creation ex nihilo and the Translation of *tōhû wābōhû*." In *Pentateuchal Traditions in the Late Second Temple Period. Proceedings of the International Workshop in Tokyo, August 28-31, 2007. (Supplements to the Journal for the Study of Judaism 158)*. Leiden: Brill, 2012, 3–22.

Tuell, S. "The Rivers of Paradise: Ezekiel 47:1-12 and Genesis 2:10-14." In *God Who Creates. Essays in Honor of W. Sibley Towner*, edited by W. P. Brown and S. D. McBride, 171–189. Grand Rapids: Eerdmans, 2000.

Van Ruiten, J. "Eden and the Temple: The Rewriting of the Genesis 2:4-3:24 in the Book of Jubilees." In *Paradise Interpreted: Representations of Biblical Paradise in Judaism and Christianity*, edited by G. P. Luttikhuizen, 63–94, Leiden: Brill, 1999.

Van Ruiten, J. and J. C. De Vos, eds. *The Land of Israel in Bible, History, and Theology: Studies in Honour of Ed Noort*. Leiden: Brill, 2009.

Van Seters, J. *Prologue to History: The Yahwist as Historian in Genesis*. Louisville: Westminster John Knox, 1992.

Vander Hart, M. D. "Possessing the Land: As Command and Promise." *Mid-America Journal of Theology* 4, no. 2 (1988): 139–155.

Vlach, Michael J. "Various Forms of Replacement Theology." *TMSJ* 20, no. 1 (Spring 2009): 57–69.

Volf, M. *Exclusion and Embrace: A Theological Exploration of Identity, Otherness, and Reconciliation*. Nashville: Abingdon Press, 1996.

Von Rad, G. *Old Testament Theology (Vol. 1): The Theology of Israel's Historical Traditions*. Translated by D. M. G. Stalker. Edinburgh and London: Oliver & Boyd, 1962.

———. "The Promised Land and Yahweh's Land in the Hexateuch." In *The Problem of the Hexateuch and Other Essays*, edited by G. Von Rad, 79–93. Edinburgh and London: Oliver & Boyd, 1966.

———. "There Remains Still a Rest for the People of God: An Investigation of a Biblical Conception." In *The Problem of the Hexateuch and Other Essays*, edited by G. Von Rad, 94–102. Edinburgh and London: Oliver & Boyd, 1966.

———. "City on a Hill." In *The Problem of the Hexateuch and Other Essays*, edited by G. Von Rad, 232–242. New York: McGraw-Hill, 1966.

———. *Genesis: A Commentary.* London: SCM Press, 1972.

Von Waldow, H. E. "Israel and Her Land: Some Theological Considerations." In *A Light unto My Path: Old Testament Studies in Memory of Jacob M. Myers,* edited by H. N. Bream, R. D. Heim and C. A. Moore, 493–508, Philadelphia: Temple University Press, 1974.

Vorster. "The Ethics of Land Restitution." *JRE* 34, no. 4 (2006): 685–707.

Walker, P. W. L. *Holy City, Holy Places?: Christian Attitudes to Jerusalem and the Holy Land in the Fourth Century.* Oxford: Oxford University Press, 1990.

———. "Jerusalem in Hebrews 13: 9-14 and the Dating of the Epistle." *Tyndale Bulletin* 45 (1994): 39–71.

———. *Jesus and the Holy City: New Testament Perspectives on Jerusalem.* Grand Rapids: Eerdmans, 1996.

———. "The Land in the Apostles' Writings." In *The Land of Promise,* edited by P. Johnston and P. Walker, 81–99. Downers Grove: InterVarsity Press, 2000a.

———. "The Land and Jesus Himself." In *The Land of Promise,* edited by P. Johnston and P. Walker, 100–120. Downers Grove: InterVarsity Press, 2000b.

———, ed. *Jerusalem: Past and Present in the Purposes of God.* Carlisle: Paternoster Press, 1994.

Wallace, H. N. *The Eden Narrative.* Atlanta: Scholars Press, 1985.

———. "Eden, Garden of." In *The Anchor Bible Dictionary,* edited by D. N. Freedman, 281–283. New York: Doubleday, 1992.

Waltke, B. K. "The Phenomenon of Conditionality within Unconditional Covenants." In *Israel's Apostasy and Restoration: Essays in Honor of Roland K. Harrison,* edited by A. Gileadi, 123–140. Grand Rapids: Baker Book House, 1988.

———. *An Old Testament Theology: An Exegetical, Canonical, and Thematic Approach.* Grand Rapids: Zondervan, 2007.

Walton, J. H. "Eden, Garden of." In *Dictionary of the Old Testament: Pentateuch,* edited by D. W. Baker and D. W. Alexander, 202–207. Downers Grove: InterVarsity Press, 2003.

———. "The Imagery of the Substitute King Ritual in Isaiah's Fourth Servant Song." *JBL* 122, no. 4 (2003): 734–743.

Ware, B. A. "The New Covenant and the People(s) of God." In *Dispensationalism, Israel and the Church: The Search for Definition,* edited by D. L. Bock, W. C. Kaiser and C. A. Blaising, 68–97. Grand Rapids: Zondervan, 1992.

Warshal, B. S. "Israel's Stake in the Land." *Theology Today Lancaster, Pa*, 35, no. 4 (1979): 413–420.

Watts, J. D. W. *Isaiah 34-66. Word Biblical Commentary.* Dallas: Word Books, 1987.

Wazana, N. "From Dan to Beer-Sheba and from the Wilderness to the Sea: Literal and Literary Images of the Promised Land in the Bible." In *Experiences of place,* edited by M. N. MacDonald, 45–85. Cambridge: Harvard University Press, 2003.

———. *All the Boundaries of the Land: The Promised Land in Biblical Thought in Light of the Ancient Near East.* Jerusalem: Bialik Institute, 2007.

Weber, H. R. "The Promise of the Land." *Study Encounter* 7, no. 4 (1971).

Weber, L. J., B. F. Evans and G. D. Cusack. *Theology of the Land.* Collegeville: Liturgical Press, 1987.

Weinfeld, M. "The Period of the Conquest and of the Judges as Seen by the Earlier and the Later Sources." *Vetus Testamentum* (1967): 93–113.

———. "The Covenant of Grant in the Old Testament and the Ancient Near East." *Journal of the American Oriental Society* 90, no. 2 (1970): 184–203.

———. 1975, "ברית." In *Theological Dictionary of the Old Testament (Vol. 2)*, edited by H. Ringgren and G. H. Botterweck, 253–278. Grand Rapids: Eerdmans, 1975.

———. *The Promise of the Land: The Inheritance of the Land of Canaan by the Israelites.* Berkeley: University of California Press, 2003.

Wells, J. B. *God's Holy People: A Theme In Biblical Theology.* Sheffield: Sheffield Academic Press, 2000.

Wenell, K. J. *Jesus and Land: Sacred and Social Space in Second Temple Judaism.* London: T&T Clark, 2007.

Wenham, G. J. *Genesis 1-15. Word Biblical Commentary.* Waco: Word Books, 1987.

———. *Genesis. 16-50. Word Biblical Commentary.* Waco: Word Books, 1994.

———. "Sanctuary Symbolism in the Garden of Eden Story." In *I Studied Inscriptions from Before the Flood: Ancient Near Eastern, Literary, and Linguistic Approaches to Genesis 1-11,* edited by R. S. Hess and D. T. Tsumura, 399–404. Winona Lake: Eisenbrauns, 1994.

———. "Genesis." In *Eerdmans Commentary on the Bible,* edited by J. Rogerson and J. Dunn, 32–71. Grand Rapids: Eerdmans, 2003.

Westermann, C. *Genesis 1-11: A Continental Commentary.* Minneapolis: Fortress Press, 1994.

Whitelam, K. W. "Israel's Traditions of Origin: Reclaiming the Land." *Journal for the Study of the Old Testament* 14, no. 44 (1989): 19.

Wilkins, M. and J. P. Moreland, eds. *Jesus Under Fire. Modern Scholarship Reinvents the Historical Jesus*. Grand Rapids: Zondervan, 1994.

Wifall, W. "The Breath of His Nostrils: Gen. 2: 7b." *CBQ* 36 (1974), 237–240.

Wilken, R. L. "Early Christian Chiliasm, Jewish Messianism, and the Idea of the Holy Land." *The Harvard Theological Review* (1986): 298–307.

———. *The Land Called Holy: Palestine in Christian History and Thought*. New Haven: Yale University Press, 1992.

Williamson, H. G. M. *A Critical and Exegetical Commentary on Isaiah 1-27 (Vol. 1)*. London: T&T Clark, 2006.

Wilshire, L. E. "The Servant-City: A New Interpretation of the 'Servant of the Lord' in the Servant Songs of Deutero-Isaiah." *JBL* 94, no. 3 (1975): 356–367.

Witherington, B. *The Jesus Quest: The Third Search for the Jew of Nazareth*, Downers Grove: InterVarsity Press, 1997.

Wolff, H. W. "The Kerygma of the Yahwist." *Interpretation* 20 (1986): 131–358.

Wolters, A. M. *Creation Regained: Biblical Basics for a Reformational Worldview*. Grand Rapids: Eerdmans, 2005.

Wright, C. J. H. *God's People in God's Land: Family, Land, and Property in the Old Testament*. Grand Rapids: Eerdmans, 1990.

———. "A Christian Approach To Old Testament Prophecy Concerning Israel." In *Jerusalem Past and Present in the Purposes of God*, edited by P. W. L. Walker, 1–19. Cambridge: Tyndale House, 1992.

———. "Biblical Reflections on Land." *Evangelical Review of Theology* 17 (1993): 153–167.

———. "God or Mammon: Biblical Perspectives On Economies in Conflict." *Mission Studies* 12, no. 1 (1995): 145–156.

———. "Implications of Conversion in the Old Testament and the New." *International Bulletin of Missionary Research* 28, no. 1 (2004): 14–15.

———. *Old Testament Ethics for the People of God*. Downers Grove: InterVarsity Press, 2004.

———. *The Mission of God: Unlocking The Bible's Grand Narrative*. Downers Grove: IVP Academic, 2006.

Wright, N. T. *The Climax of the Covenant: Christ and the Law in Pauline Theology*. Minneapolis: Fortress Press, 1992a.

———. *The New Testament and the People of God*. Minneapolis: Fortress Press, 1992b.

———. "Jerusalem in the New Testament." In *Jerusalem Past and Present in the Purposes of God,* edited by P. W. L. Walker, 53–77. Grand Rapids: Baker, 1994.

———. *Jesus and the Victory of God.* Minneapolis: Fortress Press, 1996.

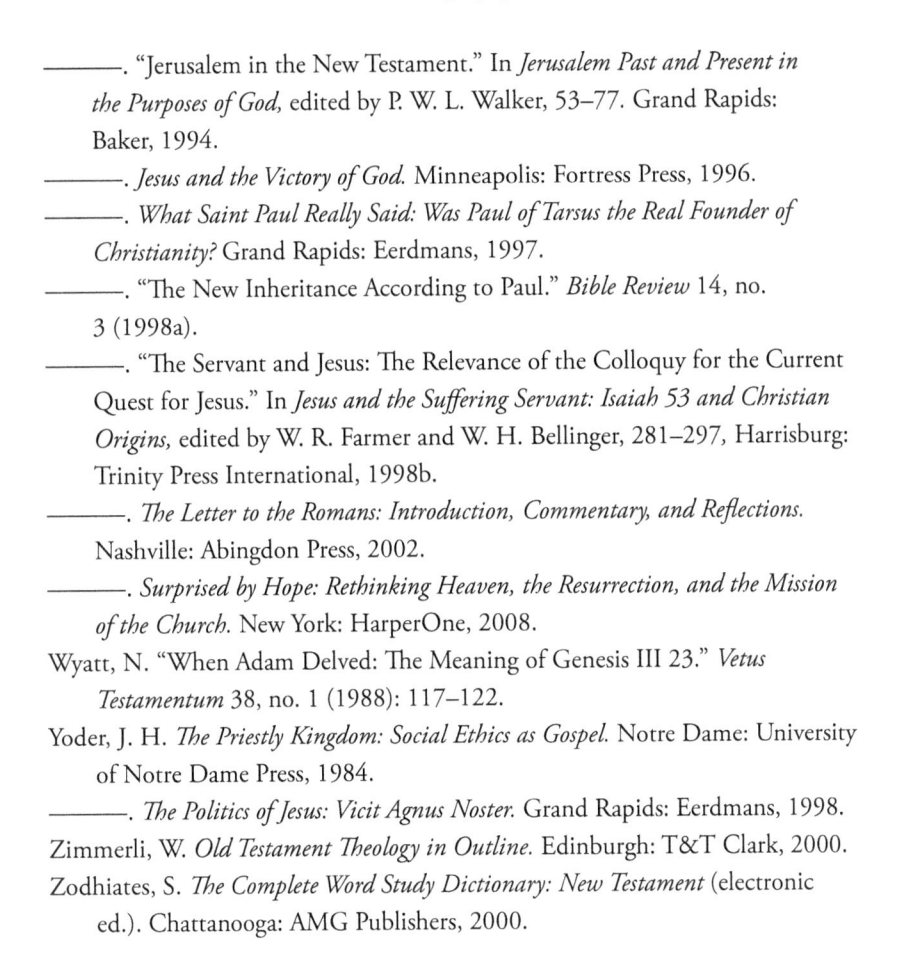

———. *What Saint Paul Really Said: Was Paul of Tarsus the Real Founder of Christianity?* Grand Rapids: Eerdmans, 1997.

———. "The New Inheritance According to Paul." *Bible Review* 14, no. 3 (1998a).

———. "The Servant and Jesus: The Relevance of the Colloquy for the Current Quest for Jesus." In *Jesus and the Suffering Servant: Isaiah 53 and Christian Origins,* edited by W. R. Farmer and W. H. Bellinger, 281–297, Harrisburg: Trinity Press International, 1998b.

———. *The Letter to the Romans: Introduction, Commentary, and Reflections.* Nashville: Abingdon Press, 2002.

———. *Surprised by Hope: Rethinking Heaven, the Resurrection, and the Mission of the Church.* New York: HarperOne, 2008.

Wyatt, N. "When Adam Delved: The Meaning of Genesis III 23." *Vetus Testamentum* 38, no. 1 (1988): 117–122.

Yoder, J. H. *The Priestly Kingdom: Social Ethics as Gospel.* Notre Dame: University of Notre Dame Press, 1984.

———. *The Politics of Jesus: Vicit Agnus Noster.* Grand Rapids: Eerdmans, 1998.

Zimmerli, W. *Old Testament Theology in Outline.* Edinburgh: T&T Clark, 2000.

Zodhiates, S. *The Complete Word Study Dictionary: New Testament* (electronic ed.). Chattanooga: AMG Publishers, 2000.

Langham Partnership

Langham Literature and its imprints are a ministry of Langham Partnership.

Langham Partnership is a global fellowship working in pursuit of the vision God entrusted to its founder John Stott –

> *to facilitate the growth of the church in maturity and Christ-likeness through raising the standards of biblical preaching and teaching.*

Our vision is to see churches in the majority world equipped for mission and growing to maturity in Christ through the ministry of pastors and leaders who believe, teach and live by the Word of God.

Our mission is to strengthen the ministry of the Word of God through:
- nurturing national movements for biblical preaching
- fostering the creation and distribution of evangelical literature
- enhancing evangelical theological education

especially in countries where churches are under-resourced.

Our ministry

Langham Preaching partners with national leaders to nurture indigenous biblical preaching movements for pastors and lay preachers all around the world. With the support of a team of trainers from many countries, a multi-level programme of seminars provides practical training, and is followed by a programme for training local facilitators. Local preachers' groups and national and regional networks ensure continuity and ongoing development, seeking to build vigorous movements committed to Bible exposition.

Langham Literature provides majority world pastors, scholars and seminary libraries with evangelical books and electronic resources through grants, discounts and distribution. The programme also fosters the creation of indigenous evangelical books for pastors in many languages, through training workshops for writers and editors, sponsored writing, translation, strengthening local evangelical publishing houses, and investment in major regional literature projects, such as one volume Bible commentaries like *The Africa Bible Commentary*.

Langham Scholars provides financial support for evangelical doctoral students from the majority world so that, when they return home, they may train pastors and other Christian leaders with sound, biblical and theological teaching. This programme equips those who equip others. Langham Scholars also works in partnership with majority world seminaries in strengthening evangelical theological education. A growing number of Langham Scholars study in high quality doctoral programmes in the majority world itself. As well as teaching the next generation of pastors, graduated Langham Scholars exercise significant influence through their writing and leadership.

To learn more about Langham Partnership and the work we do visit **langham.org**

www.ingramcontent.com/pod-product-compliance
Lightning Source LLC
LaVergne TN
LVHW021747191125
825975LV00010B/599